Killer Kane

Killer Kane

A Marine Long-Range Recon Team Leader in Vietnam, 1967–1968

ANDREW R. FINLAYSON

McFarland & Company, Inc., Publishers
Jefferson, North Carolina, and London

LIBRARY OF CONGRESS CATALOGUING-IN-PUBLICATION DATA

Finlayson, Andrew R.
Killer Kane : a Marine long-range recon team leader in
Vietnam, 1967–1968 / Andrew R. Finlayson.
p.   cm.
Includes bibliographical references and index.

ISBN 978-0-7864-7701-2
softcover : acid free paper ∞

1. Finlayson, Andrew R.   2. Vietnam War, 1961–1975—Personal narratives,
American.   3. Vietnam War, 1961–1975—Reconnaissance operations, American.
4. Vietnam War, 1961–1975—Regimental histories—United States.   5. United
States. Marine Corps. Force Reconnaissance Company, 1st.   6. United States.
Marine Corps—Officers—Biography.   I. Title.
DS559.5.F513 2013   959.704'3092—dc23   2013030622

BRITISH LIBRARY CATALOGUING DATA ARE AVAILABLE

On the cover: Andrew R. Finlayson calling in an artillery mission
on a VC column; silhouettes of members of Killer Kane;
background the Song Thu Bon River

Manufactured in the United States of America

*McFarland & Company, Inc., Publishers
Box 611, Jefferson, North Carolina 28640
www.mcfarlandpub.com*

To two extraordinary young men who gave their lives
for their country in South Vietnam. As long as I live,
I will remember them and honor their sacrifice.

2nd Lt. Thomas Brown Dowd, USMC
Killed in Action in Quang Nam Province, 1 March 1967

Captain (Capt.) Eric M. Barnes, USMC
Killed in Action in Quang Nam Province, 25 March 1967

"No one has greater love than this: to lay down his life for his friends."
John: 15:13

"Qui procol hinc, qui ante diem perit: Sed miles, sed pro patria."
("He died far from home, and before his time:
But as a soldier and for his country.")
Grave stone inscription of a Roman legionnaire

Table of Contents

Preface and
Acknowledgments

I wrote this book to provide historians and the general reader with a firsthand account of how one twenty-three-year-old United States Marine officer fought his war. Many veterans of the Vietnam War have written about their experiences and the units they served in during that war. What differentiates my book is I wrote it from the perspective of someone with a far broader and lengthier exposure to the war. I spent 32 months in South Vietnam performing three distinct combat jobs in two different geographical areas during the most critical years of the war, 1967 to 1970.

I served in Vietnam both before and after the 1968 Tet offensive, and this changed my perspective on the war dramatically. I experienced the "Search and Destroy" attrition-intensive strategy that General (Gen.) Westmoreland employed prior to Tet, and then on my second tour I served during the period known as "Vietnamization" when the U.S. began its withdrawal from the war and turned over the fighting to the South Vietnamese. These were two very distinct periods and involved different strategies and tactics. This book covers only the pre–Tet period and involves combat in only one geographical area of South Vietnam, an area approximately 25 miles west and south of the city of Da Nang. It covers the thirteen months leading up to the Tet offensive and does not cover any portion of my second tour of duty in South Vietnam, where my experiences were far more diverse and far more influential on my perspective on the war. While it might be helpful for students of the war to understand how the transition from one phase of the war to another affected one junior officer fighting in that war, I have chosen to save that analysis for another time and another book.

The book is not a critique of the war. I offer no broad generalizations within. Instead, the book reflects the feelings and observations of one young man as he fought his own personal war in the company of a small band of exceptional comrades. Although the events I describe occurred over 40 years ago, a span of time that allows for reflection, I have tried to write this book from the perspective of my younger self, rather than from the perspective of someone who has spent many years since then studying the war and drawing conclusions on the broader events that transpired. Sometimes, however, these two perspectives converge in order to offer a point of helpful comparison. I have tried to be completely honest in my portrayal of events. I made some very serious mistakes of judgment, and my decisions were not always correct or effective. These mistakes and misjudgments will be readily apparent to the reader, and I hope that young military officers will learn from my mistakes. I also hope that people who have been spared the experience of war will see how easily things can go wrong when a leader lacks good judgment.

Within these pages, I also tell the story of the men and women I knew during the war, both American and South Vietnamese. I felt compelled to do this because I knew their stories would be lost if I did not. While I was doing research on this book, I interviewed several of the people who appear on the following pages. Most of them had never spoken to their families about their experiences during the Vietnam War. Their families were completely unaware of the magnificent service they performed for their country. I did not want their heroism and sacrifice to go unsung. While this book is my story, it is also very much their story.

This book covers the first half of my Vietnam War experience: the period from my arrival in South Vietnam in early 1967 to the end of 1968, when I volunteered to return to South Vietnam for a second tour of duty. While it is my personal account, it is also the story of the men who made up one of the most successful U.S. Marine Corps' long-range reconnaissance teams of the war. That team was code-named Killer Kane. The patrols they conducted deep inside enemy-controlled territory were some of the most exciting and dramatic patrols performed by U.S. Marines during that war. By telling their story along with mine, I hope to do justice to their bravery and provide their families and future generations of Americans with an example of the uncommon valor they displayed doing some of the most dangerous work the military is called upon to do.

Finally, I wanted to write a book that explained why I volunteered to fight for my country and then volunteered again to return to combat when I was not required to do so. The Vietnam War was the one great lyric passage of my life; everything else I did in my life paled in significance when measured against that experience. I joined the military and served for twenty-five years in the U.S. Marine Corps because I wanted the people I knew and loved in my small town to respect and love me. I did not serve out of a great sense of patriotism or the pursuit of an adventurous life. While I loved and respected the Marines I served with, I did not fight because of my pride in the Marine Corps or a sense of obligation to the leaders of my country or its institutions. What motivated me was a need formed when I was a teenager to do something in my life that would make the people of Merchantville, New Jersey, proud of me. In a sense, the words that Pericles spoke at a funeral for dead Athenian soldiers over 2,000 years ago best describes the underlying rationale for my decision to fight in the Vietnam War. In Pericles's famous funeral oration for Athenian soldiers who died in combat defending the city of Athens, as related by Thucydides in his *History of the Peloponnesian War*, he called upon that city's citizens to love the greatness and goodness of their city, and to be willing to sacrifice everything, including their lives, to preserve it. Merchantville, New Jersey, was my Athens, and I was determined to honor my hometown by defending it.

Of the failures and disappointments in my life, the one that hurt the most was the realization that I never accomplished anything that merited their pride in me. It was this vain attempt to win their praise that made me fight in the Vietnam War, and it was also the reason I spent so many years in the U.S. Marine Corps trying to redeem myself for failing to win that war.

The primary sources for this book were the official United States Marine Corps Command Chronologies on file with the History Division at Headquarters Marine Corps, Quantico, Virginia. All that are cited in the text are 1st Force Recon Company Command Chronologies, so this may be assumed by the reader and has been left out of the citations in the interest of brevity and readability; consequently, only the specific team that is its subject and the date of the report are given in the text. I relied heavily on these official unit histories because they provided a solid, factual basis for the events described. I wanted to avoid the tendency of some writers to inject information that might be colored by fading memory or personal prejudice. I also relied on my complete file of the letters I wrote to my parents on a weekly basis during my 25-year Marine Corps career. These letters were my personal journal of events. The level of detail I provided in these letters often provoked a sense of dread for my parents, but I wanted to ensure that the events I lived through during that time were not obscured by time or the terse prose contained in official reports. These letters also served the purpose of providing details about the men I served with, the Vietnamese civilians I knew as friends and my life in Camp Reasoner when I was not on patrol. Additionally, I retained the original copies of my patrol reports with the 1st Force Reconnaissance Company, along with several other original documents from that period, such as maps, photos, and captured enemy documents. Using the sources mentioned above, I have tried to rely almost exclusively on primary sources. Books and articles that helped to form my thinking on the war and, in part, pertain to aspects addressed in the book are included in a Recommended Reading section, after the text.

This book would not have been possible to write without the kind assistance of many people. I am particularly grateful to Lt. Col. George W. T. "Digger" O'Dell, USMC (Ret.), Col. Frederick J. Vogel, USMCR (Ret.), Lt. Col. Charles Kershaw, USMC (Ret.), Michael C. Henry, Bart Russell, Robert Garcia, Rick Rabenold, Rudy Enders, Andy Vaart, and Charles O. Stainback. These individuals provided steadfast support and valuable firsthand information on the events discussed in this book. They also read portions of the book or the entire manuscript and offered many useful comments and suggestions.

Richard Botkin, a friend and author, was a constant source of encouragement as I wrote this book. He was a student of mine when I was teaching at the University of Michigan, and he pursued a career as a Marine officer both on active duty and in the Marine Corps Reserve. He read the initial manuscript of my book and convinced me that the book needed to be published. Without his advice and assistance, this book would not have been written.

I am also indebted to the families of 2nd Lt. Thomas Dowd, USMC, and Capt. Eric Barnes, USMC, for their support during the writing of this book. The Dowd family's friendship over the years and their undying love for Tom inspired me to dedicate this book to him. After many years of fruitless searching, I was finally able to locate in 2012 Deirdre B. Harris, the daughter of Capt. Eric Barnes. She provided many facts pertaining to Eric's life before he died in South Vietnam and how his family dealt with the aftermath of his death.

I was given many useful leads and advice from Charles D. Melson and Kenneth H.

Williams of the U.S. Marine Corps Historical Division at Quantico, Virginia. These gentlemen allowed me to have complete access to the Marine Corps historical archives and pointed me in the right direction when I became lost in the files. Williams also provided many valuable insights on how the book could be better organized so as to be more concise and better suited for publication.

A close friend and colleague, Mary Davisson, typed the manuscript and provided several useful suggestions on how to improve portions of the book. She was always responsive to my numerous requests for revision of the text. Her expertise, encouragement and friendship kept me focused on my writing.

Melissa Solomon, Ph.D, was instrumental in providing critical and substantive suggestions on how to improve the text of the book. During several months of review and editing, she patiently helped me to transform my manuscript into something readable. I deeply appreciate her kind assistance and professional recommendations.

The maps for this book were developed by Becky Wilkes, a cartographer with the Carolina Population Center at the University of North Carolina–Chapel Hill. She was able to take my rough outlines and turn them into finished maps, which identified the key locations mentioned in the text of the book. I sincerely appreciate her helpful and professional assistance.

I would also like to express my deep gratitude to Dr. Mark Moyer, noted historian on the Vietnam War, for inspiring me to put down on paper my experiences during that war.

Finally, I would like to thank my wife, Sarah, for putting up with the many hours of research and writing that this book demanded. Her patience, loyalty, love, and support played a major role in the creation of this book.

1

Preparing for Battle

While my preparation for war began long before I entered the U.S. Marine Corps, it did not take a truly tangible form until I graduated from the U.S. Naval Academy in 1966. On that sunny, June day in Annapolis, Maryland, a day that marked the end of four frustrating and largely unhappy years of academic and athletic struggle, I joined my classmates at the football stadium for the graduation ceremony and took my commission as a second lieutenant in the U.S. Marine Corps. My parents saw me graduate, and I could see in their eyes both the pride they had in my successful completion of my studies and the apprehension they had about my decision to serve in the Marine Corps, which they considered the most dangerous military branch. In addition to the joy I felt at leaving the Naval Academy and starting on a new career, two events stand out in my mind. One was seeing the legendary Navy baseball coach, Mr. Joe Duff, who came up to me after graduation and told me he was proud of me even though I could not hit worth a damn. The other was the moment my mother and father pinned my second lieutenant bars on my uniform. While this was being done my mother mentioned the new Naval Academy class ring I was wearing. I looked down at it and saw engraved on the ring our class motto, "Non Sibi Sed Patria," the Latin inscription for "Not for Self, but for Country." That phrase would provide direction and guidance for me in the years to come and throughout my life.

After a brief vacation following my graduation from the Naval Academy, I left my hometown of Merchantville, New Jersey, in my new Triumph TR-4 roadster and drove south to the Marine Corps base at Quantico, Virginia, to begin my career as an officer of Marines. The day of my departure from my hometown was bright, sunny and warm, and the trip down Route 95 through Delaware, the District of Columbia, and into northern Virginia took only four hours. My destination was the Basic School, the first stop in a Marine officer's career, where I would spend the next twenty-two weeks learning my trade. I was anxious to do well at Quantico and not to fall short the way I had at the Naval Academy. I was determined to do everything in my power to measure up to the standards of the Marine Corps, standards that I knew were stringent and unyielding. As I drove south on my way to my first Marine Corps duty station, I began to feel exhilarated by the prospect of testing myself against the other officers in my Basic School Class of 1–67.

I found myself thinking of some of the useful training I had received prior to graduation from the Academy. I thought about my last year at the Academy and the classes Major (Maj.) Jarvis Lynch had taught me and the other First Class midshipmen who had expressed a desire to select commissioning as second lieutenants in the Marine Corps. His classes were held on several evenings just prior to graduation, and he attempted to explain to us what we could expect at the Basic School and how we should prepare ourselves for it. For example, he taught us some useful things that were essential for newly commissioned officers in the Marine Corps, but were not on the curriculum at the Naval Academy. Among the things he taught us were how to organize a standard issue Marine Corps pack and what to put in it; how to care for the equipment we would be issued at the Basic School, and how to tune and maintain a PRC-10 radio. He also covered such useful and practical subjects as personal finance, insurance, and military customs particular to the Marine Corps. One of the most valuable lectures he arranged for us was given by a Marine First Sergeant (1st Sgt.) with more than 20 years' experience in the Corps who told us what to expect from a Marine Corps Staff Non-Commissioned Officer (SNCO) and how to deal with a SNCO so we worked as a team, each of us with separate responsibilities and tasks to perform. This wise 1st Sgt. stressed the importance of an officer not trying to

Midshipman Andrew R. Finlayson, 1966.

do the SNCO's job, giving practical examples of how to avoid this problem. As a result of these informal classes during the last few weeks of my time at the Naval Academy, I came away with the feeling that I would succeed at the Basic School and get off to a good start in my Marine Corps career.

My daydreaming came to an end as I exited Route 95 at the Quantico-Triangle exit and approached the main gate of the base. A Marine sentry at the gate looked at the decal on my car, stood at attention, and gave me the kind of sharp, crisp salute that I would come to expect from every sentry I encountered on any gate guarded by Marines. Receiving that salute made me feel both proud and humbled. I wondered if I was worthy of the respect that salute conveyed.

After checking in with the Officer of the Day (OD), I was directed to drive to the Basic School and report there for billeting. At the Basic School I was told that I would be a member of the first platoon of Alpha Company, Basic School Class 1–67. I was also assigned to a room on the second floor of O'Bannon Hall, the BOQ for the Basic School. My roommates were Curtis D. Floyd and Thomas "Tim" Flournoy, two southern boys who were both fun to be around and easy to live with. One of the first things we did together the next day was to go on a run while other new officers reported aboard to the

Basic School. Like most young officers we were all in good physical condition. I had been warned by Marine officers at the Naval Academy that the 2nd lieutenants I would encounter at the Basic School would be better prepared physically and professionally than I since they would have benefited from attendance at Officers Candidate School (OCS). When we started our run, I fully expected my roommates to run me into the ground, but I was pleasantly surprised by my ability to keep up easily as we jogged five miles along the base's roads. My anxiety about my ability to measure up to my brother officers dissipated the more I got to know my roommates and to discover they were just as anxious as I was about succeeding in our new profession.

As I recall, Curtis Floyd was from North Carolina and Tim Flournoy was from South Carolina or Georgia. Like me, they were both single. Curtis was a tall, lanky young man who took life and his commitment to the Marine Corps very seriously. We often spent many hours talking about military history, and on those occasions he would demonstrate a comprehensive knowledge of the American Civil War, especially anything that had to do with Stonewall Jackson. He was very reliable and sensible, two traits that made him both popular and respected by his fellow officers.

Tim Flournoy was, to put it mildly, a "character," who had a lively and sophisticated sense of humor. He was shorter than Curtis and had a stocky build. His eyes sparkled with mischief and his general demeanor was one of a person supremely confident in himself and at peace with his world. He had just finished law school on a government scholarship. He was a few years older than us, but in many ways he was childlike in his love of practical jokes and his ability to come up with colorful and humorous stories and descriptive words. I loved the way he talked and the language he used. His smooth southern drawl and his penchant for florid phrases were a delight to hear, making him one of the most popular officers in our Basic School class. I admired and enjoyed the company of both of these men, but like so many of my Basic School classmates, I lost contact with them after leaving the Basic School.

My company commander at the Basic School was Maj. Robert J. Woeckener and our company executive officer was Henry "Mac" Radcliffe, two impressive officers who guided our training every step of the way while serving in these leadership positions. Similar to most of the officers assigned to the Basic School as instructors, these two men were recent combat veterans of the Vietnam War and perfect role models for a young Marine officer to emulate.

I had the highest respect and admiration for my platoon commander, Maj. Robert H. Philon. He was a "Mustang" in the parlance of the Marine Corps, meaning he had served as an enlisted Marine before he was commissioned as an officer. All of the lieutenants in our platoon idolized him and sought his approval. He treated each of us with respect, and I never once heard him raise his voice or use profanity. He was calm, professional, unflappable, and highly competent in everything he did and said. He was, in my opinion, a natural leader of men. Whenever he wore his uniform, it was impeccable, setting a very high standard for the men in his platoon to aspire to, no matter what the task or goal. We all felt he had our interests at heart and that he was motivated by a sincere and profound desire to make us ready to lead Marines in combat. His informal lectures during our break periods between classes or on the ranges were filled with practical advice on how to take care of our Marines and how to prepare ourselves for war. For example, on one break during a field exercise, he gathered his platoon around him and, using his experience as an advisor in South Vietnam, he explained why it was vitally important to supervise every aspect concerned with the preparation of night defensive positions. His graphic description of the fatal consequences of poor supervision left an indelible impression on everyone in the platoon. He carried an old smoking pipe with him whenever we went to the field for training, and I have fixed in my mind the slow deliberate way he took his pipe tobacco out of an old, weathered leather pouch, tamping it down into the bowl of that pipe, and at the same time imparting some arcane yet highly valuable lesson he had learned over a long career. When we graduated from the Basic School, our platoon presented him with a new and rather expensive pipe as a parting gift. When we saw his reaction as he opened the box and saw the new pipe, we knew we had made the right selection. For once, he was so touched by this expression of our respect and esteem he did not say a word but only looked up at us with a look of joyful surprise. Tom Dowd, who idolized Maj. Philon, led us in a cheer for him, and I noticed Maj. Philon's eyes were moist, which told us more than any words could.

Three of my Basic School instructors made a lasting impression on me. One was Capt. Jack Kelly, a big, strong Irishman from New England, who taught us tactics. Another was Capt. "Mortars" Murphy who taught us everything we would need to know if we were given the job of mortar platoon commander. He was later killed in action on his second tour in Vietnam. Both of these officers had keen wits and sharp minds which resulted in informative and entertaining classes that I eagerly looked forward to whenever I saw their names on my syllabus. They were famous among the students for the way they laced their classes with humorous anecdotes and jokes, all with the timing and humor one would expect from a professional comedian. Invariably they would begin each of their classes with what they called their "attention getters," highly risqué jokes that had some tangential relationship to the course material covered. Since only men were in my Basic School class, these "attention getters" often went far over the line in terms of propriety. However, they did serve their purpose of gaining our attention at the beginning of a class.

Capt. "Paddy" Collins was another officer who made a strong impression on me. He was a legend in the Marine Corps and had recently returned from South Vietnam where he had been a reconnaissance company commander. He taught scouting and patrolling, and his classes provided many practical tips on how to conduct recon and combat patrols, all of which would benefit me later in South Vietnam. He retired as a colonel (Col.), and throughout his long career he was considered one of the Marine Corps' top experts on ground reconnaissance and special warfare.

Although life at the Basic School was not what most people would call "relaxed" it was a significant improvement over the Naval Academy, where the midshipmen were treated as children in most cases and given very little freedom of thought or action. At the Basic School we were treated as Marine officers, and as long as we maintained ourselves as "officers and gentlemen" we were afforded a great deal of freedom and initiative when we were not in class or in the field training. In addition to our classroom work, we spent a great deal of time in the field conducting realistic training. Unlike my time spent at the

Naval Academy, I enjoyed each day at the Basic School and considered the time spent there meaningful and productive. The instruction was interesting and comprehensive, the living conditions Spartan but comfortable, the instructors on the staff impressive and inspiring, the food in the officers mess excellent, and the feeling of being part of an elite military organization exhilarating. The six months I spent at Quantico were happy times for me.

Unlike most of my colleagues at the Basic School, I seldom went on liberty at night or on the weekends. I wanted to do well at the Basic School, and for me this meant spending extra time studying and preparing myself for the exams and practical exercises that were graded. Many of my fellow officers drove north to Washington, D.C., to meet young women at "mixers" arranged by a group known as the Junior Officers and Professionals Organization, or JOPA. These dances brought together young military officers, civil servants and professionals at dances held at various bars and hotels in the Washington, D.C., area. Many of my friends found their future wives at these JOPA gatherings. I never attended a single one of the JOPA events. Other Marine lieutenants at the Basic School would drive south to the campus of Mary Washington College, an all-women's college in Fredericksburg, Virginia, in pursuit of feminine friendship. Again, several of my fellow officers met their future wives while visiting this college.

I had literally no social life during my first two months at the Basic School. However, in late August, I attended the wedding of one of my Naval Academy classmates, and there I met an attractive blond undergraduate student named "Jane," who was one of the maids of honor. "Jane" and I hit it off right away. She was the 20-year-old daughter of a naval officer and, therefore, was familiar with military life and what that life demanded of a wife and family. She had moved recently from San Diego to attend George Washington University and was living with family friends in McLean, Virginia, until her parents and younger sister could join her that fall. For the last few months of my time at the Basic School, I would drive up to McLean to see "Jane" on the weekends, and we would spend many enjoyable hours in each other's company walking along the barge canal in Georgetown, going to the movies, shopping at Tyson's Corner, and eating in several restaurants in the Washington, D.C., and Northern Virginia areas. Several weekends, we went to the Harry Lee Hall Officers' Club on the Quantico base where we could have an excellent meal at a very reasonable price. I also took her to her sorority's formal dance on the George Washington University campus. I wore my dress blue uniform, and she looked stunning in her evening gown. It was one of the only times in my life when I actually enjoyed dancing.

As my Basic School training progressed I began to find that my scores on both my academic and military subjects placed me near the top of my class of 187 officer students. Aside from a rather poor grade in my test on mortars, I usually scored in the mid- to high– 90s on my tests. I had my highest scores on my instructor evaluations for the practical military applications, such as leading the squad live fire attack, night land navigation, the single and double running of the obstacle course, ceremonial drill, and marksmanship. I was especially proud of my performance on the rifle range where I scored "expert," the highest qualification.

A few weeks prior to graduation from the Basic School, we were asked to make three choices for our Military Occupational Specialty (MOS). This would be the career field we would work in, and we all gave our choices a great deal of thought. We knew there was a war being fought in South Vietnam and that most of us would be given orders there after graduation. We also knew from the countless stories we heard from friends and news reports that combat arms officers were the most likely to be killed or wounded. "Combat arms" meant infantry, armor, artillery, and aviation MOSs. I pondered my choices carefully. Since our Basic School Class 1–67 contained many Naval Academy and NROTC officers who possessed regular commissions, the Marine Corps wanted to spread them out over many MOSs with the view of maintaining a cadre of regular officers in all of the career fields. This meant that there were many MOSs open that were not combat arms MOSs, a fact that bothered me because I did not want any other MOS than infantry. I knew I would have to stand high in my class if I wanted to obtain the infantry MOS.

We were given a weekend to think over our three choices and to submit them first thing on Monday to our platoon commander. I had told Maj. Philon shortly after I arrived at Quantico that I wanted to be an infantry officer, but when I told him this he sternly told me that I must score high in all of my military skills subjects and demonstrate leadership ability if I wanted to secure one of the few infantry MOS slots for our class. He stressed that leading Marines was a privilege that had to be earned and that meant hard work and total dedication. He warned me that he would be keeping an eye on me throughout our training and, if he saw anything in my character or approach to training that might cost the life of a Marine, he would not recommend me for any of the combat arms MOSs. His little talk with me served to focus my attention on my studies and performance during the tests and practical applications that followed.

On the Monday when we were to submit our choices I put down in order of preference Infantry, Armor and Artillery. Shortly thereafter, Maj. Philon came up to me and told me that he had recommended I be given the Infantry MOS, and the selection board had approved his recommendation. I was elated and immediately called my parents to give them the "good news." I could tell from their voices on the phone that they were not as enthusiastic as I was over my new MOS. My father, who was a Navy veteran of World War II and saw the vicious fighting on the islands of the Central Pacific Drive, knew the risks associated with being a Marine infantry officer, so his comments to me were measured and candid. He said he was proud of me and that my grandfather, who was an infantry officer in the U.S. Army, would certainly be proud of me, if he were alive. My mother was largely silent, saying only that she hoped I would be careful and not take unnecessary risks. My mother was not given to displays of emotion, but I could hear the catch in her voice as she spoke to me. It suddenly dawned on me that my decision to become an officer of Marines and to do so in the combat field of the infantry was a decision that caused great anxiety to my parents. The call to my parents put a damper on my enthusiasm. I had expected them to be as joyful as I was at my new MOS, but that phone call told me that my decision filled them with apprehension. Instead, they were badly worried. I wanted them to be proud of me, but now I knew all they felt was concern for my safety.

Although I did not realize it at the time, one part of my training at the Basic School would later affect a future duty assignment. Throughout our six months of training we were taught military drill, concentrating on platoon and company formations, inspections and parades. The final assessment of our drill instruction was a company parade in preparation for graduation. Since I had been in the Marine Reserves and had a lot of experience at the Naval Academy with drill, I was given command of my platoon for the graduation parade. I did not know it at the time, but my Basic School fitness report contained a comment that I was highly proficient in drill and "should be considered for ceremonial duties." This innocent comment on my graduation fitness report would result in my future assignment as a ceremonial guard officer at the most prestigious post in the Marine Corps, the Marine Barracks in Washington, D.C.

The culmination of our training at the Basic School came in November when all of the lieutenants conducted the "Three Day War," an exercise where we put into practice all of the lessons we had learned during the previous six months. Adding to the realism of this exercise and to its difficulty, the "aggressors," the "enemy forces" we would be tested against, were members of the Schools Demonstration Troops, a company of battle-hardened Marines fresh from the war in South Vietnam. We all realized that the "Three Day War" would test us to the limit and point out any flaws in our training. Because I was rated near the top of my class, I was made platoon commander with 40 other lieutenants under my supervision. Once the war started there was no let up. For 24 hours a day we did the things that an infantry company in combat would be expected to do. We conducted combat and reconnaissance patrols, we assaulted fortified positions, we launched attacks in daylight and at night, we prepared defensive positions, and we called in artillery and mortar missions and air strikes. Just about every conceivable tactical scenario was covered. Throughout the exercise our instructors and the "aggressors" evaluated our performance, giving us valuable feedback on how we performed on each phase of the "war." The "war" took place as winter was approaching, resulting in weather that was both cold and rainy for the entire three days we were in the field. We had very little sleep during this exercise, perhaps only three or four hours, during the entire three days. We were wet, miserable, and bone tired at the end of the "war" but we were all filled with pride and exhilaration since we realized we had performed well and our instructors had recognized this in their verbal and written evaluations.

Our last event at the Basic School was graduation. The number one graduate in our class of 187 second lieutenants was Steve Berkheiser, who excelled in every aspect of our training. He went on to have a distinguished career culminating in promotion to Brigadier General (BGen.). He was the only member of our class to reach the flag officer ranks. I did not know it at the time, but Steve and I would serve together again in a year's time.

I had received my orders a week before graduation, and I was not surprised when I saw that I was to report to the 1st Marine Division in South Vietnam for duty. I had volunteered for this duty so I was pleased that I had not been assigned to a stateside school or some assignment other than one in South Vietnam. I firmly believed that the only way I could achieve my goal of making the people of my hometown proud of me was to fight and win wars in their behalf. I could only do this if I got to South Vietnam and the sooner the better.

After graduating from the Basic School I had a month of leave before I had to report to Staging Battalion at Camp Pendleton, California, for a few weeks of training before departing for South Vietnam. I spent the first few days of my leave with "Jane" in Virginia. Her classes took up a lot of her time but we managed to spend two weekends together enjoying the fall foliage during long walks near her home. It was difficult leaving "Jane" but I knew I was keeping her from her studies, which were very important to her. After a tearful parting, I drove up to my hometown to spend the remainder of my leave with my parents.

My mother suggested that I apply for a job as a substitute teacher with the Cherry Hill public school system while I was on leave. I was immediately given a week-long job teaching physical education at Cherry Hill High School. I enjoyed the opportunity to work for my old high school basketball coach, Reese Ruediger, and to practice with the Cherry Hill High School basketball team at the end of each school day. The next week, I found another teaching job at an elementary school taking over for the sixth grade teacher. At the end of my leave, I resigned my position as a substitute teacher and received a very nice letter from the Cherry Hill school system's superintendent of schools thanking me for my service and recommending me for any similar position in the future.

On the day I left for the Staging Battalion at Camp Pendleton, my parents drove me to the Philadelphia International Airport to see me off. I said my goodbyes to my brothers and sisters at our home and then loaded my foot locker and B-4 flight bag into the trunk of our car, trying not to let my emotions show. As we pulled out of our driveway, I waved to them and it suddenly hit me that I might never see them again. I looked at them over my shoulder until they disappeared in the distance. At the airport, I checked in and then went to the boarding gate with my parents, who were strangely quiet. When the flight was ready for boarding, I turned to my mother and father, and for a moment I thought my emotions would get the better of me. I felt a strong sense of homesickness, and I had not yet left the airport! I shook my father's hand, and he wished me luck. He said something about keeping my "eye on the ball" and to be sure "to write your mother." When I turned to my mother, I could see she was pale and was trying very hard to smile, but was not quite succeeding. I kissed my mother, and she clung to me as if she did not want me to go. She did not say a word, but I said, "I love you Mom. Don't worry. I'll be all right." She did not answer; she just looked at me and straightened the tie to my uniform. I then turned and went through the gate and down a flight of stairs to the plane which was parked on the tarmac. As I climbed the stairs to the plane's door, I turned and saw my mother and father standing in the window above me. I waved and my father waved back, but my mother only stood there hugging my father tightly. I entered the plane and settled into my seat. I looked out of the window of the plane, and I could still see my parents standing by the window at the boarding gate. My mother's head was buried in my father's shoulder, and I could see her sobbing. She had held back, not wanting to make me feel bad but now that I was on the plane she broke down. I felt terrible and had to fight the urge to leave the plane and run to her one more time. I felt as if I would cry myself if I continued to look her way, so I turned away and fastened my seatbelt. As I did, I heard a voice to my right say, "Are you Andy Finlayson?" I turned and saw a man who looked vaguely familiar. He was dressed in an American Airlines uniform but he was not part of the crew. When I acknowledged him he said, "I'm Tom Wright. We used to play baseball together at Wellwood Park before I moved to Moorestown." I recognized him as one of my best friends when I was 12 years old.

He noticed my Marine Corps uniform and asked me if I was going to Vietnam. I said I was going to California and then on to Vietnam. We chatted for a moment about our childhood friends, and then he told me to follow him up to the front of the plane. As we went into the first-class cabin, he approached the cabin attendant there and told her I was going to Vietnam. He told her I was a close friend, and asked if she would please find a seat in the first-class cabin for me. He then shook my hand and left the plane. I never saw him again. She gave me a first-class seat and treated me royally during the entire flight to California.

When I reported to the Staging Battalion at Camp Pendleton, California, I was delighted to find that Tom Dowd, my good friend from the Basic School, was assigned to the same replacement company, and we would be the only two officers among the 300 Marines with this unit. Our duties were primarily administrative, but fortunately for us, we had a few very good Marine administrative personnel in our company, so Tom and I did little more than sign orders and service record book entries each day when we were not in the field with our company participating in training.

For the most part, our training was very rudimentary and totally focused on lessons to prepare us for combat in South Vietnam. We received classes on patrolling, ambushes, land navigation, Vietnamese culture, mines and booby traps, U.S. policy in South Vietnam, field fortifications, field sanitation, first aid, and escape and evasion. For the Marines in our company, especially those who were recent boot camp graduates, the training was of some value, but Tom and I agreed that we had covered all of the subject matter before in the Basic School.

During my time at Staging Battalion, I got to know Tom Dowd quite well. We sought out each other's company both during training and after hours. We ate our meals together at the mess hall and officers' club, roomed next to each other in the BOQ, went to mass together each Sunday, and spent all day together training with our staging company. Although we were good friends at the Basic School, I never got to know the details of his life while the two of us were at Quantico. During conversations with Tom at Camp Pendleton, I found out that Tom had graduated from John Carroll High School in Birmingham, Alabama, and then went on to graduate from Saint Bernard's College in Cullman, Alabama, where he was a small-college All-American soccer player. Tom told me that, like me, he came from a large Irish-Catholic family. His father was the president of Gertz Department stores, and his family had recently moved from Alabama to Manhasset, New York, because of his father's work. Tom loved his family deeply. He would often regale me with amusing tales about the adventures of his brothers and sisters as they grew up. When he was in a serious mood he would also tell me with great pride about the accomplishments of his family members. He was especially proud of his father's stand against segregation during the turbulent civil rights period of the early 1960s when his family lived in Alabama. To say that Tom was idealistic would be a huge understatement — he was one of the most idealistic and dedicated men I have ever met.

Each day, after our training and administrative duties were complete, Tom and I would take a run in the hills behind the BOQ. Our run would end with a sprint up a small but steep hill where we would rest on some large rocks and take a few minutes to talk. Like most young men going off to war, Tom and I hid our apprehension with a false bravado, but after a while it was apparent that we both had the same fears about the fate that awaited us in South Vietnam. While Tom and I shared many things in common, we also found that we possessed some different traits that became apparent during these late afternoon talks on that rocky, windblown hill overlooking the desert-like terrain of Camp Pendleton. For instance, Tom was gregarious and fun-loving, while I was more laconic and introspective. Tom also had different aspirations. He did not intend to make the Marine Corps a career, but wanted to become a college professor or college-level soccer coach; I only wanted to be a Marine and did not even think about a civilian career. Tom was also very interested in finding the right woman and getting married. He wanted to have a large family, similar to the one he grew up in. I thought marriage would be a burden for me as a Marine officer, and I never felt keen about having a family. We both viewed the Marine Corps as a calling, something akin to the priesthood, but with Tom this calling would only be temporary, a passage on the way to something else in life. Several times, Tom told me that I was too committed to the Marine Corps, to the point of obsession. I did not share his view of my attitude about the Marine Corps, but I could see he found my lack of any aspirations outside of the Marine Corps to be a bit strange and even unhealthy. He told me on more than one occasion that I was far too serious and needed to lighten up a bit.

Near the end of our training, I received a call from my old roommate at the Naval Academy, George Philip, who was on Christmas leave with his family at Camp Pendleton. His father, Col. Wilbur Helmer, was stationed at Camp Pendleton, and one night George invited me to come over to their home for dinner. After a very nice meal, Col. Helmer, George, and I went out on the front porch of their home to talk for a while. It was during this talk that a wave of apprehension came over me. I wondered if I would be able to lead Marines in combat. I feared that I might make mistakes that would get my men killed. I questioned whether I was sufficiently trained or properly motivated to be a capable Marine officer. I shared my concerns with Col. Helmer and sought his advice since I knew he had extensive combat experience, and he knew how men reacted in combat. He leaned back in his chair, as if to collect his thoughts, choosing his words carefully before he responded to my question. He told me not to worry. He told me that I had all the training I needed to do my job as a second lieutenant and that the screening process at the Naval Academy and at the Basic School was more than enough to prove my motivation was up to the task. He then offered me some practical advice, based as he put it "from a trench line view of life." He told me,

> Andy, a Marine officer must never think of himself; that will always lead to trouble. Think only about your job and how to do it better than anyone else. Trust and use your SNCO's because without them you cannot be a good officer. They are the backbone of the Corps. You, as an officer, will plan and supervise, but they will execute. Don't try to do their job for them. Tell them what you want done and then stand back while they do it. In combat, you must always be thinking like a chess player — think several moves ahead — and when you do this you will be able to respond to any situation. Always ask, "What if" type questions. What if the enemy does

this? What if that hill has a reverse slope defense on it? What if the enemy tries to attack my position from this direction or that one? What if? What if? What if? If you are always thinking like this, you will not have time to be frightened and you will not fail your men. They expect tactical proficiency from you. That is all. They do not want you to be their friend, and you will never be their hero. You are the guy who knows his job and that knowledge will keep them alive. That is what they have to know, and that is what you must do if you want to be a good combat leader.

When I left Col. Helmer that evening and drove back to Staging Battalion I felt at ease with myself and filled with a new sense of confidence. I began a lifetime of asking "What if" questions that evening and charting the path that Col. Helmer laid out for me.

In late January 1967, our three weeks of training at the Staging Battalion ended. I called my parents and "Jane" the night before I was due to ship out for South Vietnam, using the pay telephone that was in the hallway of the BOQ. I knew I would be talking for a long time, so I went to the bank on base and had ten dollars converted into change. I poured the ten dollars of quarters and dimes into that pay phone, trying to squeeze out a few last words to the people I cared about, desperately searching for the right words to express my feelings. My mother and father wished me luck and told me not to take any unnecessary chances before finally telling me to write to them as soon as I got to South Vietnam.

My call to "Jane" was far more emotional and difficult. I had called her every other day while I was at Camp Pendleton, but this call was much harder to make. It dawned on me that I would not see "Jane" again for over a year, and I wondered if our relationship would last while I was deployed to the war zone. She promised to write to me often and to share any news from me with my mother. As I ran out of change for the telephone, the last words I heard from "Jane" were, "I love you, Andy. Please don't forget me. I will be waiting for you when you return."

The next day early in the morning, Tom Dowd and I boarded a chartered commercial airliner, along with 200 other Marines, and flew to Okinawa. I was finally on my way to war. As the plane lifted off into the sky, I wondered if I would ever hear the voices of my parents and "Jane" again.

After a very long plane ride over the Pacific, we landed on Okinawa and were told we would wait for a few days until our transportation to the war zone "down south" could be scheduled. Tom and I spent two days at Camp Hansen, the large Marine Corps base on Okinawa, before we were finally informed that a plane would be leaving that evening for South Vietnam and we should be packed and ready to take a bus to the airfield. Tom and I ate one last meal at the Camp Hansen officers' club, made sure we packed all of our bags, set our alarm clocks, and turned in for the night. I was still not over my jet lag so I woke up in the middle of the night, got out of bed, and sat down in an armchair near my bed trying to read and, periodically, drifting in and out of sleep.

The next thing I knew I heard a voice telling me, "Get up Andy, it's time to go, get up." I had fallen asleep in the chair in my BOQ room, relying on my alarm clock to wake me. I looked up to see Tom Dowd in front of me with a worried look on his face. I then looked at my watch and saw the time was 0315, fifteen minutes after I had set my alarm clock to go off. For some reason the alarm clock had not gone off, and now I had to scramble to gather up my B-4 flight bag and my footlocker and stumble out the door with Tom helping me with my luggage. Tom told me the bus was supposed to leave at 0315, but the driver agreed to wait while Tom searched for me. Had Tom not come to get me, I would have "missed movement," a very serious breach of military conduct akin to going AWOL, but more serious. Thoughts of a possible court-martial raced through my head as Tom and I raced breathlessly through the night to the parking lot, stumbling a few times under the weight of my luggage. The bus driver, a young corporal (Cpl.), opened the door of the bus, and we climbed aboard. I felt mortified that I was late, and I could tell a few of the Marines in the bus were surprised to see an officer in such an embarrassing position. Tom and I sat next to each other, but neither one of us said a word on the 30-minute ride to the airfield. When we arrived, we had our baggage tagged, our orders inspected, and then we boarded a U.S. Marine Corps C-130 transport plane. We sat facing each other inside the fuselage, shoulder to shoulder with the other Marines, shifting our position in the uncomfortable webbing that passed for a seat. It was dark, noisy, hot and uncomfortable, but at last I was on my way to the war. Next stop, South Vietnam.

A wall of monsoon clouds hid the shoreline as we approached the coast of South Vietnam. Turning in my seat I could, with some difficulty and discomfort, see through one of the small windows of the C-130 and catch brief glimpses of the South China Sea and some small fishing boats below us as we descended. A minute later, I could make out the shoreline under us. Through some breaking clouds, I observed the patchwork of verdant rice paddies below and the reflection of the sun's bright rays against the corrugated metal roofs of Vietnamese houses. As the huge transport plane turned to begin its final approach to the Da Nang Airfield, I glanced out of the window again and caught a glimpse of the dark, steel gray mountains to the west. The thick, leaden clouds cast dark shadows over the mountains and hid their peaks from my eyes. There was something ominous and sinister about the mountains, something foreboding, yet I marveled at their beauty and, in some odd way, I felt these mountains were going to be important to me. Little did I realize that in the coming months these mountains would be my home, my refuge, and my battleground for my war against the Vietnamese communists.

The C-130 touched down on the runway, roaring and shuddering like some huge metal beast, until it finally slowed down and made a sharp turn toward the Da Nang air terminal apron. When the plane stopped, the rear cargo hatch lowered, letting in the bright noon sun, the stifling heat, and the choking dust. Tom and I, along with the other 60-odd passengers, exited the plane, retrieved our baggage on the sweltering tarmac, and trudged off to the terminal's receiving area 100 yards away. The date was 2 February 1967, the middle of South Vietnam's winter monsoon season. The heat and humidity quickly turned our uniforms into sodden, moist shrouds that clung to our bodies, giving us the appearance of green prunes. Inside the terminal, nothing more than a wooden hut that measured 60 feet by 120 feet with a corrugated metal roof, we approached a long counter manned by several enlisted Marines. They checked our paperwork in silence and told us to wait for transportation to take us to transit billeting. A group of cocky and jubilant Marines dressed in clean khaki uniforms were standing on one side of the terminal. They were Marines who had completed their 13-month tour of duty in South Vietnam and now were eagerly waiting to board a plane that would return them to "the world," as they called the U.S. I heard one of these veterans tell a young Marine Private First Class (PFC) who had arrived with us,

"You'll be sorry!" I simply shrugged off this comment as the bravado of a veteran of 13 months of combat. In a few months, his words would become abundantly clear to me.

After we had completed our paperwork, a Marine Staff Noncommissioned Officer (SNCO) arrived and announced that transportation for both the enlisted men and the officers was waiting outside. The enlisted men boarded two busses, while I, Tom, and four other officers climbed into the back of a Marine "Six By" truck, along with all of our baggage. We did not get off to an auspicious start because the truck had some transmission problems, and the driver, a Marine corporal, obviously fancied himself to be a drag race driver. The truck jolted forward, jolted again, and then began to grind its gears as we pulled out of the terminal parking lot and began speeding toward our destination, the Officers Transient BOQ at 1st Marine Division Headquarters at Hill 327, which was located only a few miles west of Da Nang.

The trip from the airport to the division headquarters was a short one, about 15 minutes. As we drove along, I eagerly took in my new surroundings. Just outside the airfield's perimeter fence, we passed through the village of Phouc Tuong, better known as Dogpatch to the Marines. This ramshackle village of huts and garish shops had once been open to Marines on liberty, but after a few unfortunate incidents involving the deaths of several Marines, it had been placed "off limits" to all U.S. personnel. Its main street led directly to the division command post (CP) a few miles northwest of the village. This street was choked with military traffic and Vietnamese civilians walking and riding on motorbikes. The fumes from the numerous vehicles filled the air with acrid, gray plumes of smoke, and their wheels churned up a fine dust that swirled and eddied everywhere.

After a bumpy and dusty ride, our truck arrived at the base of Hill 327 and made a

Dogpatch Village, Quang Nam Province, RVN.

sharp left turn into the parking area for the 1st Marine Division CP. The driver lowered the back of the truck and we jumped out, taking our baggage with us. We were taken to the division personnel office and told that Major General (MGen.) Herman Nickerson, the Commanding General of the division, was extremely busy and would not be able to talk to us until the following morning, so we would have to spend the night in the transient officers' quarters just below the CP. Tom Dowd and I welcomed this respite after our long flight and dusty trip to the CP and decided we could certainly wait another 24 hours before we went to war. We took our baggage down to the transient officers' quarters, a collection of SEA huts nestled on the side of Hill 327 just a few yards uphill from the division officers' club. We found two empty cots, stowed our gear under the cots, and waited for dinner to be served in the officers' club.

We both had time to write a letter home and to talk about what the next day might bring. We had heard from the personnel officer at the CP that it was likely Gen. Nickerson would assign us to the 1st Marine Regiment since they were short officers. Tom and I hoped that we could be assigned to the same unit, and we greeted this news with enthusiasm. After a surprisingly good meal in the officers' club, we watched a movie with the division's staff officers and had a few beers before retiring for the night. We both found the food and accommodations at the division CP to be better than we expected, but we knew full well such luxury and comfort did not await us in a Marine infantry regiment. As we settled in for the night, we found it difficult to sleep soundly because we could hear outgoing artillery fire and see flares in the distance, two reminders that we were in a war zone, and fighting was going on just a few miles away in the rice paddies and hills of Quang Nam Province.

The next morning we rose early, shaved and washed in the communal head, and waited for our meeting with Gen. Nickerson and our assignment orders. We did not have long to wait. We reported to the division personnel office at 0800, and within minutes we were told a decision had been made on our assignments. Tom would be going to the 1st Marines, as expected, but my orders had been changed overnight, assigning me to the 1st Force Reconnaissance Company. When the personnel officer told me of my new assignment, I could not believe my ears, and then a deep sense of fear set in. I had heard that force reconnaissance Marines did some of the most dangerous work in the war, and they often operated in areas completely controlled by the enemy. Everything I had heard about recon Marines and the rigorous entry requirements an officer had to meet to join such an elite, highly trained unit, made me think some big mistake had been made. I felt that I was woefully unprepared for such an assignment, especially considering the fact that I was a newly minted 2nd lieutenant fresh out of the Basic School. When I learned this news, Tom turned to me with a look in his eyes that told me he was worried for me. I asked the personnel officer why my orders were changed from the 1st Marines and he said, "Lieutenant, you are being sent to 1st Force Recon because they lost a lieutenant there yesterday, and they need a replacement officer, one who is parachute qualified. You fit the bill." His answer did nothing to assuage my apprehension.

After a two-hour wait, we went into the office of Gen. Nickerson and stood at attention in front of his desk. Gen. Nickerson was a tall, dark, distinguished looking gentleman with a serious but pleasant demeanor. He shook our hands and welcomed us to his division. Then he let us know in no uncertain terms what he expected of us. He told us he did not want us to kill Marines by making stupid mistakes, or to kill innocent civilians by the profligate use of supporting arms, or to allow our Marines to harm each other by having accidental discharges. He asked us a few questions about our families, and then the meeting ended. It had taken only a few minutes. We returned to the personnel office, picked up our orders, and then Tom boarded a two-and-a-half-ton truck that would take him to the 1st Marines. I began to walk down Hill 327 to the headquarters of 1st Reconnaissance Battalion, nestled at the bottom of the hill directly across the road from the entrance to the division CP. As I walked down the dusty road to my new assignment, the truck carrying Tom and several enlisted Marines destined for the 1st Marines passed me, and Tom smiled broadly, waving to me from the back of the truck as it passed. Above the sound of the truck's engine I heard him say, "Keep your head down, Andy." I returned the wave and shouted that he should visit me whenever he got the chance. That was the last time I saw my good friend because he was killed in action just a few weeks later. To this day, I can still see Tom's smiling face as he drove away from me. He was a prince of a man, and I made it a point to visit his grave in Arlington National Cemetery several times in later years whenever I was stationed in the Washington, D.C., area.

As I approached the gate of Camp Reasoner, the home of the 1st Reconnaissance Battalion and the attached 1st Force Reconnaissance Company, a sentry noticed I was struggling with my footlocker and B-4 bag. He suggested I leave my baggage with him, and he would arrange for a vehicle to take it to my new quarters. I thanked him and asked for directions to the battalion headquarters, which he quickly pointed out among the dozens of SEA huts and other buildings inside the barbed wire perimeter of Camp

Camp Reasoner, home of the 1st Reconnaissance Battalion.

Camp Reasoner, Hill 327.

Reasoner. As I walked to the battalion headquarters, an officer approached me and asked
me if I knew where I was going. I instantly recognized him from my days at the Naval
Academy. It was Capt. Michael D. Ceretta, and he remembered my name immediately. He
told me I should report to the headquarters of 1st Force Reconnaissance Company before
going to the battalion headquarters. Maj. Bill Lowrey, the company's Commanding Officer
(CO), was expecting me, and he wanted to talk to me before I was given my assignment
in the company. I felt instantly at ease seeing Capt. Ceretta. He was a familiar face since
I took his chemistry class during my plebe year at Annapolis, and I had always admired
him for his professionalism and approachability. I followed him along a path of wooden
pallets winding along the side of the hill until we came upon a nondescript SEA hut with
a scarlet and gold wooden sign outside that read "First Force Reconnaissance Company,
Home of the Night Stalkers." Below the lettering were large, gold, Marine Corps parachute
jump wings. We entered the screen door and were met by the company 1st Sgt. and the
company gunnery sergeant (GySgt.). The senior SNCOs were friendly, but I could tell they
were sizing me up. They noticed the gold jump wings I was wearing on my utility uniform
and asked me if I had served in a "stateside recon outfit" before. I told them I had not. I
could sense they were a bit taken aback that a young second lieutenant would have qualified
for gold jump wings without being assigned to one of the few USMC units that could issue
these wings. I earned my Navy-Marine Corps jump wings while I was at the Naval Academy, foregoing my summer leave one year to attend the U.S. Army's airborne school at
Fort Benning, Georgia, and then took several days from my Christmas vacation my senior

year to make the additional parachute jumps needed to qualify for my wings. I did not bother to explain this to them since they did not ask. In addition to the two SNCOs, there were a few clerks in the office, and one of them was instructed to take my paperwork up to battalion. Maj. Lowrey was out running, but I was told he would be back momentarily, so I took a seat and waited for him. The 1st Sgt. returned to his desk and the gunny left the SEA hut, leaving me to wait for Maj. Lowrey in silence. The only noise in the office was the sound of typewriters hammering away on the paperwork needed to make the Marine Corps function, such as endorsements for orders, unit diaries, muster rolls, command chronologies, and patrol reports.

After 20 minutes, the screen door of the company office swung open, and a trim, physically fit man with close-cropped hair strode in. He appeared to be in his early thirties and was very confident in himself. He looked every bit the CO of an elite unit despite the absence of any rank insignia and the fact that he was dressed solely in Marine Corps khaki running shorts and combat boots. He was sweating profusely from his run, but he immediately came up to me, smiled broadly, and greeted me with a warm, but very moist, handshake. He told me to stand at ease and follow him into his small, hot office at the back of the SEA hut where he motioned me to sit down while he reached into a small refrigerator and pulled out two cans of Coke. He offered me one while he pulled my Officer Record Book (ORB) from a stack of papers in his "in" box and began silently to look through it, as if searching for some hidden information that might explain why this very young 2nd lieutenant was sitting in his office with orders to join his command.

For a fleeting moment, it occurred to me that he might not want me under his command, especially given my lack

Headquarters of the 1st Force Reconnaissance Company, Camp Reasoner as seen from the officers' hootch.

of experience with reconnaissance work and my obvious lack of any specialized reconnaissance training that would benefit such an elite unit. However, my fears were assuaged when he looked up, smiled, and said, "Welcome aboard, Finlayson. I have been waiting for you to show up because we have a lot of work that needs to be done, and I think you are the man to help us do it." With that he endorsed my orders and told me to stand by to see the commanding officer of the 1st Reconnaissance Battalion, Col. Donald N. McKeon, who, he assured me, was eager to meet me and tell me something about my new duties. Maj. Lowrey explained that the 1st Force Reconnaissance Company had been assigned "OPCON" to the 1st Reconnaissance Battalion ever since the company had returned a few months ago from Dong Ha near the DMZ. After a few more minutes of conversation concerning my training back in the States, Maj. Lowrey took me to the SEA hut nearby that served as both Lt. Col. McKeon's office and living quarters.

I stepped into Lt. Col. McKeon's office and he rose behind his desk to greet me. He was a distinguished looking man, confident in himself and fully in command. I immediately felt I was in the presence of a truly superior officer who knew what he was doing and knew how to lead men in combat. From his close-cropped hair and chiseled features to his starched utility uniform and spit-shined boots, he was the picture of a Marine leader.

After introducing me, Maj. Lowrey excused himself and told me to see him after my interview with Lt. Col. McKeon was finished; he wanted to show me my quarters and have me meet several other key individuals. Lt. Col. McKeon made me feel very much at ease, asking questions about my family, my training prior to coming to Vietnam, and whether or not I was adapting to the heat and humidity. He told me that the mission of the 1st Reconnaissance Battalion was to serve as the "eyes and ears" for the 1st Marine Division, and the battalion did this by conducting two types of patrols, primarily in areas controlled by the enemy and far from friendly lines. He explained that the two types of patrols were called "Stingray" patrols and deep reconnaissance patrols. I had never heard of these types of patrols at the Basic School, so Col. McKeon described them to me. A "Stingray" patrol was a patrol where a small reconnaissance team would be "inserted" into an area controlled by the enemy but within range of friendly artillery so the patrol could call in artillery fire, or close air support, on any enemy sighted by the patrol. Deep reconnaissance patrols were patrols in enemy-controlled territory also, but outside the artillery fan and, thus, were more dangerous and required more stealth since the patrol would not have artillery to protect it if it got into trouble.

Col. McKeon reminded me that my company, 1st Force Reconnaissance Company, had been created by the Marine Corps specifically for deep reconnaissance and that the majority of these deep reconnaissance missions west of Da Nang would be carried out by my company. He also told me that my company used smaller teams than the teams sent out by the battalion, usually only six to eight Marines, because our table of organization (T/O) had platoons of only 15 men while the battalion platoons had 26 men. Most battalion teams went on patrol with 10–12 men. While the missions assigned to both the battalion and force teams were the same in most cases, the size, equipment, and the methods used were somewhat different. Lt. Col. McKeon ended our conversation by again welcoming me to the battalion and cautioning me about adapting to the heat. He also told me that it was his policy to send all new patrol leaders out on three "snap in" patrols where the new officer would act as an observer. In this way, a new patrol leader would learn his trade before actually taking his own team into the areas controlled by the enemy.

After my meeting with Lt. Col. McKeon, I was taken to the SEA hut office of the Intelligence Officer for the battalion, 1st Lt. Mike St. Clair. Mike was a former Marine SNCO who received a meritorious commission. When I met him I was immediately impressed by his knowledge of, and passion for, his job. He appeared to be very busy, but he took a considerable amount of his time to explain to me the enemy situation in the 1st Marine Division's Tactical Area of Responsibility (TAOR), stressing how important the work of the reconnaissance teams was in developing our knowledge of the enemy. He showed me a map with the locations of enemy units marked in red on it, and he pointed out places where I could be expected to conduct my patrols.

I was surprised and somewhat fascinated by the names of the places he mentioned, and I had difficulty remembering them as he rattled them off. Starting in the north of the TAOR he mentioned the A Shau Valley far to the west near the Laotian border before pointing out several locations north and west of Da Nang with names such as Elephant Valley, the Garden of Eden, the Enchanted Forest, Happy Valley, Charlie Ridge, the Ong Thu Slope, Base Area 112, and Antenna Valley. These names were a blur to me then as Mike ran his hand over the map from north to south, but in the coming months I would come to know each of these areas quite well.

Mike also spent a few minutes explaining to me that before each patrol, I would be given a patrol order from the battalion S-3, and from this I would prepare my own patrol order, which I would use to brief my team. He gave me several samples of what he considered good patrol orders to study. He also told me that after each patrol a recon team would be debriefed immediately so he could write a patrol report and send it to the division G-2 within hours of the patrol's completion. He handed me several of these patrol reports and explained that such items as the location of trails and streams in the patrol area, any enemy sightings and contacts, and a strip map made of the patrol route within its assigned No Fire Zone (NFZ) were always included in these reports. He went on to explain the patrol's NFZ was a block of territory assigned to each patrol that varied in size but normally was 3000 meters by 3000 meters. He told me the NFZ was necessary to prevent any friendly units from operating in it and to require any artillery fires or air strikes to be cleared by the patrol before they could be used. This was done to prevent friendly fires from killing or wounding members of the patrol. Mike stressed that he kept very detailed records of the patrols, and it was a wise patrol leader who came to him prior to a patrol to review the reports he had on file that pertained to an area for an upcoming patrol. I made a quick note in my patrol leader's notebook to be sure to do this prior to every patrol, and I was later thankful that I took Mike's advice.

My next stop was the Operations Office, or S-3 shop as most of us called it, which was located in an enlarged SEA hut surrounded with sandbags for protection. There I met the Operations Officer for the battalion, Maj. Charles M. Welzant, another former Marine SNCO who was commissioned due to the expanding Corps' need for officers. Tall, blond, sinewy and professional, Maj. Welzant was a no-nonsense individual who took his job as operations officer very seriously, as evidenced by the highly organized appearance of his operations center and the very serious demeanor of the enlisted Marines who worked there.

His operations chief was 1st Sgt. Clovis Coffman, a former patrol leader on his second tour in Vietnam. Coffman was revered by the Marines he served with for his combat experience in both the Korean and Vietnam Wars and his extraordinary heroism and multiple Purple Hearts. I was to find out later that most of the doctrine written for the "Stingray" concept had been written by 1st Sgt. Coffman. Maj. Welzant and 1st Sgt. Clovis Coffman gave me a tour of the Operations Center and explained to me how they continuously monitored the progress of as many as 24 recon patrols operating at any given time throughout the division's TAOR. Each day, they organized and executed as many as a dozen recon patrol insertions and extractions, primarily by helicopter but on occasion by rubber boat or truck. It was evident they had to keep a lot of balls in the air with so many patrols operating in enemy-controlled areas at the same time.

At one end of the Operations Office was the communications area where one or two communicators sat in front of a bank of radios monitoring the radio frequencies of the recon patrols, as well as the frequencies of other units that might be called upon to assist a patrol in trouble, such as the 1st Marine Air Wing and the 12th Marines, the division's artillery regiment. As I listened to the radio traffic, I noticed that these transmissions were distinctly different than those of other Marine units. The recon teams in the field did not talk in a normal tone of voice, but instead they whispered their messages into their radio handsets. I also noted that the S-3 communicators were busy writing down messages from the recon patrols and handing them to 1st Sgt. Coffman, who logged them into a book and then posted the information they contained on the huge situation map that covered one wall of the operations center.

These reports from the recon teams, which I would soon be writing myself from the field, were called SALUTE reports, and they contained the essential information needed concerning a sighting of the enemy. SALUTE stood for the first letters of each paragraph of the report. The S stood for "sighting," the A for "activity," the L for "location" in map grid coordinates, the U for "uniforms," the T for "time of sighting," and the E for "equipment." I made it a point to visit the S-3 shop each day to read the incoming SALUTE reports from the teams in the field, a practice that enabled me to get a good picture of what the enemy was up to and to form in my mind an initial idea of their intentions. If Maj. Welzant or 1st Sgt. Coffman were in the S-3 shop during my daily visit, I would ask them what the SALUTE reports were telling them about the enemy's activities and intentions. After many months of doing this, it became apparent to me that the enemy was, like most humans, a creature of habit since sightings of the enemy seemed to repeat themselves in the same areas of the TAOR.

On Maj. Welzant's desk at the other end of the operations office was a bank of telephones that he used to contact the Division G-2 (Intelligence), the 12th Marines, the 1st Marine Air Wing operations center at the Da Nang airfield, and several other key units that either needed to have information from our recon teams or were needed to respond to a request generated by a recon team.

Before I left the Operations Center, Maj. Welzant told me that on the day of my team's insertion, I would meet with the pilots of the helicopters that would be inserting the team so both I and the pilots could receive a briefing from him on the mission of the team, the enemy situation near the patrol's NFZ, and the locations for the insertion and extraction Landing Zones (LZs), as well as any alternate LZs nearby. I came away from my meeting with Maj. Welzant and 1st Sgt. Coffman deeply impressed by their knowledge and attention to detail. In the coming months, my respect for both of these men would only grow.

As I walked out of the Operations Center into the searing heat and the bright sunlight, I heard a voice behind me say, "Lieutenant, would you like to eat some lunch?" It was 1st Sgt. Clovis Coffman. He guided me to the battalion's mess hall, located on the north side of the camp, a short walk from the Operations Center. This building was different from all the rest of the buildings on the camp, which were primarily SEA huts. It was rather large with three sections. One section housed the kitchen. Another was for enlisted Marines in the rank of sergeant (Sgt.) and below. The third section, which Clovis Coffman guided me to, was for the officers and SNCO's, and it was raised off the ground 5–6 feet, giving a view from its interior to most of the camp and the rice paddies and villages that stretched out to the east toward the city of Da Nang.

I was very surprised when I walked into this mess hall since it was so different from what I had expected to find in a combat zone. There were a dozen tables for 4–6 people in it, and each table had a red and white checkered table cloth and place setting with stainless steel flatware and paper table napkins. Against one side of the mess hall was a milk machine, an unheard-of luxury for most Marines serving in the Da Nang TAOR, and a freezer with real ice cream containers in it, another extremely rare culinary treat for any Marine serving in combat. Against another wall was a long table filled with food,

The SNCO and Officers Mess at Camp Reasoner.

including individual plates of mixed salad, hot trays of various meats and vegetables, and individual plates of desserts. I was astounded that such good food would be available to me in Vietnam, having been conditioned to expect nothing but C rations. I was to find out that this magnificent mess hall was run by an E-5 Sgt. in his late forties who had been in the Marine Raiders during World War II. He had reached the rank of master sergeant (MSgt.) after the war, but he was court-martialed for taking meat home in his automobile and reduced to the rank of private. He was an exceptionally good cook and administrator, but the court-martial conviction resulted in his terminal rank of Sgt. after over 30 years of service. During my entire career in the Marine Corps, I never ate in a better mess hall than the one run by this crusty old sergeant.

After lunch, I returned to the company office to meet again with Maj. Lowrey. When I arrived I noticed that my personal luggage had already been taken from his office and delivered to my "home" for the next ten months, a SEA hut that housed the company grade officers of the 1st Force Reconnaissance Company. Maj. Lowrey pointed to the SEA hut that housed his officers and asked me to follow him. The hut was located on the north side of the camp along a path that hugged the side of the hill. The path was made of wooden pallets and lined with banana trees and waist-high grass. Unlike many SEA huts, it had a back porch, and below the porch was an outdoor, cold water shower that had been constructed from a discarded external fuel tank once the property of some Marine aviation unit.

Inside, I met the officer I was to replace, Lt. John King. He welcomed me warmly and told me that I could have his rack since he was leaving and he could not take it with him. This rack was actually a hospital bed that someone had "borrowed" from "Charlie Med" down the road. Again, I was surprised to find such a comfortable bed in a combat zone since I was told back at the Basic School that I could expect only the hard ground or, if lucky, a canvas cot to sleep on while in Vietnam. John even gave me his bed sheets and pillow cases, which had a very musty smell to them, the result of too many washes in rice paddy water. I was beginning to like the luxury I saw at Camp Reasoner, but I suspected there might be some price to pay for all of this unexpected good food and comfort.

John introduced me to two other officers in the hut, Lt. Ken Carlisle and Lt. Mike Henry, and told me that Lt. Lenny Torres and Lt. Eric Barnes were out on patrol. As I dropped my gear at the foot of my newly acquired bed, I looked around the interior of the SEA hut. Several distinct living areas had been apportioned so that each of the six officers living in the hut had their own private space. Each space was different and reflected the personal preferences of the officer who occupied it. There were locally made wooden footlockers and roughly constructed chests and tables in each of the individual areas, along with cots with mosquito netting covering them. The mattresses on the cots ran the gamut from rubber air mattresses to locally made, brightly colored quilts. Field packs, cartridge belts, combat boots, rifles and other bits of field equipment hung from nails on the walls and the cross boards of the hut and seemed to stand out from the other objects that were less discernible. On the floor were several C ration boxes with various meals missing from them. The entire "hootch," as we called it, smelled of diesel oil which had been liberally spread on the deck to keep the dust down, a recurrent problem since the camp's helicopter pad, LZ Finch, was only 50 yards below our hootch, and each helicopter's arrival and departure produced swirling clouds of fine dust that permeated everything nearby. I was told that I must never leave the back door of the hootch open since this would result in everything in the hootch receiving a fine "dusting" whenever a helicopter used our LZ. An old, battered refrigerator was along the back wall of the hootch next to the back door, and on a table made of ammunition boxes in the middle of the hootch were a record player and a few albums of popular music of dubious origin. There were never more than a half dozen records in our collection, but two of them were played endlessly by my fellow lieutenants: the "Greatest Hits of the Lettermen" and a collection of "Golden Oldies" from the 1950s and early 1960s.

After settling in and stowing my gear under my newly acquired bed, I went out on the back porch of our hootch and sat down in one of the crudely made "deck chairs" that had been constructed out of old ammunition boxes and other pieces of salvaged lumber. The view from our back porch was truly magnificent and one that will always be fixed in my mind. Because Camp Reasoner was built on the side of Hill 327, our hootch's entrance was at ground level, but the rear was elevated by ten feet, making the porch more like a deck than a patio. Below me and to my right was LZ Finch and beyond that was the camp's perimeter of barbed wire and, at 50-yard intervals, sandbagged defensive bunkers. Beyond the perimeter were the deep, emerald green rice paddy fields and dark tree lines of Da Son and Phuoc Ly hamlets. Beyond the hamlets was a vista that stretched all the way to the city of Da Nang. I always felt a sense of peace and tranquility when I sat on

Camp Reasoner and LZ Finch aerial view.

the porch and looked out in the direction of the South China Sea several miles away to the northeast. During the day, there was often a cool breeze rising up from the paddies and the green rice fields below us. On many days, I would sit on this back porch and gaze out at the rural scene in front of me, taking in the rich blue of the sky and the varying shades of green in the fields and tree lines. I followed the languid movements of the water buffaloes roaming near our perimeter wire or the daily routine of farmers tending their paddies. These scenes set my soul at peace and transported me to a level of consciousness far removed from the stress of long-range patrolling. In the evenings, the twinkling lights from the villages and Da Nang under a clear, star-studded sky gave the impression that no war was being fought, although this tranquil scene was often interrupted by periodic artillery fire and the eerie, ghostlike appearance of flares in the distance or the piercing trajectories of red tracers arching through the sky. For the next ten months the back porch of our hootch was the place where field gear was cleaned, coffee sipped, patrol orders written, letters read and replied to, and conversations struck. It was our social gathering spot and refuge from the war.

I spent four days at Camp Reasoner before I went on my first patrol. Maj. Lowrey informed me that since I was a recent graduate of the Basic School and had no previous reconnaissance training I did not yet possess the skills necessary to lead a long-range reconnaissance patrol. The solution to this deficiency was a requirement to go on three "snap in" or orientation patrols as an "observer" before I would be allowed to lead my first patrol. On these "snap in" patrols, I would observe the actions of the patrol leaders and learn from them. He informed me that the first of my "snap in" patrols would be as a member of Sgt. McDonald's team. He was the acting platoon commander of the 5th Platoon, the platoon I was most likely to be officially assigned, since that had been Lt. King's platoon. Sgt. McDonald was a veteran of over 30 patrols and had only two more

Landing Zone Finch, Camp Reasoner.

months left on his 13-month tour of duty. Maj. Lowrey said that Sgt. McDonald was one of the best patrol leaders in the company, and I should carefully note everything he did before and during the patrol. After I had completed this first patrol with Sgt. McDonald and his team, I would be assigned to two other patrol leaders, one from the battalion so I could compare their techniques with those of the company, and the other with one of the company's officers. He stressed that after I had successfully completed these three patrols, the comments of the three patrol leaders would be taken into consideration to determine whether or not I was ready to assume the duties of a patrol leader and take out my first patrol on my own.

During the four days prior to my first patrol, I busied myself by drawing all of my field equipment, studying old patrol reports in the S-2 office, running three miles a day with the 5th Platoon, reviewing my Basic School notes on field communications and the use of supporting arms, and talking to the other officers in my hootch about what I needed to know for my first patrol. In the evenings, I spent my time in the S-3 shop monitoring the progress of patrols in the field as they reported in via radio and tracking their progress on the large map of the Da Nang–Chu Lai TAOR. In the S-3 shop's dim light, amid the crackling of the radios and the intermittent clapping of a typewriter, I tried to digest as much information as I could about the area I would be making my patrols in. In the next ten months, I would spend many hours in the S-3 shop doing the same thing: trying to find out all I could about where I was going. I was never sorry I did this. It was time very well spent.

2

Lost Friends and Deep in Enemy-Held Territory

The days before my first patrol passed quickly, too quickly perhaps, because even though Sgt. McDonald and my hootch mates helped me as much as they could, I felt I was somewhat ill-prepared for my first trip into enemy-controlled territory. The lieutenants in my hootch — Eric Barnes, Mike Henry, Ken Carlyle, John King, Lenny Torres, and Frank Guderman — all were very helpful and went out of their way to answer any questions I had, freely offering their advice based upon their experience. All of them, with the exception of Frank Guderman, who was the supply officer, had led patrols, so their advice was very welcome, indeed.

Early in the day before my first patrol's insertion, Sgt. McDonald came to my hootch and invited me to join the other members of the patrol, code-named Brisbane, so I could

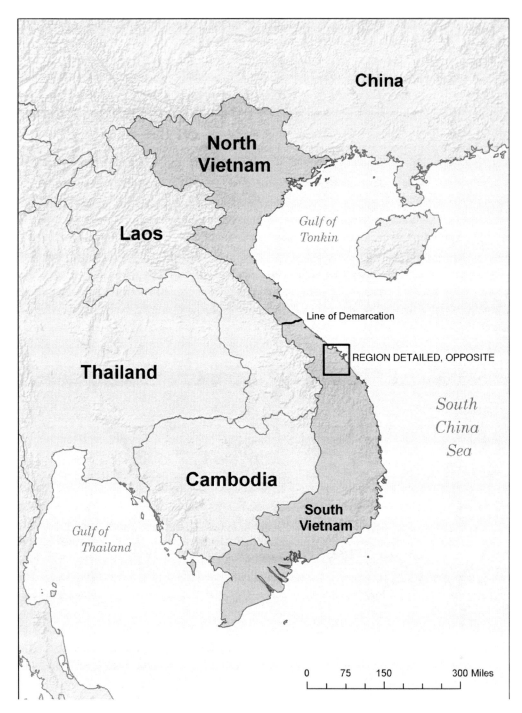

be introduced to them. I could tell that every Marine in the patrol was sizing me up and wondering whether or not I would be a hindrance or a help on the patrol. They did not say anything, but I could read the apprehension in their eyes. They knew I would soon become a patrol leader for one of the platoon's two patrols, Brisbane or Killer Kane, so their interest in me was not casual or insignificant. I was determined to make the correct

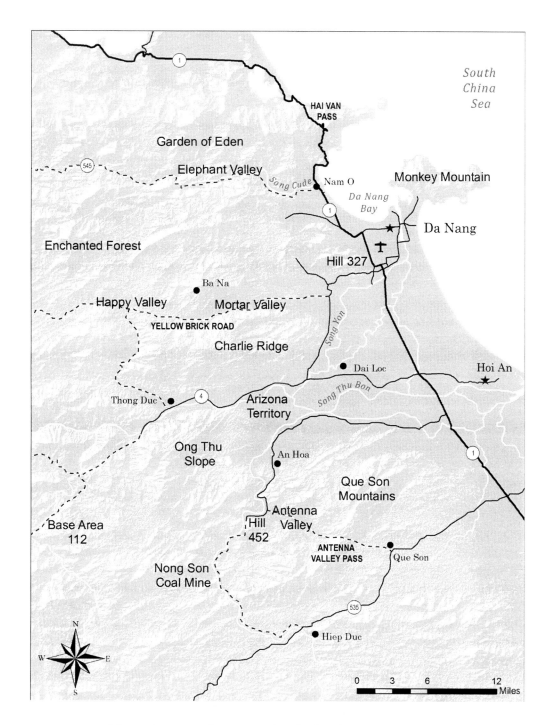

The region around Da Nang, in which Killer Kane operated.

impression and to do everything possible to assuage their apprehension, but I knew this would take time. These first few minutes were important since they were my only chance to make a good impression. Sgt. McDonald asked me if I wanted to say anything to the team. I did not feel it was the time or place for any long-winded speech, so I merely stated that I was very proud to be among them and that I realized I had a lot to learn about reconnaissance patrolling. I asked them to share their knowledge with me and always to feel free to talk to me if they had any ideas about how I might improve the conduct of a patrol.

After my introduction, Sgt. McDonald sat us down and gave a detailed patrol order. I was amazed by the level of detail in his order. It seemed as if he had thought of everything and left nothing to chance. I could see that every member of the team had complete confidence in his abilities. After listening to his patrol order, I felt the same way. He told us we would be patrolling on Charlie Ridge, a large, jungle-covered mountain southwest of Da Nang that was notorious for the many enemy contacts made there by our recon teams. He also told us about the weather and terrain and what enemy units might be encountered. He went over the general conduct of the patrol, but he also carefully informed each man of his job on the patrol, what equipment and ammunition we were to take with us, and how such items as Claymore mines, demolition kits, and binoculars would be apportioned among the patrol members. He went over the radio call signs and frequencies we would be using, the artillery positions that would be supporting us, the locations of nearby recon teams and friendly infantry units who might come to our assistance, and a myriad of other details. He took over an hour to brief us fully.

When the patrol order was finished, he took us to the test-fire pit near the perimeter wire adjacent to the helicopter landing pad and had each of us test-fire the weapons we would be taking on patrol to make sure they functioned properly. I had been issued both a standard Model 1911 .45-caliber semi-automatic pistol and an M-14 rifle to take on patrol, which I test-fired into the pit. When I had finished, Sgt. McDonald asked me if I would like to take a new rifle with me on patrol, one he had recently "traded for" with the Air Force. He said it was a good rifle, much lighter than the M-14, and would allow me to carry more ammunition since the .556 mm round used in this weapon was much lighter than the standard NATO 7.62 mm round used by the M-14. He handed me the odd looking weapon and told me it was a Colt AR-15. I decided I would take this lighter rifle with me on patrol since it allowed me to carry more ammunition and its short barrel length made it easier to maneuver in dense jungle growth.

After everyone had finished test-firing their weapons, Sgt. McDonald took us over to the helicopter landing pad where he went over the patrol's immediate action drills in the event we encountered the enemy while we were on patrol. He had us walk through "action front," "action left," "action right," and "action rear," and then he had us run through these drills at normal speed until we reacted to his commands as if they were second nature. He also rehearsed the "hasty ambush" drill in the event we had the opportunity to surprise a North Vietnamese Army (NVA) or Viet Cong (VC) unit. In such an instance, we would systematically search the ambush "killing zone" using CS gas to cover our movements and find out if any of the enemy were "playing dead." He even went over the proper way to secure a prisoner with parachute cord that he had cut to the proper length for tying a prisoner's hands behind his back.

We broke for lunch after Sgt. McDonald dismissed the team, but he reminded me that I would be accompanying him that afternoon on an "overflight" or aerial reconnaissance of the insertion and extraction LZs on Charlie Ridge. I agreed to meet him at the camp's LZ as soon as the recon helos landed.

After lunch, I went to the S-2 shop and borrowed a Polaroid land camera from Lt.

St. Clair and told him I needed it to take some pictures of the LZs we would be using the next day. I also asked him for a map that included Charlie Ridge and asked to see the last three or four patrol reports for patrols on Charlie Ridge so I could get a feel for what it was like to patrol on that mountain. The words of Lt. St. Clair and my reading of the patrol reports did nothing to ease my mind since any logical conclusion drawn from both sources indicated Charlie Ridge was a very dangerous place. All three reports contained comments about NVA sightings, and one report told of a patrol that had gotten into a serious firefight requiring an emergency extraction under fire. I began to see why Charlie Ridge had the reputation it did.

The recon helicopter for our overflight, a CH-46 Sea Knight, arrived late in the afternoon, and Sgt. McDonald and I climbed aboard using the rear ramp. Sgt. McDonald had a laminated map in his hand with several spots marked in grease pencil indicating the proposed insertion and extraction LZs. He asked the crew chief for a headset so he could talk to the pilots and he settled into a seat near the gunner's port. I sat next to him, and soon the helicopter lifted off and climbed into the sky. I felt the air change as we ascended. The heat at ground level gave way to cool and then cold air as we climbed into the sky and headed southwest. After 15 or 20 minutes flight time, I saw a large, dark mass appear ahead of us. To the west of this dark, ominous shape all I could see were mountains. They stretched as far as the eye could see. Somewhere far to the west was the Laotian border. I looked out the other side of the helicopter and saw the endless patchwork of light green paddy fields, dark tree lines, and tiny villages that made up the coastal plain of Quang Nam Province. I also noted that there were many bomb craters scarring the land.

The helicopter pitched violently and descended until we were only a few hundred feet above the trees on Charlie Ridge. All I could make out were tall, dark, 100-foot-high trees with thick foliage. The noise in the helicopter made talking very difficult, so Sgt. McDonald resorted to sign language most of the time. Sgt. McDonald pointed to his map and then pointed out the starboard port of the C-46, indicating the LZ on his map as we passed over it. I was so excited by this information and in awe of Sgt. McDonald's ability to locate the LZ from the maze of jungle below I forgot the Polaroid camera on my lap. He pointed to the camera and then he spoke into the headset to the pilot, and immediately the helicopter began to make a wide turn. Within a few seconds, we were over the same LZ again, a small cleared area in the jungle on the side of the mountain not more than 50 yards long and 20 yards wide. I quickly leaned out the gunner's port and took two pictures of the LZ. Sgt. McDonald smiled at me and used hand signals to indicate we were not finished. He instructed the pilot to fly over two other LZs; one was an alternate zone in case we were unable to land in our primary zone for some reason, and the other was our extract zone where the helicopters would pick us up when our patrol was complete. I took pictures of these LZs as well. We had been over Charlie Ridge for only a minute or two, and then the helicopter flew back to LZ Finch at Camp Reasoner.

That evening after dinner, I went over the notes I had taken when Sgt. McDonald gave his patrol order, made another map study of the terrain in our NFZ, checked my equipment one last time, and tried to assuage my anxiety by talking to the other lieutenants on our back porch. I found it difficult to sleep that night. It finally dawned on me that I was going into harm's way for the first time — this was no training exercise. I was going on a combat recon patrol with seven young Marines and a Navy corpsman into an area controlled by the enemy and known for danger and death. Only our training and luck would protect us and prevent the enemy from detecting us. It seemed as if morning came just an hour after I went to sleep but my traveling alarm clock indicated I had been in bed for six hours. I was not hungry, so I did not eat breakfast, a mistake I would not make again. Instead, I put all of my patrol gear on the back porch and waited for the insertion helicopters to arrive.

When the insertion helicopter package of two C-46 helicopters arrived at LZ Finch and shut down, I joined the pilots with Sgt. McDonald and the other team leaders scheduled for insertion that day in the S-3 shop for a briefing by Maj. Welzant. He went over each patrol's mission, the coordinates of the insertion LZs, the call signs and frequencies, and several other essential details so both the patrol leaders and the pilots had all the information they would need for a successful insertion. He also briefed the pilots on the patrols to be extracted that day, providing the same important information needed by the pilots, especially the information on any reported contacts with the enemy by the patrols. After the briefings, I went back to my hootch to get my gear for the patrol and await the call from Sgt. McDonald that our helicopters were ready for our insertion.

Our insertion was due for the early morning of February 8, but weather and the delayed extraction of another team resulted in delaying our insertion until mid-afternoon. All morning I waited on the back porch for the insertion helicopters to arrive, and with each passing moment, my anxiety and apprehension built. This uneasy feeling deep in the pit of my stomach just before an insertion would never be allayed with time. I always felt a pang of fear before each insertion, and it always lasted until the helicopter landed and the patrol began. Once I was on the ground, the conduct of the patrol and the process of always thinking in advance as to what we were to do kept my fear at bay. It was not dissimilar to the feeling I experienced before a big basketball game in high school or a school yard fight, yet the feeling was far more intense before a reconnaissance patrol into enemy territory because the stakes were infinitely higher than the outcome of a game or a fistfight.

Our ride to the insertion zone lasted less than 30 minutes. I watched as Sgt. McDonald left his pack on his seat and moved into a position between the pilot and copilot of the CH-46 helicopter. He pointed to the map and showed the pilots the Polaroid pictures I had taken of the LZ on the overflight the day before. They nodded, and then Sgt. McDonald returned to his seat and put his pack back on. Seated next to me he placed his mouth close to my ear and shouted, "We are going into a false LZ first, so don't move from your seat until I tell you to." I had no real idea what he was talking about, but I knew I was not going to move until he told me to. The helicopter began a rapid, spiraling descent that seemed to force my stomach into my mouth. As we descended, I saw the trees come into view outside and heard a distinctive cracking sound. I suddenly realized we were taking fire from somewhere near the LZ. The helicopter briefly touched down in some elephant grass and then with a shudder it began to rise up out of the LZ and gain altitude. Sgt. McDonald again put his mouth to my ear and yelled, "That was a false insertion. We did it to fool the enemy into thinking we had actually landed there. It was a good thing because they were waiting for us. That was the shooting." The thought struck me:

This was the first time in my life someone had shot at me, and I thanked God that they had missed.

Our helicopter and "chase bird" circled another LZ not too far from the false insertion zone while Huey gunships prepped the LZ with machine gun fire. After prepping the LZ, the gunships flew in beside our helicopter and followed us down as we again began to spiral toward the earth in what appeared to me to be "crash mode." As we descended into our LZ, Sgt. McDonald instructed all of us to take the safeties of our weapons off and get ready to exit the helicopter. The helicopter shuddered violently as it lowered into the LZ. When we exited the helicopter, we had to jump off the rear ramp because the CH-46 could only get partially landed in the small zone. I was the third person off the ramp, and I dropped about four feet through the elephant grass onto the hard ground. The weight of my 70-pound pack made my drop seem like the height was a lot higher than four feet, and it sent a shock through my spine. Our eight-man team scurried to cover in the dense jungle while the helicopter shook itself loose from the bounds of earth and lifted slowly into the air like some huge, primeval insect, sending dirt, grass and other debris into the air around us. As the helicopter flew away and the sound of its rotors became more distant, we huddled in silence, straining our ears for any telltale signs that the enemy was near. Sgt. McDonald had told me that the enemy often waited until the helicopters and the fixed-wing escort planes departed to hit a recon patrol, so we stayed on alert in a small circle facing outboard, our ears and eyes straining to pick up any sound or movement that might indicate the enemy had seen us land and were preparing to attack us. We wondered if the VC who fired at us during the false insertion would attempt to find us in our new location.

After twenty minutes and no signs of the enemy, Sgt. McDonald whispered to our radio operator to send a message to base that we were safely inserted and were beginning our patrol. When the message had been passed to one of our radio relay stations, Sgt. McDonald used his hand and arm signals to indicate we were to move out in a column uphill in a westerly direction through the jungle. My position was in the middle of the column, right behind Sgt. McDonald so I could observe him during the patrol and learn from him as he went about his duties.

The patrol, which had developed its procedures through trial and error over time, began to move slowly through the thick secondary growth at a pace I initially thought was excessively slow; however, I soon realized this was the proper pace so as not to make any noise. The point man, Lance Corporal (LCpl.) Bart Russell, set the pace. He would often stop to take out his K-bar knife so he could slowly and noiselessly cut vines and small branches that impeded our way or might make a loud noise if someone caused them to spring back after passing. Every 20 minutes the patrol would stop and sit down with each man in the patrol facing outboard in staggered fashion so all 360 degrees around the patrol were covered. No one spoke; all communication between the patrol members was done using hand and arm signals. During these stops, we listened to ascertain if we were being followed. After each ten-minute rest period, Sgt. McDonald would signal us to continue. We struggled to rise under the weight of our packs, which made us walk in a stooped fashion and often caused us to stop and hitch our packs up on our backs to gain some comfort from the weight.

Within minutes, I was perspiring profusely, and the heat and humidity seemed to sap my strength. It was the heat of the day when we inserted, and after two hours of struggling uphill through the tangled undergrowth beneath the thick jungle canopy, I was near exhaustion. However, I was determined not to let the other members of the patrol see my discomfort or to ask them to stop and allow me to rest. Nervous tension and my concern about how the other members of the patrol would view me made me push on without complaint, secretly anticipating the next ten-minute respite the patrol would be taking as a security break.

As light began to fade, we stopped and formed a circle with each man facing outboard. Sgt. McDonald came over to me and took out his map. I took out my map also and he showed me where we were and told me to watch him as he wrote a Situation Report (SITREP) that would be sent via radio back to base informing them that we were stopped for the day and would soon be occupying a night harbor site. Sgt. McDonald showed me the SITREP, which he had written on yellow message paper, and whispered to me that the harbor site location was approximately 100 meters from our present location and that we would move to it as soon as it became dark. In this way, if the enemy had spotted us and wanted to attack us after dark, they would hit our present location and not the real harbor site 100 yards distant. We would have a distinct advantage using this technique. While the radio man whispered the SITREP over the radio, Sgt. McDonald signaled to us to eat. We carefully and noiselessly took a can of C rations from our packs and then quietly and slowly used our P-38 (John Wayne) can openers to open the cans. Sgt. McDonald did not allow his men to cook their meals since the smell of cooking food traveled far in the jungle and it could give our position away. He also did not allow anyone to smoke while on patrol, which resulted in most of the men chewing tobacco.

I opened a C ration can of beans and franks and slowly consumed it. Despite being cold, it tasted very good. In the days ahead this meal would always be my favorite one among the culinary offerings of C rations. When I was finished, we collected the empty cans, and one of the patrol members took the one entrenching tool the patrol carried, dug a shallow hole, and deposited the empty cans and any other trash we had in the hole before filling it in and covering it with leaves to hide it. After our meal, Sgt. McDonald told us to make our last "head call" since he did not want anyone to venture outside the harbor site during the night to relieve themselves. After this, we stood up and moved to our night harbor site, a very thick stand of brush on a finger overlooking our insertion LZ. I was surprised to note that we had moved less than 500 meters from our insertion LZ, but this was far from unusual for a recon patrol. The very careful and slow pace over rough terrain with frequent stops every 20 minutes greatly reduced the distance the patrol would cover. It was not uncommon for a patrol to travel less than 1,000 meters in a full day of patrolling in the jungle. While the slow pace restricted the amount of territory covered by a patrol, there were several distinct advantages to conducting a patrol at a slow, deliberate pace. First, rapid movement in the jungle was loud and could easily alert the enemy if they were nearby. Second, any loud movement prevented the patrol from hearing the telltale noises that indicated the enemy's presence. Sound, especially man-made sound, traveled far in the jungle. Third, a slow pace did not tire the patrol members and make them careless. Finally, a slow pace allowed the patrol to take note of all of its surroundings so that later, during the patrol's debriefing at Camp Reasoner, the area covered could be accurately described. Such information as trails, streams, ambush sites, enemy bunkers, and the like, could be described in detail so future patrols or infantry units would have a good idea of the terrain and enemy activities in the area covered by the patrol.

My first night in the field in Vietnam passed quietly. Our harbor site, which we crawled into on our hands and knees because it was so thick with tangled foliage, was ideal, since anyone trying to get close to us during the night would make an awful racket fighting their way through the thick brush, thus giving us advance warning of their approach. We slept in a tight circle with our feet facing inboard and our heads and weapons facing outboard next to us so we could quietly retrieve them in the darkness if needed. The patrol's two radios were placed in the center of our circle so anyone of us could use them during the night. Sgt. McDonald assigned each member of the patrol a one-hour radio watch, and these assignments went in a clockwise direction around the circle of men so it would be easy for the man on watch to quietly wake up the man next to him and pass him the radio handset. Sgt. McDonald probably sensed that I was dog tired, so he gave me the last watch before dawn so I would get eight hours of unbroken sleep before taking over the radio watch. I was grateful for this consideration, but made a mental note never to allow myself this luxury when I was a patrol leader. In future, I would take the mid-watches, those watches around midnight, and give the early and late watches to my point men who needed to be fully rested to do their dangerous work.

As I curled up in my poncho on the moist jungle floor, I soon found myself the target of a host of noisy and very aggressive mosquitoes. I knew I would be unable to sleep if the mosquitoes continued to bite my face and hands, so as quietly as possible I retrieved a pair of aviator's gloves and an insect head net from my pack and put them on. I was grateful to Mike Henry for his gift of the pilot's gloves which were light and flexible and for the mosquito head net my mother had given me prior to leaving the States. These two items would spare me a lot of discomfort in the months ahead. Without them, I would have been devoured by mosquitoes and other insect predators on my numerous sojourns into the fields and jungles of South Vietnam.

The next day, an hour before daylight, Sgt. McDonald woke all of us, and we "stood to" facing outboard with our weapons at the ready. Reconnaissance men knew that the most likely time for the enemy to attack a recon patrol was at dawn or at last light, so the patrol often was on full alert, or "standing to" as it was referred to, listening for the enemy approaching and ready to fight back without delay. Straining our ears for any sign of the enemy, we waited until an hour after daylight to resume our patrol route up the hill.

Around noon we came upon a trail running east and west in the direction that the patrol wanted to take. Normally, recon patrols avoid walking on trails for the simple reason that it is along trails that the enemy travels, and we wanted to remain undetected. However, Sgt. McDonald assessed that this trail had not been used recently, and it was safe for the patrol to travel on it for a short distance. We walked west along the trail for approximately 100 meters until we came upon an abandoned hut and several old trench lines that the enemy had built. There was also a dilapidated "lean-to" made of bamboo with broken glass and pottery shards strewn about it. Nearby, we found what appeared to be a handmade 60 mm mortar tube the enemy had fashioned from steel tubing. More ominously, we found a very well-prepared ambush site the enemy had built just off the trail and camouflaged so effectively it was impossible for someone walking on the trail to see it. If we had not been moving slowly and carefully, observing all of our surroundings, we would have missed this ambush site with its ground-level fighting holes running parallel to the trail and facing downhill. I looked at these fighting holes and came away with a respect for the people who made them. They were completely flush with the ground, about four feet deep, and the sides had been reinforced with woven twigs and branches to keep the dirt from caving in. One of the fighting positions had a parapet in it so a machine gun could be placed on it with the barrel only an inch or two above ground level. I felt very grateful that the enemy was not occupying this ambush site.

Farther on, we found a handrail made of bamboo and steps cut into the trail near the top of the ridgeline running north-south. This was clear evidence that this trail was used by the enemy in the recent past, and we took this warning seriously, especially in view of the previous day's experience in the false LZ. We decided to leave the trail and establish an observation post (OP) just south of the trail on a small finger overlooking the valley to the south, a valley that was called "Mortar Valley" because the VC often launched mortar and rocket attacks from it.

When we came to a spot on the finger that afforded good observation of the terrain to our south, Sgt. McDonald divided the patrol into three elements. One element was the observation element, and it consisted of Sgt. McDonald, me and the radio operator; the other two elements, consisting of three men each, were security elements with the mission of watching the trail to our north and any approaches into the OP from that direction. We maintained the OP for the remainder of the second day of the patrol and into the third, but we saw no enemy activity on either the trail or in Mortar Valley.

However, the time I spent with the observation element was beneficial since I was able to learn from Sgt. McDonald the best way to observe for enemy activity using a team approach. Sgt. McDonald told me to take out the 7 × 50 binoculars he had given me to take on the patrol while he took out a 30-power spotter's scope with a small tripod attached. He told me to take the binoculars and to slowly scan back and forth over an arc of approximately 90 degrees. He told me to look for movement since that was the best indicator of the enemy and to concentrate on any trails or terrain features that the enemy might use, such as stream crossings, hilltops, or open spaces. One piece of information he gave me was invaluable: Unlike Marine units, who always tried to set up their defensive positions on the high ground, NVA units usually bivouacked in the low ground along streams. Because of this, it was never a good idea to move parallel to a stream, and it was necessary to avoid spending much time in any low ground that had a stream running through it.

Sgt. McDonald instructed me to let him know as soon as I spotted something that looked suspicious so he could use the spotting scope's greater, but more restricted, power to try to identify what I had picked up with my broad sweeps. The radio operator stayed close to his radio so he could rapidly send in a request for artillery or air support in the event we actually spotted the enemy. We laid out a map on the ground between us so we could quickly assign a grid coordinate for our sighting, and both Sgt. McDonald and I had compasses ready to get an azimuth to any potential target. This three-man observation team was organized in such a way that we could rapidly observe any enemy target in our line of sight, identify its location on a map, obtain a range and azimuth to it, and report it quickly so artillery or air support could be used to destroy it. I had never been taught this technique during my previous training, but I saw that it was infinitely superior to having just one individual do all the tasks involved. I made a mental note to make sure I used this same system on every future patrol I took out where we would establish an OP.

At the end of our third day of patrolling, we began moving to our extraction LZ 1,000 meters uphill and to our north. Using a compass heading of zero degrees, we carefully covered the distance in three hours. Along the way, we found an unoccupied enemy company-sized harbor site with a dozen bunkers made of logs. When we reached our extraction LZ, Sgt. McDonald instructed the patrol to search the area around it to make sure there were no booby traps or enemy fighting positions. It was a larger LZ than our insertion LZ, capable of easily accommodating two CH-46 helicopters. We kept watch on the zone until it was nearly dark, and then we moved 100 meters into some thick secondary growth and established our night harbor site.

During the night I was awoken by Sgt. McDonald and PFC J. D. Glor. Sgt. McDonald put his hand over my mouth and whispered, "VC lights," and then he pointed to PFC Glor who was staring up Charlie Ridge through the jungle canopy. I moved to Glor's location and observed 50 lights in a row winding their way down Charlie Ridge parallel to us and approximately 500 meters away. Charlie was on the move. Later at 0600, we saw the same lights moving west away from us. We reported both sightings, but Sgt. McDonald decided not to call in an artillery fire mission on the lights since it was very difficult to observe the area where they were last seen, and he did not like to fire artillery "blind," as he put it.

After first light, the patrol moved to the extraction LZ, set up security, and waited for the extract helicopters to arrive. We sat and waited until late in the afternoon for our extraction and suffered because of it. We had filled our canteens in a small stream on the second day of our patrol, but now we were out of water, and the heat and humidity gave all of us a powerful thirst. We dreaded the thought that we might be extended another day since we would have to find water, and that meant we would have to travel downhill at least 1,000 meters to find a stream.

After what seemed like an eternity, we finally received a radio message telling us the extraction "package" of two CH-46 helicopters and two Huey gunship helicopters was on the way and would arrive at our position in less than 30 minutes. The gunships arrived first and contacted us via radio. They asked us to use a smoke grenade to mark our position and give them an indication of the wind direction. Sgt. McDonald took a yellow smoke grenade and tossed it into the center of the LZ. The gunship pilot then asked us what color smoke we were using. We never told helicopters or fixed wing aircraft what color smoke we would be using before we actually used it because the enemy often listened to our radio transmissions, and they would attempt to lure our helicopters into an ambush at another nearby LZ using smoke grenades they had captured from U.S. or ARVN units. When the gunship spotted our smoke and we had confirmed the color as yellow, they called in the extraction helicopter while the "chase bird," a CH-46, circled in the near distance ready to come in and rescue us and the helicopter crew if it was shot down. The sounds of the friendly helicopter rotor blades had a very soothing effect on all of us since that distinctive sound meant we would be safe soon and on our way back home at Camp Reasoner. To this day, the sound of helicopter rotor blades beating the air makes me feel calm and content.

Our extraction helicopter descended rapidly into the LZ, and we scrambled aboard, happy to be safely out of harm's way. We returned to LZ Finch at 1600 where we were quickly sent to the S-2 shop for a debriefing by Lt. St. Claire. For the next hour Lt. St. Claire debriefed the patrol asking questions about the names of the patrol members, the times of insertion and extraction, the route the patrol took, the terrain encountered, and any enemy sightings (Team Brisbane Patrol Report, 11 Feb. 1967). He told us he would type the patrol report that evening and deliver it to the Division G-2 on Hill 327 as soon as it was completed. I asked him if I could have a copy of the patrol report, and he said he would have one for me in the morning.

After the debriefing, we immediately went to the mess hall and ate dinner. Our faces were still covered with camouflage paint, and our jungle utility uniforms were wet and dirty, but that did not deter us in the slightest as we wolfed down the first hot meal we had had in four days. After dinner, I returned to my hootch and took a cold shower beneath the porch and shaved in a tub of cold water on the back porch. Lt. Lenny Torres noted that I was having trouble getting all of the camouflage face paint off using cold water and soap, so he volunteered another great piece of good advice — use insect repellent to wash the paint off. It worked like a charm and made it infinitely easier to shave off the four days of beard I had on my face.

During the next few days, I prepared for my second "snap in" patrol as an observer. This time I was to go on patrol with another 1st Force Reconnaissance Company team called Countersign. Mike Henry, the company's communications officer, was to take this patrol out because the company was short a platoon leader, and he often volunteered to take out patrols whenever a backup team leader was needed. I went through much of the same procedure that I went through with my first patrol with an overflight with Mike of the intended NFZ, the issuance of Mike's patrol order to the team, the test-firing of my weapons, and the packing of my gear into my rucksack.

There was a shortage of personal field equipment, such as rucksacks and 782 gear, a situation that forced many Marines to use captured enemy equipment or items bought from the ARVN. I had been given a captured NVA rucksack for my first patrol, and I found it difficult and uncomfortable to use. I spoke to Mike Henry about this, and he recommended I go to the small shop down the road from the Division CP and buy an ARVN rucksack since these were actually the best field packs for recon work. I took Mike's advice, and for the sum of $3.00 I purchased a new ARVN rucksack from this store. It occurred to me that this item of equipment had previously been issued to an ARVN soldier who found it expedient or profitable to sell it to the Vietnamese entrepreneur turning it over to me. I wondered if this sort of transaction was carried out between our allies and the NVA, but thought it better to forget about it. The nice thing about the ARVN rucksack was it was just the right size to hold the equipment, ammunition and rations needed for a normal four-day patrol.

After I had brought the ARVN rucksack back to the hootch, I began to reflect on the equipment I was taking to the field and how it seemed to demonstrate a lack of supply preparedness by the Marine Corps. I was wearing a camouflage jungle uniform from the U.S. Air Force along with an Air Force AR-15 rifle, and my rucksack was standard ARVN issue, as were my field suspenders. I carried an East German 8 × 30 set of binoculars that had been captured from a North Vietnamese soldier and given to me by Lt. Eric Barnes. Some of my equipment, like my mosquito net and rain suit, was obtained through commercial U.S. sources. All of this did not reflect well on the Marine Corps supply system, since most of my colleagues in the reconnaissance business were similarly outfitted

Lt. Mike Henry at Camp Reasoner.

with disparate items that the Marine Corps was unable to provide. We did not let this prevent us from doing our job, but we were all aware that the Marine Corps' penchant for tightening its belt in peacetime had a price in wartime. We had been fighting in South Vietnam for two years when I arrived in country, and still the supply system seemed to be woefully short of the basic items needed to equip our Marines properly.

My patrol with Mike Henry and team Countersign was uneventful. Our team spent 76 hours on the ground inside an NFZ west of the combat base of An Hoa in the foothills of the Ong Thu Slope, a rugged escarpment that was used as a shield for the 2nd NVA Division, who had their base camps hugging the western slope of this large massif. Artillery could not fire effectively on the steep western slope of this escarpment, making it ideal for the NVA to establish their base camps there. These widely dispersed NVA base camps west of the Ong Thu Slope occupied an area the enemy called Base Area 112, and it covered nearly 25 square miles of dense jungle-clad mountains and deep, narrow valleys.

Team Countersign spent most of its 76 hours on the ground moving from one OP site to another in the hope of finding a spot that would allow us to see enemy movement in the villages below us. On one such movement, we found an old trail that led from the foothills down into the Arizona Territory, but it was evident that it had not been used recently. On the day before our extraction, we got a scare when we heard voices near us. We froze and waited to see if the voices came closer, but after a few minutes the voices moved away and we did not see who was doing this talking. Mike suspected they were probably not NVA but woodcutters who often went into the hills to cut firewood to sell back in the lowland villages. In any event, we did not see any enemy, and there was no indication that the enemy was active in the area of our patrol. In the parlance of the time, this patrol was "a walk in the sun." Although the patrol was uneventful, I learned a great deal by watching Mike Henry and his men, especially the way Mike planned artillery concentrations around our harbor sites at night. This precaution allowed Mike and the radio operator to quickly call in these pre-fired artillery concentrations if the enemy attacked us (Team Countersign Patrol Report, 17 Feb. 1967).

My final "snap in" patrol was with team Coventry from Company C, 1st Reconnaissance Battalion, led by one of the best patrol leaders in that battalion, Lt. Lance Woodburn. I was very impressed by the methodical way Lt. Woodburn went about preparing himself and his team for the patrol. He not only rehearsed all of us in the procedures to be executed if we made contact with the enemy, but he also had us lay out all of the equipment we intended to take with us so he could inspect each item to make sure the equipment was

The Arizona Territory looking north with the Ong Thu Slope on the left and Charlie Ridge in the background.

in good working order. His patrol order was very detailed, and he even used aerial photos of the patrol area and a sand table to familiarize us with the terrain. One thing I noticed immediately about team Coventry was its size; it was much larger than the two patrols from 1st Force Reconnaissance Company I had gone on. Team Coventry consisted of 13 men, and they would be taking a lot more gear and ammunition with them than the lighter and smaller patrols from my force reconnaissance company. In addition, the team was also taking a scout dog named Rip and his Marine handler with them. As I stated earlier, the difference in patrol size between the battalion patrols and the force reconnaissance patrols was due to the size of their respective platoons. 1st Force Reconnaissance Company had platoons of 15 men, while 1st Reconnaissance Battalion platoons had 26 men. Since each platoon was required to field two teams, this meant the Force Reconnaissance Company normally sent out patrols with only seven or eight men, while the 1st Reconnaissance Battalion sent out patrols with 12 or 13 men.

Team Coventry was inserted late in the day on 21 February into a good, two helicopter LZ on the southern slopes of Charlie Ridge with the mission of climbing up the mountain to its peak. Lt. Woodburn told us no patrol had ever succeeded in reaching the summit of Charlie Ridge because the "VC owned the top of the mountain," and they did not want any Marine units there. This was understandable since Charlie Ridge was an excellent position from which to observe the area around the Da Nang TAOR and the airfield south of the city. It was also only one day's march from the mountain to locations just west of the city where mortar and rocket attacks against Marine positions and the airfield could be mounted. Our intelligence briefings also identified Charlie Ridge as the terminus of a spoke of the Ho Chi Minh Trail that ran east from Laos, as well as a base for one of the 2nd NVA Division's regiments. In this sense, Charlie Ridge was key terrain for the enemy, and they would fight to keep Marine units from occupying it. Lt. Woodburn expected contact with the enemy somewhere during our ascent, so he instructed us to take extra ammunition for the M-60 machine gun and the M-79 grenade launcher the patrol carried. He also had the patrol carry four Claymore mines and six anti-personnel mines which he thought might be needed if we were forced to defend a position on the mountain. Needless to say, my rucksack was filled with more weight than I would normally take on a patrol. When it was fully packed, I estimated its weight at nearly 80 pounds.

After our insertion, the patrol quickly moved off the LZ and headed west toward a trail we knew existed from reading the report made by another patrol that had passed through this area several months previously. The distance we traveled was only 2,000 meters, but it was cross compartment, meaning we were going up and down steep ridges between deep ravines, a very slow and difficult way to move. All of us struggled under the weight of our packs, but the scout dog had the most difficult time. It was obvious that the dog was not used to the heat and the steep jungle terrain, and several times we had to stop to give the dog a rest and allow it to drink water.

In the ravines, we found numerous leeches which managed to find their way into our clothing and onto our skin. On one stop I looked down and saw that my crotch area was soaked in blood. A leech had affixed itself to my penis, gorged itself on blood and then dropped down the leg of my trousers and was caught in my blousing garters. Needless to say, I found this not to my liking. The corpsman in the patrol came over to me and

Patrolling on the slope of Charlie Ridge.

gave me a stick of coagulant to stop the bleeding. Later I found the blood-filled leech in my trousers and dispatched it with a fingertip of insect repellent, the common way of killing these nuisances. I had seen leeches during my training in Panama, but the leeches in South Vietnam were bigger and far more aggressive, a fact that always made me look down while on patrol to see if they were lurking along the trails or streams I passed. I was told later that the best way to prevent leeches from getting inside your clothing was to soak your clothes and jungle boots with insect repellent before going on patrol. This technique seemed to work quite well for me in the ensuing months.

After struggling through the torrid jungle for two days, we came upon the well-used trail system that we were to take north to the summit of Charlie Ridge. Since it was evident this trail was heavily traveled, Lt. Woodburn decided it was too dangerous for the patrol to use it. Instead, he told us it would be wiser to establish an ambush along the trail and then find some alternate route to the mountain's summit. We slowly walked along the trail for 20 minutes, looking for a good ambush site, until we came upon a small stream where the trail took a sharp bend that offered a good killing zone for our ambush. We were just setting in our ambush when I looked up the trail and saw two North Vietnamese soldiers wearing khaki uniforms and carrying rifles. They were walking down the trail only 50 yards away and obviously oblivious of our presence. I quietly signaled to the Marine behind me, who was moving into a position where he could fire on the trail, that I had seen the enemy. He froze immediately, but I saw that he had silently taken the safety on his rifle off. I then turned and raised my rifle to my shoulder, ready to fire as soon as the enemy came into our killing zone. Only five Marines had taken up their positions in the ambush because Lt. Woodburn wanted to use some of the patrol as a security element. Despite this, we had more than enough firepower to take care of these two soldiers, if they were the only ones coming down the trail.

A few tense seconds passed as we waited for Lt. Woodburn to initiate the ambush by firing his rifle. Just as he was about to open fire, the NVA soldiers stopped and started to look down at their feet. They were now only a dozen yards from us. I had the lead NVA soldier in my sights, and my heart was pounding so hard I could see the front site of my rifle jumping up and down with each heartbeat.

All of a sudden I heard the scout dog, Rip, bark. Immediately, the two NVA soldiers bolted back up the trail before we could fire a shot. After berating the dog handler for allowing his dog to bark instead of giving the normal silent alert, Lt. Woodburn ordered us to abandon the ambush site and move back in the direction we had come toward an LZ we had passed the previous day. There we set up security waiting to see if the NVA soldiers would bring their friends to look for us. After passing a quiet night in a good harbor site, we moved to the extraction LZ and waited for the helicopters to extract us.

At noon on the 24th of February, we were told the helicopters were on the way to pick us up. Our LZ was large enough for one CH-46 to land in, but it had a steep slope and tall trees surrounding it, so landing would be difficult. As the first helicopter came in to land, we noticed it was having some difficulty maintaining its position in the LZ and began to drift downhill as we approached it to climb aboard via the rear ramp. For some reason, the helicopter suddenly lurched downhill, and its rear rotor blades hit several tall trees. The helicopter crashed, and one member of the patrol was seriously injured with a broken leg from parts of the flying rotor blades. I was doused in pink hydraulic fluid which for a moment led me to believe I was soaked in the blood of one of my fellow Marines. We ran over to the downed helicopter and were relieved to find that no one inside of it was hurt. A second helicopter came in and rescued the helicopter crew and the wounded recon Marine, but the remainder of our patrol was instructed to stay with the helicopter and provide security for it until it could be either destroyed or recovered. A platoon of infantry was flown into the LZ a few hours later to relieve us, and we were then allowed to depart for Camp Reasoner on the same helicopters that brought in the infantry (Team Coventry Patrol Report, 24 Feb. 1967).

Now that I had completed my three "snap in" patrols as an observer, I was eager to take my first patrol out as a patrol leader and to assume my first command as a Marine officer. I had learned a lot from each patrol leader, and I was grateful for the opportunity to observe the various patrol techniques they employed on my three "snap in" patrols. From these three patrols, I was able to choose what I considered to be the best techniques and procedures from them. I knew that I was far from a seasoned recon Marine. I still had a lot to learn, but I felt confident that I could take out a patrol as a patrol leader and do a credible job. Evidently Maj. Lowrey felt the same way because after the patrol debriefing at Camp Reasoner that evening, he took me aside and told me he was giving me command of the 5th Platoon and wanted me to take out team Killer Kane on my next patrol. He also told me that while the three "snap in" patrols had helped me learn my trade, none of these patrols had afforded me much of an opportunity to call in and adjust supporting arms, one of the most important skills a patrol leader needed. To remedy this he said he was sending Killer Kane to the reconnaissance OP and radio relay site on Hill 452 south of An Hoa for a week so I could practice this vital skill. The team was scheduled to leave on 3 March.

During the days prior to taking my first patrol out as a team leader, I took command of the 5th Platoon. I assembled the entire platoon after the morning formation, told them I was honored to be their platoon commander, and described how I intended to lead the platoon. I reminded them that I was open to any suggestion they might have on how to improve the functioning of the platoon since I knew that collectively the members of the platoon possessed literally years of patrolling experience. I interviewed each Marine individually so they would get to know me and I would get to know them. I kept a platoon commander's log with a page devoted to each Marine's personal data. It contained basic information on them, such as their home address, their date of birth, identification number, blood type, parent's names, rifle serial number, religion, and other items of information that might prove useful to know. Some of them I knew from the first patrol, but others were completely new to me. I knew I had to find out about them quickly since that knowledge would determine how they would be used on patrol.

In the course of my interviews with the men of my platoon, I found each of them to be exceptional in some way. The most common characteristics were their devotion to each other and their ability to think clearly and act quickly under conditions of extreme stress. For instance, Sgt. McDonald told me that LCpl. Bart Russell, a native of Ocean City, New Jersey, was a good example of the type of Marine in our platoon. He related to me an incident involving LCpl. Russell that was illustrative. Russell had been released from the hospital a few months before my arrival after receiving treatment for a severe infection which would not heal properly. He was in a very weakened condition when he returned to the company. Despite his need for rest, however, Russell insisted on going on a morning run while he waited for his team to return from patrol. During the run, he fell and cut his knee badly and passed out for a

Bart Russell, whose bravery and skill saved Killer Kane on several patrols.

moment due to his weakened condition. An unfeeling officer, who was leading the run and did not know Russell, berated him and told him that if he did not complete the run, he would recommend Russell be dropped from the reconnaissance company. At the time, Russell was nearly a mile from the gate of Camp Reasoner and barely able to stand, but he refused to give up and literally crawled the last 400 yards to the gate. Standing at attention with blood running down his leg and with a fever over 100 degrees, Russell addressed the officer who had left him on the road. He said, "Sir, I completed the run." Bart Russell was tough and determined, the kind of man who would never give up, even if sick or injured. I felt honored and privileged that I would be in the company of Marines like Bart Russell and I knew any success we might enjoy would come from the bravery and talents of men like him in Killer Kane.

In many respects, a reconnaissance team is very much like an athletic team. Each member of the recon team possessed certain traits and abilities that were appropriate for his job within the team. For instance, a point man had to have keen eyesight and hearing, patience, stamina, and lightning fast reflexes. A radio man had to be able to carry the extra weight of the PRC-25 radio along with all of his other equipment, and he had to be able to call in and adjust supporting arms under any conditions since the patrol leader might not have the time to do so or might be a casualty and unable to perform this duty. The team's machine gunner had to be able to carry the extra weight of the machine gun and its ammunition, but he also had to be thoroughly competent in its use, especially in a meeting engagement with the enemy at close range since the firepower of the machine gun was often the only way the patrol could break contact quickly or establish fire superiority. Every job required special skills, so I had to know which man could best fill each position in order to maximize the aggregate efficiency of the patrol.

A few days before my first patrol to Hill 452, I went with Lt. Lenny Torres and Lt. Mike Henry to the Freedom Hill PX to buy a few luxury items I needed to make my hootch accommodations even more comfortable than they were. I was always amazed at both the size of the Freedom Hill PX and the variety of items they had on sale, some of which seemed out place for both a war zone and a hot climate. For instance, every imaginable electronics and photographic product made anywhere in the world seemed available for sale at this huge PX. There were men's and women's fur coats on sale also, which seemed bizarre given we were living in a country that often was only a few degrees colder than hell. Exotic and expensive perfumes and lingerie were also on sale, ostensibly so the military personnel could purchase these items and send them home to their loved ones. It was pretty obvious, however, that a lot of the items on sale were there to help fuel the extensive and pervasive black market in such goods. Some servicemen in the rear often bought these luxury items and immediately resold them to Vietnamese who then sold them on the black market in Da Nang. This went on for years, and it always seemed strange to me that nothing was ever done about it even though it contributed to rampant corruption and inflation in the country. On this trip to the PX, I purchased a set of new sheets and pillowcases for my hospital bed to replace the mildewed and rather odiferous ones given to me by Lt. King. I also bought film for a small Canon 35 mm camera I had purchased from a Marine in my platoon who was going home and did not want it any longer. Finally, I bought a case of Coke to put in the refrigerator in our hootch and some small cans of apple juice and deviled ham that I intended to take with me on patrol to supplement my C rations.

The night of 27 February, I was awakened by the sound of what I thought was artillery landing near the Da Nang Airbase. At first I ignored the noise since I had already been exposed to loud noises at night, and I considered these noises a "normal" part of living in a combat zone. However, I heard another officer outside on the porch yell, "Hey, take a look at this shit; they're hitting the airfield." I got up, dressed only in my skivvies, and went out on the back porch where I found the other lieutenants staring off into the night in the direction of the Da Nang Airbase. From our vantage point, it appeared that there were several fires burning inside the airbase's perimeter. I could see the bright flashes as the enemy 140 mm rockets impacted, followed a few seconds later by the distinctive "carumph" sound of the explosion. Flares hung over the scene, giving everything a ghostly appearance.

This VC attack set off a barrage of return fire from artillery batteries in the surrounding area and caused skittish Marines manning bunkers at the various installations near the airfield to fire their weapons at imaginary targets. Every few seconds we could see red tracer rounds arcing gracefully into the night sky. We watched for several minutes, and then when it was over we went back to our cots. The next day, we were told that eleven U.S. military men had been killed and 18 aircraft destroyed in the first enemy 140 mm rocket attack of the war.

I did not know it at the time, but the enemy's use of 140 mm rockets posed a new and potentially lethal threat to the Da Nang Airbase, causing the 1st Reconnaissance Battalion to increase their patrols along the "Rocket Belt" surrounding the Da Nang Airbase. With the addition of the 140 mm rocket in the enemy's inventory of weapons, the "Rocket Belt" was extended several more miles to the west into the eastern slopes of the Annamite Mountains, and this placed new demands on the 1st Reconnaissance Battalion to screen this expanded area. For months to come, the battalion would send out numerous patrols searching for the source of these rocket attacks.

Since my first patrol as a team leader was going to be a "milk run" on a static OP, there was no need for an overflight. The day before the patrol set off, I had the eight Marines going with me to the OP assemble for my first patrol order. I wanted to make a good impression with this order, even if it was not the type of order that I would normally give for a long-range patrol. I carefully went over every paragraph of the order, stressing the latest intelligence I had on the area we would be observing and the names and call signs of the other recon teams we would be providing radio relay services for. I inspected the equipment we would be taking with us, including a week's worth of food and water. One item on my equipment list would prove to be very helpful on the patrol: an artillery spotting scope that had a 30-power lens. This powerful scope could reach out and identify targets miles away. Since we would be on the top of a mountain 452 meters above sea level, we would have an unrestricted view of the surrounding terrain for several miles, allowing us easily to spot any enemy moving along the many trails below our vantage point.

Hill 452 was one of two radio relay sites in Quang Nam Province that the 1st Reconnaissance Battalion had established to improve communications with its far flung recon teams. Hill 452, actually a small mountain, was located a few miles south of the Marine combat base at An Hoa, and its height and location made it a perfect site for the relay of line of sight FM radio signals. Its summit consisted of a narrow ridge line that ran for only 100 feet, and on three sides of the summit were incredibly steep 100-foot cliffs. The northern side of the summit had a more gradual slope, but it was still quite steep. Because the terrain near the summit was so steep, no helicopters could safely land on it. However, on a saddle just below the peak, there was a man-made, wooden landing platform that had been recently constructed by Marine engineers. This structure looked very much like the deck one would see behind a suburban U.S. home. It was only 30 feet by 30 feet, so this meant a CH-46 helicopter could not fully land on it, only place its back wheels down, lower its ramp, and allow Marines to exit the helicopter onto the few feet of LZ left after this dangerous maneuver had been accomplished. From the air this man-made LZ looked like a postage stamp. Once Marines had landed safely and unloaded their gear, the recon team they were replacing would board the helicopter carrying their empty water cans and bags of trash with them as they departed. The team going in for its week-long stay on the summit would then haul their heavy water cans and boxes of C rations up the extremely narrow and steep trail 100 meters to the summit. It was arduous going and took nearly an hour to accomplish.

At the top of Hill 452, there was a defensive position with four bunkers made out of six-inch by six-inch timber and sandbags with firing ports facing along the most likely avenues of approach to the summit. The largest bunker was on the exact summit, and the relay team and radios were stationed there. A 30-foot-tall RC-292 radio antenna was attached to the side of the radio relay bunker and secured with wires and engineer stakes

A precarious insertion on the summit of Hill 452.

since the winds at the summit sometimes were quite strong. Surrounding the entire sum-mit was barbed wire. All of the vegetation had been removed for 100 yards, so the Marines had unobstructed fields of fire for their weapons. The bunkers could accommodate a maximum of 12 Marines.

Our insertion on Hill 452 on 3 March was normal insofar as it scared me as much as it we were going into a hot zone. The CH-46 carrying us and our gear had to make two approaches because the first one was aborted just a few feet from touchdown. We could tell that landing on the small, man-made landing platform was no easy task even for a good pilot. On the first attempt to land, the helicopter shuddered as it fought to maintain altitude while slowing enough to land on the platform. It missed the platform and dropped over the steep side of the mountain, nearly stalling as it rapidly lost altitude and hurtled toward the valley below.

For an instant I thought we were going to crash, but the pilot regained altitude and circled for another attempt. Over the headphone, he joked with me about the failed attempt, saying, "That first landing was just a drill, now we are going to do it for real." I was trying to keep the contents of my stomach in place, so I did not bother to reply. On the second attempt, another "white knuckle" landing for us, the rear wheels of the chopper established themselves on the platform while the front of the helicopter hovered over the deep drop on the south side of the mountain. None of us wanted to stay in the helicopter in this precarious position, so we quickly exited the helicopter as soon as the rear ramp was lowered. We formed a human chain and began unloading the water cans and C ration boxes from the helicopter, while the team that had been on the OP waited in column to board. They carried their empty water cans with them, but their load was considerably lighter than ours, so they were aboard the chopper and in the air quickly. As the helicopters flew away in the direction of Da Nang, we began the arduous task of moving our packs, water cans, and C rations to the summit. It was only 0800 in the morn-ing, but already the fierce heat of Vietnam was stifling, making our journey to the summit a slow, hot, and difficult one.

Once on top of Hill 452, we occupied our bunkers and began the routine that would last for the next seven days. This routine consisted of observing the vast panorama of rice paddies, villages and trails that stretched out before us for several miles. Based upon the intelligence we had received prior to our departure from Camp Reasoner, we placed special emphasis on the approaches to the An Hoa Combat Base to our north, the trail networks to the south that led to the Que Son Mountains, and the Song Thu Bon River to the west which ran below us like a dark serpent winding its way south to the dark, mist-shrouded mountains that formed the western half of Quang Nam Province. To our east, just a blue sliver on the horizon, we could see the South China Sea. I marveled at how much of Quang Nam Province we could see from the summit of Hill 452 and quickly came to appreciate how important this OP was.

We used the team approach to observation. I set up a two-man watch team sitting on top of the radio relay bunker. Several metal engineering stakes were attached to the sides of this bunker which allowed us to attach ponchos to shade the observers from the intense sunlight. Two PRC-25 radios were placed between the men so one of them could quickly call in a SALUTE report on any sightings of the enemy and the other could be

The Song Thu Bon River.

used to contact the closest artillery battery and call for an artillery fire mission on the enemy. The observer team also had a pair of 7 × 50 binoculars and the 30-power artillery spotting scope. In addition to observing for enemy activity, the observer team was responsible for relaying any recon team radio transmissions 24 hours a day back to Camp Reasoner. Since the terrain in the province had many "dead spaces" that prevented the recon teams from sending their radio messages directly back to Camp Reasoner, the OP on Hill 452 was often the only way these teams could communicate with recon's headquarters. Since Marine recon teams carried the PRC-25 radio and it was an FM radio that needed "line of sight" to function properly, any team operating in the mountains often found itself in areas where it was impossible to maintain communications with Camp Reasoner. For those teams, the radio relay stations were the only means of maintaining continuous communications. Even with the relay stations, recon teams often found themselves in areas where their radios were incapable of communicating with friendly units. If a radio relay team lost radio contact with a recon team for more than a few hours, the relay team would report this to Camp Reasoner, and the S-3 would request the 1st Marine Air Wing, located at Marble Mountain, to send an observation plane to the last known location of the patrol and attempt to make radio contact with it. A recon team without communications was in great danger, so the relay sites were crucial to the survival of these teams.

The view from the summit of Hill 452 was breathtakingly beautiful. In the early morning hours, as the sun came up in the east out of the South China Sea and began to hover over the Que Son Mountains, the valleys below us were filled with a thick, snow-white fog called "cracin." This white fog was so thick it blanketed the entire area around the summit and made it appear as if we could walk off the summit on a floor of clouds. Temple bells rang out in the valleys below and the voices of children playing and adults talking could be heard clearly below the clouds. Around 1000 in the morning the "cracin" would burn off, or rise like a white, billowy blanket above the mountains, revealing the rich, verdant valleys below with their dark tree lines, emerald-colored rice paddy fields, and brown, thatch-roofed houses grouped together in tight clusters that hugged streams or tree lines. Here and there, we could see village schools, Buddhist temples, and village defense forts. On the Song Thu Bon River we observed the V-shaped fish traps and small sampans used by local fishermen. The sight was deceptively tranquil and serene. The view was so beautiful at times it seemed to me that heaven might look like what I was gazing upon. I wanted my parents to see this beauty, so I took several photos of the morning "cracin" and the peaks of distant mountains wreathed in mist. On the back of these photos I wrote, "A view from Hill 452 — What Heaven might look like."

Despite the beauty of the scene we saw each morning from Hill 452, we were keenly aware that the land below us was decidedly not heaven, and we had a deadly business to conduct from our lofty perch. We could be distracted at times by the beauty of our surroundings, but we knew our only reason for being on this hill was to find the enemy and kill him, so we fought off the urge to lose ourselves in the beauty and to concentrate instead on the task at hand. For hours on end we manned our OPs, scanning the terrain below us looking for the VC.

We did not have long to wait. Around 2200 in the evening of our first day on the OP, we observed 30 to 50 VC sitting around campfires a mile south of our OP. We called in artillery fire on the campfires, but we were unable to observe the results due to the darkness. The next day at 2000 in the evening, we saw 50 flashlights and torches moving into the village of Ninh Dinh (4), which was located a mile due south of our OP. Since we could not see well enough to identify these lights as belonging to VC, we did not call in a fire mission. Using lights after dark was forbidden by law unless approved in advance by local authorities, so any large grouping of lights like this was certainly the result of VC moving about. Despite this knowledge, the rules of engagement did not allow us to fire on these lights unless we were certain they were VC. Even so, any fire mission we called in had to be cleared with the GVN district first before any rounds were fired. Later on that evening, a unit of Fox Company, 2/5, operating near the Nong Son coal mine, reported that a Combined Action Platoon (CAP) had moved into the village of Ninh Dinh (4) the night before. We watched the lights for nearly an hour before they went out, and the area around the village of Ninh Dinh 4 was again wrapped in total darkness. We never found out who had been using these lights that night, and the CAP never reported seeing them, despite their close proximity to the CAP fort.

During the next three days, we did not see any enemy activity, but all of that changed on our last day on Hill 452. On 8 March, a CAP unit reported that 300 enemy troops had been sighted in the hills near the village of Tu Phu several miles southwest of our OP and just east of the Song Thu Bon River. Cpl. Mike Borecky and Sgt. Dave Pugh scanned the area with the binoculars and the spotting scope trying to find these 300 enemy troops. After a few minutes, around noon, they located and identified a large group of armed, uniformed enemy troops moving along a trail near the village. I took the binoculars and confirmed the sighting and immediately worked up a fire mission. I had pre-registered several artillery concentrations near the location of the enemy, so I was able to contact

Mike Borecky calling in an air strike from OP Hill 452.

the artillery battery and ask them to adjust from the concentrations I had already established the first day on the OP. Within minutes, we could hear the artillery firing behind us from the An Hoa Combat Base. It made a "whishing" sound as it passed over our heads on its way toward the enemy. In the distance, we could see the flash of the artillery shells impacting, and then several seconds later we could hear the loud "carumpf" sound of the explosion. We fired several artillery missions while Cpl. Borecky and Sgt. Pugh relayed adjustments to me so I could radio the artillery battery to shift the fires to get better coverage of the target. After the artillery had fired their missions, an Aerial Observer (AO) arrived on the scene in his single engine Cessna airplane and began to direct Marine and Air Force fixed-wing aircraft onto the impact area of our artillery fires. The planes dropped napalm canisters and 500-pound bombs on the enemy, after which the AO flew over the target and reported seeing fifteen enemy bodies strewn on the ground.

Later in the afternoon, we observed two enemy soldiers emplacing two .50-caliber heavy machine guns near the village of Ninh Khanh (2). We called in air strikes on these two weapons, and an AO reported that both weapons were destroyed and three enemy soldiers had been killed.

As our last day came to a close, we tallied up the artillery missions and fixed-wing sorties we had used during our stay at the OP. We found that we had called in eight artillery missions and three air strikes using two F-8s, two A-4s, and eight F-4s to deliver napalm and bombs on the enemy. In addition, I had the opportunity to practice requesting and adjusting both artillery fire and air strikes. This practice would pay off in the coming months.

On 9 March, Killer Kane left Hill 452 and returned to Camp Reasoner (Team Killer Kane Patrol Report, 9 March 1967). On the 10th of March, we watched Armed Forces Television and saw the air strikes we had called in on the enemy the previous day and an interview with one of the AOs who controlled the air strikes. On this same day, the other recon team from our platoon, Team Brisbane, led by Sgt. Barry "Rabbit" Preston, made contact with the enemy and suffered two wounded Marines. Both Marines had been shot in the legs so they were unable to move. Sgt. Preston organized a quick defense so the remaining members of his patrol, including four South Vietnamese PRU soldiers who were accompanying the patrol as part of their Reconnaissance Indoctrination Program (RIP) training, were able to fight off the enemy long enough for a UH-34 helicopter to fly in and hoist the wounded Marines to safety. Sgt. Preston and his patrol killed four of the enemy in this firefight and later used artillery fire to break contact and move to an extraction LZ. I was very impressed with the courage and ability of Sgt. Preston and another Marine on this patrol so I thought it appropriate to recommend both of these brave Marines for a Bronze Star medal. This was my first attempt to obtain awards for my Marines, and it would serve to sour me on the Marine Corps awards system.

When I broached this subject with Maj. Lowrey, he told me that 1st Force Reconnaissance Marines were not put in for individual awards; instead, their actions would be recorded and then used to determine whether they received a Bronze Star or a Navy Commendation as an "end of tour" award. I had never heard of an "end of tour" award, and I did not like Maj. Lowrey's rationale for the policy. After spending the better part of a day writing up the Bronze Star award recommendations, I was not very happy with this situation, and I let Maj. Lowrey know it. I learned, both at the Naval Academy and at the Marine Corps Basic School, that it was my responsibility as an officer to make sure deserving Marines received promotions and brave Marines received awards for superior performance in combat. I felt this policy of giving an award to everyone in our company at the end of their tour of duty was not conducive to good morale or proper leadership. I decided to save the award recommendations I had written and wait for a time when either Maj. Lowrey was transferred or the policy changed.

While waiting in camp before my next patrol, I helped Lt. Mike Henry, who was our battalion's civic action officer, to go on a Medcap to the village of Phuoc Ly, population 402. Our little group included a Navy medical doctor, an interpreter, and a few Marines and Navy corpsmen. Just about every week one of these Medcaps would be conducted in Phuoc Ly village. They proved very popular with the locals, who did not have ready access to the kind of medical care our Navy medical personnel could provide. These visits often involved providing free inoculations for the children, medical screening for anyone needing it, routine dental work, lectures on water treatment and disease prevention, the treatment of injuries and minor illnesses, and the dispensing of antibiotics, vitamins, and soap.

Whenever we went to Phuoc Ly, we met with the village chief, and he arranged for his people to be treated by organizing them in the priority of treatment. He also made sure that the soap we provided was distributed fairly and evenly. We often sat down with the village elders and drank warm tea, but most of the time we spent with the corpsmen asking the villagers what they thought the most pressing medical needs in their village were. This led to special projects, such as the drilling of two concrete wells for fresh, clean water and the construction of a shower area that gave the women of the village a place to shower in private when they came in from the fields. Another project was the construction of a new three-room school house for the children of primary school age. These projects were small, but welcome.

I probably made a dozen Medcap visits to Phuoc Ly during my year in South Vietnam. With each visit, I learned more about village life. Life was not easy in a Vietnamese village, even in peacetime, but war made it far more difficult. Talking to the village chief, I found that the Marine presence near his village caused many problems for the locals. Waste water flowing from the Marine encampments on Hill 327 had damaged the rice crops of Phuoc Ly; artillery H and I fires frightened the animals and made it impossible to sleep outside of a family bunker at night; Marine trucks often sped through the village's main road, causing accidents and fear among the inhabitants. While the village chief told us that most villagers were grateful for the work on the Marine bases and for the Medcaps, they still would have preferred a more normal life and one not subject to the presence of so many foreigners and the dangers of war.

My fifth patrol was one of the strangest. On this patrol, Killer Kane took along Lt. John Danko as an observer, giving us a total of two officers and seven enlisted Marines. We were inserted by CH-46 into Elephant Valley on a grassy ridgeline overlooking the Song Cu De River early in the morning of 13 March. The LZ consisted of waist-high elephant grass and was rather exposed, so I had the patrol move quickly into some dense undergrowth where we waited and listened until we were confident no enemy troops were nearby. I took out my map and compass to make sure I knew where I was, and then I had the patrol move off in a northerly direction toward a spot where I hoped we could establish a good OP.

It was unusually hot and humid, taking a toll on all of us, but especially on LCpl. Gaston, who fainted and took several minutes to recover from his heat exhaustion. I was about to call an emergency medical evacuation (medevac) for him, but some water and shade brought him around, and he insisted he was able to continue on the patrol. I decided to take it easy and not stress the men on the patrol since I knew fatigue often led to serious lapses in security with deadly consequences.

We moved slowly downhill toward Elephant Valley, which stretched several miles toward the west and was uninhabited. Due to the heat and the condition of LCpl. Gaston, I decided to find an OP on the south side of the valley where some high trees afforded adequate shade from the sun. We found a good site for an OP on a small ledge outcropping, one that allowed us to see clearly into the valley below us. I established rear and flank security for the OP and began to search the valley for any signs of the enemy. It was obvious that at one time the valley had been used extensively for agriculture but was now abandoned. There was a stream running through the valley, and we could see the outlines of old paddy fields and overgrown irrigation canals from our position about 500 meters away.

On the second day of the patrol, the 14th of March, we heard 27 rounds of enemy 82 mm mortar fire landing approximately 500 meters away from our position. The sound of the mortar fire indicated the mortar tubes were farther to the north on a magnetic azimuth of 70 degrees. We also heard a 12.7mm. heavy machine gun firing as two USMC helicopters passed over the valley. We called in an artillery fire mission on the suspected mortar position. We were unable to observe the impact area, and so we could not determine if the artillery fire had any effect.

On the 15th of March, I had the patrol move 200 yards northwest to a new OP site on the side of the hill. This new OP was an improvement over the previous one since it afforded good observation of the valley and had some trees that provided welcome shade. We spent the entire day looking for the enemy who had fired the mortars and the .50-caliber machine gun, but the day passed with no sign of the enemy, although we heard the distant trumpet of elephants late in the day just before sunset. As I sat up against a tree under a poncho and stared out over the dark valley below me, I realized this was the first time in my life I had ever heard an elephant outside of a zoo. As I drifted off to sleep under a star-filled sky, the only sound I heard was the hum of mosquitoes vainly trying to get at me through my head net.

The next day, the 16th, I decided to maintain our OP for another 24 hours, something recon patrols rarely did because it was our policy never to stay in one position longer than 24 hours. This policy of moving every 24 hours was a good one, based upon some very hard lessons learned. Moving every 24 hours made it very difficult for the enemy to organize an attack against a recon team's OP or harbor site. But in this case, I decided the OP was in a secure location, and we had not seen any indication the enemy had observed us. It was a risk I was willing to take this time.

Around noon, Cpl. Bill Ellison and I were using the two 7 × 50 binoculars we had brought with us to scan Elephant Valley when he leaned over and whispered, "Lieutenant, VC, 300 meters at 11 o'clock on the trail." I took my binoculars and looked in the direction he indicated. Immediately, I saw three VC moving east on the trail parallel to the stream. They were wearing black pajamas and coolie hats, and two of the VC appeared to be injured. One had a khaki bandage on his arm and a rifle slung on his back, while the other was unarmed but limping on his left leg.

I put down the binoculars, took a quick compass heading, located the position of the VC on my map, and then called in a fire mission 200 yards ahead of them in their direction of travel. I hoped that the fire mission would be cleared and fired just as they entered the impact area. The VC were moving slowly, but after five minutes, they were approaching the impact area for our artillery mission. There was no radio transmission to us indicating the artillery mission was close to being fired. I radioed the artillery battery and asked them to expedite the fire mission, or I would have to amend it and shift the fires another 100 meters east. While I was talking to the artillery battery, the first spotting round, a smoke round, impacted far to the west, causing the VC to seek cover in the high elephant grass near the stream. I asked the battery why they had not given me a "Shot over" or a "Splash" warning for the artillery round, but they did not answer. I asked them to shift their fires 500 meters east from their spotting round and to "fire for effect" using High Explosive (HE) rounds since I did not want the VC to have another chance at escaping. The fire mission involved a battery firing powerful 8-inch rounds, but coverage of the target was poor, and we were unable to observe whether or not they had hit any of the VC. I felt frustrated with this fire mission and learned a valuable lesson from it. That lesson was never to use smoke rounds as spotting rounds, since they told the enemy they had been observed and someone was adjusting fire on them. From that moment on, I would only use HE rounds to spot targets since the enemy often thought single HE rounds were unobserved "H and I" fires and, therefore, they usually did not take evasive action.

Three hours later, we again observed VC in the valley. This time we saw four VC moving northeast along a trail that passed through the long abandoned village of Hoi An Thuong. They were in a column spaced approximately 20 meters apart and heading toward us. I had Sgt. Ellison call a fire mission, but I knew we would probably not have the mission cleared and fired in time. I decided we should engage these four VC when they came closest to us in an open area near a stream 300 meters directly in front of our OP. I instructed Cpl. Borecky, who was carrying our M-79 grenade launcher, to prepare to take the enemy under fire when they reached the open space next to the stream. Lt. Danko and I positioned ourselves so we could fire our rifles on the approaching VC. I took up a standard sitting position, while he placed his rifle in the crook of a tree for better stability.

We waited and waited for the artillery to fire but nothing happened. After ten minutes, we saw the VC approaching the ambush killing zone, but no artillery had been fired. Since it was apparent we would be using small arms fire instead of artillery on the VC, I took a few seconds to take some extra magazines of ammunition from my web belt. As I was doing this, Sgt. Pugh, who had taken over observing the VC with the binoculars, whispered, "Hey, one of these bastards looks like a white guy." I took the binoculars from him and asked him which one he was talking about. He replied that it was the third one in the column, "the tall guy in the khaki uniform." Since this individual was now only about 300 meters in front of us and 100 feet below us, I got a very good look at him. His appearance clearly set him apart from his traveling companions. He was taller than the other VC by about a foot. He was dressed in a khaki uniform with the sleeves rolled up, and he had a short-brimmed, light-green bush hat on his head. He was carrying a large khaki rucksack and a rifle that looked a lot like a Belgium FLN. In addition to his appearance, he acted differently than his colleagues; he did not look at the ground but scanned the sky and the hills around him in an almost arrogant manner. As he came closer, I could see he had distinctive web gear; it was made of what appeared to be black leather, something I had never seen before on a VC or NVA soldier. I saw his face clearly as he turned to look up in our direction and it was obvious that his facial features were European and not Asian. I remembered I had my camera in my pack and asked LCpl. Dave Powell to get it quickly and take some pictures of this Caucasian-looking VC. As Powell was aiming my camera at the odd-looking VC, Lt. Danko said he had a good bead on the lead VC, and he requested to fire. I gave my permission, and almost in unison Lt. Danko, Cpl. Borecky, and I opened fire. The first two VC dropped in the grass and appeared to be crawling away while the other two began to run into some high elephant grass. Lt. Danko and I fired several magazines of M-16 rounds at the fleeing VC, and Cpl. Borecky fired his M-79 multiple times, getting very good coverage of the area where we last saw the VC. Both Lt. Danko and I felt we had hit the two lead VC, but we could not see any bodies due to the high grass and brush. Cpl. Borecky continued to fire his M-79 grenade launcher into the area below while I took over the radio and adjusted an artillery fire mission back and forth over the area where we last saw the VC. I asked LCpl. Powell if he had gotten any good pictures of the Caucasian-looking VC, and he said he had taken 4 or 5 pictures of him before we opened fire.

I debated whether or not to go down the hill and into the valley to search for the VC but decided against it since searching for the enemy in elephant grass was very dangerous, and I knew it would take us at least an hour to reach the ambush site safely. My decision to remain in our OP became moot when I received a radio message from Camp Reasoner that a Marine infantry reaction force from F Company, Second Battalion, 26th Marines was on its way to search the valley for the Caucasian-looking VC. They gave me the call sign and frequency of the infantry unit, and we waited for the helicopters with the reaction force to arrive. Within an hour, the reaction force landed 200 meters west of the ambush site and began to sweep the valley along both sides of the trail. I spoke with the reaction force commander and gave him directions, but he found it difficult to maneuver his Marines quickly to the ambush site.

Finally, after about 30 minutes, a squad of Marines entered the open area we had used for our ambush, and they began to conduct a search. They found blood trails, some bandages, and a Chinese hand grenade, but no bodies. After 45 minutes on the ground, the reaction force left via helicopter. Since we had given our OP position away, I moved the patrol down the hill into the southern edge of the valley. We set up a harbor site in some thick bamboo and spent a quiet night there.

Early the next morning, as we prepared to be extracted, we observed two VC in black pajamas moving in a tree line northeast of our position. They were carrying large packs which were camouflaged with foliage to make them look like moving bushes. While we were observing them, two Marine helicopters flew over the valley, and the VC froze in place, leaned over, and held that position until the helicopters had flown by. I am sure no one could have seen them from the air given the excellent camouflage job they had done on their packs. It was even difficult for us to make them out when they did this, and we were relatively close to them. The thought struck me that my patrol could probably pass right by such well-camouflaged enemy troops and pay a heavy price for it.

Ever since we had moved off the high ground and on to the valley floor, our radios did not work well. This communication problem made it impossible for us to call in a fire mission on these VC. We could only watch as they moved away out of our sight to the east. Later in the day, we moved to the trail near the stream and placed several psychological warfare leaflets on trees and brush nearby. These Vietnamese language leaflets had a large eye printed on them and warned the enemy that "Marines are watching you — rally or die." We often took these propaganda leaflets with us on patrol, but we made sure we placed them on the last day of any patrol, so the enemy would only find them long after we were gone.

In the late afternoon, we were extracted from Elephant Valley by helicopter and returned to Camp Reasoner. Lt. St. Claire immediately debriefed us, and told us there was a great deal of interest in the Caucasian-looking VC the patrol had encountered (Team Killer Kane Patrol Report, 17 March 1967). He asked me to write a special report describing this strange-looking VC, so he could make it an attachment to the normal patrol report sent to the Division G-2. Sgt. Ellison, LCpl. Powell, Lt. Danko and I were each interviewed separately to see if there were any discrepancies in our observations, but all of us reported the identical characteristics. Lt. St. Claire took the film we had taken of this strange VC and sent it to the Division G-2 for processing. It was highly unusual for our film to be confiscated. In fact, this was the only occasion when this unusual step was taken. However, given the intense interest in our report of a tall, fair-skinned VC, it seemed like the logical thing to do. We never heard anything about the photos, and we did not receive any of the other photos taken on the role of film. Lt. St. Claire told us later that the film had been flown to Camp Smith, Hawaii, for processing and analysis.

March 1967 was a transformative month for me and for my team, Killer Kane. Two tragic events that deeply affected me took place that month and caused me to adopt a radically different approach to the business of conducting reconnaissance patrols. The first of these occurred on 1 March when my good friend, 2nd Lt. Thomas Dowd, was killed leading his Marines. Tom had been assigned to Company E, 2nd Battalion, 1st Marine Regiment, when he arrived with me in South Vietnam, and he quickly made a favorable impression on his CO and the men of his platoon. He was aggressive, yet not foolhardy, a trait his company commander noted with satisfaction. He was also a quick learner who listened to and learned from the experienced men in his platoon and from his fellow platoon commanders. Despite his natural leadership and careful approach to

Thomas Dowd.

his job, luck ran out for Tom on an operation southwest of Da Nang when he was killed by a hand grenade thrown by a VC he was chasing. When I saw Tom's name on a list of those killed, I was sitting on the back porch of my hootch cleaning my equipment from my last patrol. At first, I thought there might be some mistake, but when I went to the company office and asked the personnel NCO to check the casualty lists at Division headquarters, the sad news was confirmed. I felt sick at Tom's passing. He was the first person I knew who had been killed in the war. Tom was such a vibrant, witty, and charismatic young man it did not seem possible that he was dead. I felt physically ill at hearing the news, but then I began to feel a rage well up inside of me, a rage that grew with every moment I thought of Tom and his grieving family. I wanted to strike out against the enemy that had deprived me of my friend.

Then on 25 March tragedy struck again, even closer to home. Team Countersign, led by Capt. Eric Barnes, was patrolling in an area southeast of the An Hoa Combat Base when someone in the patrol stepped on a land mine. The blast killed both Eric and Sgt. Godfred Blankenship, the assistant patrol leader. What was particularly tragic about Eric's death was he did not have to be on this patrol. He had recently been promoted to captain, and captains did not take out patrols. He had volunteered to take the patrol out because there was a shortage of experienced patrol leaders. Afterward, he would take over duties as the operations officer for the company. He had just returned from R and R in Hawaii, where he met his wife and two young children. While he was on R and R, Eric had told his wife that he would not be taking out any more patrols since his promotion meant he would be assigned to a staff position for the few remaining months he was to be in Vietnam.

I had been out on my seventh patrol when Eric was killed. Our insertion mode for this patrol was unusual. We were inserted by truck because bad weather and mechanical problems for the CH-46 helicopter fleet had grounded these helicopters. Our patrol was inserted on 23 March on Highway 1 north of Da Nang on the north side of the Song Cu De River. The insertion location was a bad one, since it was close to the bridge across the river and there were many villages in the vicinity. I had the patrol move rapidly west into the hills and began climbing the slopes of the Ti Tau Mountain. The purpose of our patrol was to locate where the VC we had spotted during our previous patrol might have been heading. We spent 78 hours hiking in dense and steep jungle terrain, but we only made one sighting of four VC with packs and AK-47 rifles in Elephant Valley not far from where we had spotted the Caucasian VC.

After sighting the four VC, we attempted to follow them in the hope of killing or capturing them. However, they moved away from us quickly, and we were unable to pick up their trail. As we chased after the VC, we found several platoon-sized enemy harbor sites but no indication these sites had been used recently. We covered a lot of ground on this patrol, much of it along a rocky stream bed, making our movement slow, tedious, and difficult. During one of our stops along the patrol route, we saw the face of an entire cliff covered with beautiful orchids set against black stone. Most of the orchids were white or purple but a few were a blend of several colors. The area of this beautiful scene was close to the Garden of Eden, so I began to understand why my recon colleagues had chosen such an apt name for the area. As I stared at the beauty of the scene, I wondered why God had placed such beauty in a place where only a patrol of Marines or some wandering VC would ever see it (Team Killer Kane Patrol Report, 26 March 1967).

As soon as the patrol returned, we were greeted by Maj. Bill Lowrey and several others

Eric Barnes.

National Highway 1 north of Da Nang.

who informed us of Eric's and Sgt. Blankenship's deaths. We were stunned. Without waiting for our debriefing or washing up, I joined Maj. Lowrey, GySgt. Gabbert, and Lt. Mike Henry and went to Company C, 1st Medical Battalion, a short jeep drive from Camp Reasoner on the road to Dogpatch Village. There we viewed the bodies of both of our fallen comrades at Graves Registration.

I was sickened by the deaths of Tom Dowd and Eric Barnes, both of whom I knew and respected. Since Eric lived in the same hootch with me, slept directly opposite me, and was the officer I most admired in our company, I was overcome with grief. I thought about how sad his wife and young children would feel when the news reached them back in New England. It all seemed so unfair that Eric and Sgt. Blankenship, two of the very best men in our company, should die. That evening as I lay in my bed, sweltering in the heat, I vowed that I would make the enemy pay for what they had done to Tom, Eric and Sgt. Blankenship. For hours that night I thought about how I could take revenge on the enemy. The answer would come the next morning.

After breakfast in the mess hall, I was sitting on the back porch cleaning my rifle and other gear when I heard a voice with a thick Irish accent coming from the front door of our hootch. The Irish voice asked Lt. Lenny Torres, "Is Andy here? I need to speak to him." While I was not the strictest officer, I was not used to an enlisted Marine referring to me by my first name, and I was a bit put off by what I considered a lack of respect on the part of this "voice." Lt. Torres brought the "voice" to the back porch where I immediately saw that the "voice" belonged to Cpl. Roy L. Watson, a member of Team Countersign.

Instead of saluting, as any normal Marine would do, he simply walked up and said, "Ah, there you are, Andy." I stood up and asked him what he wanted, and he said, "Andy, can we talk in private? I mean I don't want anyone but you to hear what I have to say." I was beginning to get really annoyed by his lack of military courtesy and the continued use of my first name, so I told him if he wanted to talk to me, I would be glad to do so but only if he used "Sir" or "Lieutenant" when addressing me. Undeterred by my show of annoyance, Cpl. Watson simply assumed a feigned attitude of contrition that was far from convincing. I knew something of his background, which was unique: He was an Irish citizen, but had volunteered to serve in the U.S. Marine Corps after serving for eight years as a British Royal Marine fighting in Kenya and Yemen. I also knew he had a reputation in the company for eccentric behavior. With a hurt look on his face more theatrical than sincere, he said, "Sorry, Andy, but in the Royal Marines, we use our officers' first names in the field."

I told him we were not in the field, and we were not Royal Marines. He got my point and standing at attention with eyes fixed ahead, he formally asked again if we could talk in confidence "about a small matter that needs to be taken care of." Since he belatedly used "sir" at the end of his question, I said I would be glad to talk to him. Then in a very conspiratorial manner, he whispered that he and the men of Team Countersign wanted to propose something to me. What he told me and what we carried

Roy Watson at Camp Reasoner.

out as a result of that conversation would change the way Killer Kane would operate against the enemy from that moment on with dramatic results.

3

Killer Kane Goes on the Attack

"Lieutenant, our team is angry about the deaths of Capt. Barnes and Sgt. Blankenship, and we want to avenge their deaths. We need you to help us do this," Sgt. Watson whispered.

He went on to lay out the rationale for this request.

"We want you to lead a combined patrol of the men from Countersign and Killer Kane, so we can go back to the Antenna Valley Pass and ambush the bastards who killed our friends. Our team talked it over, and we decided we wanted you to lead this patrol because we know you are not one of the patrol leaders who just goes out and hides from the enemy. You ambushed that Caucasian guy in Elephant Valley, and you were not afraid to try to ambush some VC on your last patrol. Your team says you are aggressive, and that is the kind of team leader we need on a mission like this. Besides, we know you go to the S-3 and request patrols, so no one would be suspicious if you requested a patrol near the Antenna Valley Pass."

At first I thought the idea was a bad one. I knew it would be risky to go back into an area that was mined, but I also was aware of the dangers of ambushing a well-used trail far from any friendly units. I also did not like the idea of taking Marines from another patrol along with my men since I would not know these men and how they would react under my command. I also was aware of the eccentric and manipulative character of Sgt. Watson. My initial reaction to his idea was to reject it, but then I felt the rage well up inside me about Tom Dowd's and Eric Barnes's deaths. Despite my misgivings, I told Sgt. Watson to come with me into the hootch, where I took out one of my maps of Antenna Valley so the two of us could study it. He pointed out where Team Countersign had been inserted on a ridgeline north of the pass and the path they had taken before they hit the land mine that killed Capt. Barnes and Sgt. Blankenship. I noticed that the Antenna Valley Pass was both long and very narrow with steep mountains on the north and south sides, which would make it an ideal place to establish ambush sites. The more I studied the map with Sgt. Watson, the more I liked his idea of setting an ambush in the pass. I told Sgt. Watson to choose four of the best men from Team Countersign, and I would pick three of my best men to make up the combined patrol using my call sign of Killer Kane. I also had him swear to secrecy about what we intended to do on this patrol. He waited for me on the back porch while I went to the S-3 office to request a patrol for Killer Kane that would take us into the Antenna Valley Pass area.

When I entered the S-3 office, I saw that Maj. Welzant was not there, but MSgt. Clovis Coffman was, so I approached him and casually asked him where he thought my next patrol would be. He and I had had conversations previously about where I would take my team, so he was not surprised when I asked him if he thought he could send our team into the Antenna Valley Pass area. He went over to the large S-3 situation map on the wall and looked at the active and planned recon team NFZ's, focusing his attention in the area around Antenna Valley. After a quick glance, he turned to me and informed me that no decision had been made yet about where to send Killer Kane on its next patrol. Before he could make a suggestion on a NFZ for my team, I pointed to the situation map and queried him about the feasibility of assigning Killer Kane to an NFZ on the south side of Antenna Valley near the "Old French Fort," an abandoned concrete blockhouse the French had built during the First Indochina War. Clovis Coffman was a battle-hardened Marine who had been awarded several Purple Hearts and the Navy Cross for valor, and I could tell he sensed that I might have something in mind when I requested such a patrol. But all he said was, "Lieutenant, you need to be careful here because Capt. Barnes' team hit that land mine on the north side of the pass, and there may be more mines there. I recommend you stay off the ridgelines and that trail below in the valley, or you might end up getting killed."

I replied, "Don't worry, Top, we will be careful and not take any risks. Just take your trusty grease pencil and give us an NFZ near the 'Old French Fort,' and we will try to find a good OP site to observe that trail." He took his grease pencil and gave my team an NFZ exactly where I wanted it, and he even pointed out several good LZs we might use inside of it. I waited for a few minutes until I heard him get on the landline phone to the Division G-2 and pass on the grid coordinates for Killer Kane's next patrol. When he hung up the phone, I thanked him and left the S-3 office.

Later that night, Sgt. Watson and Cpl. Robert J. Garcia joined me on the back porch for a planning session. I included Cpl. Garcia in our conspiracy because he had impressed me with his skills as a point man, and I knew with the danger of land mines it was essential that he be mentally prepared to avoid them when we moved down to the valley floor for our ambush. We decided that the best approach was to be inserted into an LZ on a ridge adjacent to the one that Team Countersign had used on its tragic patrol. We would then move cross compartment, avoiding any trails and ridge lines, to a position where we could observe as much of the trail as possible, but low enough so we could quickly get down to the trail to establish an ambush. We looked at the contour lines on the map and a few black and white aerial reconnaissance photos of the pass that I had obtained from Lt. St. Claire's S-2 shop so we could plot a good patrol route. Sgt. Watson, Cpl. Garcia and I were the only people involved with the planning of this ambush patrol.

I had wanted to include LCpl. Bart Russell on this patrol because I considered him one of the best recon men in my platoon, but I decided to leave him behind and have

Robert Garcia, the perfect point man.

him go out with our other team, Brisbane, since they were short one man and they needed a good point man. Instead of taking LCpl. Russell, the patrol would include another officer, one making his first patrol as an observer, Lt. Tom Williamson. Maj. Lowrey wanted Tom to make his first "snap in" with our team. I was not worried about having Tom go with us since he had impressed me with his knowledge and attitude in the few days he had been with the company. I liked his aggressive outlook. Still, I felt a patrol like this one needed the special talents of someone like Bart Russell, and his absence was a cause of concern for me.

Bart Russell was the son and grandson of Marines. His desire to become a Marine was so strong he left college to join the Corps and to volunteer to fight in South Vietnam. He was tough, highly intelligent, aggressive and skillful, the perfect field Marine. He had all the tools needed to be a patrol leader, and he would have been one had he been more senior in rank. Sgt. Watson assured me that he and his men, along with Cpl. Garcia, would be able to compensate for not having LCpl. Russell on this patrol, but he agreed with me that LCpl. Russell was one of the best Marines in the entire company. Throughout my time as a patrol leader I often solicited the advice of LCpl. Russell and Cpl. Garcia since they were highly experienced and capable men who seemed to have an almost instinctive knowledge of the craft of ground reconnaissance. Their advice and assistance proved invaluable to me and our team time and again.

When I went over the roster of men making up the patrol I felt very good about its composition. In addition to Sgt. Watson, Cpl. Garcia, and Lt. Williamson, the patrol included Cpl. Jeptha Carter, Cpl. Maxwell B. Carter and four other junior enlisted men: Daniel Bowser, J. D. Morris, Davis Powell and a Marine named Swatsell. With the exception of Lt. Williamson, who was new to the company, each of the enlisted men was a seasoned reconnaissance Marine. As I reflected on the capabilities of the men who were to make up this patrol, I thought of the rosters of baseball and basketball teams I had played on as a youth. Similar to a sports team roster, these patrol rosters placed the best men in the positions where their skills and talents could prove the most beneficial. This roster had "All-Star Team" written all over it.

The next day, Sgt. Watson and I went over the particulars of the patrol so I could write my patrol order and arrange for an overflight of our intended NFZ. We paid special attention to the equipment we were to carry. In addition to the two PRC-25 radios, we included an M-60 machine gun, two 7 × 50 binoculars, an M-79 grenade launcher, and one of the new, experimental Stoner carbines. We also made sure that each man carried 300 rounds of ammunition and two M-26 fragmentation hand grenades and one CS tear gas grenade. Since we were going on an ambush patrol, we wanted to have all the firepower we could carry. Also, since we intended to use CS gas before we entered the killing zone of our ambush, we decided that we would make sure each man had a new filter in his gas mask and make sure the masks had no leaks. Every recon team member always took a gas mask as part of his standard patrol equipment, primarily because recon teams could use CS gas to cover a withdrawal under fire during a meeting engagement with the enemy. In our case, however, we needed to use CS gas in the killing zone because we wanted to determine if any wounded enemy were feigning death before the search team entered the killing zone to search it. A wounded or unwounded enemy would not be able to remain immobile once he breathed the CS gas, so the search team would be alerted and take the necessary precautionary action. We also took along several three-foot parachute cords that we could use to secure any captured enemy and a few extra field bandanas to cover their eyes while we transported them back to base. Mentally, Sgt. Watson and I walked through the patrol route, the selection of the ambush site, the occupation of the ambush site, the conduct of the ambush, and the search procedure for the killing zone.

After I wrote my patrol order, Sgt. Watson, Lt. Williamson and I went on an overflight of the NFZ, the one we had been assigned by MSgt. Coffman on the south side of the Antenna Valley Pass. After going through the motions of identifying insert and extract LZs, I had the pilots fly over the north side of the pass so I could identify the insertion zone we wanted to use for our "real" patrol. The more time I spent on overflights, the better I became at finding terrain features on the ground that I had previously plotted on a map. Using my wrist compass to orient my map, I was able to find terrain features on the ground from a helicopter with relative ease. I could then talk to the pilots over the headset and direct them to the LZs I wanted to observe. As part of my routine on an overflight, I took along a Polaroid camera so I could photograph the insertion and extraction LZs. These photos could then be used during my patrol order to familiarize the team members with the LZs and to brief the insertion pilots prior to liftoff on the day of the patrol.

On this overflight, both Sgt. Watson and I had on intercom headsets so we could talk to the pilots. Sgt. Watson knew exactly what the terrain looked like for the "real insertion" since he had covered the area with Team Countersign a few days earlier. The pilots did not know we were looking for an LZ outside of our NFZ when I asked them to make a few passes on the north side of the pass. They probably assumed we were interested in seeing if there were some alternate LZs in the vicinity.

Upon our return to Camp Reasoner's LZ Finch, I told Sgt. Watson that I would issue my patrol order the next day at 1300, and we would conduct our ambush training immediately afterward. I also informed Lt. Williamson of our little conspiracy and asked him not to talk to anyone about it. Tom agreed and seemed eager to participate. Tom would later develop into an extremely capable patrol leader and a close friend. That evening after dinner, I went to the S-2 office and reviewed several patrol reports from recon teams that had patrolled near the Antenna Valley Pass. Then I walked over to the Division G-2 to see if they had any recent information on the enemy units operating in this area.

The next morning I wrote my patrol order and went over it with Tom Williamson to see if he could spot any problems with it. He made a couple of useful suggestions, and I incorporated them into the patrol order. At 1300, Sgt. Watson brought the members of the patrol over to my back porch, and I gave them the order. At this time I also told them that we would concentrate on the trail running east and west in the pass, and we intended to ambush this trail if we observed its use by the enemy. When I finished reading my order, I asked the team members if they had any questions or any insights that might benefit us. One of the Marines from Team Countersign said he had been on two patrols in this area, and he knew that there were several good OP sites on the north side of the pass that would give us clear observation for 500 meters or more in each direction. I asked him to point these potential OP sites out on my map. This information would prove very valuable to us while we were on the patrol.

We then went down to the helipad area and test-fired all of our weapons with the exception of the grenade launcher. Then we went over the hand and arm signals we would be using on the patrol because our team was a combination of two teams from separate platoons, and I did not want to find out on the patrol that we used different hand and arm signals. Since we rarely talked on patrol, these hand and arm signals needed to be fully understood by each member of the patrol. It was essential that everyone could quickly and accurately communicate in silence. We also positioned everyone in their respective positions for the patrol, and we rehearsed our quick reaction drills for countering an ambush and breaking contact to include our use of CS gas grenades during both situations. I inspected each man's gas mask to ensure the filters were new, required each man to don his gas mask, and made them clear their masks to ensure there were no leaks. Finally, we divided the team into three elements: two security teams of two men each and an assault element for the ambush consisting of six men. Each element was briefed on their responsibilities. We then spent an hour going over how we would conduct the ambush, practicing several iterations of the various phases for the ambush: moving into position, posting security for the assault element, conducting the ambush, searching the killing zone, and executing a safe withdrawal. Just before evening chow, I again gathered the team together and asked them if I had missed anything or they had any last-minute suggestions on how to improve the patrol. No one spoke up, so I said we needed to get a good night's sleep that night, and I reminded them that no one outside of the patrol should know about our intentions.

The next day, March 31, I attended the briefing of the insertion pilots in the S-3 office. Maj. Welzant gave the pilots the coordinates of the boundaries of the patrol's NFZ and the primary and secondary insertion LZs. He also gave them the latest intelligence on the enemy situation. I gave two Polaroid photos to the pilots that I had taken on the overflight, but I did not tell them of my plan to land in an entirely new LZ 1,000 meters north and west of the NFZ. When our team boarded the helicopters for the insertion, I took a moment to tell the pilots that we might have to land in another LZ since I was worried about land mines near the Old French Fort.

After a 30-minute flight south toward An Hoa and the Hiep Duc Mountains, we approached the Antenna Valley Pass. When we were within a few miles of the pass, I told the pilot that I had a new LZ for the insertion, and I pointed it out to him on my map. He did not question my change of plans, but simply nodded his head, took my map, examined the location of the new LZ, and handed it back to me. In less than a minute, the pilot located the new LZ on the ground, and we began our descent. We began a steep dive, giving the team just enough time to take their weapons off safe and prepare for our landing. As we drew closer to the ground, the air in the helicopter changed from cold to cool and then hot, all within the space of a few seconds. At altitude, the air inside a helicopter is cool and rather pleasant, but as the helicopter descends, the air inside becomes hot and humid rapidly.

When we stepped outside into the elephant grass on a narrow ridgeline, we were met with a blast of hot air, like stepping into the mouth of a furnace. We moved off the LZ into some thick brush as the helicopter rose and joined up with the chase bird and the gun ships. The pilot radioed us and asked us if we were "all secure." I replied that we were on the ground, had not taken any fire, and had seen no signs of the enemy. The pilot wished us luck, and soon the sounds of the helicopters' rotor blades faded into the distance. Sweating intensely and feeling apprehensive as we always were immediately after landing in an insertion zone, we spent 20 minutes sitting quietly, our ears straining to pick up any indication the enemy had spotted us and were moving toward us. During this time, all we heard were the normal sounds of the jungle, the chirping of birds, the hum of insects, and the whistling of the wind in the tall elephant grass.

Confident that the enemy was not near the LZ, we began our patrol. Cpl. Bob Garcia and Cpl. Jeptha Carter led the way as point and backup point, followed by me and the rest of the patrol. As we moved through the thick brush, I marveled at the way Cpl. Garcia moved. He seemed to glide noiselessly through the thickets and elephant grass with slow, deliberate motion, aware of everything around him. From time to time, he would raise his hand to signal us to stop, and then I would watch him scan the area ahead and cup his ear to pick up any faint sound that would indicate the presence of the enemy. Nothing seemed to escape Bob Garcia's attention. Every man on the patrol knew we owed our lives to Bob and the skills and experience he possessed. Bob Garcia was to the job of point man what Picasso was to art — a master of his craft.

We headed in a southeasterly direction going downhill until we came to an open area in a ravine with a small stream running through it. The stream ran downhill 500 meters toward the trail that ran through the Antenna Valley Pass. It was evident that the ravine had been cultivated at some time in the recent past because a small plot of rice paddy hugged the floor of the ravine, and the irrigation dikes for the paddy had been tended within the past year. I thought it strange that someone would tend such a small plot so far from any habitation. I did not know whether this plot had been farmed by an innocent peasant or the VC. Regardless of the source of the cultivation of this small rice paddy, I considered it a danger area and treated it as such.

As we began to move, we heard voices coming from the trail to the south. We froze in our tracks. After a few minutes the male voices moved away to the west, and we were left in silence again. Although it meant more time and effort, I decided to move around the open area to the south staying inside the thick brush. We were hot and sweating heavily as we pushed through the thick brush, but it was safer than moving through an open area where we could become an easy target for any enemy lurking in the vicinity.

After crossing the ravine, we began to ascend the opposite hill, struggling under the weight of our full packs and the intense heat. The patrol moved slowly and methodically, thanks to the skills of the two point men, Garcia and Carter. Still, it took us nearly two hours to climb to the opposite ridgeline, a distance of only 300 meters from the bottom of the ravine. On the ridgeline, I set up security by breaking the patrol into three groups. One group of three men would face up the ridgeline to the north while another three-man team would look south toward the valley. These two groups would cover the two most likely avenues of approach along the ridgeline and protect the middle group consisting of me, the primary radio operator, our Navy corpsman, and Lt. Williamson. I drafted a Position Report (PosRep) and had the radio operator send it to the radio relay station on Hill 452 for retransmission to Camp Reasoner.

While I was on the ridgeline, I noticed that it afforded very good visibility of the trail in the pass below, so I decided to set up an OP on the ridgeline and begin watching for foot traffic on the trail. It was extremely hot, but we found a small stand of 15-foot-high brush and bamboo that afforded some shade from the sun. For the rest of the day we took turns using our two sets of binoculars to scan the western and eastern approaches of the trail. The only traffic on the trail that we observed consisted of a dozen or so civilian farmers dressed in the ubiquitous black pajamas moving in both directions. They might have been VC, but since we did not observe any packs or weapons, we assumed they were not and let them pass unmolested.

As darkness fell on our first day, we ate our evening meal of C rations and then assembled the patrol 100 meters further up the ridgeline where we could hide for the night. Throughout the night we could hear artillery fire in the distance and see the occasional flare as it hung from its parachute, lighting up the black sky as it drifted toward the earth, sending ominous shadows across the landscape. The night passed peacefully for Killer Kane, and the cool of the night was a welcome respite after a day in the hot, tropical sun.

Our second day was spent moving over to another ridgeline farther east where we thought we had a better chance to observe any enemy moving into our ambush site. This was accomplished after two hours of negotiating some steep terrain which required us to literally crawl uphill to reach the next ridgeline. We found a spot approximately 100 meters north of the trail that was ideal for our purposes, so I chose it for our OP. I was pleased to see that we could observe over 200 yards along the trail in either direction and to be able to fire our weapons into any killing zone we set up below.

Sgt. Watson and I, along with two other Marines, moved down the ridgeline to the trail to reconnoiter a possible ambush site. We found one almost immediately near a stream that crossed the trail. After stopping for a half hour to fill our canteens with the fresh mountain stream water, we moved along the trail for another 50 yards until we found another excellent ambush site with a small grass-covered berm that would provide both cover and concealment for a small ambush team. We stayed in this second ambush site for two hours. Only a few old peasants walked by us, so we decided to abandon the ambush for the day and move back up the ridgeline where we had left the observation team.

The last few hours of the day were devoted to establishing the best location for our combination OP and fire-support site on the ridgeline and quenching our thirst with the cool, clean water we found in the stream earlier. As the tropical sky turned a murky blue and a thick mist descended over the ridgeline, we moved to another safe harbor site farther up the ridgeline and deeper into lush green foliage. Under a cloudless sky, filled with bright stars, we spent the night enjoying the cool mountain breezes after a day of intense heat and humidity.

The morning of the third day of the patrol was breathless and windless, a clear indication that the day would be an unusually hot one. The valley below us was shrouded in a grey mist, but the rising sun was soon beginning to clear it away. I had originally intended to use two security elements and an assault element for our ambush, but the terrain we found offered us a unique opportunity: the chance to use our OP site team as both a security element and fire-support element for the ambush team 100 feet below us. I decided I would stay with the OP team of five men while Sgt. Watson would take the other men down to the valley floor to set up an ambush in the first ambush site we had found the previous day. LCpl. Dave Powell and I each took binoculars and watched the trail. I took the portion of the trail to the west. As I scanned the terrain below me, I found that I could see anyone approaching from the west as far away as 1,000 meters and track their advance right into the killing zone. We had one radio with us in the OP, and Lt. Williamson took the other radio with him down into the valley. With this arrangement, I could use our radios to inform the ambush team well in advance of any enemy moving along the trail toward their ambush.

Only a few minutes after Lt. Williamson radioed us to tell us the ambush site was manned and ready for business, LCpl. Powell whispered to me that he saw VC 500 meters away on the trail moving west toward the ambush. I quickly scanned my binoculars to where he pointed and saw three VC. They were all dressed in black pajamas and carrying packs and weapons. Two of them wore the distinctive pith helmets of the communist forces. I took the radio and contacted Lt. Williamson, informing him that three armed VC would enter his ambush in approximately five minutes. I then had the four Marines with me get into good firing positions so they could fire into the killing zone, adding our firepower to the Marines below. I told them not to open fire until Sgt. Watson triggered the ambush.

What seemed like an eternity passed before we saw the lead enemy soldier walk into the killing zone below us. A second enemy soldier, following the first by about ten yards, entered the killing zone, and we heard the sharp report of Sgt. Watson's M-14 rifle, followed almost simultaneously by the rifle fire of the other members of his ambush team. I aimed at the lead enemy soldier and fired 5 or 6 rounds at him. He stumbled but did not fall. He disappeared into the high elephant grass on the far side of the trail, and I continued to fire at him although I could not see him. I could see one body in the killing zone, but no others.

Lt. Williamson's excited voice came over the radio telling me that Sgt. Watson was going to search the killing zone, so I had everyone in our group cease firing and shift their positions so they could cover any escape routes the enemy might take to the east and west of the ambush site. Cpl. Carter and I moved quickly down the ridgeline to the ambush location while LCpl. Powell scanned the valley to the east and west to make sure no more VC were coming in our direction. We did not want Sgt. Watson and his men caught unawares in the valley if more VC were on their way to find out what all the firing was about. When Cpl. Carter and I got to the ambush site, we found Sgt. Watson and the others searching one of the bodies. The other VC was missing and presumed dead since his pack and pith helmet lay in the trail, and there was a blood trail leading into the high elephant grass on the opposite side of the trail. Cpl. Carter had an M-79 grenade launcher, and he fired several 40 mm grenade rounds into the area where the VC was last seen. We decided it was too dangerous to search for the body of this VC in the high grass, so we took the body of the dead VC and placed it off the trail where it could not be seen. We took care to make sure the ambush killing zone had nothing in it that might warn the VC that it had been used. We even policed up the grass near the trail and covered the blood with dirt. Sgt. Watson wanted to continue to occupy the ambush site, but I decided we were now compromised since the third VC had probably escaped unharmed and would be warning his comrades of our presence. I decided it would be best to move back up the ridgeline to our OP and observe the trail from that location. If we saw any more VC we could call in artillery on them.

It was nearly noon when our team reassembled in the OP on the ridgeline. There Sgt. Watson showed me what he had found after searching the killing zone. He had taken the two pith helmets, a red propaganda flag, some Vietnamese cigarettes, a magazine with 15 rounds of ammunition in it, and a plastic poncho. I asked him about the weapons we saw the enemy carrying, and he told me he had retrieved one of them but he did not want me to report it in my SALUTE report to Camp Reasoner. He explained that he had the weapon disassembled in his pack and he wanted it for "trading material" back in the rear. He contended that if it was reported, the S-2 would take it, and he would never see it again. I told him I would think about it, but that I did not like to withhold anything of intelligence value from the S-2. He gave me a curious look, and then in his heavy Irish accent, he said, "Andy, you are right. We should never withhold a single shred of important intelligence from the people in the rear. I know you will always do what is right, but we need these weapons because we can get all sorts of good things for our team back in the rear with them. We can trade them to the Air Force for their AR-15 rifles, survival equipment and camouflage uniforms. We can take them over to the First Marine Air Wing and trade them for pilots' gloves and whiskey. We can get ARVN rucksacks and other goodies we need. So you see, I know you will do what is right, won't you?"

Sgt. Watson had a way with words, and I knew he was doing his best to manipulate me, but I did not think it was the time or place to waste any time discussing this matter, so I simply nodded my head that I understood. I could see the logic of his argument, but it irked me to know he was using me and trying to make me complicit in his conspiracy to obviate our orders to turn over all captured weapons. I wanted to think about what was the correct course of action, so I decided I would not report the capture of this weapon in my SALUTE Report and wait until our return to Camp Reasoner to decide on its disposition. My silence was taken as acceptance by Sgt. Watson. He took the pieces of the weapon out of his pack, and with a broad smile, he reassembled it. Displaying it with pride, he showed me a well-worn French MAT-49 submachine gun. It was prize trading material, indeed.

There was a hot shimmering haze covering the Antenna Valley Pass that afternoon, but we only observed one VC on the trail. He, like his unfortunate predecessors, was moving toward the west. He had a large pack on his back that he had camouflaged with leaves. He often looked up at the ridgelines above him and his gait was both cautious and rapid. It was obvious that he suspected Marines were nearby, and it was possible he had been sent to ascertain what had happened to the VC we had ambushed earlier in the morning. I decided not to call in an artillery fire mission since observed fire would clearly tell the VC that Marines saw him and were nearby. Instead, I thought it better to let this one VC go in the hope that a larger group might be following him. With this in mind, I later called in and registered two artillery missions on the trail; one to the west and one to the east, each about 1,000 meters distant. Although we watched the trail until daylight faded into dusk, no more VC used the trail that day.

The next day, 3 April, our fourth day observing the pass, I modified our ambush somewhat. I had Lt. Williamson stay with the OP element while I went with Sgt. Watson down into the valley to our second ambush site. On our way down to the ambush site, Lt. Williamson reported that several Vietnamese civilians carrying baskets on poles were moving on the trail in a westerly direction. As we got within a few yards of the ambush site, we saw these civilians passing by rapidly. After they had passed, we asked Lt. Williamson if the trail was clear, and he told us it was. We had hardly gotten into position when Lt. Williamson radioed us again and told us that two VC were approaching our ambush site from the east and that they should be in our killing zone in a few minutes. I asked him if he could see any VC behind these two, and he said he could see for 1000 meters behind them and no other VC were in sight. I had asked this because I knew the VC would often divide their forces into front and rear guard elements when they moved large units, and I thought these two VC might just be scouts for a larger force following them. It was possible that the civilians we had just seen pass in front of us had been sent ahead of the VC as scouts but there was no way of knowing this. With the information provided by Lt. Williamson, we prepared to ambush the two VC he had spotted.

Our ambush site was a good one, a berm 20 yards long on the north side of the trail that afforded our ambush team excellent cover and concealment. There was a slight dogleg in the trail on the western side, which gave two of us an almost perfect field of fire for 30 yards. I was the westernmost Marine in our ambush team, so I covered this dogleg, along with Cpl. Garcia. We both crouched down behind the berm and leveled our rifles through the grass, moving as noiselessly as possible. As the minutes passed, we tried not to move because even the slightest sound might alert the enemy to our presence. Perspiration ran down our faces and stung our eyes. I silently released the safety on my rifle and took up a good firing position.

In a flash, we both heard the other members of the team open fire. It was over in an instant, and Cpl. Garcia and I had not fired a shot. Cpl. Garcia and I looked back at the other members of the ambush team, and we saw that Sgt. Watson was kneeling on the berm, his weapon trained on the killing zone in front of him. He had triggered the ambush and had killed both of the VC himself. All of the other shooting was redundant. We donned our gas masks, threw two CS grenades into the killing zone next to the bodies, and waited to see if the gas produced any movement by the VC. The CS gas drifted over their bodies and one of them moved slightly. Sgt. Watson fired two rounds into the moving VC and the movement stopped. While Cpl. Garcia and I moved out onto the trail to secure the approach from the west, two other Marines moved into the trail and covered the approaches from the east. Sgt. Watson and one other Marine searched the bodies and retrieved the gear they had been carrying. We then moved back up the ridgeline to the OP and rejoined Lt. Williamson and the three men with him. The climb back up the ridgeline was very uncomfortable due to the added weight of the enemy gear we had captured. The CS gas had also permeated our clothing and caused a stinging sensation all over our bodies when combined with our perspiration.

Since I had not seen the VC we had killed until after the ambush had been triggered, I did not know what they looked like or what they were carrying. As it turned out, we had obtained some very valuable intelligence from one of the two VC we had killed. Both VC were dressed in a combination of khaki and black clothing and both carried weapons and packs. One of them, however, was clearly different. He appeared to be an officer or senior communist cadre. He was the older and the taller of the two, and he carried a pistol and a dispatch case, two items that indicated he was an officer or party official. When we returned to the OP, we began to take an inventory of the weapons, equipment, and documents found on these dead VC. The smaller of the two VC had an NVA rucksack that contained assorted clothing, green plastic material, sights for a 12.7 mm heavy machine gun, several black and white photos of him and his family, and a sock filled with rice. He was also carrying a Chinese Type 50 submachine gun.

The taller VC, the one who appeared to be an officer or senior communist cadre, was carrying a U.S. Marine Corps haversack which contained some clothing, 9,800 South Vietnamese piasters, a canteen, a Chinese compass, a pair of East German binoculars and a leather dispatch case. We opened the dispatch case and found pens, ink, pencils, writing paper, a diary, communist propaganda material, a hand-drawn map of Antenna Valley, a list of names and villages, and two red flags with the communist hammer and sickle on them. This VC was carrying a U.S. M1911 .45-caliber pistol in a holster attached to a black leather Sam Browne belt. It was obvious from the weapon he was carrying and the documents in his dispatch case that he was an important person, probably a member of the Viet Cong Infrastructure (VCI) that exercised political control over the rural population in the area. After our inventory was completed, I reported the results of the ambush by SALUTE message to our base. Within minutes of sending our SALUTE message Maj. Welzant was on the radio informing us that he was sending helicopters to extract us a day early so we could bring back the contents of the dispatch case. He told me that there was a lot of interest in the dispatch case at the Division G-2 and to expect our extract helicopters in an hour or two.

At 1140, we were contacted by the lead pilot of our extract helicopters. He informed us that he was about 15 minutes from our position, and we should be prepared to use a smoke grenade to mark our position. I gave him a zone briefing and waited for him to arrive. Two Huey gunships arrived first to provide cover for the extract helicopters as they approached the LZ. The CH-46 pilot asked me to "pop smoke," and I threw a smoke grenade into the center of the small LZ on the ridgeline. The pilot saw my smoke and asked me to confirm its color. A minute later, he landed his helicopter, and we all boarded it. As was our routine, I boarded last and made a quick head count to ensure we did not leave anyone behind. Once aboard, we sat on the floor as the helicopter slowly lifted off the ridgeline, struggled to gain altitude, and finally climbed to 1,500 feet. After four days in the intense heat, the cold air at 1,500 feet was both refreshing and invigorating, making our flight back to Camp Reasoner a welcome one (Team Killer Kane Patrol Report, 3 April 1967; see also Stubbe and Lanning, pp. 211–213).

When our chopper landed at Camp Reasoner, Col. McKeon, Maj. Welzant, Maj. Lowrey, and an officer from the G-2 section of the 1st Marine Division met us on the heli-pad. We dropped our gear in our hootches and immediately went to the S-2 shop for our patrol debrief with Lt. St. Claire. We turned over the dispatch case and the two weapons we had captured on the last ambush to the officer from the Division G-2, and then we gave our report to Lt. St. Claire. When the debrief was over, Lt. St. Claire and Col. McKeon asked me to remain behind saying they wanted to talk to me alone. As my team filed out of the debriefing room, I could tell by the demeanor of both Lt. St. Claire and Col. McKeon that I was in for some difficulty. I was not wrong!

What followed was a major league ass-chewing by both gentlemen. Their comments went this way:

> Lieutenant, when we assign you an NFZ, we expect you to use that NFZ and not decide on your own that you will go somewhere else. Not only did you go into an area where two recon Marines, Capt. Barnes and Sgt. Blankenship, were just killed, but you fully intended to do this without telling anyone in advance that you were going to do it. We put you into an NFZ for a specific reason. By deciding on your own to go somewhere else, you not only placed your team in danger from friendly fires, you also disregarded the mission we sent you on. You may think it is cool to ambush the enemy, but that is not what you were sent to do. You could have gotten your entire team killed and, perhaps, jeopardized the operations the 5th Marines were conducting to your east. In short, you were disobeying orders, and you did not exercise good judgment. We have half a mind to give you an Article 15.

I sat there in silence feeling the sting of their comments. I knew they were right and that I had exercised bad judgment and risked the lives of my team for no other reason than my anger at the death of my friends. I also knew that I had not told the truth when I told everyone outside of my team that I was going into the assigned NFZ when I knew full well that I had no intention of doing so. I had also not been honest when I failed to report the weapon Sgt. Watson had hidden in his pack, or some of the other items we had found on the dead bodies. Lurking in the back of my mind I knew I had allowed Sgt. Watson to influence me to do things that I would normally not have done. The realization that he had chosen me for his scheme began to sink in. He knew I was a new lieutenant, and he thought he could take advantage of my lack of experience. I allowed this to happen because I placed emotion before reason, a serious mistake for an officer to make. My desire to avenge the death of my two friends caused me to willingly go along with Sgt. Watson's scheme and to disregard my orders and to do so in a deceitful manner. I was wrong and I knew it. All I could do was sit in the debriefing room and listen to two officers I greatly respected berate me for my actions. When they finished, I told them the truth about why I chose to disregard my orders and conduct an ambush patrol instead of a reconnaissance patrol. They listened and then Col. McKeon said, "Lieutenant, you are new to the Marine Corps and to this unit, but that is no excuse for your rashness and disregard for orders. You probably deserve a letter of reprimand, but I am going to give you one more chance. Don't make me regret it. From now on, you will carry out your orders to the letter. I am not sure whether you are brave or crazy — maybe both — but I don't have room in my battalion for officers who disobey orders. Now go get cleaned up and go to chow. We will forget about this from now on, unless there is a repeat."

Feeling very dejected and chastised, I went to my hootch, cleaned the camouflage paint off my face, shaved off the four days of beard that had accumulated while I was on patrol, took a cold shower, and put on a clean utility uniform. It was too late to eat noon chow, so I sat on the back porch and cooked a can of beans and franks and drank one of the Cokes in our refrigerator. I was dog tired, dejected, and alone in the hootch so I took what I thought would be a short nap, only to be awakened several hours later by Lt. Mike Henry, who asked me if I was going to evening chow in the mess hall. I got up and went with Mike to eat dinner, a meal I can remember clearly to this day; it was pork cutlets, mashed potatoes, tomato gravy, string beans and ice-cold orange Kool Aid. As I sat eating with Mike, Lt. Lenny Torres came up with Lt. John Danko, and they began to tell me about how excited everyone was over the documents that we had taken off the body of the VC officer. They told me that the Division G-2 had determined that the officer we had killed had been a district-level VC political officer who had just finished a round of meetings with other VC cadres in Antenna Valley. Of great importance was a list he carried that identified over 100 VC agents and cadres in Antenna Valley and the Que Son Valley. Later, Mike St. Claire told me this list of enemy agents was turned over to the CIA for their action. This information resulted in the capture or death of several communist spies and political cadres in these two valleys in southern Quang Nam Province.

Having just been subjected to a severe tongue-lashing from Lt. St. Claire and Col. McKeon, this exciting news did not lift my spirits very much, so I excused myself and went back to my hootch to clean my rifle and field gear. As I sat on the back porch I heard a voice from below call to me in a stage whisper, "Andy, are you there? It's me, Sgt. Watson." I looked over the edge of the porch, and there ten feet below me stood Sgt. Watson, still dressed in his dirty field uniform and his face still covered with green and black face paint. He said, "Andy, I heard you got your ass chewed for taking us out on patrol, so I thought I would come over and talk to you about it." Then he added, "Let's bring the team over. They are feeling a wee bit down after hearing about the trouble you got into. OK?"

I was really in no mood to talk and it annoyed me that Sgt. Watson still persisted in calling me by my first name, so I said, "God damn it, Sgt. Watson, I told you not to call me by my first name. Let's maintain some military courtesy. OK?"

"Sure, Lieutenant, I'm sorry," he responded with a feigned look of remorse that did little to convince me that he would not do it again. He left, but five minutes later, he returned with the other members of the patrol. They brought with them a case of warm beer, and soon we were talking about our patrol and how Capt. Barnes and Sgt. Blankenship had been avenged. As we drank beer and I heard these men talk, my sadness over the day's events dissipated, and I found myself enjoying their company. I listened to them talk of home and girlfriends and boot camp and how much they enjoyed being recon Marines. Lt. Tom Williamson joined us later on, and we talked about his father, who was a career Marine who had fought in Korea and the early stages of the Vietnam War. We listened to Sgt. Watson relate his experiences in Kenya and Yemen with the Royal Marines and how this elite British organization differed from the U.S. Marine Corps.

As the hours slipped away and we consumed several cases of beer, Sgt. Watson led us in Irish songs of revolution, lost causes, and sadness. We finally ended our little party when the lieutenants in my hootch came out and requested we secure our party, since it was time for "lights out" in the division area. As we broke up, Sgt. Watson asked if he might make a toast before we departed. He stood at attention with a beer can in his hand and said, "To Killer Kane, To Capt. Barnes, and To Sgt. Blankenship." We all rose and repeated the toast. Then my teammates from Killer Kane staggered back to their hootches, and I fell on my bunk and slept like a baby. As I drifted off to sleep, I thought to myself that I might be a failure as a recon platoon leader, but I was blessed by God to have the privilege of serving with such brave and loyal friends. I prayed to God that night that I would never fail them.

The next day, the Mutual Broadcasting System came by Camp Reasoner to interview me about the ambush patrol. They recorded the interview and told me that it would be edited and then broadcast over their radio stations in the U.S. in a week or two. I was warned by Maj. Lowrey to be careful about what I said to the press, so I was rather nervous when the interview began in the S-2 debriefing room. An enlisted Marine from the division's public affairs office was also present. The interviewer seemed genuinely interested in what happened on the patrol, but he kept trying to ask me questions about how I felt when I shot at the enemy. When I told him I really didn't think about anything other than killing the enemy soldier in my sights, I could see the Public Affairs (PA) Marine wince. Afterwards, the PA Marine took me aside and told me the interview went well, but I had to remember many members of the press corps covering the war were not our friends and they would use anything we said in an unguarded moment against the Marine

Corps. Having no experience with the press prior to this, I made a mental note to always be on my guard when talking to the press. Later on, I would come to realize how truthful that Marine's warning was.

After this patrol, I had another unpleasant encounter with the Marine Corps awards system. I was very impressed with the heroism of Sgt. Watson on the ambush patrol in the Antenna Valley Pass, and I still had the award recommendations I had written for Sgt. "Rabbit" Preston and another Marine for a previous patrol, so I decided to try again to submit the paperwork needed to recognize the bravery of these fine young Marines. I asked our Administration Sergeant, Staff Sergeant (SSgt.) John Cole, what I needed to submit an award for the actions of my Marines, and he gave me a copy of the 1st Marine Division order on the subject. I read the order and spent several hours getting statements from witnesses and writing my own statement for Sgt. Watson. I also made a copy of a sample award recommendation which was an enclosure to the order so I could closely approximate it for my three award submissions.

In the evening, I wrote up the award recommendation for Sgt. Watson and refined the two others I had written previously. The next morning, I submitted them to the company office, fully expecting that all three awards would be approved, since they clearly reflected uncommon bravery on the part of the three Marines. How wrong I was! Two days later, SSgt. Cole, who was a great help to me in preparing the award recommendations and made sure they were correct in every respect, gave me the bad news that the award recommendations had not even made it out of the battalion and had been returned with a note to keep them on file so they could be used for input for an "end of tour award."

Needless to say, I was very disappointed with this news and asked to see Maj. Lowrey about it. Once again, he told me that it was currently the policy not to award medals for individual acts of bravery but to include these acts in an "end of tour" award. He went on to say that Bronze Stars would be awarded for individuals who had a record of superior service and instances of demonstrated heroism and that the others would receive Navy Commendation Medals. Everyone who went on patrol would receive one or the other of these awards at the end of their 13-month tour in Vietnam. He then astounded me with his next comment when he said, "There would be too many awards given if it was done every time a patrol got into a firefight because recon Marines do this all the time."

I listened politely, but when he was finished, I told him I did not agree with this policy. I tried to point out that it was both unfair and detrimental to morale not to recognize quickly those Marines who risked their lives on patrol and performed exceptional acts of heroism and to do so each time these acts were performed. Not surprisingly, Maj. Lowrey angrily disagreed. Since I was in enough hot water already for my last patrol, I decided not to make more of an issue of it. It was, however, the beginning of my disenchantment with the entire Marine Corps policy concerning awards and decorations, the results of which would cause me to reject the policy completely in a very personal way.

This ambush patrol by Killer Kane in the Antenna Valley Pass marked the beginning of a new chapter in the way Killer Kane would conduct future patrols. While I had made several serious mistakes in judgment on the patrol, mistakes I was justly criticized for, the patrol proved to me that the only way to obtain really useful information about the enemy was to either capture a prisoner or search the bodies of enemy dead for documents of intelligence value. Before this patrol we were not unlike other recon teams in that we considered it essential to remain covert and only engage the enemy with air strikes and artillery fire. From now on, we would deliberately seek out the enemy and engage them at close range with small arms if the tactical situation looked favorable. We would continue to use the Stingray techniques of using supporting arms to kill the enemy, but we would not pass up any opportunity to kill them with small-arms fire also. We would be far more aggressive and spend less time hiding and more time seeking the enemy. We would ambush the enemy and attempt to obtain prisoners. Killer Kane was about to embark on a one-team campaign to kill the enemy wherever we found them and to ask to go on patrols in areas that everyone knew contained significant numbers of VC and NVA troops. Killer Kane was going on the attack.

4

More Patrols

Maj. Welzant decided that Killer Kane needed some rest time, so he told me I would be leading on another "milk run" patrol to the radio relay site on top of Hill 452. I was not particularly pleased with this return to the lofty heights of Hill 452, but I realized I was in enough hot water over the last patrol, so I kept my mouth shut. Secretly, I thought that his motivation for this respite from another long-range patrol was his desire to keep our team somewhere where we would not be able to ambush anyone. Whatever his reason was, I went about the normal routine, preparing for a week-long stay in the bunkers high atop Hill 452. In preparation for this easy patrol, I read the latest patrol reports of recon teams that had recently manned the radio relay site and spoke with two of the team leaders from the 1st Reconnaissance Battalion who had been on Hill 452 within the past month. Sightings of the enemy had been sparse.

In addition to doing our daily physical training, which consisted of 20 minutes of calisthenics on the Camp Reasoner helipad followed by a three-mile run to the Freedom Hill PX and back, Killer Kane also spent a few mornings rappelling out of a CH-46 helicopter. Often recon teams had to be inserted into areas where there were no LZs, and this required the teams to rappel through primary and secondary jungle growth often as high as 150 feet. Each man in Killer Kane rappelled from the rear ramp of the CH-46 several times until we felt we were capable of doing it flawlessly. We carried our packs and rifles with us when we rappelled, adding to our weight and the speed of our descent. Many of us learned quickly that despite wearing rappelling gloves, it was easy to get bad friction burns if you made the mistake of clutching the ropes too tightly. We also learned that it was very important to make sure the helicopter's ramp edge was covered with a thick, padded tarp since the sharp edges of the ramp could cut the ropes and send a Marine 150 feet below to his death. The concept of "fast roping" had not been developed, so recon Marines during the Vietnam War used rope harnesses, snap links, and rappelling rope to get from a hovering helicopter through jungle canopy to the ground. It was both dangerous and time-consuming, since only one Marine at a time could be on the rope.

Due to my upcoming mission at the radio relay site, I would be missing a party Mike Henry was organizing for the villagers of Phuoc Ly hamlet. To finance this event, Mike had asked every Marine in the battalion to contribute 50 cents, and I eagerly told him my platoon would donate their fair share. Mike planned to hold a MEDCAP in conjunction with the party and to organize foot races and some other athletic contests between the Marines and the local youths. Mike also arranged to purchase over 100 South Vietnamese flags and distribute them at the party so the villagers would be able to display a flag from each house. I enjoyed the visits to Phuoc Ly, so I felt a bit disappointed to miss this event.

Shortly after speaking with Mike about his party, one of the men in my platoon told me that a girl who worked in a small laundry concession in the village next to Phuoc Ly had asked him and several other Marines some very unusual questions about his job. He was so suspicious of these questions he decided to bring it to my attention. I really did not think much about it, but I reported it to Lt. St. Claire anyway and brought the Marine along with me to provide the details. Mike St. Claire notified the South Vietnamese authorities, and the girl was arrested the next day. The police found evidence that she had been communicating with a VC agent. We later found out that the local security chief in this village had suspected this girl for some time and had asked her neighbors to watch her and her family. Her arrest served to remind us that it was possible to have a VC spy living only 400 meters away from our main gate.

On the day before Killer Kane was to depart for its week on Hill 452, I came down with a very severe case of gastroenteritis, probably the result of drinking too much water from the stream we found in the Antenna Valley Pass. I awoke very early in the morning with severe stomach cramps followed rapidly by diarrhea and nausea. I checked into sick bay and was sent to Charlie Med for evaluation. The doctors there then conducted several blood tests to determine what had caused my sickness. I ran a high fever for two days, causing me to hallucinate in between frequent runs to the head, where I found myself making the hard choice of either defecating or vomiting, often finding it was possible to do both at the same time. I made quite a mess of myself several times, but in my fevered state I really did not care. A sympathetic Navy doctor gave me some medicine, and my fever finally broke. I was also able to eat some solid food and keep it down. On the third day, I was well enough to return to Camp Reasoner. I told Maj. Welzant I wanted to go out on patrol with my other team, Brisbane, but he told me that I was not completely well, and I must wait until Killer Kane returned from Hill 452 before he would allow me to go on patrol again.

Mike Henry asked me if I would like to go with him to help locate a Marine colonel who had disappeared after going out to inspect some damage to a bridge north of Da Nang. Our mission would be to search the waters downstream of the bridge. Since this mission likely would require us to make dives around the bridge, two qualified scuba divers accompanied us: Capt. Ostrie, the Operations Officer for our company, and SSgt. Valerio, the man in charge of our Scuba locker. We left in the early morning and drove north along Highway 1 toward the bridge. We took a Dodge Weapons Carrier with a rubber boat and outboard engine in the back and a jeep with diving equipment loaded in its trailer. When we arrived at the bridge, we were told our trip had been a waste of time. The body of the missing colonel had been retrieved from the river and had been taken to Charlie Med to ascertain the cause of his death.

Since we were not needed, we took the rubber boat to a nearby U.S. Coast Guard station and put it in the water. We took our weapons, a couple of spear guns, and our flippers with us in the boat and set sail for a U.S. Navy recreational area called "Spanish Cove." There we found a group of U.S. sailors having a beach party, and they invited us to join them for a beer and some chicken they had cooked on two homemade barbeque grills. These grills, which were ubiquitous to military units in South Vietnam at the time, consisted of one-half of a 55-gallon steel drum cut along its long axis and laid on a frame made of lumber and metal. The rounded bottoms of these homemade grills concentrated the heat of the coals burning inside, making them an excellent tool for grilling meat.

We swam in the cove's protected waters, drank some beer, ate some chicken, and then thanked the sailors for their hospitality before taking our rubber boat back to where we had left our vehicles. On our drive back to Camp Reasoner, we talked about how odd our time at Spanish Cove seemed to us. Anyone who came to Spanish Cove or the other big recreation area near Da Nang, China Beach, might wonder if a war was actually going on. There were sun and sand, palm trees, cool ocean breezes, plenty of cold beer and Coca Cola, and all the steak and chicken one could eat. While these resort-like places were similar to other tropical beaches in Asia, they were different in one big respect: the total absence of women. Still, a day or two at these R and R locations made for a welcome and relaxing respite for many a war-weary soldier, airman, sailor or Marine. During my 13-month tour of duty, I spent a grand total of three days at the R and R centers on the shores of the East China Sea. I enjoyed myself each time. I suspect my enjoyment had less to do with the safe and pleasant surroundings these seaside R and R facilities provided and more to do with the memories they provoked of the happy days I spent with my family on the beaches of Cape May, New Jersey. For a few glorious moments, it was almost like being home.

On 17 April, I again took part in another MEDCAP which I described in some detail in a letter home to my parents:

Today I really felt as if I had accomplished something worthwhile. Mike Henry, a Navy corpsman, two U.S. Army doctors, and about six enlisted Marines went over to Phuoc Ly to give the entire hamlet plague shots. It was a real success, and the people showed their appreciation as never before. After the shots we conducted a MEDCAP for any of the villagers who were sick, and we treated 35 people for everything from skin diseases to headaches. We distributed vitamins to everyone and gave two bars of soap to each family. One of the Marines had received a box of clothing from home, and he gave this to the village chief to distribute to the neediest families. While we were there, Mike discussed plans for the building of a new cement and steel water well. Our interpreter, Mr. Minh, assured the chief that we could get the materials for the new well, but the labor had to be provided by the villagers. This was agreed upon, so tomorrow Mike will deliver the materials. Next week we will give cholera shots to the entire hamlet.

While I was waiting for Killer Kane to return from Hill 452, I took advantage of my imposed stay at Camp Reasoner to go with the other lieutenants in our hootch to the U.S. Navy Officers' Club, the Stone Elephant, in the city of Da Nang. This was my first visit to the city, and I was impressed with its broad streets, French colonial villas, crowded open air markets, and busy seaport. I could not help but notice that it was very crowded, the result of an influx of refugees fleeing from the war in the rural areas surrounding it. As we drove to the Stone Elephant in the Dodge Weapons Carrier (WC) we had checked out of the motor pool, I could not restrain the feeling that I was driving through some mysterious, exotic, colonial town that had escaped from the pages of a Graham Greene novel. With its bustling traffic, vibrant commerce, colonial architecture, and frenetic pace of life, Da Nang was far different from the rural villages of Quang Nam Province.

As we pulled up in front of the Stone Elephant and got out of the WC, I was struck by the gleaming white walls of this officers' club and how orderly it appeared in comparison to the other buildings nearby. We passed a checkpoint outside the main entrance manned by several Marines who stood in a sandbagged bunker, checking the ID's of anyone not in uniform. Inside we checked our weapons. I always wore a .45-caliber pistol in a USMC issue shoulder holster whenever I drove outside of Camp Reasoner, so I took it off and hung it on one of the empty pegs.

The interior of the club was clean and modern with a strong air-conditioning system that made for a welcome relief from the blazing heat outside. Our first destination was the club's mess area, which was very much like a stateside restaurant, complete with

The city of Da Nang.

tables covered with white linen and set with ceramic plates and stainless steel eating utensils. This was the height of luxury for anyone serving in Vietnam, and we reveled in it. We all ordered steak and French red wine for dinner, and I was amazed at how delicious the food and wine were. Perhaps it was the fact that we had not eaten like this for several months or that the place had the feel of a nice, private club in the States. Whatever the reason, we enjoyed this respite from the war immensely. Later, I would often reflect on the vast divide that separated those who served their tour of duty in South Vietnam in the rear areas and had access to facilities such as the Stone Elephant and those who endured their war far from such luxuries in the heat and stench of South Vietnam's jungles and rice paddies.

After dinner, we went into the club's large lounge and took a table near a small stage. There were seven of us, so we pushed two tables together. We ordered drinks and talked to a few naval officers who were seated near us. After a few minutes, a Vietnamese band called "The Shotguns" came out and began to play. They played songs such as "We Gotta Get Out of This Place" and "The Green, Green Grass of Home," all meant to appeal to an audience of Americans far from home. Like many Marines, we were a bit overzealous in the way we showed our appreciation for the entertainment, and several times the manager of the club came to our table and asked us to either restrain ourselves or to leave. This proved to be a mistake on his part. We took his comments as a challenge, so we continued to talk and laugh a little too boisterously for most of the naval officers and civilians sitting near us. The club manager disappeared for a few minutes and when he returned, he brought four Marine MPs with him. They were all heading straight for our table. The MPs politely but firmly informed us that we could either keep quiet or they would arrest us. We told them we were just about to leave, but they evidently did not believe us because they continued to stand behind our table with their night sticks prominently displayed.

Capt. John Danko, the most senior and the most sober of us, suggested we leave immediately since we were not wanted in the club and the club manager obviously did not have a sense of humor. We walked out, followed closely by the MPs and the club manager. After we had retrieved our weapons, the MPs and the manager saw us to the door and escorted us to our vehicle in the parking lot where they bid us a fond farewell and warned us that if we ever came back and acted rowdy again, we would end up in the brig. As we drove back to Camp Reasoner, we agreed that we had had a very good time, but the club manager lacked a true sense of hospitality. The next day, Col. McKeon asked us to visit him in his office, where he told us he had received an interesting telephone call the previous evening from the Shore Patrol headquarters in Da Nang. As a result, he advised us in very strong terms to stay away from the Stone Elephant for the foreseeable future.

After my bout with gastroenteritis, the dressing down by Col. McKeon for taking my patrol outside of its assigned NFZ, and then making an ass of myself at the Stone Elephant, it was good to escape Camp Reasoner and go out on patrol again. Killer Kane made two rather uneventful patrols in April, both of which were in the Que Son Mountains. The second of these patrols was noteworthy because of a very unusual discovery we made on a hillside overlooking Antenna Valley.

Our patrol began early on the morning of 20 April with an insertion on the side of a mountain covered in thick undergrowth and jungle canopy. The LZ a mile southeast of Hill 452 was large enough for two CH-46s to land in easily, making our insertion rapid and simple. We did not encounter any signs of enemy activity as we walked downhill along a ridgeline toward Antenna Valley. The going was slow as we cut our way through heavy brush, high elephant grass and tangled vines. Since our mission for this patrol was to observe enemy activity in Antenna Valley and call in supporting arms on any enemy we observed, we searched all day in the oppressive heat for a good OP sight from which to observe the valley below. Despite our efforts, we found none.

The next day we continued to move in a northerly direction searching father down the mountain for a suitable OP. We had started before dawn, and there was a heavy gray mist on the mountain that reduced visibility to approximately 50 yards. This grey mist gave the jungle a rather sinister, ghostlike appearance, but it also hid us from any enemy that might be in the area. We had gone about 200 yards when we came upon an odd opening in the jungle that afforded some limited observation of the valley below. We stopped the patrol for a moment to see if we could use this spot for an OP. As we quietly set up an all-around defense, Sgt. Watson, who had been temporarily assigned to Killer Kane again, noticed a large stone at the southern edge of this jungle clearing and he drew my attention to it. There, tangled in jungle vines, was a five-foot-high grave-stone. We pulled some of the jungle growth away from the gravestone and found that it had an inscription in French on it. In this isolated clearing on the side of a mountain far from civilization, we had stumbled upon the grave of a young French woman named Nicole who had died in 1936 at the

age of 26. We wondered who this French woman had been and why she had chosen to be buried on this mountain. It was clearly an odd place for a grave, so lonely and far from any hamlet or village.

While we examined her grave-stone, I turned and looked downhill from it. On the opposite side of the clearing there was an opening in the jungle canopy that offered a beautiful, serene view of the valley below. We surmised that this location had once been a favorite spot for her to look out over the valley. We even thought that, perhaps, she had lived in Antenna Val-

Steep terrain encountered in the Que Son Mountains.

ley or owned a villa somewhere on the mountain during French colonial times. Someone had loved her deeply to bury her here and give her such a large and ornately inscribed gravestone. We wondered why she died so young and whether or not she had been married. All of us felt a bit sad seeing this abandoned grave for Nicole, and we felt we were imposing on her rest by spending any more time there. I decided to leave her alone and search for an OP elsewhere. As we left, I heard Sgt. Watson whisper, "Au revoir, Nicole."

Roy Watson standing in front of Nicole's grave.

This patrol did not result in any appreciable intelligence gained. We saw only one armed VC during the entire patrol, and we did not call a fire mission on him because there were too many women and children in the area. We did see several helicopter traps in the valley below: poles about 12 feet high with barbed wire strung between them. These simple, yet deadly devices were difficult for helicopter pilots to see from the air, a problem that often resulted in a helicopter's rotor blades becoming entangled in the trap's wires, causing the helicopter to crash. We duly noted them so we could include them in our patrol report. We also noticed there was a great deal of activity in Antenna Valley with scores of peasants working in the fields and transporting rice and other commodities on village trails and paddy dikes. Although Antenna Valley was considered an area with a strong VC presence in it, our patrol did not observe any indication that the enemy was in the valley in force.

It was a rather dull patrol until the day of our extraction when our extract helicopters took approximately 40 rounds of small-arms fire from the vicinity of Hill 170. Our door gunners on the CH-46 returned fire with unknown results. As we lifted away from our LZ, we could see that the escort choppers were in the process of calling in air strikes (Team Killer Kane Patrol Report, 24 April 1967).

No sooner had we arrived back from patrol at Camp Reasoner when we were informed that we were to be placed on two-hour standby for a new patrol. Killer Kane only had time to be debriefed and clean up before we were issued a new order for a patrol near the Song Ly Ly River. This patrol was precipitated by an NVA attack against Fox Company, Second Battalion, 1st Marines, which resulted in many Marine casualties. An NVA regiment from the 2nd NVA Division had made this attack, and the commanding general of our division, MGen. Nickerson, wanted as many recon teams deployed as possible so we could locate this enemy regiment before it escaped to the mountains. Every conceivable escape route was to be covered by a recon team.

Because we were on such a short leash and did not know exactly when we might be inserted, the team prepared for the patrol in a rather truncated fashion, dispensing with the normal overflight of our NFZ and some of the routine coordination we would normally do. Despite the haste, I prepared a patrol order using old patrol reports from the files of the S-2, along with some aerial photos I obtained from the Division G-2. I made my map study trying to read the minds of the enemy soldiers who wanted to escape to the mountains west of the river.

I began to notice that I could "read" or "sense" how terrain looked from a map, creating in my mind a picture of what the land actually looked like by analyzing the contour lines and the shading of our military maps. In a way, maps began to "talk" to me. Every contour line told me how steep a gradient was on the side of a hill, and from this information I could tell how long it would take our team to traverse this terrain. Every fold in the earth gave me a hint about whether or not I might find running water there. Ridge-lines told me they might have trails on them, and the colors on the maps told me a lot about the kind of vegetation I might encounter. These 1:50,000 (1 inch on the map equated to 50,000 inches on the ground) military maps became my valuable companions and a source of increasing information each time I used them. There was no Global Positioning System (GPS) available to assist a patrol navigating in the jungle or any other technological wonder to make land navigation simple; all we had to rely on were a map and a compass to find our way under the jungle canopy. Because of this, we valued greatly those Marines who had the training and skill necessary to use these navigational implements properly. A recon team's survival was often a function of how well it knew its location on the ground since this information was essential if the team needed to use supporting arms or request an emergency extraction.

Maps were precious to me, so I made sure the map I used on patrol was well protected from the elements and organized so that I could use it quickly and easily under any conditions. I constructed my own map case out of cardboard, clear plastic, and rigger's tape that could be folded neatly in the carrying pockets of my jungle utility trousers. I always folded my maps in this case so I could readily see my entire NFZ as soon as I opened it. The Marine Corps had standard issue map cases, but these were too large and unwieldy for anyone traveling with a recon team, so most of the patrol leaders fashioned their own map cases out of the materials I had used. Also in this small, compact map case, I would have a card with the call signs and radio frequencies I would need on the patrol, including any friendly infantry units nearby and artillery batteries within firing distance.

Prior to most patrols, I would memorize two grid coordinates: one 1,000 meters to the north of my intended insertion LZ and the other 1,000 meters to the south of it. I did this so I would be able quickly to call in and adjust an artillery mission or an air strike without having to take out my map case and lenzatic compass. I knew that if the enemy hit our team right after we were inserted, we would need to react quickly. This small effort to cut seconds off a request for artillery or air support might mean the difference between escaping unharmed or losing our entire team.

Killer Kane's next patrol took us back to Elephant Valley. Our eight-man patrol was inserted on 27 April into a rather large LZ at the western extreme of Elephant Valley near a mountain called Hon Cao, overlooking the Song Cu De River to the south.

In a letter home to my parents I wrote about this rather uneventful patrol:

> Well, another patrol has come and gone. Instead of going south where all the action is going on with Operation Union, they sent my team up north into Elephant Valley to screen an infantry sweep. We were inserted at 0630 on the 29th of April in a little valley that had a stream in it that fed into the Song Cu De River to the south. We climbed a small hill and set up the first of three OPs we used on this patrol and waited for the infantry to arrive the next day.
>
> That night a Navy ship off the coast fired Harassment and Interdiction (H&I) rounds into our NFZ, so we had to radio Camp Reasoner and have them tell the Navy to knock it off. Early the next morning, the 30th, an AO flew over and began to prep the area with artillery. This was fine until the artillery rounds began to fall around our position. It seems the infantry or someone forgot to tell him we were in the area. Trees began to fall down and the earth shook. Doc Willis, my Navy corpsman, took a small piece of fragmentation an inch above the eye, but he wasn't hurt seriously, and he refused evacuation. I realized the AO did not know we were in the area so I radioed our relay station on Ba Na Mountain and asked them for his frequency. As soon as they passed the AO's frequency to me, I switched the radio to his frequency and told him, in no uncertain terms, to call off his fire mission. He was really surprised to hear from us, since no one had told him friendlies were in the area, and he was just about to call in an air strike on our position. About this time, I looked at my rifle and noticed that it had a big hole in it where a piece of shrapnel from the artillery fire had gone through it.

For the remainder of this patrol I carried a worthless rifle around with me.

Our mission for this patrol was to support infantry operations in the Song Cu De River area by screening their northern and western flanks. When an infantry company from 2/7 landed in the valley below us, we heard the enemy open fire on them from across the river to the south. The infantry called in artillery and Huey gunships on the enemy positions, and this silenced them. We watched as the rifle company spread out and established a 360-degree defensive perimeter. I contacted the rifle company commander on my extra PRC-25 radio and passed on any sighting we made of the enemy. As the infantry began to send out patrols from their perimeter, we began to see groups of the enemy moving toward them from the west. Throughout the day, we observed these small groups of the enemy, and we called in numerous artillery missions on them, resulting in very good coverage of the targets and grateful comments from the infantry company commander. That evening, we also saw four torches or flashlights moving south on top of Hill 441, but we did not call in a fire mission. This target was difficult to locate accurately in the

"Doc" Willis, U.S. Navy Corpsman.

darkness, and we were not sure if the Marine infantry company had any patrols in that area.

The next day, the Marine infantry unit concluded its sweep and was heli-lifted out, leaving us on our own. Since the infantry no longer needed us to observe their movements and screen the western portion of their area of operations, we moved west along a wide, ridgeline trail to a new OP location near the summit of Hill 324. We normally avoided trails, but this trail had not been used for a long time. We knew this because there were numerous cobwebs stretching across it and many fallen leaves covering it. We moved very slowly on the trail, no more than 100 yards an hour, stopping frequently to listen and to observe. Mike Borecky and Bob Garcia took turns as lead point man as we moved west along the trail. These two men were experts as point men and could read signs of activity on a trail better than anyone else in the platoon. Once we reached the summit of Hill 324, we set up our OP so we could observe directly south toward the Song Cu De River. We had been told by our S-2 that the river in that area was being used by the enemy to move supplies on small sampans, so we hoped our new OP would offer us an opportunity to spot these sampans and call in artillery on them. For one reason or another, we did not observe any sampans on the river during the two days we had OPs on Hill 324. We did sight several groups of NVA soldiers south of us moving east along a trail, and we called in artillery on these groups, killing several of them and causing one secondary explosion.

On the last day of this patrol, I moved the team down from Hill 324 to a very good ambush site at a junction of a large, north-south running stream and the Song Cu De River. We saw several recently made Ho Chi Minh sandal prints in the mud at this junction, indicating the enemy had used this crossing point within the past 24 hours, so we decided we would set in our ambush there in the hopes of catching the enemy as they crossed the stream. We remained in the ambush site for several hours, but no enemy walked into our trap. Late in the afternoon, I decided to abandon our ambush site and move to an extraction LZ nearby where we were picked up by helicopter and flown back to Camp Reasoner.

One event of particular interest occurred on this patrol: the enemy attempted to use captured U.S. communications equipment to entrap us. It occurred on the evening of our second night around 2300 and continued off and on for several hours. Sgt. Pugh was on radio watch at the time, and he awoke me to tell me that someone was on the radio calling for Killer Kane, but the person calling us sounded Vietnamese to him. Sgt. Pugh had taken Vietnamese language training and was relatively fluent in the language. It had been raining that night, so I huddled with Sgt. Pugh under his poncho and listened to the handset. At first I heard only static, but after a few minutes I heard a voice say, "Killer Kane, Killer Kane, this is 'Gallant.' How do you hear me, over?" The voice had a distinct Vietnamese accent but the English was correct in all respects. At first, I thought it might be a Vietnamese unit or a U.S. Special Forces CIDG unit operating within radio range, but I did not reply. Instead, I switched to our alternate frequency and called our radio relay site at Ba Na, asking them to check to determine whether any Vietnamese units using the call sign "Gallant" were within radio range of our patrol. They radioed back that there were no Vietnamese units within 15 miles of us, and there were no units with the call sign "Gallant." Sgt. Pugh and I listened for approximately an hour. Periodically the Vietnamese voice would call us and ask for our position. We remained silent.

Later that night, the "Gallant" station came up on our frequency again and asked us to key our handset twice if we were secure. This was a common radio procedure used by recon units since it allowed a radio operator or someone on radio watch to inform one of our relay stations that we were "all secure" without speaking. When we returned from this patrol, we were told that Marine intelli-

The ruined French hotel which was used for a radio relay site on Ba Na Mountain.

gence suspected the Vietnamese radio operator trying to contact us was using one of the three PRC-25 radios captured from a U.S. Marine unit at the beginning of Operation Union I. The enemy abandoned his attempt to get our location after several hours. The radio relay site on Ba Na Mountain stated afterwards that whenever they asked us to key our handset twice to indicate we were "all secure," this enemy station clicked their handset for us. Had we been fooled by this English-speaking enemy soldier and had given him our location, we probably would have been attacked soon thereafter by one of their counter-reconnaissance teams. This was the first, but not the last, time an enemy radio operator attempted to contact us and obtain information from us (Team Killer Kane Patrol Report, 1 May 1967).

Killer Kane's first patrol in the month of May took it to an area never patrolled previously by any Marine recon team. Our team entered an area south of the An Hoa Basin that was suspected of serving as a major resupply route for the NVA forces fighting the 5th Marine Regiment during Operation Union II. The patrol covered the period 6–10 May, and it offered our team the opportunity to conduct a successful ambush and to close, at least temporarily, a major enemy north-south supply route between the villages of Thach Bich, Ninh Long (2), and Ninh Long (1).

Our seven-man patrol began at 0800 with our insertion by CH-46 helicopter into an old, abandoned rice paddy nestled between two jungle-covered hills. Soon after we landed, our insertion helicopters radioed that they had received small-arms fire coming from the hill to our east, so I decided to take the team in a westerly direction away from this potential danger. We climbed a steep hill, often resorting to using tree trunks and low-hanging branches to haul ourselves up its wet, slippery slope. It took us an hour to reach the top of the hill, where we rested for 20 minutes. While we sat in our 360-degree defense, we listened for any tell-tale sounds of enemy activity. I placed two men to cover the route we used to climb the hill in the event we had been followed, but I suspected no one would be able to climb the steep slope without making a lot of noise, giving us plenty of time to react.

When we resumed our patrol, we continued to move in a westerly direction downhill. At the bottom of the hill, we came upon a small, fast-moving stream, so I set up security and allowed the team to refill their canteens. While we were doing this, we heard voices of women and children close by. We pulled back into some thick growth and waited for a half hour to see if the voices came closer. After a while, the voices faded, and we decided the patrol should move northwest, away from the voices.

Almost immediately after we crossed the stream we came upon a very well-used trail that did not show on our map. Since I did not want to go back in the direction of the voices, I took the chance of moving along the trail until we could reach a better location to hide in. We moved approximately 100 yards along the trail until we again heard voices, this time directly in front of us. I had the patrol move off the trail in a northerly direction, but we had not gone more than 20 yards when our point man, Cpl. Borecky, raised his hand to signal he had spotted enemy to his left. I crawled up next to him and looked in the direction he was pointing. There, only a few yards in front of us, were several huts hidden under the jungle canopy. Beyond, there were huts for as far as we could see. It looked like an entire VC village had been built under the thick jungle canopy.

Fortunately for us, we had avoided walking directly into this hidden village by leaving the trail only a few minutes earlier. We could see only one woman near one of the huts, but we could hear many voices in the vicinity. I had a serious decision to make. I could stay where we were and risk a villager finding us. I could move back in the direction we came and risk encountering villagers at the stream crossing. Or I could take the patrol in a northerly direction parallel to the trail system and risk the villagers hearing us move. It was a dilemma for us, but I decided we had been sent on this patrol to locate the enemy's resupply route, and we would not be able to do this if we took either of the first two options. I told Cpl. Borecky to move out to our north and to do so very, very slowly.

Sgt. Paul, one of the new men in our patrol and a Marine reservist who had been a state highway patrolman prior to going on active duty, came up to me on one of our stops and suggested we call in a fire mission on this hidden village so the sound of the artillery rounds would mask any noise we made by moving in the jungle. I told him we could not do that. We did not

Clarence Williams.

know for certain that this hidden village, which did not appear on our map, was a VC village, and we could not just call in an artillery mission on civilians, even if we were certain they were VC sympathizers. I did not have time to argue the point with Sgt. Paul, so I told him to get back to his position in the patrol, and we continued on our way.

Fortunately, we were not discovered by any villagers, and Cpl. Borecky led us noiselessly through the jungle for several hundred yards until we came to a large, open area with a trail five feet wide running through it in a north-south direction. This area had been a large rice paddy in the past with paddy dikes still visible but worn down by time and rain. On the east side of this old rice paddy area, an area 300 yards long and 200 yards wide, was a large, black volcanic rock jutting out of the jungle. The rock was approximately 30 feet high with two steep sides on the west and north facings and more gradual slopes on the east and south facings. I decided that this rock, although completely exposed to the sun, would make an excellent OP from which to observe the wide trail, which I suspected might be the resupply trail we were looking for. It was getting dark, so I had the patrol move into the jungle behind this rock and set up a night harbor site. We passed the night without incident, but several of the men reported they heard voices early in the evening coming from the direction of the hidden village.

The next day, I posted two men on the rock OP to watch the trail while the other five men stayed in the shade of the jungle and rested. Because of the intense heat on the rock, I replaced the two men with two fresh scouts every two hours. I also radioed an artillery battery at the An Hoa Combat Base and had the battery preregister two artillery concentrations on the trail, one south of us and one north of us, so I could rapidly call in an artillery mission if we spotted any enemy using the trail. I was becoming fairly proficient in the adjustment of artillery fire so it did not take me long to adjust the registration rounds precisely where I wanted them for my artillery ambush. As the hours passed, we did not see any sign of movement on the trail, which was only 100 yards west of our rock OP. The absence of movement was probably due to my calling in artillery fire on the trail. Any enemy in the area would know this fire was not random, meaning Marines were in the area. Their caution kept them from using the trail until they were sure it was clear. We would soon witness their method for clearing a trail.

Around noon, while I was taking my turn on the rock OP with Cpl. Clarence Williams, I observed an old man dressed in white pajamas walking rapidly down the trail away from the direction of the hidden village and north toward An Hoa. Using my East German binoculars, I could easily make out his facial characteristics, and it was evident he was very apprehensive and wary. His head darted back and forth as he made his way through the open area in front of us, and he appeared to be looking for a place quickly to hide or seek cover. A half hour after the old man passed our Op, two other unarmed old men followed him in the same direction. The enemy was using unarmed villagers to walk down the trail to see if it was safe.

I had Mike Borecky join me on the rock, and we discussed the possibility of setting up an ambush on the trail and how we might best do this. I remembered from a book I had read about fighting guerrillas in Malaysia how the British would divide their small patrols into two equal groups when ambushing a trail with both providing advance notice for the other depending on the direction of the enemy. With this method, the two groups would serve both as a security element and an assault element for an ambush. I told Mike Borecky that we could do the same thing. He seemed to like this idea so we divided our seven-man patrol into two groups: three men with Sgt. Paul would take one radio and set up an ambush/security site at the north end of the open area, and I would take two men, Mike Borecky and Rick Belinski, and set up a similar position on the south end of the open area. The position I chose was a good one, located behind a worn down and overgrown rice paddy dike that allowed us to remain hidden yet able to see for 50 yards in either direction. Cpl. Borecky was on the left, or northern, side of our ambush, and I was positioned on the right. Our killing zone was approximately 20 yards long. Before we left the OP, I told everyone that we would not trigger an ambush if the size of the enemy force walking into it was more than three, the limit we could quickly kill. I did not want to get into a firefight with a large enemy force in this relatively open area, since I knew we would be unable to maneuver against them unless we had fire superiority.

When we reached the trail, I decided to check it out in the direction of the hidden village because I wasn't sure how far the village was from our ambush site. I did not want to have the villagers running down the trail as soon as we triggered the ambush. I took the patrol down the trail for 50 yards, and there on the side of the trail we saw several large stone jars camouflaged with palm leaves. Inside of these stone jars, which were at least four feet high, we found over 500 pounds of rice and 30 pounds of salt. I took some

Mike Borecky and me, uncovering a VC rice cache near the hidden village.

pictures of Cpl. Borecky with the jars, and then we turned them over and spilled their contents into the surrounding jungle. No normal villager would hide rice in this manner so we knew it was meant for the VC to pick up. I radioed Camp Reasoner and told them about the rice cache we had found and my intention to ambush the trail nearby. We received approval to conduct the ambush, so I immediately took the patrol back to the trail to set it up.

It was oppressively hot as we crouched behind the old paddy dike. Mosquitoes added to our discomfort by feasting hungrily on us as we waited impatiently for the enemy to enter our ambush. Several civilians passed by but no enemy. Despite the intense heat, I did not allow any of us to take our canteens out to drink for fear of making a noise that might alert the enemy. As the hours passed, I was about to abandon the ambush and move back to the rock OP when I heard Sgt. Paul whispering into my radio handset that VC were approaching my position and they should arrive in about one minute. His team had spotted two VC moving south in the direction of the hidden village. I asked him if they were armed, but before he could answer me, I heard the report of an M-14 rifle being fired to the left of me, followed by several individual shots a second later. Cpl. Borecky had fired those shots. I put down the radio handset and looked out into the trail and saw two VC clad in black pajamas lying in the trail. One was obviously dead, but the other was moaning and moving his arm slightly. I was about to shoot the wounded VC when Cpl. Borecky fired again, and I saw the VC jerk under the impact of the 7.62 mm rounds as they entered his back. He lay still after that.

We quickly began to search the bodies, but we heard voices coming from the direction of the hidden village. We hurriedly moved back to the jungle, leaving the bodies on the trail. PFC Belinski picked up a pack that one of the VC was carrying but we left the other pack on the body of its owner. We moved through the jungle, skirting the open area, and arrived back at the rock OP as it was getting dark. We hid in a harbor site that evening, daring not to move, whisper, drink or eat since we continued to hear voices to our south. During the night, I asked Rick Belinski about the pack, and he said it contained glutinous rice in a USMC sock, two NVA grey uniforms, a poncho and a knife. I examined the uniforms because I knew the enemy often marked their uniforms with a numbering system that revealed the owner's unit, but these uniforms had no markings at all. I told him to put the pack in his rucksack, but since it contained nothing of value in terms of intelligence, I told him he could keep the contents.

In the morning, I asked Sgt. Paul why he had taken so long to warn us of the approaching VC. He said he was afraid to speak on the radio because he thought the VC might hear him. I told him his "minute" for their arrival at our ambush site was more like "a second," and I told him that the next time he acted as a security element, he had better give the assault element more time and a better description of the people moving into the ambush. Cpl. Borecky had no warning at all of the approaching VC and had to react instantly when he saw the two VC in front of him. Fortunately for our team, there were only two VC approaching our ambush site, and they were walking close together. Had there been more enemy and more space between them, all three of us could have been killed. I realized that Sgt. Paul was new, and I chalked up his mistake to having very little field experience. However, I made a mental note to keep an eye on him for the remainder of the patrol and to give him some remedial training when we returned to Camp Reasoner.

Instead of moving back to the trail, I decided to continue using the rock OP in the hope that we might be able to execute the artillery ambush we had established. This was probably not a wise decision, since our location had been compromised by the ambush, but I allowed my aggressive tendencies to overrule common sense. I thought the enemy would try to find out what happened at our ambush site, and I wanted to use my prefired artillery ambush to hit them when they came to investigate. It did not take long for this opportunity to present itself. At 0730, we saw a single VC carrying a rifle walking north on the trail 200 meters to our left front. I called the artillery battery, but they were in a check fire, so I decided we would open fire on this individual VC from our position on top of the rock. This was rather foolhardy on my part because doing so would clearly give away our OP position to any enemy nearby. But my frustration with the check fire and my determination to attack the enemy at every opportunity caused me to act in a way that placed all of us in danger. I had all seven of us take up firing positions near or on the rock. Sgt. Paul had a sniper rifle with a powerful scope, and he had told me he was an expert with this weapon, so I told him to take the first shot. He fired and the VC began to run along the trail unhurt. He fired a second round and again he missed. I ordered everyone to open fire before the VC moved out of sight, but none of us hit our target. Either that VC was very lucky, or we were terrible marksmen. He just continued at a dog trot pace for 100 yards as rounds went whistling over his head or hitting the ground around him. As he disappeared, the artillery battery called to tell us they were out of their check fire condition and were prepared to fire for us. I told them to fire 500 meters north of my northern concentration in the vain hope that a lucky round might catch our fleeing VC. After firing one marking round using a HE round, I called in a "fire for effect," meaning I wanted the battery to fire enough rounds to adequately cover the target area. However, I knew it was a futile effort given the distance the VC had traveled after we last sighted him. As I reflect on this incident, I realize my decision to engage the enemy with small arms, instead of waiting for the artillery check fire to be lifted, was a bad one. I had given my team's position away, a position that was dangerously exposed and close to an enemy village. The value of killing one enemy soldier did not outweigh the risk to my team. I compounded this poor decision by remaining in our compromised OP. I should have moved to a new OP site immediately after we triggered our first ambush of the trail.

For the next few hours, no one used the trail. However, late in the afternoon, we saw eight individuals appear on the south end of the trail walking north. In front was an old man dressed in white, and behind him were seven young men dressed in black pajamas carrying heavy loads on carrying poles. The first young man in the column also had a rifle slung over his shoulder. The old man acted as their point man, cautiously examining the terrain in front of them and pausing on occasion to see if he could locate any Marines. The fact that there were two dead bodies on the trail where they were traveling did nothing to put their minds at ease. It was obvious that this was a VC resupply column, the type of enemy activity we were sent to find, and it was moving north to resupply enemy forces fighting the 5th Marines. I again called the artillery battery, telling them to fire the northern concentration "for effect" as soon as I gave them the command to fire. I also reminded them to be sure to give me a "shot out" and "splash" voice message. When the VC column was approximately 100 yards from the artillery concentration, I radioed the artillery battery and told them to fire the concentration "for effect," which should have been four 8-inch howitzer rounds. As the VC column continued to walk toward the concentration, I waited for the battery to tell me "shot out," meaning they had fired the mission and rounds were complete. I waited and waited, but there was no message. The VC were almost in the artillery ambush concentration, so I radioed the battery a second time and asked them if they had fired yet. The artillery radio operator told me they had not fired the mission yet, and I told them to do so immediately. By the time I heard "shot out" from the artillery battery, the VC had entered the artillery ambush area. When I heard the "splash" warning from the artillery battery, meaning the rounds would be impacting in seconds, the VC had already passed through the concentration.

To my amazement and anger, I saw one 8-inch round burst 100 yards south of the ambush site and only 50 yards from our position sending shrapnel over our heads. I quickly radioed the artillery battery and told them to shift their fire 300 meters in the direction of the VC and to fire again. A minute later, four 8-inch rounds thundered into the northern edge of the rice paddy sending dirt, grass and twigs flying into the air. The coverage of the target was good, but we could not observe whether they had hit the VC column. I asked them to fire the mission again but to move the impact of the rounds a further 200 yards to the north. The artillery radio operator asked me if we had a "BDA" (Bomb Damage Assessment) of their artillery mission. When I told them they had fired too late and I could not observe the results of their mission, their battery commander got on the radio and asked me if I intended to search the impact area so his battery could get credit for any confirmed kills. I told him I had no intention of searching the impact area and that I was disappointed with the performance of his battery. I told him now was not a propitious time to discuss the source of my disappointment, but I would be glad to discuss it with the 12th Marines, his parent unit, when I returned from patrol. He promised that he would take a personal interest in any future fire missions we called in, and he understood why we were not able to search the artillery impact area. Since we had certainly given our presence away by the day's events, I decided to pick a new, more distant harbor site for our team that night. I also wanted to find a source of water because we had exhausted ours. Fortunately, we found a small stream not too far from the rock OP, and we were able to refill our canteens with fresh, cool water just as darkness began to fall.

On 9 May, we moved back to the rock OP to continue our observation of the north-south trail. I knew it was extremely dangerous to do this but I also knew our mission was to find the enemy north-south resupply route, and to do this we needed to observe the trail. During the morning hours, no more than a dozen people used the trail, and all of them exhibited furtive and fearful movements. We also noted that the bodies of the two VC we had killed and left on the trail had been removed during the night. At around 0940, we observed five VC dressed in camouflage and black uniforms and carrying packs and rifles moving south on the trail. They moved in a staggered column with at least 30 to 40 meters between each man. By their actions, it was obvious they were looking for us and not transiting the area. I pulled the two men on watch off the rock OP and arranged the patrol in a line of skirmishers facing the direction of the trail, expecting the enemy to attack us if they found our position. When I had done this, the thought occurred to me that this squad of enemy troops might be a decoy for another larger force maneuvering behind us in the jungle, so I had two men take up positions to our rear to deal with this possible threat. I then got on the radio and called in a fire mission to the artillery battery that had fired for us the previous day. This time, the battery was more responsive, but once again, instead of firing for effect, they fired a single marking round which alerted the VC squad that they were under observed fire. They immediately retreated to the north while I adjusted the fire mission further north in the hope of hitting them with a full fire for effect instead of a single round. I could see that we had excellent coverage of the area the VC retreated to but I was unable to observe the results of this fire mission. Later that day, a village chief and a U.S. Marine CAP unit reported to the 5th Marines that three VC had been killed by this artillery mission.

The next day, our team was extracted by CH-46 helicopter and returned to Camp Reasoner (Team Killer Kane Patrol Report, 10 May 1967). This patrol, which lasted 98 hours, was judged a success by the Division G-2 because we had found a probable VC village, an unmarked trail network, and the north-south resupply route used by the local VC to supply the enemy mobile units fighting the 5th Marines. In the process, we also conducted a successful ambush that resulted in two confirmed enemy killed and several artillery fire missions that resulted in three probable kills. This patrol produced some important lessons learned about the vagaries of using artillery for ambushes and the importance of never using more than one marking round before firing for effect on a moving target. It also reinforced the policy of never staying in one location for more than 24 hours. We were lucky on this patrol that the enemy never reacted quickly or competently to our presence, but my decision to remain in the area of our first ambush could have led to disastrous results.

After giving my patrol report, I went to the headquarters of the 12th Marines, the artillery regiment for the 1st Marine Division, where I met with their operations officer to discuss the problems I had with the firing battery on my last patrol. I solicited his advice on how we could improve the use of supporting arms in an ambush. At first, he was a bit defensive, but when he saw that we had lost two good opportunities to decisively engage and destroy the enemy because the firing battery had not performed as expected, he became very helpful and even volunteered to give some classes to my team on calling and adjusting artillery in the most efficient and timely fashion. I took him up on his offer, and later that month my entire platoon attended special day-long classes that were arranged just for us. These classes included live firing from a battery near Camp Reasoner, in which every man in my platoon had the opportunity to call in and adjust an actual fire mission and see how the fire direction center (FDC) and the artillery gun line carried out their duties. These day-long classes were some of the best and most useful classes I have ever received. After completing this training, I felt confident that any man in my platoon could call in an artillery mission, a capability that would allow a patrol to survive even if a team leader or radio operator was killed or wounded. It would also allow me to turn over a fire mission to one of my team members while I performed some other task.

From that moment on, I often visited the headquarters of the 12th Marines to talk to their operations officer and training officer about how we could work together to produce better results.

It was about this time I became aware of a secret training program at Camp Reasoner for a shadowy group of South Vietnamese special operations units called the Provincial Reconnaissance Units (PRU). We were told very little about these PRU soldiers, aside from what their training entailed, which was instruction in basic reconnaissance skills and English. They wore no rank insignia or unit identification on their tiger-striped uniforms, and they appeared older and tougher than the average South Vietnamese soldier. When I asked Maj. Lowrey who these PRU soldiers were and why their training was so secretive, all he would tell me was they belonged to the CIA and they were being trained for special missions as part of the newly created Phoenix Program. I had not heard of the Phoenix Program or the PRU before, but on my second tour of duty in South Vietnam I would have firsthand experience with both.

Killer Kane's next patrol drew a lot of attention from both the commanding general of the 1st Marine Division and the Marine Corps' History Division, who interviewed the team for its Oral History Program after we had returned from the field. The patrol's destination was far to the south, near the Hiep Duc Valley at the very southern edge of the 1st Marine Division's TAOR. Few Marine units had operated in this area, and the Division G-2 suspected the enemy was using it as either a forward base or a transit route for the 2nd NVA Division. Killer Kane's mission was to conduct reconnaissance and surveillance of this little-known area and determine whether or not the enemy was active in it.

Early in the morning of 15 May, Killer Kane's seven-man team was inserted by CH-46 helicopter into a small LZ south of Hill 498 on a finger just north of a hill where we intended to establish an OP. After landing and quickly hiding in the dense jungle on the south side of the LZ, the patrol began moving toward the OP site. We soon encountered a large, swift-running stream. We crossed it and then climbed a large hill that had a jungle canopy consisting of trees reaching heights of over 100 feet. It took us most of the day to climb the steep hill, a task that was made even more strenuous by the oppressive heat. That evening, tired and exhausted from our climb, we harbored in some thick brush on the north slope of the hill.

The next day at 0730, we started downhill and soon lost communications with our radio relay site on Hill 452. We descended into a steep ravine thick with vines and secondary growth until we came to a stream where we stopped, set up security, and refilled our empty canteens. As we started up the opposite slope toward our intended OP site, an AO that had been dispatched by Maj. Welzant came on station and asked us for a SitRep. The AO suggested we should get to high ground as soon as possible so we could again establish radio contact with Hill 452, but the terrain was so thick and steep we could only proceed in a southerly direction along a rocky stream bed. The rocks in the stream were slippery and covered with green algae, making it very difficult to follow the stream without constantly slipping and falling under the weight of our rucksacks. The farther south we went in the stream, the higher the rocky slopes on both sides of it became. Just as I started to think about going back the way we came, there appeared a very good trail that had been cut out of the rock facing on both sides of the stream perpendicular

The stream near Hill 498.

to our direction of travel. Although I knew it was dangerous to follow a man-made trail, especially one that did not appear on our map, I decided to take the risk since we were making a lot of noise moving in the stream, and we were forced to look constantly down in front of us to avoid falling on the slippery rocks, something that prevented us from paying close attention to our front and flanks for the enemy. I knew if the enemy found us in the stream bed, we would be at a distinct disadvantage and unable to maneuver out of any ambush.

I took the lesser of two evils and had the point man, Bart Russell, take the patrol up the trail to the south. We ascended the trail for an hour until we came upon the main east-west Hiep Duc Trail. The patrol moved east on this trail for several hundred meters, finding several enemy harbor sites and one 200-yard portion of the trail that had been cut into the ground to a depth of four feet on each side. The trail was hidden from observation from the sky by thick, lush foliage, and we observed several signs that clearly indicated the trail had been used recently by the enemy. There were no cobwebs on the trail, and we found a few Ho Chi Minh sandal tracks in areas where the trail was muddy. Bart Russell moved the patrol very cautiously along this trail, never faster than a few, slow steps at a time, pausing every 20 minutes so we could set up a hasty ambush. Bart whispered to me several times that he "sensed" the presence of the enemy ahead of us, so we decided it was best to leave the trail and look for a harbor site. We did not want to push our luck any further by walking on this well-used trail.

As darkness approached, we moved to a harbor site 100 meters off the trail and spent most of the night under our ponchos as heavy thunderstorms soaked the jungle and sent flashes of lightning across the tropic sky. We set up a radio watch, but we were unable to establish radio contact with anyone, a situation a recon team never wanted to find itself in since it meant if the enemy attacked us, we would not be able to summon help. To add to our discomfort, we soon were aware that the area we picked for our harbor site was infested with bloodthirsty leeches. Fortunately, we were spared many bites since we used an abundant amount of insect repellent on our clothing, hands, and faces before we settled in for the night.

The next day, I decided it was too dangerous to continue walking on the trail, especially given our lack of radio communications with Hill 452, so I had the patrol move to higher ground where I hoped to reestablish communications. Hill 203 looked like a good piece of high ground with a direct line of sight to Hill 452, so I made that our destination. My choice was not the best idea since Hill 203 was steep and very wet from the recent rain, making our movement up the hill slow and difficult, especially for our radio operators who had to carry the extra 25 pounds our radios weighed. Several times, members of the patrol lost their footing, causing them to fall 20 feet or more downhill. I used my rifle like a climbing stick, and we all helped each other over the particularly difficult parts of our ascent. The heat added to our discomfort: the kind of mind-numbing, strength-sapping heat that is the enemy of situational awareness.

By the time we reached the top of Hill 203, everyone in the patrol was exhausted, and several of us felt faint from the exertion of our climb. At such times, discipline can slip, and this can spell great danger for a patrol. The top of a hill can be a dangerous place, used by the enemy for any number of reasons. For this reason, I was thankful that the patrol did not succumb to their fatigue, but immediately took up their routine defensive posture. We sat in a 360-degree defense with each man looking outboard and listening for any sign of the enemy. In the jungle, the enemy is often heard long before he is seen, so we all strained our ears to pick up even the faintest sound that seemed out of place.

I looked across at PFC Bingham, a new man in the platoon, and saw that he was breathing heavily and sweating profusely, but still he kept his eyes alert and his rifle close to his shoulder, ready to fire if he needed to. I glanced at his shoulder and saw a large, slimy brown leech inching up his collar toward his neck. I did not want to startle him, so I reached over to him with my forefinger raised to my lips and then I quietly brushed the leech off his neck. He shuddered at the sight of the leech, the normal reaction of a new man, but he did not move or say anything. I took out some insect repellent, put a drop on my finger, and then touched the leech on its head. Immediately, the leech contracted and fell dead. Leeches hated insect repellent and for good reason. It caused instant death. I noticed on subsequent patrols that PFC Bingham always carried extra insect repellent in a pouch on his cartridge belt.

After resting and listening for a half hour, we found a good spot for an OP a few hundred meters south of Hill 203 and only a hundred meters from the narrow valley floor below us. We did not see any VC that day, but late the next day, we observed seven enemy soldiers moving toward us along the main east-west trail. I took a quick compass reading in their direction and then called in a fire mission to the nearest artillery battery. As always, I whispered my fire mission into the radio, "Arnica Delta, this is Killer Kane.

I have one fire mission, can you copy, over?" The artillery battery radio operator called back and said he was ready to copy my fire mission request. I keyed the handset and sent my fire request, "Arnica Delta, this is Killer Kane. Grid Alpha Tango 854270, direction 185 degrees magnetic, troops in the open moving west, request one round hotel echo in adjustment, battery five hotel echo in effect, how copy, over?"

We waited for the first round to land, but I could see the enemy was moving away from the grid coordinates I had called in, greatly decreasing the likelihood that my HE marking round would cause any casualties. In my frustration over the enemy moving away from the artillery impact area, I decided to open fire on this group of seven enemy soldiers, even though I knew it would give away our position. They were approximately 250 meters away from our position and 100 feet below us in the valley, well within effective small arms range. I told every man in the patrol to get ready to fire and assigned them sections of the enemy column to fire at. I took the lead enemy soldier and I used the crook of a tree to steady my rifle. On my command, all seven Marines opened fire. The enemy soldier I fired on fell and did not move while the rest fell back into some bushes. The patrol continued to fire into the bushes where the enemy had fled, and we were fairly confident that we had hit several of them. Cpl. Borecky fired a dozen M-79 grenades into the bushes with his usual outstanding accuracy.

After the patrol had fired nearly 300 rounds at the enemy, Sgt. Paul tapped me on the shoulder and pointed to the right of the area we had been firing on. There, to my astonishment and horror, was a very large force of North Vietnamese regulars dressed in their distinctive light green field uniforms and pith helmets moving on line toward our position. There were approximately 100 of these NVA troops, and they were only 200 yards away in front of a tree line, moving tactically, and firing their weapons in our direction. I had never seen so many enemy troops before and the sight of them so close and firing at us made my stomach wrench with fear. In my mind, I knew there were few options open to us. We could attempt to run from them and hide in the jungle, but this would cause us to leave the relatively good defensive position we were in on top of a hill and move downhill into a ravine where we would not have any radio communications. Then the enemy would have the advantage of the high ground. We could stand and fight, and hope the artillery would fire their mission soon, but if the artillery did not fire soon, we would probably be overrun by this superior enemy force. Since both options seemed to be bad, I decided to stand and fight.

We opened fire on the approaching enemy, and they returned our fire. Luckily for us, they seemed to think we were at ground level and not above them on the hill so most of their rifle fire hit the trees below us. As we fired on them, I could hear the sound of an artillery round passing over us, and a second later I saw it impact near the approaching enemy, followed quickly by the sound of the explosion. The marking round was close enough to the enemy that I immediately radioed the artillery battery and told them to fire for effect.

Within seconds, the ground around the enemy erupted as 8-inch howitzer rounds exploded, sending earth and debris into the air and shrapnel into the enemy. While this was going on, the quick thinking Cpl. Russell had used our primary radio to called Camp Reasoner via the radio relay site on Hill 452 to tell them of our contact with this large enemy force. Shortly thereafter, an AO was over our position calling in air strikes as soon as the artillery had ceased firing. The enemy had been stopped dead in their tracks and began running back into the tree line they had emerged from earlier. Air strikes were then directed on the tree line by the AO. Marine Corps F-4 Phantom jets dropped napalm canisters, rockets, and 500-pound fragmentation bombs into the tree line with outstanding coverage, sending columns of dirt and parts of trees into the air while destroying an estimated 15 enemy.

After thanking the artillery battery and the AO for saving our lives, I took the patrol into some very thick foliage north of our OP, and we harbored for the night. Few of us were able to sleep that night since we all envisioned hordes of the enemy finding us and attacking in the dark. The sight of so many enemy troops attacking us was frightening, and everyone realized we had escaped being overrun and killed by a very small margin. I pondered my decision to open fire and whether or not it had been a wise one. I had to be honest with myself and admit that my aggressiveness had once again placed the patrol in grave danger. I wondered whether or not the other members of the team questioned my decision to engage such a large enemy force and whether my decision had adversely affected their confidence in me. I spent several hours that night listening to mosquitoes trying to bite me and reflecting on the day's events. I decided there was no use worrying about something that had passed, and it would be far better for me to wait until I was back at Camp Reasoner to analyze what, if anything, I should have done differently.

The next morning, 18 May, at 1000 Killer Kane was extracted from a one-bird LZ a little west of our OP site (Team Killer Kane Patrol Report, 18 May 1967). When we returned to Camp Reasoner, Maj. Welzant, Maj. Lowrey and a dozen others greeted the team on the helipad and escorted us to the S-2 office for our patrol debrief with Lt. St. Claire. Our patrol report was audio-recorded by the U.S. Marine Corps History Division, and several of us were asked to comment on various aspects of the patrol. When the debriefing was over I was handed an envelope containing a handwritten note from MGen. Nickerson. It was on the general's official stationary, and it read, "Killer Kane — Seven against 100! You must be crazy but you are certainly effective — Congratulations." When I read the note to the patrol members, they all thought it was great, but it was pretty evident that Maj. Welzant did not share their enthusiasm. When everyone had left, he took me aside and said, "Andy, we both know what you did was wrong. You should not engage a large force like that again. All of you could have been killed. Remember, your mission is primarily to find the enemy and let others do the killing. One of these days, your luck will run out."

I did not argue with Maj. Welzant because I knew he was correct. I had acted rashly, and only luck and the skill of my team members and the artillery battalion had prevented a disaster. I began to question why I felt so compelled to attack the enemy, even a large enemy force. I never answered that question in any meaningful way. Whether my motivation was due to my training, my natural instincts, or my hatred of the enemy for killing Eric Barnes and Tom Dowd, I did not know. What I did know was I did not want to revert to conducting simple clandestine patrols. I would continue to attack the enemy when the opportunity presented itself. I only resolved to pick my battles more carefully and not to take unnecessary risks.

The next day, I went to the S-3 shop and spoke with MSgt. Clovis Coffman about the patrol, and he told me that he had gone to Gen. Nickerson, who it turned out was Clovis's godfather and mentor, and asked the General to send the note. I asked him why he had done this, and he said he knew most of the command was upset with my decision to attack the large enemy force. He wanted to blunt their criticism by using the congratulatory note from Gen. Nickerson to do so. I was grateful to Clovis for this act of kindness, but I knew in my heart I had to put a check on my aggressiveness or I was going to get my team into serious trouble. MSgt. Coffman had a distinguished combat record spanning two wars, Korea and Vietnam, so I always took his advice to heart. On this occasion, he gave me some good, practical advice on when to engage the enemy with small arms and when not to. One of the most important things he told me was to always fire first in any firefight. "Never let the enemy start a firefight," he said, "Fire fights are just like bar fights; whoever gets the first punch in usually wins."

After a few days' rest, Killer Kane was sent on patrol in the northern portion of the division's TAOR, this time to again search for signs that the enemy was using the old French road in Elephant Valley to move troops and supplies toward Da Nang. At 0830 on the morning of 21 May, a CH-46 carrying the nine Marines of recon team Killer Kane settled into an LZ in Elephant Valley half way between Da Nang and the Laotian border. The LZ was in six-foot-high elephant grass only a few yards north of the old French road, Route 545, which snaked along the valley floor. Our mission was to screen the western approaches of Elephant Valley for the 7th Marines, who were conducting a search and

The old French road in Elephant Valley.

destroy operation several miles east of us. Killer Kane had never been this far west before; in fact, very few recon patrols had ever been conducted in this area since it was normally well out of range of artillery. The 7th Marines had heli-lifted a battery of 105 mm howitzers into the valley four miles to our east to support them during their operation, so we could also call on them for fires if we needed artillery support.

Elephant Valley was very narrow where our patrol was inserted, no more than 20 or 30 yards wide in most places with high, steep ridgelines running down to the valley floor on both sides. Route 545, a single lane macadam road, had been built by the French many years ago during colonial times, but it had not been used in years and in most places, it was little more than a wide trail overgrown by jungle. We found a large amount of elephant feces along this old road, which should have been no surprise given the name of the valley. There were literally piles of elephant feces every few feet along the road, and we had to be careful not to step in them.

I spent the first few hours of the patrol searching for a good OP site on the north side of the valley, but the jungle was so thick we could not find a spot where we could observe the road below. In the afternoon, we searched the south side of the valley for an OP, but we encountered no sites from which we could observe movement on the valley floor. As dusk approached, I had Bart Russell move the patrol parallel to the road until we found a good harbor site near a mountain stream with cool, clean water running in it. We filled our canteens, ate some C rations, and then settled in for the night. Cpl. Garner, our radioman, sent in our SITREP at last light, and we set the radio watch with each man taking one hour monitoring the radio. Our harbor site was close enough to the trail so we could hear anyone walking down it but too far away to see anything moving on it. The harbor site was in thick brush so anyone approaching it in the dark would have to make a lot of noise, which would give us plenty of advance warning of their approach. The night passed without incident, aside from the normal problem with leeches seeking us out in the dark. Around midnight, we heard elephants calling to each other and wondered if they were going to approach our harbor site. Fortunately, they did not and we never did see a single elephant during the five days we were on this patrol; however, we heard them often during the night.

Dave Pugh on the old French road in Elephant Valley.

Having given up in our attempt to find an OP on the ridgelines overlooking the valley, I decided we should try to find a good spot near the road where we could both observe it and possibly ambush any enemy moving along it. Early in the morning of our second day of patrolling, I moved the team west along the old French road looking for a good ambush site. We slowly traveled 500 meters, crossing several old wooden bridges and stopping frequently to set up hasty ambushes just off the road. I felt it was too dangerous to continue walking on the old road, so I moved the patrol back to a spot near one of the old bridges where there was a good dogleg in the road, just right for an ambush location. We set up the M-60 machine gun along the long axis of the ambush so it had a clear field of fire for nearly 50 yards. The rest of us positioned ourselves parallel to the road at fiveyard intervals creating a killing zone approximately 50 yards long. At one end of the ambush killing zone was the old bridge; at the other was the right angle of the dogleg in the road. It was an ideal ambush site.

Each night we occupied a different harbor site near the ambush site, and each morning we would establish an ambush and watch the trail until dusk. All day long, we sat in the brush near the old road and watched to see if any enemy troops approached. It was hot, dirty and frustrating because we did not see a single human being on the old road. The road itself was rather eerie, often looking like a Hollywood set for a ghost tale, especially in the early morning hours when a creamy mist would drift down from the mountains and wrap itself around the foliage on the valley floor. Our eyes would strain to see across the old bridge, half expecting a column of enemy soldiers to appear out of the mist at any moment. But all of our vigilance was wasted. It was hard to believe that such a natural route from Laos to the heart of Quang Nam Province was not being used by the enemy, but we never encountered a single sign that the road had been used by humans. There were no footprints, no human spores, no papers, no dropped ammunition, no wood cuttings, nothing.

On the last day of the patrol, the 25th of May, we moved east along the old road until we linked up with the 7th Marines. Their defensive position straddled the old road at a point where a stream running in the valley broadened into a pool 20 yards across and two feet deep. As we approached the pool I heard a voice say, "Killer Kane, I presume." There sitting by the jungle pool was the new CO of the 1st Force Reconnaissance Company, Capt. Albert "King" Dixon, who smiled broadly at me and introduced himself. He had come out to serve as a liaison officer with the 7th Marines and stayed with them to coordinate our patrol and two other recon patrols supporting their operation.

I immediately took a liking to my new CO, and we spent nearly an hour getting acquainted sitting by the side of the stream in Elephant Valley. I found out he had been an All-American football star at the University of South Carolina before joining the Marine Corps, a fact that would endear him to the Marines he led. In many ways, his leadership style was that of a coach to his players, and I naturally took to this brand of leadership. He asked me and the other members of our team several really good questions about our patrolling techniques, and he went out of his way to praise the work we were doing. His ready smile, keen intellect, and charismatic personality made him a natural leader of men, and I felt our company would benefit greatly from having this man as our commanding officer.

After we talked for a while, he suggested the team go for a dip in the jungle pool. This idea seemed bizarre to me, but he put me at ease by saying it was foolish to worry about security when our patrol had not detected any human activity in this part of Elephant Valley, and we had a company of infantry from the 7th Marines providing security nearby. I saw the logic of his argument and asked my team if they wanted to "take a bath" in the cool, mountain waters in front of us. They looked at me with incredulity, but then several of them started to take off their clothes and wade out into the pool up to their knees. Then they crouched down in the cool waters and beckoned me to join them. Before long, we were all buck naked and lying in the incredibly luxuriant coolness of the pool's waters. We relaxed this way for nearly an hour, then got out and dressed back in our sweat-stained, foul-smelling jungle utilities. A few hours later at 1500 we were extracted from an LZ that the infantry had cut on the side of the road about 50 yards east of the pool (Team Killer Kane Patrol Report, 25 May 1967).

When the patrol returned we were saddened to hear that Lt. Larry Stone had been killed leading a patrol on Charlie Ridge. Larry had been with the 1st Reconnaissance Battalion only a month, and this patrol was one of the first ones he had taken out as a patrol leader when tragedy struck. According to the other lieutenants in our hootch, Larry had bravely attacked several VC in a hut they had found on Charlie Ridge, and in the ensuing firefight Larry killed one VC but the others returned fire, killing him. I had known Larry for only a short time but I found him to be a very likeable young man who enjoyed the respect and affection of everyone. His death was a grim reminder that conducting reconnaissance patrols in enemy-held areas was a dangerous job.

Around this time, a package containing my baseball glove, a second baseball glove and two new baseballs arrived from home. I had told my father that there were several men in our company who enjoyed playing baseball, but we had no access to baseball equipment or a suitable playing field. He took my comments to heart, found my old glove in my bedroom at home, bought a new glove and two baseballs, and shipped all of them to me. I was very grateful to receive these items and immediately invited anyone who wanted to throw a ball to join me on the helicopter pad. We whiled away the hours, usually in the late afternoons when the heat was less intense, by playing catch and fielding grounders thrown to each other. This activity was very therapeutic for me, and I think it had a similar effect on the others who joined me. Throwing a baseball back and forth seemed to ease the tension in our lives and reminded us of home in a pleasant way. To this day, whenever I hear the sound of a baseball bat making contact with a baseball or the sound of a baseball hitting the leather of a glove, a flood of pleasant memories comes back to me of warm afternoons playing pepper with my father in our backyard, or playing countless games on fields in my hometown, or playing catch with my fellow Marines on the helipad in the shadow of Hill 327 in South Vietnam.

Killer Kane's last patrol in May was a very eventful one. I had an idea we would encounter the enemy on this patrol because on the day of our overflight, our helicopter received small arms and 12.7 mm heavy machine gun fire. The S-2 told us that the NFZ we would be patrolling in had a lot of recent NVA activity, probably involving elements of the 2nd NVA Division. Normally, our patrols took us into mountainous areas where few civilians lived, but this patrol along the southern border of the 1st Marine Division's

TAOR was in an area where there were many villages and farms on three sides of our patrol's NFZ. Because of the danger of patrolling in an area with large numbers of civilians, the S-2 chose an NFZ that included Hill 381 and gave us the mission of establishing an OP there. My initial map study, followed by the overflight, gave me the impression that we would find a good OP at or near Hill 381's summit and that its steep slopes and jungle cover would make it difficult for the enemy to approach our OP without being either observed or heard.

When I gave my patrol order the day before our insertion, I showed the team the Polaroid photos I had taken of the area, and we at first all agreed that Hill 381 was the best site for an OP since it was the only high ground in our NFZ. It was also the safest given the proximity of so many farms east, south and west of it. However, Sgt. Pugh quickly pointed out that there was one obvious danger with Hill 381; there were no LZs near the top of it. This meant we would have to fight our way to an extraction zone at its base if the enemy attempted to attack us while we were on the OP. Cpl. Borecky, one of our most experienced men, reminded me that it would be difficult to find many suitable harbor sites on such a steep hill, something that would make it easier for the NVA to locate us and plan for an attack. I agreed with everything they said, but I did not see any alternative to using Hill 381 since our NFZ contained no other locations where we could effectively hide from the enemy and avoid discovery by the population in the surrounding countryside. With some trepidation, we all finally came to the conclusion that the only feasible location for an OP was on Hill 381 and that we would have to be especially vigilant on this patrol.

I had been told at the Basic School that I should always end any patrol order I gave with, "Any questions?," but I found from experience with my recon team that ending a patrol order this way only produced silence. Instead, I said, "Is there anything we should be doing differently than what I just described, anything that will improve the patrol?" This question invariably would provoke some very helpful comments from the team members. The collective experience of the team was something we needed to exploit fully if we wanted the team to perform to its maximum potential. I put a lot of effort and study into each patrol order I gave to the team, but I knew I often forgot some important aspect or detail. The patrol members invariably were able to find these oversights and provide valuable alternatives. In our line of business, there was no place for arbitrary decisions. Each member of the recon team had an important role to play, and each had a wealth of experience that we could put to good use. Although I took pride in giving a detailed patrol order, I viewed it as a rough draft that would only be complete when every member of the recon team had had an opportunity to provide input. Our team was infinitely more effective because of this.

Our patrol to establish an OP on Hill 381 started with a surprise. The gunships who preceded the insert birds radioed to our pilot that they had received some small arms fire on their approach, but the LZ itself seemed to be clear of any enemy activity. As we made our approach, I could see the gunships off to our left and right providing cover for us as the CH-46 Sea Knight helicopter descended into the LZ, a small cultivated area on top of a perfectly round hill. When we landed, we saw that there were some old graves nearby in addition to several well-tended vegetable gardens. We saw no huts or people, but we could tell this area was used for agricultural production. The people doing this work were probably hidden away out of sight not far from the LZ. Looming to our east was the dark green mass of Hill 381, less than 500 meters away.

I took the team off the small hill we landed on, stepped over a low stone fence, and descended into a grape vineyard that ran parallel to our direction of movement. Immediately, I saw we had a problem, one that no map survey or overflight would have prepared us for. In fact, my map showed this area as a rice paddy, not a grape vineyard. The problem was the grape vines were low to the ground and supported by some sort of trellis built only three feet off the ground. We could not walk across this vineyard without getting hopelessly entangled in the trellis system and, besides, the area was relatively open and afforded us no real concealment or cover. The entire distance from the small hill to the base of Hill 381 was what we called a "danger area." This sort of situation is something one can never plan for, but I knew we had to do something quickly. We could hear voices behind us, and we were very much exposed where we were. I got down on my hands and knees and saw that the area under the trellis system was relatively clear of vines and that we might be able to crawl through this vineyard under the vines until we reached the other side, some 100 meters away. Without saying a word, I used hand and arm signals to indicate to Cpl. Borecky, our point man, that the team would crawl through this vineyard. He gave me a look that indicated he understood, but one that also conveyed his opinion that this might not be the best idea I could come up with. Nevertheless, he and the others got down on their hands and knees and proceeded to begin their crawl eastward.

It took us nearly 30 minutes to crawl slowly through the vineyard. As we approached the other side, Cpl. Borecky and I stopped the patrol and crawled forward to the edge of the vineyard. There we saw a very well-used trail running north-south, another serious "danger area" we would have to cross if we wanted to get to the relative safety of the jungle clad Hill 381. As we were looking down the trail to the north we saw five NVA soldiers approaching in a staggered column. They were on guard and obviously looking for us. With our camouflage uniforms and green and black face paint, they could not see us crouching in the vineyard only a few feet from the trail as they passed. All five of these NVA soldiers were quite young, and their grey-green field uniforms and pith helmets were clean and new. Each of them carried an AK-47 assault rifle with several 30 round magazine pouches on their web belts. These were definitely regular soldiers, not local guerrillas, probably members of one of the regiments of the 2nd NVA Division.

For a moment, my aggressive instincts took over, as I contemplated the odds of Borecky and me initiating contact with these enemy soldiers. However, it occurred to me that this group of five enemy soldiers might just be the advance of a larger force, and attacking them would only expose the team while we were in a very vulnerable position in the vineyard. Reluctantly, I overcame my desire to fire upon the enemy. Cpl. Borecky watched the trail, while I crawled back to get the rest of the patrol and bring them forward. In order to cross the danger area of the trail as quickly as possible, I had the team spread out parallel to the trail and cross all at one time, thus limiting the time we were exposed on the trail. Once on the other side, I had the team set up a hasty ambush since I was worried we had been observed when we crossed the trail. If so, I wanted to be able to bring as much fire power as possible to bear on any enemy force that attempted to follow us. After waiting in the hasty ambush for 30 minutes, I had the patrol continue through some thick brush in the direction of Hill 381.

We moved very slowly with Cpl. Borecky carefully and quietly cutting a path for us using his K-bar combat knife. This rugged knife with its seven-inch blade was originally issued to Marines as a tool for maintaining the Browning Automatic Rifle (BAR), a weapon that saw extensive service with U.S. soldiers and Marines during World War Two and the Korean War. It was a prized possession since it was both a tool and a weapon. Even after the BAR was no longer used by the American military, the K-Bar knife was issued to Marine infantry units. Walking through thick brush close to a trail can be very noisy and, thus, dangerous, especially if the team moves rapidly and pushes brush aside as it moves. Tangled vines and branches need to be slowly sawed through by the point man using a K-bar combat knife, if the patrol was to maintain a silent advance. Such a process was slow and tedious, but everyone knew the noise of breaking brush was a sure way of letting the enemy know you were there.

It took the patrol nearly two hours to move 100 yards through the thick brush, but around noon we came upon a trail leading up the slope of Hill 381. Again, we were confronted with a dangerous situation. I was fairly certain the enemy had seen our insertion, that they were out looking for us, and they could figure out that Hill 381 was a likely site for a Marine recon patrol to hide. For these reasons, I was very hesitant to have our patrol walk along a trail, even one that did not seem like it had been used within the last 24 hours. I had Cpl. Borecky and Sgt. Pugh, my most experienced men, come to me and together, in barely audible voices, we discussed our options. We all agreed that we should use the trail but only for a short distance and with a two-man point, using a staggered, leapfrog approach with the lead point covering the backup point as he advanced. This system of movement would, at least, have one man with his rifle at the ready and aiming forward so he could fire immediately if any enemy troops were encountered. The rear point and rear backup point man would do the same in case the enemy was following us. We had practiced this technique before and used it whenever we were forced to walk on a trail that indicated recent use. It was dangerous, but we saw no other way to get to a point close enough to the summit of Hill 381 before darkness set in.

Fortunately for our patrol, we only had to walk on this trail, which skirted the south side of Hill 381, for a few minutes, when we came upon another trail leading up a finger to the summit. We took the trail to our left and soon found that it was no more than a game trail and almost completely overgrown with tall grass and bamboo. The going was slow, but we knew this trail had not been used by humans, which was definitely not the case with the trail we had just left.

As we moved up the finger, I noticed Cpl. Borecky was getting tired. Walking point is both tiresome and stressful, and fatigue can make a point man lose his concentration, a dangerous situation for the entire patrol. I halted the patrol and replaced Cpl. Borecky with LCpl. Bart Russell, who gave his M-60 machine gun to Cpl. Borecky and took Borecky's M-16. I also moved Sgt. Pugh up from rear point to point backup so I had two fresh and very capable point men leading the patrol. Because the trail was overgrown and steep, it took the patrol most of the afternoon to finally reach the summit.

There we found a spot that was one of the best OPs I ever encountered. On the south facing of Hill 381 there was a huge, black rock sixty feet high. The top of this rock was flat, affording the patrol an excellent place to lay prone and observe the valleys and hills to the south. We could see for miles. An added advantage of this OP was a stand of trees on the back side of the rock that provided excellent shade from the blistering hot rays of the sun.

It was getting dark so I decided to look for a harbor site. I sent out two men to search for a place that would be hard for any enemy to approach at night without making a lot of noise. They came back in a half hour and motioned to me that they had found a spot directly below the large rock we were using for our OP. I collected the patrol and followed them down the edge of the rock until we came to a large cave at the bottom of the rock's western side. The cave was twenty feet wide, six feet high, and 30 feet deep. Aside from an abundance of bird droppings on the floor of the cave, it was an excellent harbor site because every approach to it was steep and difficult to traverse. No enemy would be able to attack us without giving themselves away long before they reached the cave's entrance, and there were several good positions near the mouth of the cave where we could find cover behind large rocks.

We moved into the cave, established our radio watch for the night, ate a quick meal of C rations, and spread our ponchos on the cave floor. The cave's interior was cool, and this made for a welcome respite from the heat of the day, although the stench from the bird droppings took a bit of getting used to. As the sun began to dip behind the Annamite Mountains to the west, we heard an awful screeching in the distant sky. There, flying against the setting sun, were two of the biggest birds I had ever seen. They looked pre-historic, more like pterodactyls than birds. They were black and white with wing spans that looked to be nearly five feet. The birds flew closer and closer to our cave and squawked louder and louder as they approached. It suddenly dawned on us that this cave was their home, and we were unwelcome interlopers. They were quite aggressive, and for an instant I thought they would land inside the cave. Instead, they hovered around the entrance for a few minutes and then disappeared. On two subsequent nights, these birds returned to the cave but they only flew around it for a few minutes to see if we were still there before they flew off to the west. When I returned from this patrol, I attempted to find out what kind of bird our patrol had encountered, but when I looked at pictures of Southeast Asian birds in a book the Division G-2 had, I did not find any that looked like the birds we saw.

During the next two days on Hill 381, we used our OP on the huge rock and another OP on the north side of the hill to call in several artillery fire missions on enemy troops we saw moving in the valleys below us. We could see for miles in any direction and had every trail covered. We used our two 7 × 50 binoculars and our 30-power spotting scope to very good effect whenever we observed the enemy. We observed a total of 73 NVA troops and called in five or six fire missions resulting in 11 confirmed kills and 15 probable kills.

On 31 May, we saw four NVA soldiers attempt to recover two bodies of NVA soldiers we had killed the previous day. The NVA bodies lay in a rice paddy just a few meters off a trail between two villages, an open area approximately a half mile south of our OP. I called in a fire mission on the NVA recovery party, and the 105 mm and 155 mm howitzer rounds began to fall just as they were carrying the bodies into a hedgerow. The artillery coverage was nearly perfect with dozens of rounds impacting in and around the hedgerow. As we watched the fire mission, we were treated to something rarely seen by a recon patrol: a huge secondary explosion that looked like one of the artillery rounds had exploded an ammunition and fuel storage cache. White phosphorous and HE ammunition exploded with a thunderous roar, and orange and red flames shot forty feet high into the air, as the cache erupted in a dazzling display of fireworks. We had hit the jackpot. A half hour after the last artillery round had exploded in the hedgerow, we could still see secondary explosions going off periodically and hear small arms ammunition cooking off as small fires ignited the propellant in the cartridges. There was no doubt that some VC or NVA outfit had lost a lot of ammunition and fuel.

On the last day of the patrol, we began to move off Hill 381 before sunrise. We moved down a steep finger on the north side of the hill and then found an old trail that circled the base of the hill toward the east. The trail had a gentle descent to it, and there were no obstacles to impede our movement. After we had been on the trail for 20 minutes, the rear point, Sgt. Pugh, gave a hand signal to us to stop and listen. He thought someone was following us. We set up a hasty ambush and waited for a half hour, but we did not see or hear anything suspicious. Still, I knew Sgt. Pugh was one of my best field men and, if he thought we were being followed, he was probably right. I told Cpl. Borecky to continue down the trail since I felt we were very close to the extraction LZ, a deserted rice paddy between two fingers at the base of Hill 381. After only a few minutes on the trail, we found the deserted rice paddy, which was an excellent LZ with dimensions of 200 meters by 100 meters. We formed a 360-degree defense in the trees at the edge of the rice paddy where we could easily see anyone who might be following us along the trail we had just used. We saw nothing. But all of us sensed that we were not alone, and it put all of us on edge.

When we received a radio report that our extraction helicopters were 30 minutes out, I decided to move the team down into a large bomb crater at the edge of the rice paddy since it offered good cover in the event the enemy was waiting to attack us when the helicopters landed. As it turned out, that decision was a good one. In a letter home to my parents the following day (and as detailed in our patrol report) I described what happened:

> Just as the CH-46 descended into the rice paddy, the VC opened up at it with AK-47s from positions 100 meters to our south and east. We told the pilots where the fire was coming from, and soon Huey gunships opened up with rockets and machine guns. Jets were called in, and they dropped napalm 60 meters in front of our position in the bomb crater. The heat was really bad, but not as bad as it was for the VC. Hueys made another pass and the VC opened up again, only this time from a tree line right in front of us. The scene reminded me of a World War II documentary about Iwo Jima or some other island in the Pacific — Marines shooting like crazy from a shell crater with palm trees above. I fired four magazines in four minutes; some of my men fired eight. Cpl. Borecky laughed at the VC and taunted them as he fired. Then the choppers came back in to get us, the VC shooting notwithstanding. He landed close to our bomb crater with his crew firing their .50 caliber machine guns into the tree line. Cpl. Borecky and I covered the rest of the team as they sprinted across the paddy field to the helicopter, and then we fired one more magazine apiece and took off running toward the chopper. I think we broke the record for the 100 yard dash. I kept looking to see if anyone fell, but we all made it to the chopper all right. We kicked out the windows and began shooting out of them as the helicopter lifted out of the LZ.

When we returned to Camp Reasoner, we were met by a crowd of our fellow Marines who congratulated us for making it out safely. Maj. Lowrey, who had relieved Lt. Col. McKeon as the CO of the 1st Reconnaissance Battalion, shook my hand and the hands of each man in the team as we walked up into the camp from the helipad, but I could tell he was not at all pleased about our making contact again. After our debriefing by the S-2, he took me in his office and sat me down in front of his desk. He gave me a coke and then he told me that he was concerned about the number of firefights Killer Kane had been involved in since I had taken command of that team. He referred to some notes he had on his desk, and then he said, "Andy, your team has had more contacts with the enemy this year than any other recon team in the division. I'm not talking about artillery fire missions or air strikes; I'm talking about the firefights and ambushes your team has been involved in. I am impressed with the results, but I need to remind you that your job has always been to conduct reconnaissance and surveillance operations or to conduct Stingray operations, not ambush patrols. Just think about what you are doing. You are attacking main force enemy units far from friendly lines with what amounts to a reinforced fire team. That is foolish, and one of these days you and your team are all going to be killed."

I admired Maj. Lowrey and considered him a model officer, so his remarks stung. I understood the logic of his comments, and I did not choose to disagree with him. He was my CO, and I knew I had to obey him. I also knew he was genuinely concerned about my safety and the safety of my Marines. I told him I understood and that I would do my best to avoid contact with the enemy in the future, but sometimes the situation dictated that we take the enemy under fire. He looked like he wanted to tell me something else, but thought better of it. He then smiled, stood up, and put his arm around me. As we walked out of his office he turned to me and said something that always haunted me from that moment on. He said, "Andy, you are a strange duck. You seem obsessed sometimes. The other officers tell me you are obsessed with something. I don't know what it is, but it will get you killed if you are not more careful." He then invited me up to the officers' club and bought me a beer. I think he actually felt sorry for me.

At the time, I gave little thought to what Maj. Lowrey had said. I did not consider myself obsessed with anything, so his comments puzzled me, but did not overly concern me. Upon reflection, I think Maj. Lowrey was reflecting the views of some officers who considered the way Killer Kane operated as outside the normal scope of a reconnaissance company's mission. Their opinion, which had merit, was the mission of a reconnaissance team was to gather intelligence and use supporting arms to attack targets of opportunity, not engage the enemy with small arms unless it was absolutely necessary. They stressed the need to remain hidden from the enemy. Engaging in ambushes or firefights prevented a recon team from remaining hidden and made it more difficult to carry out the intelligence-gathering mission, which was the doctrinal imperative of a recon team. The officers who espoused this doctrinaire view and I disagreed. I was not obsessed with killing the enemy, as they often contended; I was convinced more accurate and exploitable intelligence could be obtained by capturing prisoners or searching the belongings of recently killed enemy soldiers. This was not obsessive. It was just a different approach, albeit a more risky one.

5

The Summer of Living Dangerously

With each successive patrol, Killer Kane improved. We honed our skills and practiced our techniques until each of us developed an almost reflexive response to any situation we encountered while on patrol. Despite Maj. Lowrey's words of caution, I still looked for every opportunity to ambush the NVA and VC. I figured that a successful ambush would, in all probability, produce valuable intelligence about the intentions and capabilities of the enemy. Surveillance patrols and Stingray patrols were important, but neither produced the kind of actionable intelligence an ambush could produce. Surveillance patrols could detect the movement of the enemy and give our intelligence analysts the data they needed to develop patterns of enemy movement. From these patterns the analysts could try to determine the intentions of the enemy. Stingray patrols could inflict casualties on the enemy with supporting arms and disrupt their movements to and from their base areas. Both surveillance and Stingray patrols had value, but only an ambush could produce prisoners and documents, two things that gave definitive information about what the enemy was up to.

By June of 1967 our team was the most productive team in the 1st Reconnaissance Battalion with more sightings, more enemy killed, and more weapons captured; but soon we would have a truly spectacular summer that would make our previous patrols look like routine sojourns into the hinterlands. But before I tell you about the most productive patrols of Killer Kane, it might be helpful to go over how our team was organized and how I equipped myself for each patrol.

Killer Kane went to the field with as few as five and as many as twelve Marines and Navy corpsmen, but through experience we determined that the optimum number for a patrol was eight men. How these eight men were organized and positioned in the patrol was critical to the success of the patrol. Indeed, the very survival of the team was a function of how the team functioned as a whole, with each man doing his job to perfection. I put the best men in the most important positions and tried to match each man's particular skills and talents to the requirements of the team. I put my best field man on point to lead the patrol in the direction I wanted the patrol to go. This man had to possess certain characteristics that made for a good point man, such as intelligence, endurance, excellent eyesight and hearing, lightning fast reflexes, superior marksmanship, courage, and a sense for terrain and the enemy. The life of each man in the patrol depended on the individual skills of the point man. During my time as the leader of the 5th platoon, I had several truly superior point men: Bart Russell, Robert Garcia, Mike Borecky, John Slowick, Dave Pugh, and Dwight Cobb. In many respects, I owe my life to these exceptional men. The fate of our platoon would surely have been far more tragic had these men not been on point for us when we patrolled behind enemy lines.

The second man in the patrol was the backup point man. This man had to have the same set of skills as the point man since he would often be called upon to take the point when the point man became fatigued. Often the secondary point man, as he was called, carried an M-79 grenade launcher in addition to his service rifle. This was done because the M-79 had a flechette round that could send dozens of small arrow-like metal flechettes at an enemy with one shot, very similar to what a shotgun round could do. This weapon was great for breaking contact or providing cover for the point man if the patrol encountered more than one enemy soldier on a trail.

As the patrol leader, I occupied the third position in the patrol. I felt being the third man gave me the best opportunity to assess any situation quickly and to be able to bring up any of the men behind me to support the point man and backup point man. I also knew that positioning me any further forward in the column would distract me from my primary duty as the patrol leader since I would be walking point, a job that required total concentration for that task and no distractions.

The fourth man was always the radio operator. This man had to be able to think independently and to be totally familiar with the operation of the PRC-25 radio. He had to use the radio under all conditions, even in total darkness, and he had to be able to use our various coding materials. He would write and transmit our field reports and accurately communicate my verbal reports to headquarters. The necessary skills of the radioman also included competency in map reading, land navigation, and the use of supporting arms. In essence, this man had to be able to save the patrol if it got into trouble by either relaying my instructions or taking it upon himself to communicate with higher headquarters. He kept the message pads and often could draft a SALUTE report with nothing more than verbal instructions from me. He had to be strong since the PRC-25 radio was heavy, and he had to hump the radio in addition to his other weapons and equipment. I made sure the radio operator had a map identical to mine with our NFZ marked clearly on it so he could draft both SALUTE messages and calls for supporting arms if I was not able to draft these radio messages. Next to the point man, he was the most important man in the patrol. My best radio operators were LCpl. R. Garner and Cpl. James W. Hager.

The fifth man was normally my Navy corpsman, positioned so he could react to a casualty to the front or rear rapidly. In addition to carrying a Unit 1 field medical bag, this sailor also carried a rifle and was counted upon to fight with the same ability and aggressiveness as any other member of the patrol. The best corpsmen I had in my platoon were HM2 Willis and HM3 Conner. They were skilled field medics who genuinely cared for the men on the patrol, but they were also experienced field men and aggressive fighters.

The sixth man was our machine gunner, who carried an M-60 machine gun with 300 rounds of linked 7.62 mm ammunition. Because of the weight of this weapon, the man who had this job had to be physically strong and able to endure the arduous and difficult hiking over steep jungle terrain. He also had to be able to react quickly because this weapon was the one that allowed us to achieve fire superiority in any meeting engagement with the enemy or to break contact effectively when confronted by a superior enemy force. While all of the men who held this position were good, Bart Russell was the most effective in employing this weapon. His proficient use of this weapon saved our patrol on at least two occasions when his expertise enabled us to overcome a numerically superior force of NVA soldiers.

The seventh man was the backup radio man who also doubled as the backup rear point man. This Marine normally did not have a communications MOS, but was an infantryman who acquired some proficiency with the PRC-25 radio through self-study and on-the-job training. He usually had his radio set on the frequency for the artillery battery assigned to provide fire support for our patrol or on the frequency of a friendly infantry unit that might be able to reach us if we got into trouble or needed some valuable intelligence we developed on the enemy. He had to know how to fill in for the primary radio operator, which meant he had to possess the intelligence, physical strength and proficiency to fill this demanding position. Since they often had their radio on the frequency of an artillery battery, I made sure they knew how to transmit a call for artillery fire rapidly and accurately. This required that the Marine take my verbal instructions and turn them into a complete fire mission request, a task that required him to memorize the grid coordinates of the target and the compass azimuth heading toward it. In many cases, this Marine was also the assistant patrol leader, ready to take over from me if I was killed or wounded. Like the primary radio operator, he also carried a map of the NFZ so he could know where we were at a moment's notice and use this information when sending in a request for fire support. Sgt. James Hauxhurst was one of my best backup radio operators and also one of my best assistance patrol leaders. Sgt. Hauxhurst was highly intelligent and was able to quickly request fire support whenever our team made contact with the enemy and seconds counted. He did not need an order from me to take action; he instantaneously and instinctively knew what to do, performing with complete calm even under the most stressful of situations.

The final member of the patrol was the rear point man. This Marine's job was to ensure the patrol was not being followed, to cover our trail, and to maintain constant observation to the rear. Recon patrols were often followed by NVA counter-reconnaissance patrols and trail watchers, so the job of this man was essential to the survival of the team. Several times the enemy trailed Killer Kane, and we were never surprised. Our rear point men detected their presence, and this allowed us to take the appropriate action. He had to be especially skilled at concealing our trail so the enemy would be unable to follow us, especially when we crossed a stream, used a muddy trail, or moved into a harbor site at the end of the day. Covering a trail took time, so it was imperative

James Hauxhurst, assistant patrol leader for many Killer Kane patrols.

that the patrol move slowly, allowing the rear point to make sure no telltale signs of our passage were left in our wake. I always considered the rear point man to be the point man "in waiting," someone who could fill in at point if the forward point man needed to be replaced for some reason, such as sickness or rotation back to the U.S. Two of my best rear point men were LCpl. J. D. Glor, a native of Batavia, New York, and LCpl. Dave Powell from Washington, D.C.

With few exceptions, this eight-man organization was the one Killer Kane employed on the patrols it conducted during the summer and fall of 1968.

When I first went on patrol, I listened to the advice offered by the men of my platoon and the other officer and enlisted patrol leaders in our company as to what personal equipment I should take with me on patrol. However, over time I adapted my personal equipment to the point where I felt I was taking what I needed but nothing extraneous. I was always looking for ways to lighten my load since every pound I carried exacted a price in fatigue and discomfort. We all knew that fatigue and discomfort were the enemies of vigilance and security. By the summer of 1967, I had developed my own list of personal equipment to take on a patrol.

For clothing, I wore the standard issue Marine Corps jungle utility uniform, which was made of olive green poplin material; however, I also was able to obtain some U.S. Air Force camouflage uniforms through trading with the airmen on the Da Nang Air Base. These USAF camouflage uniforms were the best uniforms for a reconnaissance patrol because they blended into the jungle better than the olive green uniform. I also wore a pair of tiger striped utilities once that I had obtained through trading with a Special Forces unit, but I found this uniform ill-fitting and hot, so I discarded it after only one patrol. On my head I wore a bush hat, a short-brimmed hat made of camouflage material and locally produced. I bought these jungle hats at a Vietnamese store near Camp Reasoner run by a man we all called Mr. Smart because he was so erudite and cultured and because the name of his store was "Smarts Clothing." We did not know his actual name. It was rumored that he had been a university instructor at a college in Da Nang or Hue before the war. I always enjoyed going to his small shop on the side of the main road outside Camp Reasoner and chatting with him about Vietnamese history and literature. I bought a surprising amount of field gear from Mr. Smart, gear that was either in short supply or unavailable from the Marine Corps supply system.

On my feet I wore the Marine Corps issue jungle boot, which I considered the best piece of gear the Marine Corps possessed. I usually wore a green T-shirt under my utility shirt, but never boxer shorts since these chafed and caused a rash when wet with rain or sweat. I sometimes dispensed with socks for the same reason.

Like most Marines, I kept my dog tags taped together with parachute rigger's tape and laced them to my boots. I never wore any rank insignia on my uniform when I went to the field or took any identification papers. If I was killed or captured, I did not want the enemy to know anything about me other than the information contained on my dog tags.

I wore a standard-issue cartridge belt and suspenders. To these items, I attached all the crucial war fighting and survival gear I needed while on patrol. On the front of the cartridge belt on both the left and right side of the buckle, I had M-14 ammunition pouches with four 20-round 5.56 mm magazines in each pouch. On the outboard side of the two ammunition pouches, I attached two M-26 fragmentation grenades. On my right hip, I carried my personal .45-caliber M1911 semi-automatic pistol in a standard USMC leather holster. Attached to my pistol was a lanyard that ran to my belt suspenders. On my left hip I had my K-bar combat knife and sheaf. On the back of my cartridge belt I carried two canteens, with a canteen cup for heating water seated in one of the canteen covers, and a jungle first aid/survival kit between the two canteens.

On my suspenders, I carried my lensatic compass, a small pen light with red lens, a strobe light, a mini-pencil flare with four flares, a smoke grenade, and a CS gas grenade. These last two items were taped to the suspenders with parachute rigger's tape. I never varied the positioning of any of these items because I wanted to be able to get to them quickly, even in the dark. Seconds often meant the difference between life and death. I even went so far as to practice changing magazines to my M-16 rifle in the dark so I could do the same if the need occurred while I was on patrol.

The most valuable item I carried on patrol was my map case which I carried in my right-side carrying pocket of my utility trousers. This item, which I constructed out of plastic, cardboard, and heavy-duty, water-resistant tape, was folded neatly in half inside my carrying pocket. Attached to the map case was one black grease pencil that allowed me to write on the plastic even when it was raining, which it frequently was. When the map case was opened, I could see approximately 100,000 square meters represented on the folded map with my NFZ marked in the middle. This ten-by-ten grid square portion of my map allowed me to accomplish 90 percent of my map-related tasks without ever taking the map out of the case.

In a small, waterproof bag, I carried a notebook and a mechanical pencil, items I needed to draft messages for the radio operator and to take down information I might need for my debriefing by the S-2 when I returned from patrol. I carried these items in the left breast pocket of my utility uniform within easy reach, along with a stick of camouflage face paint made by Helena Rubenstein's cosmetics company for the military. Each camouflage stick was fitted into a small metal container a little larger than a women's lipstick with caps on each end. Each stick was divided into two colors, and my favorite had black on one end and green on the other. I used this stick to paint my face in a pattern that broke up the contours of my face and made me virtually invisible when I was looking at something or someone with the jungle as my background.

In my ARVN rucksack from Mr. Smart's store, I carried a poncho, a camouflaged poncho liner, a mosquito head net, a small bag containing a toothbrush and toothpaste, three extra canteens of water, and a pair of 8 × 30 East German binoculars, which were superior to the U.S.–made 7 × 50 binoculars both in terms of weight and clarity of vision. They also had the added benefit of having a range-finding grid etched into the lenses, which was very beneficial when calling in artillery fire or air strikes.

I carried five days' worth of rations. On most patrols, I took the same items from the box of C rations issued to me. These items were two "heavy" cans (one each of beans and franks and spaghetti and meatballs), four cans of fruit (apple sauce, sliced peaches, pear halves, and fruit cocktail), three small cans of snacks (cheese and crackers or choco-late candy and crackers), and four small packets containing a plastic spoon, chewing gum, toilet paper, coffee, sugar, salt, pepper, and a toothpick. This was not a lot of food to last five days in the field, but I knew it was enough to keep my strength up. I had to reduce the weight I carried to the absolute minimum and food weighed a lot. It was always a careful balancing act to take just the right amount of water, food and ammunition, and nothing extra. In addition to these items, I usually took an emergency packet of rations that I would use only if my patrol was extended for some reason, such as bad flying weather during the monsoon season. This emergency packet contained two small cans of C ration peanut butter, which I found to be filling and energy producing. On rare occasions, I would replace a C ration can with a small can of tuna fish or deviled ham that my parents would mail to me. Once or twice, I took a small can or two of orange juice that I had bought at the Freedom Hill PX. I tried to limit the weight of my pack as much as possible, but it still was always nearly 50 or 60 pounds when I boarded the helicopters for insertion. Fortunately, as I ate my rations, the load was lightened with each passing day. I also experimented with American and indigenous long-range patrol rations, both of which contained freeze-dried food. I stopped using them when I realized they required far too much water to prepare. They tasted good, were lighter than C rations to carry, and easier to stow in my rucksack, but water was far too precious to waste on their preparation.

Due to the need for security, the team members of Killer Kane did not always heat their food before eating it. Eating cold C rations was not pleasant, but the smell of cooking beans and franks could give a recon team's position away, so we did not cook our food unless we were sure it was safe to do so. When we cooked, we employed two methods. One method was to use heat tabs: little square bars of flammable material that would burn for a minute or two when lighted with a match. The other method, which was preferable, was to take a small ball of C-4 plastic explosive, normally the size of a large pea, light it with a match and cook the can of food over the very intense flame the explosive produced. This required some skill since the intense heat could burn the food in the bottom of the can and leave the food in the upper portion of the can cold.

Normally, we would make a small handmade stove to do our cooking. This entailed taking one of the small C ration cans used for crackers and making several holes in the bottom of it with our "John Wayne," P-38, can openers. I carried my P-38 on a piece of parachute cord around my neck so I could get to it easily and not lose it. Once the P-38 had cut five or six holes in the can, I put a heat tab or the ball of C-4 in the can and set it on fire. The holes in the bottom of the can provided oxygen to the flame and a "heavy " C ration can of food or a canteen cup full of water could fit nicely on top of the stove for cooking. We preferred to use the C-4 because it cooked the food faster than the heat tabs and did not give off much of an odor when it burned. It was far easier to boil water for coffee using C-4 explosive, taking only ten seconds or so to bring a canteen cup of water to a boil. I am sure the Marine Corps would have frowned upon our use of C-4 explosive this way, but we were never instructed not to use it in this manner so we simply did what was convenient.

On some patrols, I took additional equipment, such as a Claymore mine or a C-4 demolition kit, but these were items that were not part of my normal load. Some patrols took more food, others more ammunition, but Killer Kane tried to take only the essentials to the field and nothing more. If we decided to go heavier, it normally involved taking more ammunition, grenades or radio batteries and then spreading these items between us. For instance, on a half-dozen patrols, I took an extra 100 rounds of belted M-60 machine gun ammunition because I anticipated making contact with the enemy. Our machine gun was the primary means at our disposal for gaining and maintaining fire superiority, so I did not want it to run out of ammunition at a critical point in a firefight.

Some patrol leaders in the battalion allowed their men to take a small commercial radio with them on patrol while others allowed their men to take reading material. I did not allow either since I considered anything that distracted us from our mission as foolhardy and dangerous. I wanted all of my men, even those resting, to be fully alert to the enemy's presence and prepared to react quickly. I made one exception to this policy. I allowed them to take reading material to Hill 452 so they could read when they were not on watch.

Our first patrol in June was rather tranquil. On 6 June, the 6th anniversary of my joining the Marine Corps Reserves in Camden, New Jersey, Killer Kane was inserted into a small LZ on a ridgeline below Nui Nhu Mountain just west of the Song Tinh Yen River. Our mission was to conduct clandestine reconnaissance and surveillance of the trail networks along the western edge of the river and to establish an OP where we could observe any enemy activity in the village of Trang Bang, a village in the southern part of the infamous area known as the Arizona Territory. The Arizona Territory was a rather large track of farm land west of the An Hoa Combat Base that was bordered on the north by the Song Vu Gia River, on the east by the Song Thu Bon River, and on the south by a spur of the Annamite Mountains. On the west was the imposing Ong Thu Slope, a dark massif that rose like a black wall against the western sky. The Arizona Territory was completely under the control of the VC and had been for many years.

Our insertion went smoothly, and soon we were inching our way up the eastern slope of Nui Nhu Mountain, struggling through very thick secondary growth and high jungle canopy, sweating profusely and stooped over from the heavy packs on our backs. As we climbed the mountain, we found several small but fast-moving streams that were not marked on our map. I carefully plotted each of them on my map so I could mention them in my patrol report and future patrols would know where to find water. We encountered no signs of the enemy or any other human activity on the mountain. As darkness began to descend, we reached a very good OP site on the northern slope of the mountain, a flat area with a perfect view of Trang Bang village to the north and the trails leading into and out of it. From this OP, we could also observe most of the Arizona Territory to the north and the An Hoa Combat Base across the river to the east. As I trained my binoculars to the east, I could see Marine transport aircraft and helicopters taking off and landing on the airstrip at An Hoa, sending up large plumes of red and yellow dust as their prop wash created little whirlpools above the airfield's short, shimmering runway. I could also see and hear the artillery batteries at An Hoa firing their howitzers, a sight that made us feel relatively secure because I knew we had direct, line of sight radio contact with these batteries. This meant our radios were not masked by any terrain feature and we would be able to obtain clearance for any fire mission quickly.

We sat in our OP for three days, moving only at night to a different harbor site to hide from the enemy and rest. We saw no enemy activity during this 79-hour patrol, but we saw dozens of women working in the fields and in a vineyard on a ridgeline a few hundred yards in front of us. They were laughing and talking, and Sgt. Pugh, who understood Vietnamese fairly well, could actually make out their conversations because their voices carried so well across the ravine between us. I wondered what they would be thinking if they knew seven recon Marines were watching their every move from dawn to dusk and listening to their private conversations. On 9 June, we were extracted without incident from a small LZ close to our OP. As we gained altitude, I looked down and saw the looks of amazement and fear on the faces of these peasant women. I think they realized we had been near them every day, watching them work in their fields, and I hoped they would convey to their husbands and brothers the fact that the eyes of the recon Marines were ever present, silently lurking in the shadows (Team Killer Kane Patrol Report, 9 June 1967).

When we returned to Camp Reasoner, I found a package of goodies from my mother. In this package, she had placed a one-pound box of Aunt Charlotte's chocolate candies: the famous, homemade candies that this small store in my hometown produced. I opened the package in the presence of my fellow lieutenants, and they eagerly volunteered to help me eat this rare treat. We consumed the entire box in less than five minutes, with each of us professing that these chocolates were the best we had ever tasted. My mother had also enclosed a few pictures taken a month earlier of my family at Cape May, New Jersey, and a paperback book she thought I would enjoy, a history of Japan by Edwin O. Reischauer. These care packages from my mother were always the highlight of my day whenever they arrived. They always contained items I enjoyed and best of all were a reminder of how much my mother loved me.

While I was out on the last patrol, the film crew for the "Huntley and Brinkley" NBC television news program came to Camp Reasoner and filmed a portion of Team Classmate's patrol near the Laotian border. There was some controversy involving this patrol, which caused many of us to assume the Marine Corps would not release the film for use on television back in the States. To this day, I do not know the details involved in this controversy or whether or not the film was ever shown in the U.S. Normally, it was the policy of the Marine Corps not to allow journalists or film crews to accompany recon patrols, so why an exception had been made in this case was, and still is, a mystery to me.

It was around this time that my best friend, 1st Lt. Mike Henry, departed the company and returned to the U.S. and his wife, Anita. I will always be grateful for the friendly advice he gave me when I first arrived at Camp Reasoner. Mike had a sharp, acerbic wit and a cynical sense of humor, and he did not suffer fools gladly. He was the intellectual in our hootch, and I always enjoyed discussing politics and history with him. He and I often would share a drink and watch a movie in the 1st Marine Division officers' club after a patrol or go together on one of Mike's civic action visits to Phuoc Ly hamlet for a MEDCAP or some other project Mike had thought of to improve our relations with the local farmers.

I got to know a lot about Mike in those first five months we served together. He was the son of a U.S. Navy officer, and he and his family had lived in England, Ireland, Hawaii,

Virginia and Puerto Rico as they followed his father from duty station to duty station. He won a Navy ROTC scholarship to Tulane University, and upon graduation he married a local beauty from Puerto Rico, Ana Margarita Tait. He was the communications officer for both our company and the 1st Reconnaissance Battalion. Unlike most staff officers, Mike actively pursued every opportunity to go on patrol, often volunteering to take out some of the more dangerous patrols. He made over twenty long-range patrols, which was highly unusual for a staff officer.

One such patrol took place just a week or two before he departed for the U.S. Mike had taken out a patrol to test some new communications equipment. While on this patrol, Mike and his team got into a horrendous firefight at very close range with an NVA platoon. In this firefight, nine NVA soldiers were killed, but the patrol suffered heavy casualties with five of its seven members wounded, including Mike, who was wounded in the head from shrapnel from a Chinese hand grenade. Mike was able to break contact with the enemy using CS gas grenades and get the team safely to an emergency LZ. It was a pretty close thing, but Mike was cool under fire and his team performed with great courage and resourcefulness.

On 12 June, I went with Mike and eleven other Marines on his last MEDCAP to Phouc Ly hamlet to help deliver 24 boxes of dry milk to the village chief and to discuss the progress of the outdoor bathhouse. He told Mike that it was nearly complete, and it would soon be "open for business." The women of the village wanted this bathhouse badly. There was no indoor plumbing in this rural hamlet so women were forced to either bathe in the open or inside an outdoor area sheltered by only a few woven mats. The new bathhouse would give them the privacy they sought and a ready source of clean water drawn from a local well and delivered via underground pipes to the spigots and shower heads inside the bathhouse. The village chief said this project was the most popular joint project the village had ever embarked upon, and he expressed the gratitude of the entire hamlet for the material provided by the Marines.

While I was in the hamlet, I took along two framed photographs of one of the village elders. I had taken the photos on a previous trip to the village and then sent the negatives home to my parents so they could develop and enlarge the photos to 8"-by-10" color prints of the old man. He had told me through our interpreter on a previous visit that he would like a simple picture of himself so he could have it put on his grave or on the small ancestor altar in his daughter's home.

Taking the interpreter with me, I walked along a dirt path past several vegetable gardens and banana plants to the home of this elderly gentleman. As we approached his home, he invited me into his house, a simple two-room thatched hut with a dirt floor. Once inside, he beckoned me to sit with him at a rough-hewn table. We talked for a few minutes, and he told me that he had been a Viet Minh soldier and had fought the French during the First Indo-China War. He also told me that his wife had died a few years earlier and that he missed her and his other children who had moved away after they grew up. Only his youngest daughter remained to care for him. His daughter brought us tea and poured it into two rather old and dirty glasses. I took the photos out of a manila envelope and gave them to him. When I did so, he looked at the pictures for a few seconds and then he wept, a very unusual thing for a Vietnamese man to do in public. He told me through the interpreter that he was "nearing death" and these photos were all he had to give to his daughter to remember him by. I felt very uncomfortable seeing him so emotional and worried that my small gift might have been a mistake since in a Confucian culture like Vietnam it is bad form to provoke emotion in another person. I was afraid that I had violated a cultural etiquette. I could not think of anything appropriate to say. I simply looked down in embarrassment and sat silently, as he stared down at the photos with tears in his eyes.

Outside, I could hear children playing and dogs barking, but inside the hut there was complete silence. His daughter, a woman in her forties who looked much older than her years, came up behind her father and gently touched his shoulder, and then she began to weep also. I did not know what to do, so I took a box of five American cigars that I had intended to give to the village chief and placed them on the table. I was not prepared for the emotional response of this elderly villager. I felt I was on the verge of tears myself, but I could not understand exactly why the old villager's tears had the effect on me that they did. I knew I would lose face if I showed emotion, so I rose from the table and left. I walked back to my jeep and drove back to Camp Reasoner. On every subsequent visit to Phuoc Ly, I would be greeted by this elderly man. He would stand in the door of his hut with his daughter and wave to me. When I returned to South Vietnam in December 1968, I went to visit Phuoc Ly to tell him of my return, but the village chief told me the old man had died while I was back in the U.S. When I approached his hut, his daughter greeted me and invited me into her home to show me her father's photograph on the family altar, along with incense sticks, rice and dried flowers. He was gone, but somehow I felt his spirit still lingered in that hut.

On 13 June, I found that I had a package waiting for me in the company mail room. I assumed it might be another care package from my parents, but I was surprised to find that this package was from the author BGen. Samuel B. Griffith, USMC (Ret.). Inside was a nice note from him and a book he had written, *Mao Tse-tung on Guerrilla Warfare*. I immediately wrote back thanking him for the book and for taking the time and effort to send it to me so far away from his home in Maine. I took the book back to my hootch and read it completely in two days. During the next few years, I would periodically correspond with both Brig. Gen. Griffith and another author, Capt. Robert Asprey, USMC (Ret.). Both of these gentlemen had helped me with my Naval Academy senior year research paper, and I valued their assistance and advice immeasurably. They both served as models for me of the soldier-scholar I aspired to be. Robert Asprey would use my letters in his famous work, *War in the Shadows*, a history of guerrilla warfare through the ages, even quoting me anonymously. My comments were rather inflammatory, and he feared I would get into trouble if the quotes were attributed directly to me (see also Asprey, p. 1186, 1389).

Killer Kane's next patrol would take it back into the same area we patrolled the previous week: the hills on the south edge of the Arizona Territory. Unlike our first patrol in this area, this patrol involved several sightings of the enemy and numerous artillery fire missions and air strikes. Our mission was the same as the previous week's patrol but with one significant difference. In addition to keeping watch on river traffic to our east and the trail networks around the village of An Bang to the north, we were to screen the advance of units of the 7th Marines, who were to cross the river north of An Hoa and

Recon OP overlooking the northern Arizona Territory and the Song Vu Gia River.

drive west to link up with other Marine units attacking south across the Song Vu Gia River. The name of the 7th Marines' operation was Operation Arizona. We hoped that these Marine infantry advances would flush out the enemy and allow us to attack them with supporting arms.

Killer Kane consisted of eight men for this patrol. Sgt. Pugh was the assistant patrol leader. LCpl. Garner and Cpl. Williams were the two radio operators. LCpl. Slowick and LCpl. Russell were the point men. PFC Boyd carried the M-79 grenade launcher and PFC Glor carried a Unit 1 medical kit since we did not have a corpsman on this patrol. We did not take a machine gun with us because each platoon had only one machine gun and my other team, Brisbane, needed it for a patrol farther west in an area that we anticipated would have more NVA in it than the area we would be patrolling.

We were inserted at dawn on the 15th of June into a small LZ on a ridgeline running off the north face of Nui Nhu Mountain. We did not take fire on our approach into the LZ, always a good sign. After waiting in the brush for half an hour to see if the enemy had any plans to follow us, we began to move slowly to a good OP site about 200 yards northeast of the LZ. Once we arrived at the OP site, I positioned two men on each flank of the OP and one two-man team directly behind the OP facing south uphill. These three security teams could cover the three approaches to the OP site from good defensive positions.

LCpl. John Slowick, a native of North Philadelphia and a superb Marine, joined me in our OP position, a slight depression that afforded good cover and concealment in addition to welcome shade from the torrid rays of the sun. From here we began scanning the Arizona Territory as it stretched out for several miles in the direction of the Song

Thu Bon River. We concentrated our efforts on the three hamlets nearest to the OP, which were known as An Bang 1, 2, and 3.

John Slowick, a native of Philadelphia, walked point for several dangerous patrols.

We were in our OP less than two hours when we had our first sighting. At 1030, we observed 20 NVA in mixed black, green and camouflage uniforms carrying rifles and packs moving north on a trail that ran between the hamlets of An Bang 2 and Tan Phuoc 1. I called in an artillery mission on them and saw two secondary explosions, but we could not see any bodies. Then at 1700 we saw 21 NVA soldiers with rifles and large packs moving north in a well-spaced column where two trails met on the southern side of Tan Phuoc 1. Again, I called in a fire mission, and this time we saw several large secondary explosions which we thought might be rockets or mortar shells they were carrying. Since the coverage was outstanding and we had such large secondary explosions, we reported ten enemy probable kills. An hour later we saw seven NVA soldiers wearing grey field uniforms, carrying packs, cartridge belts and AK-47 and SKS rifles, moving along a tree line near the main trail leading from An Bang (2) east to the Song Tinh Yen River. Using the artillery concentration we had fired an hour earlier, but adjusting it to take into account the new location, I called for a fire for effect, dispensing with the use of a marking or sensing round. Either by luck or skill, twenty-five rounds of 105 mm artillery shells tore into the enemy column killing all seven of them. For the rest of the day, the bodies of these dead NVA soldiers lay where they fell in the hot sun. No one approached the bodies out of fear that we would call in additional artillery fire on anyone attempting to retrieve them. During the night, I gathered the team together, and we harbored in thick vegetation 100 yards south of the OP site. Since I suspected the enemy would try to retrieve their dead comrades under the cover of darkness, I radioed the artillery battery at An Hoa and had them fire H and I rounds where the bodies were last seen. Every hour or so during the night we could hear these H and I rounds impact to our north, and we hoped any enemy body recovery teams would be killed while they worked.

The next day, shortly after sunrise, we saw two VC in black pajamas carrying large packs moving north in the area where we had killed the NVA soldiers the day before. Because there were many civilians in the area, we decided not to call a fire mission, and the VC moved out of sight. I could tell my team was not happy with my decision since we all knew the civilians in the Arizona Territory were considered VC sympathizers.

However, there was no way of knowing who was a VC, a VC sympathizer, or an innocent civilian. I reminded them that we were only authorized to call in supporting arms on people carrying weapons or packs, not people working in their fields. No one complained but I could tell they felt I had let the enemy escape out of some misguided compassion for innocent civilians. At the time, my decision was based more on my understanding of the orders given to me by Gen. Nickerson when I first arrived in country. He had stated firmly that I was not to abuse or kill unarmed civilians. Later, during my second tour of duty in South Vietnam, I came to realize that most of the people who lived under VC control were not VC or even VC sympathizers so it was counterproductive, as well as immoral, to call in artillery on unarmed peasants. The profligate usage of supporting arms does not win the hearts and minds of the people subjected to it.

Around noon that day, as LCpl. Slowick and I were scanning the valley with our binoculars, a Marine AO arrived and began to call in air strikes in support of the 7th Marines. While we watched the Marine F-4's drop their bombs along the advance of the infantry, we heard what sounded like brush breaking 100 yards below us. We were not sure what caused this sound, but we suspected it was the enemy climbing up the hill toward our position and having difficulty remaining silent. I had Slowick alert the other members of the team and have them move to our position where there were several small depressions in the ground similar to shallow foxholes. Within a minute or two, we were all in position listening to the brush crack and snap below us and pointing our rifles toward the sound of the enemy moving uphill toward us.

Suddenly the noise ceased, and after a minute or so we heard the distinctive report of an AK-47 round as it cracked over our heads. This was followed by several other single shots in our general direction. We all knew what the enemy was attempting to do. They were probing for us. They knew we were somewhere on the finger above them, but they did not want to advance further without knowing exactly where we were. The shots they fired were meant to flush us out or make us return fire revealing our position. We did not return fire but kept completely silent and immobile with our weapons at the ready. Then, as we prepared to beat back what we expected would be an attack on our position, we saw that the enemy had set fire to the brush below us and were using the brush fire to screen their movement and force us to move from our position. Within minutes, the smoke from the fire drifted uphill, and we could see a wall of flames only a few yards below us.

I was not sure whether the enemy really knew where we were, so I decided to risk a run for it. I thought our best option was to run in the direction of the LZ we had used on our patrol the previous week. I knew exactly where it was, and it had no terrain over-looking it. It also possessed several good fighting positions if we needed to engage the enemy in a firefight. Fortunately for us, the fire served to shield our movement both in terms of sound and sight. With LCpl. Russell walking point, the team moved northeast off the finger in the direction of our old LZ. We moved quickly, trying to keep ourselves shielded from the enemy by using the natural contour of the ridgeline and avoiding any open areas. Within an hour, we reached our old OP site and the LZ nearby. There we waited to see if the enemy had picked up our trail and followed us, but after a few hours it appeared that they had not been able to find us. I attributed this primarily to the fine work done by our rear point, LCpl. Slowick, who took the time to carefully cover our trail by folding brush back over where we had passed.

Around 1845 we heard several probing rounds of AK-47 rifle fire that seemed to come from a spot 200 meters northwest of us, so I called an artillery fire mission on that area but with unknown results. That night, our patrol harbored in the same harbor site we had used the previous week, only this time we kept half the patrol awake and on watch throughout the night. We did this because we sensed the enemy knew where we were, and we thought they might try to attack us in the dark. I lay awake most of the night and, despite the precarious position our patrol found itself in, I wondered at the beauty of the night sky, the dark mountains surrounding us, and the black and silver ribbon of the Song Tinh Yen River winding its way north into the lowlands. The night was beautiful and clear with large luminous stars standing out on a black velvet sky. There was even a cool wind that kept the mosquitoes at bay, a rare but welcome relief for us. Throughout the night, we could hear small-arms fire and mortars in the Arizona Territory north of us as the 7th Marines moved west and encountered small patrols of NVA soldiers. At times, ghostly flares lit up the night sky and cast eerie shadows across the paddies and tree lines below us. The thought struck me that war made us more aware of the beauty we found.

On the 17th we continued our observation of the terrain north of us. Three times, we spotted small groups of NVA soldiers maneuvering to avoid contact with the advancing infantry, tanks and amtracs of the 7th Marines. Each time we spotted the enemy, we called in artillery fire on them achieving varying results. At the end of this 105-hour patrol, we tallied up our score and found we had nine separate sightings of the enemy totaling 73 individual enemy soldiers with eight confirmed kills with artillery and 15 probable kills. Late in the day of the 17th, we were extracted without incident from the same LZ we had used the previous week (Team Killer Kane Patrol Report, 19 June 1967).

From 25 to 30 June, Killer Kane conducted a patrol that I described in a letter to my parents as "a dud." Because we had the mission of establishing an OP in support of Operation Calhoun in the Que Son Mountains and would be forced to stay in one location for the entire five days of the patrol, we were sent out "loaded for bear," as Maj. Welzant described it. Instead of wearing our normal light clothing on patrol, we were instructed to don flak jackets and steel helmets. In most respects, we looked just like an infantry outfit. We also took both teams, Killer Kane and Brisbane, which gave us a total strength of 17 men. My platoon Sgt., SSgt. Thompson, was the assistant patrol leader. We took a lot of extra firepower and equipment with us, including the experimental Stoner Light Machine Gun, an M-60 machine gun, an M-79 grenade launcher, and several Claymore mines.

We landed in a good LZ close to the summit of Nui Ba Hoa Mountain. After we landed, I knew this was a dangerous LZ to use because it was a natural bowl of high elephant grass dominated on all sides by high ground. If the enemy had chosen to occupy that high ground, our helicopters would have been sitting ducks for them. I had the patrol move off the LZ quickly and found a good place to hide where we waited for a half hour to see if we had been discovered. Once I was sure we were not being followed, I had our point man begin our climb up the hill to the summit. After an hour of climbing, we

The Que Son Valley.

established our OP on the summit, which consisted of brush and rocks but little shade from the sun. From the OP, we began to observe mountain trails to our north and the Que Son Valley to our south. Since we found several old, two- and four-man, enemy harbor sites, but no signs of recent activity during our climb to the summit, I sent in a report to Camp Reasoner with this information so they could relay it to the infantry. I wanted them to know that the high ground north of them was clear of the enemy, at least on the slopes of Nui Ba Hoa Mountain. Despite our having an excellent OP site and spotting several small groups of enemy soldiers during our stay on the mountain, the patrol was a dud because each time we called in an artillery fire mission we were denied clearance, and the enemy escaped.

We spent 120 hours on the OP and suffered greatly because of the heat and the absence of any water. Our thirst became so bad, I asked for a night parachute resupply of water, something unheard of in a recon unit. It was decided not to resupply us at night but to send helicopters to us during daylight hours. I knew this was highly dangerous since it would definitely be seen by everyone within miles of our OP, but I also knew I would soon have medical emergencies with heat exhaustion if we did not receive water soon. Helicopters were dispatched from Camp Reasoner late in the afternoon of the 28th with two packages of what we were told would be water cans attached to T-10 parachutes. We used a signal mirror, instead of a smoke grenade, to guide the pilots over our position; but when the parachutes were dropped from the helicopter, they drifted away from us and down into a ravine several hundred feet below.

SSgt. Thompson volunteered to take five men into the ravine to retrieve the water

East of the An Hoa Combat Base, overlooking the foothills and lakes north of the Que Son Mountains.

cans and haul them back up the hill to the OP. It took him nearly three hours to do this, and when he returned he was livid. Instead of water cans, the resupply packages contained boxes of C rations and ammunition. Not a single drop of water had been delivered! I radioed Camp Reasoner and asked why rations and ammo had been sent instead of the water I had requested. Their reply was, "You got what you requested."

With SSgt. Thompson gasping for air and fuming intensely by my side, I restrained myself and told the radio operator to put Maj. Welzant on the radio immediately. Maj. Welzant and I straightened things out, and two hours later just as it was getting dark, two more helicopters flew over our position. This time, they used poncho parachutes rigged by GySgt. Gabbert to deliver the precious load of water, and they all landed perfectly in the middle of our OP. Twenty plastic water containers filled with cool, refreshing water were nestled inside the netting attached to the poncho parachutes. As the helicopters passed back over us, I could see Gunny Gabbert leaning out of the helicopter waving to us. We all felt like cheering. When we returned to Camp Reasoner on 30 June, we all went to see the Gunny to thank him personally for taking charge of the parachute drop. There are few things in life that one can always count on, but we knew we could always count on Gunny Gabbert to take care of us whenever we needed him (Team Killer Kane Patrol Report, 30 June 1967).

Our next patrol was one of our most memorable and dangerous ones we ever made, and it was the first of several very exciting patrols into the infamous enemy base area called Happy Valley. For recon teams, there were two places in Quang Nam Province that

The infamous Happy Valley.

we knew we could always expect to find trouble: Charlie Ridge and Happy Valley. Most recon teams made contact with the enemy in these two places and the results were not always favorable for our teams. The NVA fiercely defended both places, and any Marine recon patrol could expect to encounter well-trained and very aggressive NVA anti-recon teams who were determined to destroy us. These specially trained, NVA anti-recon teams often had dogs with them, and they employed a sophisticated warning and communications system that employed drums and rifle shots to coordinate their movements. We would often joke about patrols in Happy Valley, saying it was not necessary to take any water or food, just ammunition, because you would not be on the ground long enough to get thirsty or hungry. Most patrols in Happy Valley ended with emergency extractions, and for this reason it was one of the least popular places the helicopter pilots of the 1st Marine Air Wing had to fly into.

Happy Valley was located north of Nui Son Ga Mountain, commonly referred to as Charlie Ridge by the Marines. At one time it had some small hill farms in it, but those had long been abandoned due to the war. Historically, it had been a refuge for political dissidents and bandits, but in 1967 it was a base area for NVA units and a terminus for one of the trails that diverged from the Ho Chi Minh Trail in Laos and headed due east toward Da Nang. In fact, the main east-west trail in the valley, which we called "The Yellow Brick Road," ran all the way to the Laotian border 30 miles to the west where it linked up with another trail that led north to the A Shau Valley in Thua Thien Province. A few Catu montagnard tribesmen lived in small villages on some of the mountain ridgelines of the valley, but most of its inhabitants were NVA and main force VC units who used the valley as a refuge and staging area for attacks on the Quang Nam lowlands ten miles to the east. The valley floor had many open areas but few LZs because these open areas were studded with decaying tree trunks that often reached heights of 30 feet or more. Old trails, dense jungle, thick hedgerows, overgrown paddy fields, and worn down paddy dikes could be found interspersed throughout the valley. The mountains to the east, south and west were steep and covered with high double and triple canopy jungle. The ridgelines were infested with large, blood-sucking leeches that lay in ambush along every trail, and the smell of rotting jungle vegetation hung in the air and clung to our clothing whenever we came in contact with the ground. Often the mountains and ravines were shrouded in the thick mist called "crachin" making it impossible for helicopters to operate, a situation the enemy could take advantage of when they decided to trap a recon patrol during bad weather. The nearest friendly units were many miles to the east and south, and most parts of the valley were outside the range of friendly artillery. In short, Happy Valley was a dangerous place, almost primeval in its dark, dank, and misty appearance. For some, it was a place to avoid at all costs.

When Maj. Welzant brought me into the S-3 office on 2 July to give me my patrol assignment, he told me that Killer Kane was going to be inserted into an area never patrolled before by any Marine unit, and it would be far from friendly lines and, more importantly, far from any artillery support. He pointed to a spot on the operations map

Patrolling along the stream in Happy Valley.

about halfway between Da Nang and the Laotian border. There were no other NFZs anywhere near the one that had our name on it. He told me that Division G-2 suspected that
there might be an enemy unit somewhere in the vicinity of Hills 537 and 372 deep inside
Happy Valley, but he did not tell me why the intelligence officers at division suspected
there was an enemy unit where we would be patrolling. I knew that when he was tight-
lipped about the source of intelligence on the enemy, it was usually because the information was gained from communications intercepts by Radio Battalion, a secretive Marine
unit that collected and decrypted enemy radio transmissions. Radio Battalion was a very
effective collector of actionable intelligence, and the enemy knew this because they often
relied on couriers instead of any electronic means for transmitting important messages.

Maj. Welzant told me my overflight was scheduled for later that day, and he gave
me the grid coordinates for several potential LZs to check out. He warned me to find
more than two zones and to make sure I patrolled along a route with ready access to one
of these LZs. I knew why he told me this. The probability of making contact was great,
and it would be essential for Killer Kane to find an LZ quickly in the event we needed an
emergency extraction. He also told me that it would take at least 30 minutes for a helicopter to reach us since we were to patrol so far west of Da Nang. The tone of his comments conveyed more than the facts. He and I both knew this patrol was not going to be
a cake walk.

My overflight did nothing to assuage my sense of foreboding. The flight west was
longer than most of our reconnaissance flights due to the distance. When we arrived over
our NFZ, I had difficulty finding any suitable LZs. The valley floor was shrouded in
crachin and, aside from a few slash-and-burn fields on the steep mountain slopes, there
were only a handful of
LZs that could accom-
modate one helicopter
safely. The paucity of
LZs meant the enemy
could afford to place
watch teams on these
few LZs. I noted each
LZ on my map and told
the pilot to head for
home. I did not want
to spend more than a
minute or two over the
NFZ since this would
attract the attention of
the enemy.

That evening after
chow, I wrote my patrol
order and told Sgt.
Pugh, my assistant
patrol leader, to assem-

**Corporal R. Garner, Killer Kane's radio operator, in Happy Val-
ley.**

ble the team early the next morning for the patrol order, rehearsal, and weapons testing. I also gave him a list of names for the patrol. Since I knew this was going to be a difficult and dangerous patrol, I wanted to have an all-star team of recon men with me. In addition to the very competent Sgt. Pugh, I had Garner and Williams as my radio operators, HN2 "Doc" Willis as my corpsman, Slowick and Glor as my front and rear point men respectively, and Bart Russell as my machine gunner. Bart would be taking the highly effective and lightweight Stoner light machine gun (LMG) with him since we all recognized this weapon was better suited for a recon patrol than the heavier and more cumbersome M-60 machine gun. These seven men were all highly professional and experienced recon men. I could count on them to think for themselves and act with decisiveness and resourcefulness. If we ran into trouble on this patrol, I knew I would have the best team of men available to respond to it.

Sgt. Pugh asked me if I had any special instructions for the logistics of the patrol. I told him to tell each man to carry an extra five magazines of ammunition for their rifles and to have Bart Russell carry 400 rounds of linked 5.56 ball ammunition for his Stoner light machine gun. I also told him to draw four fragmentation hand grenades per man, instead of the normal two. When I told Sgt. Pugh about the added ammunition requirements, the laconic native of Alabama knew immediately where the patrol was going. He simply looked at me with a wry smile on his face and, "We are headed for Happy Valley, aren't we Lieutenant?" I answered, "Yeah!" No more words were spoken between us. We both knew what a patrol in Happy Valley entailed.

On the 2nd of July, I issued the patrol order, and then we spent an hour going over our immediate action drills for meeting engagements, followed by several iterations of our counter-ambush drill. After the drills, we test-fired our weapons to make sure they were all in working order, and I checked each man's gas mask and filter to make sure they were serviceable. Sgt. Pugh and I inspected all of the equipment we would be taking with us, and then we broke up and went back to our hootches to clean our weapons, load our magazines, and pack our rucksacks.

The next morning, I attended the briefing in the S-3 shop for all the pilots who would be inserting teams that day. Because we would be going into Happy Valley, it was decided we would be the last team to be inserted that day. The rationale for this did nothing to inspire our confidence. Maj. Welzant and the pilots all agreed that the prospect for an emergency extraction was greatest in Happy Valley, and it was not uncommon for helicopters to take hits going in or coming out of that infamous place. One of the pilots came up to me after the briefing and said, "Lieutenant, I wouldn't do your job for all the money in the world." I gave him a weak smile and left the S-3 shop trying to forget his comment. I walked down to where my team was assembled in a small open hut off the heli-pad and told them to go back to their hootch since we would be the last team inserted that day. Around noon, I expected to get the call to assemble on the heli-pad for insertion but Lt. St. Claire came into my hootch and told me the weather in Happy Valley was so bad we might have to cancel the insertion for the day. Evidently, the weather cleared enough to try an insert later on because we launched from LZ Finch at 1715 and headed west toward the Annamite Mountains into the dark, gray rain clouds that hovered over Happy Valley.

We flew west for over 30 minutes. I could see that the pilot was guiding on the stream in Happy Valley as it snaked its way west, deeper and deeper into the valley toward Laos. Much of the terrain was shrouded in mist and rain, making it difficult to use my map for dead reckoning. However, every once in a while I could catch sight of a key terrain feature beneath the cloud cover. I huddled with the pilots in the cockpit, hunched over in between them as the three of us tried to find the LZs I had spotted on my overflight. Just when I thought we would not be able to find one of the LZs, the co-pilot pointed to his right, and I confirmed that it was the primary LZ I had chosen and marked on my map the previous day. It appeared to be a small cultivated field on top of a ridgeline. We began a circular dive into the zone but, just as we reached a height of 100 feet above it, we began to take ground fire, and the pilots pulled the helicopter up abruptly and gained altitude. We circled in the clouds as we searched for one of my alternate LZs. We found one about 1,000 meters away from the one where we had received ground fire, and the pilot again began to descend. Just as we were about to land in what looked like a small hill farm, we received ground fire again.

The pilots, who were looking rather anxious by this time, asked me if I wanted to abort the mission and return to Camp Reasoner. For some odd reason, certainly not based upon good logic, I said I wanted to continue looking for a LZ somewhere in the vicinity of our NFZ. I could tell that the pilots were not very keen on this suggestion, but they started to circle the valley again looking for another LZ. I strained my eyes trying to penetrate the intermittent clouds and crachin to see if there were any more suitable LZs below us. After a few minutes, the pilot beckoned to a small opening on the top of a ridgeline, and I gave him the "thumbs up" signal indicating we should land there. I went back to my seat in the helicopter's cabin and gave the hand signal to the team that we were going in.

Our new LZ was not even in our NFZ, and I had no idea what the grid coordinates were for this LZ. But I knew it was important to get into this area, so it would have to do. I would locate it on the map after I was on the ground.

I could feel the temperature in the cabin change as we descended. It went from cool to hot in a matter of seconds. Just as we settled into the LZ and exited the helicopter we received fire from three different directions. The crew chief motioned to us to return to the helicopter, but I waved him off and told the pilot on our radio to leave. While the decision I made to stay on the ground after taking fire might sound like an unwise one, I knew we had made two previous landing attempts, which we referred to as "dummy inserts," which I hoped had confused the enemy as to which LZ we had actually used. With head-high elephant grass, it was impossible for the enemy to see whether or not we had actually left the helicopter, and I hoped this would make it possible for us to escape detection.

The Huey gunships made several strafing runs on the three locations that had fired on us and then they and the insert helicopters gained altitude and flew into the clouds. As the sound of their rotor blades faded into the distance, our team huddled in the tall grass straining our ears for any sign that the enemy was near. It wasn't long before we heard voices in the valley 50 to 100 meters below us. I had the team remain on the edge of the LZ waiting to see if the voices we had heard came any closer, but the voices faded and then disappeared after an hour of anxious waiting. As night fell, we heard several single rifle shots in the valley to our west. We all knew the enemy used these signal shots to warn others that a Marine recon team had been inserted nearby. A light rain fell, and the mist shrouded us as we formed a small defensive circle on the south side of the LZ. We did not take our equipment off or even take a sip of water that night for fear of making a noise that would give our position away. I set up a 50 percent watch, but few of us slept more than an hour or two that night due to the stress and the constant rain.

On the morning of the 4th of July, we ate some cold food, reapplied our camouflage face paint that had been washed away in the rain, and removed the leeches that had found their way onto our bodies during the night despite the saturation of our clothing with insect repellent. While this was going on, I looked at my map to see if I could tell where we were. I used my compass to take a few back azimuths from prominent terrain features nearby, and soon I determined that we were on a southern finger of Hill 582, also known as Kon Chay Mountain, and just 100 meters from its summit. I radioed a POSREP to the radio relay station on Ba Na Mountain for retransmission to Camp Reasoner, and then we began our patrol. We moved off the southern edge of the LZ into some dense jungle and proceeded slowly until we came upon a well-used trail that ran along the valley floor: the much feared "Yellow Brick Road" that served the NVA as their primary infiltration route into Quang Nam Province. The trail had harbor sites on both sides of it, handrails made of bamboo, and steps cut into the parts that were steep and difficult to walk on. We moved along the trail for 400 meters in a southwesterly direction. The large number of Ho Chi Minh sandal tracks on this trail told us it had been used extensively and recently, so I decided it was too dangerous to continue using it. We needed to find an OP somewhere off the trail where we could safely observe it.

Just as we were about to leave the trail, our point man, LCpl. Slowick, turned and put his hand in front of his face giving us the signal that he had observed the enemy to his front. He then turned, while LCpl. Russell moved forward and took up a firing position to Slowick's right. Both men raised their weapons and pointed them down the trail. I was the third man in our column and just about to move forward when I saw what they had seen. There moving toward us, no more than 20 yards away, was an NVA soldier. He was dressed in the distinctive light-green field uniform of the NVA, and he was carrying an AK-47. Close behind him were two more NVA soldiers. Because we were not moving and were wearing camouflage uniforms and face paint, they did not see us until it was too late. Slowick and Russell opened fire almost simultaneously, and the lead NVA soldier fell backward as if he had been jerked back by some invisible rope attached to his body. He lay in the trail riddled with bullets. His two companions ran into the bush as Slowick, Russell and I fired after them. Since we were not sure whether or not we had hit the other two NVA soldiers and whether or not there were more behind these three, I decided not to search the body of the enemy soldier we had just killed. Instead, I had Slowick, Russell and Pugh throw CS gas grenades down the trail while we moved back up the way we came. It was still early morning, which we knew would give the NVA plenty of time to find us and attack unless we hid ourselves quickly. Since I did not know of any good LZs nearby, I decided it would be best if we hid somewhere in close proximity to our insertion zone. If the enemy found us, we would be able to fight our way to that zone for an emergency extraction. With this in mind, I had the patrol return to the place on the trail where we had entered it that morning. There we left the trail and moved north for 50 meters before stopping in an area of very thick brush and bamboo. We waited in our hide for four hours, not moving a muscle, and straining our ears for any indication that the NVA were searching for us.

We were beginning to think we had lost the NVA because we heard nothing but the normal sounds of the jungle. We were very tense and tired as we gripped our weapons and faced outboard in a tight circle, but as the hours passed we began to think it might be safe to continue patrolling. Then at 1300, in the heat of the day, we heard voices on the trail coming from the southwest. The voices seemed to pass the place where we had left the trail. However, after a few minutes, our worst fears were realized when we heard brush breaking in the direction of the trail. We knew it was the enemy, and they had found where we had left the trail. My rear point, PFC Glor, was an expert at covering our tracks, but I suspected he had missed a footprint or some other indication of our presence and that this had attracted the attention of the NVA.

The closest man to the enemy was LCpl. Russell, and he slowly and quietly placed himself in a good sitting position, raised his Stoner machine gun to his shoulder, and waited. The rest of us gripped our weapons and readied ourselves for the inevitable confrontation that awaited us. We continued to hear the brush breaking near the trail, and then we saw the brush slowly part only a few yards away. As the brush parted, we saw an NVA soldier and his AK-47 rifle pointing right at us, his eyes searching in front of him with a grim look on his face.

Unfortunately for him, he did not see us as soon as we saw him, and he paid for it with his life. LCpl. Russell fired a five-round burst with his Stoner light machine gun, and the NVA soldier dropped as if his legs had been cut out from under him. There was a brief silence, and then we heard the crack of AK-47 rounds going over our heads. From where I was, I could not see any other NVA soldiers, but LCpl. Russell said he saw several enemy soldiers behind the one he killed. He thought he had hit a second one with the same burst he used to kill the one who peered into our position. A short firefight ensued, but the enemy must have been below us since their fire passed harmlessly over our heads. Either they gave up once they saw they were taking casualties, or they did not want to maneuver against us while Russell had a machine gun trained in their direction. For whatever reason, they stopped shooting and began to move away from us toward the trail. I asked LCpl. Russell how many NVA he had seen, and he replied that he had seen three, but he suspected there were at least four more behind these. Russell wanted to crawl out to the dead NVA soldier to retrieve his weapon and any documents he might be carrying, but I did not want to risk a body search when I knew there were several well-armed NVA soldiers nearby. I told Russell to forget the search and, instead, told him we needed to get to an extract LZ as soon as possible since our presence was known to the enemy. They would probably attempt to ambush us soon if we continued on our patrol. I had Killer Kane move back toward our insert LZ and found a good place to hide in high elephant grass about 100 meters west of the extract LZ. We all expected the enemy to hit us again before dark, but the rest of the afternoon passed without incident, although we did hear signal drums and rifle shots to our east and west. I radioed for an emergency extraction, but the relay station on Ba Na Mountain told us we would have to wait until morning. As darkness fell, the weather cleared, and we could see a luminous, white moon above us in the wine-dark sky. I hoped the weather would hold since I knew rain and crachin could make it impossible for the extract helicopters to find us or land. All we could do now was set a 50 percent watch and wait until morning. During the night, we heard voices to our west, north and east, along with several distant rifle shots which we guessed were either signal shots or an enemy attempt to probe for our location. We felt very alone and very vulnerable.

Just before dawn the next morning, I had the entire team "stand to" just in case the enemy chose to attack us at dawn. Dawn came and nothing happened. We received a radio message from Ba Na Mountain that the extraction helicopters would be lifting off from Camp Reasoner soon and to expect them over our position in about an hour. We all felt a sense of relief knowing that we had solid communications with our relay station and the extract helicopters were only an hour away. As it turned out, our sense of relief was short-lived.

Since we had not eaten much food since we had been inserted, I had half the team eat cold C rations while the other half stood watch with their weapons in their hands. The first group was just finishing breakfast when Sgt. Pugh quietly tapped me and LCpl. Russell on the shoulder and held his hand in front of his face to indicate he had seen the enemy. Actually, he had heard the enemy, not seen him. He held up his finger to his ear and motioned to everyone in the team to listen. Very carefully, Cpl. Williams and LCpl. Garner put down their C ration cans and leaned over to pick up their rifles. As they did so, I heard what Sgt. Pugh had heard. It was the distinctive sound of bamboo breaking, a clear indication that someone or something was moving up the hill toward us. We heard it again and again, only it was getting closer. Every second or so, we heard the "crack, crack, crack" of brush and bamboo breaking. Then we heard something that removed all doubt: the sound of metal on metal, probably a rifle striking a canteen. Following this, we heard a Vietnamese voice coming from the same direction as the metallic sound. It was now obvious that the source of these sounds was only a few yards below us on the northwestern side of the hill. Even more disconcerting, we realized that the sound of breaking brush was now coming from two sides of the hill, from the northwest and the east. It appeared that we were surrounded, that the enemy knew where we were, and that they were coming to get us.

I expected that contact would be made to our west or east, but I was wrong. Our corpsman, Doc Willis, who always took an M-14 rifle with a rifle grenade launcher attached to it on patrol, was covering our position to the south in the direction of the trail where we had made contact the previous day. I saw him move out of the corner of my eye, and as he did I glanced in front of him. Then I saw what he saw: an NVA soldier standing directly in front of him peering through the tall elephant grass. The enemy soldier was only a few yards from Doc Willis, but just as he made eye contact with him, Doc fired his M-14 rifle at point-blank range, dropping the enemy soldier with a round in the middle of his chest. Doc then emptied his magazine into the grass in front of him while the rest of us opened up on the other NVA moving at us from the west and the east. We were surrounded, and the enemy was aggressively firing at us. We had never encountered this kind of aggressive behavior before and at such close range. Fortunately for us, LCpl. Russell was able to use his Stoner light machine gun to great effect, firing his entire 100-round box magazine at the enemy in seconds and literally cutting down the elephant grass in front of him in a 180-degree arc. We could hear the moaning of several NVA soldiers we had hit as we continued to fire magazine after magazine in an attempt to beat back their attack. As the enemy fire began to slacken, two Chinese hand grenades sailed through the air and landed in front of Cpl. Williams and LCpl. Russell. I saw one of the NVA soldiers who threw a grenade, and I shot him in his mid-section from a range of only ten yards. He fell back into a four-foot-deep ravine. For a second or two, nothing happened as both Williams and Russell continued to fire at the enemy, but then I heard the explosions and saw that both men were bleeding. With a firefight going on, we could not afford to tend to the medical needs of these two Marines, so I was relieved when both men shook off the effects of the grenades and continued to fight. Bleeding, cursing, and in pain, they stayed in the fight.

Then something happened that lifted our spirits and dispelled any fear we felt. Someone, I don't know who, started to laugh out loud and taunt the NVA. Soon, all of us were laughing and yelling at the enemy to come and get us. I took the four grenades I had brought with me and began to throw them in the direction of the moaning we had heard. Others followed suit and soon we had hurled most of our grenades. I am not sure whether it was the heavy volume of fire we poured into the enemy, or the laughing, or the grenades, but whatever it was, the enemy stopped firing and moved away from us. We had definitely hurt them badly because we could see at least five dead NVA soldiers lying in the grass in front of us.

I took a quick inventory of the ammunition and grenades we had left. I realized we had been rather profligate in the use of these two items because we only had three magazines left per man and only four hand grenades left for the entire team. Fortunately, Sgt. Pugh still had twelve 40 mm grenades left for his M-79. Regardless, I knew we would probably run out of ammunition if the enemy returned for a second try at overrunning us.

LCpl. Garner got on his PRC-25 radio and informed Ba Na that we were in contact and that we needed an emergency extraction as soon as possible. Fortunately for us, an AO was in the air nearby and Ba Na directed him to our location where he called in several fixed-wing air strikes on the hills surrounding our position. Garner did an excellent job of directing the AO and the air strikes, even standing up to use a signal mirror to signal to the AO where our position was. While the Marine F-4s were dropping napalm and 500-pound bombs on the enemy, Marine Huey gunships came on station and soon they were using their machine guns and rockets on the enemy. As I saw the pin-point accuracy of the Marine aircraft deliver their deadly loads and saw how low they flew between the hills only a few hundred feet above our heads, I thanked God for Marine aviation. Marine pilots are trained as infantry, just like all Marines, so they understand how important close air support is to the Marines on the ground, and this was reflected in their willingness to fly very low in order to ensure their bombs fell accurately. Without their timely arrival and their accurate bombing, our team probably would have been wiped out when the enemy regrouped and launched another attack.

LCpl. Garner informed me that the extract helicopters were only a few minutes away, so I had the team assemble and move to the LZ 50 meters to our east. When we arrived at the LZ, a few rounds snapped above our heads, indicating the enemy had seen us and knew we were waiting for our helicopters to pick us up. We could see the helicopters flying down the valley, such a welcome sight! I took the radio from Garner and told the pilots that I was marking the zone with smoke, but to be careful since we had recently taken fire from the east very close to the LZ. The pilot told me to "pop smoke" and I threw a purple smoke grenade into the middle of the LZ. As the extract bird came into the LZ to land, we noticed it was on a direct heading toward us which meant we would have to run around to the back of the helicopter through the high elephant grass to board it, a situation that would keep the helicopter in the LZ longer than normal and expose it to enemy ground fire. I knew this would be bad news with the enemy nearby, but it was too late to change the pilot's approach. I was always the last man to board a helicopter since I had to be certain we did not leave anyone behind, and this extract was no exception. The team labored through the waist-high grass to the rear of the helicopter with LCpl. Slowick leading the way. Sgt. Pugh was the next to last man right in front of me. Just as we came abreast of the helicopter, we both saw an NVA soldier stand up to our right and begin firing at the helicopter. Sgt. Pugh and I simultaneously fired on the NVA soldier and saw him fall. The door gunner of the CH-46 helicopter also saw the enemy soldier and he fired his .50-caliber machine gun at him, nearly hitting Sgt. Pugh and me. We continued to run to the rear of the CH-46, and I signaled to the crew chief that everyone was aboard. We lifted off with the door gunner and most of Killer Kane firing their weapons at the enemy as we gained altitude. We later found out that the extract helicopter took several hits, and the crew chief pointed to some pink hydraulic fluid running down the bulkhead of the chopper where the lines had been cut by enemy small-arms fire. When I looked into the cockpit, I could see little red lights flashing on the pilot's console, and I said a prayer that those lights did not mean we were going to crash (Team Killer Kane Patrol Report, 5 July 1967).

On the way back to Camp Reasoner, we stopped at Charlie Med to drop off LCpl. Russell and Cpl. Williams so they could have their wounds treated. Both had metal grenade fragments in them. Bart Russell had a superficial wound to his face, but Williams had several pieces of shrapnel in his back which needed to be taken out by a surgeon.

This patrol was the most dangerous one we had been on since I joined the platoon, and we were lucky we were not overrun. Several things helped us survive this patrol. One was the decision to move to a known LZ after making our initial contact with the enemy. Another was our camouflage uniforms and face paint, which allowed us to see the enemy before they could see us and, thus, allow us to initiate the contact, giving us the element of surprise. And finally, the rapid arrival of Marine close air support gave our patrol a decisive advantage over the NVA attacking us. Without that air support, we would not have survived another determined attack by the enemy.

What most impressed me about my team on this patrol was not the cool professionalism they showed while conducting the patrol or the effective way they beat off the enemy attack but the way they laughed at the enemy in the face of death. These were extraordinary men, and I felt such a strong sense of pride in them and affection for them that I thanked

God in my prayers every night during 1967 for the privilege of living among them and helping them as we went about our dangerous work. The word hero is often used loosely to describe celebrities and sports figures, but the men of Killer Kane were truly heroes. These were ordinary American men, but they did extraordinary things for their country and for each other. How they performed their duty could mean the difference between life and death for them and their friends. They were the finest men I have ever known.

When Killer Kane returned from this patrol, SSgt. John Cole told me that our entire patrol had been recommended for the Vietnamese Cross of Gallantry for the patrol near Hiep Duc where we took on 100 NVA. I was pleased to see that after five months of patrols we were to receive some official recognition for the results we had achieved, but this news also angered me for it told me the South Vietnamese valued our performance more than the U.S. Marine Corps did. This point gnawed at me all day until I finally went to see Capt. Dixon to discuss it with him. I told him that no one in our company had been given a personal decoration for a specific act of heroism since I had joined the company in February. I went on to tell him that I had questioned this before with Maj. Lowrey, and he had told me that everyone would receive an "end of tour" award which would include all the singular acts of heroism that an individual performed during his entire year with the company. Capt. Dixon said he was unaware of this policy, and it did not sound like a good policy to him. He promised he would take it up with Maj. Lowrey, the acting CO of the battalion, at their next staff meeting. I told him I wanted to submit recommendations for the Silver Star medal for LCpl. Russell and LCpl. Garner since they had performed so bravely and effectively on the last patrol in Happy Valley. He told me to go ahead and get written statements from the other members of the patrol and write a draft award recommendation for both men. If Maj. Lowrey had no objection, then I was to go ahead and submit the package to SSgt. Cole to be typed up. If not, he would make sure the statements were retained for the "end of tour" awards for these men. He came back to me the next day and told me that he was going to wait a few weeks until Maj. Lowrey rotated back to the U.S., and then he intended to submit my award recommendations. I could tell from his words that the policy I had told him about was still in effect and would not change until we had a new battalion commander. Although he did not say it, I could also tell he did not approve of the policy, but he was not in a position yet to change it.

Although we did not know it at the time, a momentous event occurred while we were on our patrol in Happy Valley. Sometime during the first week of July, the commander of all the communist forces in the COSVN area of South Vietnam, Gen. Nguyen Chi Thanh, had died. Later, we would hear several reasons for his demise. One was he had died of a heart attack or cancer in Hanoi, while another attributed his death to a B-52 strike on the COSVN Headquarters in either Cambodia or Tay Ninh Province in South Vietnam. His death was a major loss to the communist cause since he was a southern communist and knew the situation in the south far better than the Lao Dong leadership in Hanoi. More importantly, he was a keen advocate of a large-scale offensive strategy, and his ideas would be played out with dramatic consequences when the communists launched their Tet offensive in February, 1968.

On 7 July, Maj. Welzant told me that Killer Kane should be ready in full field gear and face paint for a "dog and pony" demonstration followed by an interview with two staff members from the Senate Armed Services Preparedness Committee who were on a fact-finding visit to South Vietnam. I told Killer Kane to get their gear ready and to report to the S-3 shop at 1400 for the demonstration. I could tell this was not what most of the men would consider the best use of their time, but they understood how important it was to provide accurate information to our elected officials, so they did exactly as I told them without any outward sign of disappointment. After our demonstration, the Senate staffers asked us questions about what we did, what we thought of the enemy situation, and how we felt about the conduct of the war. We answered their questions to the best of our ability and the answers must have been satisfactory because after they left Maj. Welzant told me we had done a great job.

Little did I know that this first demonstration would become a regular occurrence for Killer Kane. For the next five months just about every visiting dignitary to the 1st Marine Division would visit us and talk to Killer Kane. This included Admiral Hyland, the Commander of the U.S. Navy's 7th Fleet; Hanson Baldwin, the famous *New York Times* military affairs reporter, and General of the Army Omar Bradley and his wife. Gen. Bradley asked several good questions of me about what we did when we encountered the enemy, but to my great chagrin he also asked a question that I was unable to answer correctly. He wanted to know the muzzle velocity of the M-16s we carried, and I gave him the chamber pressure by mistake. He immediately knew I was wrong, but I was able to correct myself after a few seconds of embarrassing silence. He was old and infirm, but he was very sharp and asked the most probing questions of any visitor concerning how the war was progressing. He even asked us if the anti-war movement in the U.S. was having any effect on morale. I told him that we had read about the anti-war movement in *Stars and Stripes* and some of us had heard about it in letters from home, but we really did not give it much thought. This was true because we were not very interested in political developments in the United States. We were interested in doing our job and surviving. These two tasks dominated our lives, not the demonstrations and protests in America. We also did not have access to American television or newspapers unless they were sent from home. In a way, we were insulated from the negative reporting on the war and the anti-war movement in the U.S. My answer to Gen. Bradley would have been different if he had asked me this question after my first tour of duty in South Vietnam had ended. When Mrs. Bradley returned to the U.S. she wrote a very warm and thoughtful letter to my mother, informing her that she and Gen. Bradley had visited with me and that I was well. My mother cherished that letter and kept it among her prized personal items until the day she died.

While we were resting and preparing for our next patrol, I made another trip to Phuoc Ly hamlet where our MEDCAP team and a counter-intelligence team (CIT) worked together to obtain photos of the families in the hamlet. We were able to take photos of 37 out of the 44 families living in the hamlet on this trip, and we also received some valuable intelligence from the hamlet chief. He told us "people from insecure areas" had been passing through Phuoc Ly recently to work on the rock quarry on Hill 387. This was only a mile from the division headquarters. He told us he had heard that these people were making drawings of the defenses around the division's perimeter. We gave this information to the division G-2, and we later learned the Vietnamese National Police and local Popular Forces (PF) arrested several people at the rock quarry based upon the information given to us by the Phuoc Ly hamlet chief.

On 8 July, Maj. Welzant called me into the S-3 shop and told me Killer Kane was going out again into Happy Valley, only this time we were going even farther than we had on our previous patrol. This patrol would take us to the very end of the valley, a distance only seven miles from the Laotian border. We were to conduct "a clandestine reconnaissance" to detect "possible enemy troop movement or possible arms infiltration through Happy Valley. This patrol was to pay special attention to the trails that paralleled the Tam Talou Tributary and the trail network that ran between Hill 678 and Hill 800. Again, we would be patrolling in an area far from friendly lines and far outside the range of friendly artillery. I asked him if we had any old patrol orders for this area, and he only laughed and said no Marine had ever set foot within miles of where we were going. This did not make me feel very confident about the prospects for Killer Kane on this patrol, but I knew they would not be sending us on such a mission unless they had a good reason to do so. Given the difficulties we had just encountered on our last patrol, I wondered about our ability to conduct anything like a "clandestine" patrol in Happy Valley.

Since this patrol was going to be a truly "deep reconnaissance" patrol, I decided Killer Kane would only take a small number of men since it was a lot easier for a small patrol to hide than a large one. I selected five men to go with me: Pugh, Garner, Slowick, Glor, and Willis. I had wanted to take Russell and Williams with me, but both were recovering from their wounds and unavailable. Sgt. Pugh and I waited all day for an overflight but bad weather in Happy Valley made this impossible. Instead, we worked together on my patrol order using our maps and some aerial photos I obtained from the division G-2.

We started by making a thorough map study of the patrol's NFZ. We marked the LZs Maj. Welzant had told us were in our area and plotted our proposed patrol route. We both noted that there were no signs of habitation anywhere within 20 miles of this mountainous region we were to patrol in. We also knew a flight from LZ Finch at Camp Reasoner to our projected insertion zone would take nearly 45 minutes. If we got into trouble, it would take a long time for anyone to come to our rescue. I was concerned that we would not be able to take an overflight since I knew from previous experience it was impossible to locate good LZs from just a map study. We called these insertions where we had not benefited from an overflight "blind drops," and we tried to avoid them at all costs since such insertions often meant we would be lost for days.

We sat on the back porch of my hootch and spent an hour or two on my patrol order. I told Sgt. Pugh that since our patrol would only consist of six men, we would have to choose the equipment and ammunition we would be taking with us with great care. We needed to take what we needed, not what we wanted, since too much extra weight would put us at a disadvantage if we wanted to move silently and quickly in steep terrain. We both feared that if we made contact with the enemy that far from base, we would be overrun before help could arrive. Remaining as covert as possible would be our best strategy for survival.

Since the patrol was in Happy Valley we decided to take all the ammunition we could safely carry. With this in mind, I had each man take 400 rounds of ammunition and four M-26 hand grenades. We also decided to take two PRC-25 radios and a small RT-10 survival radio so that 50 percent of the patrol would be capable of contacting the radio relay site on Ba Na Mountain. We dispensed with the 7 × 50 binoculars since we did not see much opportunity for long-range observation in such dense jungle terrain. We did not take a demolition kit or any Claymore mines since they added a lot of weight, and we did not think we would have any use for them on this patrol. We told each man to take six canteens of water and only two "heavy" C ration cans in their pack to last us for four days. I took two smoke grenades and so did each of the radio operators. We would need these smoke grenades to mark our position for any fixed wing sent to support us and to mark our extract LZ. I finally instructed Sgt. Pugh to have each man take a map with him and a survival kit since we knew we might find it necessary to "escape and evade" (E&E) back to friendly lines. Operating so far west meant any E & E would take several days of hard travel through mountainous jungle before we would reach the safety of friendly lines.

At dawn on the morning of the 10th of July, Killer Kane launched out of LZ Finch and began its long journey west into the Annamite Mountains. Our six-man patrol was in one CH-46 while another accompanied us as the "chase" bird. This second helicopter would be used to extract us if we were shot down during the insertion. An escort package of two Huey gunships flew ahead to find the insertion LZ and check out the area for any enemy activity. In addition, Maj. Welzant had an AO and two fixed-wing aircraft on station a few miles to the south of our insertion LZ in the event we needed them.

Unlike the weather on our previous patrol in Happy Valley, the crachin was hugging the upper slopes of the mountains, leaving most of the valley floor clear and bright with sunshine. Our pilots followed the stream that ran the length of Happy Valley due west. We climbed higher and higher as we flew deeper into the Annamite Mountains until we could see the Hueys circling in the distance. The crew chief told me they wanted to make a fast insertion because the Hueys had taken ground fire near our LZ. I wanted to confirm the insertion LZ with the pilots so I walked up to the cockpit and stood between the pilots trying to see the LZ they had picked out, but they motioned me to prepare to land, so I went back to my seat and had everyone prepare for insertion. As we descended, I knew immediately that we were not landing in the LZ I had picked out from my map study the day before. That LZ was on a finger on the north side of the valley, but we were landing in a small LZ on the valley floor 500 meters south of Hill 594 only a few meters from the stream that ran through the valley and emptied into the A Vuong River to the west. As we approached the LZ, two enemy soldiers dressed in camouflage uniforms fired approximately ten rounds at our helicopter. I did not see these enemy soldiers, but I heard the distinctive sound their AK-47 rifle fire made. Doc Willis and LCpl. Glor in the rear of the helicopter were the only men to see the enemy soldiers firing at our chopper.

As the helicopter settled into the elephant grass of the LZ and the rear ramp lowered, we exited the helicopter and moved quickly out onto the LZ and into the jungle canopy on the north side of the narrow valley. After the helicopter lifted off, we heard it take smallarms fire from the high ground 200 meters to our south. We gave the pilots the "all secure" over the radio, and soon they departed for Da Nang Airbase, leaving us to listen silently for the enemy. I knew an LZ was a very dangerous place to be if there were enemy in the area, so I moved the team deeper into the canopy and up a steep hill where we hid for 30 minutes listening to see if the enemy was following us.

We did not hear anything other than the normal sounds of the jungle, so we proceeded to climb up the steep slope in a northerly direction. I wanted to get to some high ground so I could take a resection with my compass and establish our location. I radioed Ba Na relay station and asked them to contact the insert birds to find out the grid coordinates they had landed us in and then relay this information in code back to us. I had no idea where we were and this was a situation I had never been in before. I could not accurately report on the enemy if I did not know my own location, and I could not direct air strikes if we got into trouble. I thought my best bet was either to find an open spot in the canopy for my resection or climb a tree to get a back azimuth off one of the prominent hills nearby. All I knew for sure was Killer Kane was miles from friendly lines and somewhere in the far west of Quang Nam Province.

We spent the morning slowly climbing higher and taking 20-minute breaks every 30 minutes to rest and listen to see if we were being followed. Around 1300, we heard Vietnamese voices. It appeared that there were two groups of ten or more Vietnamese talking to each other in loud voices below us and to the west. We froze for a few minutes and then continued up a finger until we came upon a trail. It did not look like it had been used recently but it had handrails and steps cut into it, so we were very careful as we turned onto it. We had gone only a few yards when Cpl. Slowick, our point man, stopped and picked up several 7.52 mm Russian rimmed rifle cartridge casings. I looked at them, and it was evident from their bright, clean condition that they had been fired recently. We immediately thought that these rounds had been fired at our insertion helicopters and that the people who fired those shots must be close by.

We again heard Vietnamese voices below us, so we continued to move north on the trail. Using a trail is dangerous but not as dangerous as moving through thick undergrowth near a trail when the enemy is looking for you. It was a risk we had to take unless we wanted to get into a firefight with an enemy force that clearly outnumbered us. We did not have radio contact with Ba Na. We were far from any friendly support, and we had an enemy force following us. Given the constraints, movement on the trail was our best option.

We moved 100 yards on the trail until we came upon a sight that truly took our breath away. At the top of the ridgeline, we found a fence made of bamboo, a large signal drum, a well-made bunker, and a huge flat area that measured 300 feet by 400 feet on the top of a hill completely hidden under jungle canopy 100 feet high. Inside this area was a well-constructed, fortified base camp. On the camp's perimeter were large punji stake "gardens" and a dozen bunkers flush with the ground that had logs for overhead cover and logs on the floor to keep an occupant's feet dry. At each end of the fortified village was a guard tower on ten-foot-high stilts. I counted eight well-constructed huts that were big enough to house a squad of enemy soldiers. In addition to the huts, there was a large animal pen with pigs in it, a hut used as a kitchen with several large cooking pots and urns visible beside it, a raised stage with a roof over it, and a very large, two-story building made of finished lumber, bamboo, and thatch with a balcony on one side of the second floor. The size and sophistication of this camp shocked us. We had never encountered anything like this before, and we hardly expected to find such a camp in the Annamite Mountains so far from any village or hamlet.

We did not see anyone in the camp. It appeared completely deserted. We thought this was very strange although we suspected the people who lived here were aware of our presence and were only waiting for us to show ourselves so they could attack us. The entire scene was extremely eerie and bizarre. This huge jungle complex could easily serve as a barracks for 150 men or more. I was beginning to panic since I did not want to proceed further and risk giving ourselves away to anyone hiding in the base camp, but I also knew the enemy was following us and would soon come up behind us if we did not move. My options did not look good.

I could tell by the expression on the faces of my companions that they expected me to make a decision quickly, so I told everyone to get on line and cross over the ridgeline and through the camp to the other side. By doing this, we minimized the time of our exposure and reduced the chance that we would be observed and fired upon. We stepped over a low fence made of bamboo and then walked through the camp to the other side, expecting at any moment to hear a warning being given by some sentry or getting shot at. To our surprise and relief, we made it across the camp without incident and moved down the other side of the hill a few yards, half expecting the worst. We looked back into the camp and found that we were lying right in front of a large cave or bunker built into the side of the hill just below the perimeter fence. We also noted that there was a large wooden sign in the middle of the camp in front of the stage. The sign was written in Vietnamese, which told us that this was certainly no Montagnard village because they did not have a written language. Sgt. Pugh copied down the writing on the sign, and later we gave this to the division G-2 for translation.

As we lay there on the north side of the camp, we again heard voices that sounded as if they were coming toward the base camp from the western edge of the camp near the sentry tower. I decided it was too dangerous to remain near this camp, so I had LCpl. Slowick take the patrol down the slope of the hill 200 meters while LCpl. Glor carefully, quietly, and slowly covered our trail. Glor's job was critical. If the enemy picked up our trail while we were hours away from rescue and without supporting arms or reliable radio communications, we faced almost certain death.

When we reached a location that was very thick with undergrowth, I had the patrol stop and set up a 360-degree defense. We remained there for the next two days, barely breathing in fear of being discovered. We continued to hear voices above us but no one came after us. It is difficult for anyone who has never been in such a situation to understand how stressful and fearful hiding like this can be. Spending days on the side of a mountain while your enemy is living and working just 200 yards away is about as stressful a situation as one can imagine. We were so fearful we literally did not move for hours at a time and then only to slowly take out a canteen to drink some water. We remained on alert all day long, and half of us were on alert all night long, straining our ears for the telltale sound of brush breaking near us.

LCpl. Garner was afraid to whisper even into the radio, but fortunately for us the radio relay site on Ba Na Mountain was able for the first time to communicate with us.

Although we could not speak on the radio, we were able to send messages to them using the handset to signal our condition. For instance, Ba Na would ask us, "If you are all secure, click your handset three distinct times." LCpl. Garner would simply depress his handset noiselessly, indicating to the relay station his answer. LCpl. Garner knew Morse code, so he used it to send short messages to the relay site. He informed the relay site that we did not know our location, and they told him the location given to them by the insertion pilots. After decoding the coordinates given to us by the relay site, I looked at my map, and for the first time in two days, I had a fairly good idea of where I was. LCpl. Garner was also able to tell Ba Na that we were very close to the enemy and could not move without being detected. Ba Na asked us if we were near an extraction LZ. Oh, how I wished we were! I had Garner send a Morse code message informing them that we did not know of any LZ close to us, but we would try to find one. Ba Na came back and said they would send an AO out to our position to give us directions to the nearest LZ, but the weather was closing in and it may take some time to get the AO out to us.

We spent the 11th and 12th of July huddled together on the side of the hill in dense brush, too frightened to move in any direction for fear of alerting the enemy. We whiled away the hours listening to the voices above us and looking at the abundant insect life that surrounded us. Huge centipedes and millipedes scurried around our feet, along with large black beetles and the obsequious three-inch-long leeches. We amused ourselves killing leeches with insect repellent and watching centipedes hunt and kill small lizards. It might sound strange to those who have never found themselves in the position we were in, but watching these insects seemed to take our minds off the predicament we were in and helped us kill time until the safety of darkness enveloped us. Several times during the day, I prayed for night to fall since darkness provided us with a measure of safety.

On the 12th an AO, call sign Black Coat, finally arrived in the sky near us and contacted us on our radio frequency. He knew of our predicament and did not try to make us speak but only asked us to give him a mark when he flew over us. LCpl. Garner whispered that he was flying 20 degrees magnetic from our position. The AO then said he was banking left and would be heading toward us. When the AO's plane came over us, LCpl. Garner whispered, "Mark, Mark" which let the AO know we were directly below the plane. A few minutes later, the AO radioed to us the position of two LZ's we could use. One was over a click away, but the other was only 300 meters to the south of our position. Ba Na monitored the radio traffic between us and the AO, and they told us that we would be extracted the next day if we could get to the closest extract LZ. That was all I needed to know. At first light on the 13th of July, our patrol moved out toward the extract LZ the AO had found for us. I hoped the enemy was not waiting in ambush for our arrival, but we really had no other recourse. We found a stream that led in the direction of the LZ and followed it for an hour until we came upon a small open area suitable for one CH-46 to land in. Unfortunately for us, our movement to the LZ took us into a dead space where we could not reach the Ba Na relay site. We were without communications again. Our only hope once we lost communications was that Ba Na would tell Camp Reasoner to launch our extract birds without confirmation that we had safely arrived at the LZ.

We waited in the jungle beside our LZ for several hours, always expecting at any moment for the enemy to find us and attack. The tension of the past four days was beginning to tell on us, and I noticed that several of the men were unable to stay awake. As each hour passed, I began to doubt that we would be extracted that day, and I began to think about where we would be able to harbor for the night. Then, at around 1600, we heard the welcome sound of helicopter rotor blades in the distance. A moment later we heard the voice on the radio, loud and clear, of the pilot of the lead helicopter, and he was trying to contact us. I took the radio from LCpl. Garner and whispered into the handset that Killer Kane was in our extract LZ. I described the LZ to him and gave him a recommended approach into it. I also told him about the enemy base camp and gave its location to him. I did not want to use a smoke grenade to mark the LZ because I knew the enemy was near us and would probably see it. Instead, I told the pilot to look for my signal mirror. In a minute or two he spotted the flash of my signal mirror and began his descent in a steep, circling dive. He landed and we rushed toward the helicopter eager to get aboard and out of Happy Valley. As we did, two NVA soldiers dressed in khaki and black uniforms with pith helmets began firing at the helicopter from some high ground on the opposite side of the LZ. Doc Willis and I lay on the tail ramp of the helicopter as it lifted off and fired our rifles at the enemy, but we could not see if we hit them or not. What surprised me the most about these two enemy soldiers was how audacious and foolish they were. They stood up in grass that was waist high to fire their weapons and didn't seem to care about their exposed position. They were intent upon shooting down our helicopter and cared little for their own personal safety (Team Killer Kane Patrol Report, 13 July 1967).

On the way back to base, our helicopter dropped us off at An Hoa Combat Base so it could be diverted for an emergency medevac of a wounded Marine from the 5th Marines. While we waited for another helicopter to pick us up, we sat in the shade of a small wooden and screen shack that served as a waiting room for Marines and civilians being transported from the combat base's airfield. Inside this shack were two or three Marines, a Kit Carson Scout, and a dozen Vietnamese women and children. We walked in and sat on the floor since the benches were occupied. I looked at the Vietnamese civilians and was shocked by what I saw. They were terrified of us. Children clung to their mothers and cried and the women looked at us with faces that expressed sheer terror. I wondered what it was about us that so terrified these people, but then I realized it was no mystery. Here in front of these civilians sat six men dressed in filthy, mud-encrusted camouflage uniforms. We had not shaved in four days, reeked of sweat and rotting jungle vegetation, were smeared with black and green grease paint, and each of us was carrying a lethal array of weapons, grenades and ammunition. I tried to ignore them. I was bone tired and really did not care if we frightened these people or not. All I wanted to do was get back to Camp Reasoner, drink some cold water, and get some hot food in my stomach.

Sgt. Pugh motioned the Kit Carson Scout to come over to us, and he asked this former VC turned scout for the Marines why the civilians seemed so frightened of us. The Kit Carson Scout replied that we were the dreaded "Monkey Men who walked in trees." I had never heard the term "Monkey Men" before, so I asked the Kit Carson Scout what he meant by the term. He explained that many of the local lowland civilians had heard that the recon Marines actually walked through the trees like monkeys and, worse, these same Marines killed and ate babies. Now I understood why the women clung to their children and looked upon us with horror. I wondered who was responsible for spreading this fiction, but I was in no mood to ask, so I just pulled my bush hat over my eyes and tried to sleep. In the moments before gentle slumber swept over me, I had visions of my team walking through the trees in Happy Valley.

Back at Camp Reasoner, Capt. Dixon told me that we had a new battalion commander, Lt. Col. Browman C. Steinmetz, and he thought the new CO was amenable to awards for specific actions and not just "end of tour" awards. He asked me to prepare award packages for Russell, Pugh, and Garner for the patrol in Happy Valley where we were surrounded and just barely escaped. He also said he intended to prepare an award package on me for the same patrol. I was elated at this news. It meant that for the first time Killer Kane would be getting the recognition it deserved.

My elation was rather short-lived because Capt. Dixon took this opportunity to remind me that a Marine officer had important administrative duties to perform. I needed to write fitness reports for my NCOs and assign proficiency and conduct marks for the other Marines in my platoon. He also asked me to prepare a three-hour block of instruction for a class on supporting arms: all to be done in 24 hours! As I was about to leave his office and begin spending the rest of the day on administration, Capt. Dixon suggested I go to the S-3 shop and have Maj. Welzant brief me on the next mission planned for Killer Kane. As I walked toward the S-3 shop, I did not realize that this next patrol would be one of the most exciting and productive reconnaissance patrols of the entire war.

Killer Kane's "Monkey Men"— from front to back, Donald Conner, J. D. Glor, John Slowick, R. Garner, Clarence Williams, me, and James Hauxhurst — waiting for choppers at An Hoa Combat Base.

6

The Yellow Brick Road

When Maj. Welzant pointed to the situation map on the wall of the S-3 shop, I knew immediately where he was pointing to since this area had been a fixture in my mind for the past month. It was Happy Valley. He told me my next mission was to take Killer Kane into Happy Valley so we could screen the western flank of the 1st Battalion, 7th Marines, who would be conducting a search-and-destroy mission a few miles east of our insertion LZ. The name of the operation we would be supporting was Operation Pecos. Division had decided to launch this operation because intelligence indicated an increased presence of NVA units in the valley and a possible storage facility for the 122 mm rockets that had been used to attack the Da Nang Airbase on 15 July, causing the destruction or damage of 42 aircraft and the death of eight Americans. Signals intelligence indicated the source of the rockets was an NVA artillery regiment that had recently arrived in South Vietnam and had established a base somewhere in Happy Valley. Division wanted to eliminate this threat to Da Nang Airbase as quickly as possible. Since this operation would involve Marine infantry units sweeping east to west in our direction and likely cause the NVA to pass through our NFZ, he suggested I take my entire platoon with me on this patrol. He pointed out that the NVA in Happy Valley probably would withdraw to the west away from the advancing infantry, and this would increase the likelihood we would encounter them. One good piece of news he passed along was the infantry would be bringing in a battery of 105 mm howitzers with them, which meant we would have access to a firing battery in direct support of us. This artillery battery would establish a fire support base on the valley floor, so our patrol would be within friendly artillery range, a rarity for patrols in Happy Valley.

With this information and some maps and aerial photos from our S-2 shop, I went in search of my new platoon sergeant, GySgt. Walter M. Webb, so we could plan the patrol together. Gunny Webb was a highly experienced reconnaissance Marine who had served with force reconnaissance companies several times during his long career in the Corps. He had made well over 200 parachute jumps, was scuba qualified, and had attended all the advanced reconnaissance training courses offered by the U.S. military. I took an instant liking to this seasoned SNCO and greatly valued his advice and assistance. We both decided that we would take every available man in the fifth platoon and we would go "heavy" in terms of weapons and ammunition. With this in mind, we decided to take two machine guns with us: an M 60 machine gun and a Stoner light machine gun. We would also take an M-79 grenade launcher and two Claymore mines. Each man would take at least 300 rounds of rifle ammunition and four hand grenades, while the machine gunners would take 400 linked rounds per gun.

The men on this patrol were all experienced; we were not taking any rookies. In addition to Gunny Webb, the other members of this patrol were Borecky, Pugh, Haux-hurst, Hager, Williams, Slowick, Garner, Glor, Dobson, Combs, Bingham, Gardner, and Conner. I felt supremely confident about this team. It was a highly skilled and experienced team of reconnaissance Marines and corpsmen, a team fully capable of performing any mission assigned no matter how difficult or dangerous. Events on our upcoming patrol would prove me right.

On the day of insertion, 21 July, teams Killer Kane and Circumstance were heli-lifted into a small LZ next to the shallow but swift-moving stream that ran through a narrow part of Happy Valley. The main infiltration route for the NVA, the "Yellow Brick Road," followed the stream, crossing back and forth along its path, looking from the air like two black snakes intertwined with each other. We took ground fire as we were being inserted, but I told the pilots to land us anyway because I knew this was the only location where we could effectively perform our screening mission. Team Killer Kane landed first in the LZ. We established security in the LZ and then Circumstance landed and joined us. Our two teams waited together for 20 minutes to see if the enemy had found us, but no one came down the valley trail from either the west or east. Team Circumstance then moved out to the south to their assigned NFZ on the south side of the valley, an area called Col de Ba Lien, while we moved out to the north up a steep, slippery hill where we hoped we would be able to establish an OP of the trail and also maintain radio communications with both Ba Na radio relay station and the 7th Marines to our east. The jungle canopy on this hill was quite high with most trees reaching a height of 90 to 100 feet. Beneath the canopy, which was so thick very little sunlight filtered through, there was thick secondary growth that made movement difficult and slow.

After an hour of climbing, we reached the summit of the hill and found it was a ridgeline running parallel to the valley below. On the ridgeline we found a well-used trail running in an east-west direction and several large bomb craters and trees that had been splintered badly, the result of a recent TPQ-10 bombing. I was impressed with the damage done by this mini–Arc Light. The twenty or so 500-pound bombs dropped by a Marine

Left: James Hager with his Stoner light machine gun. *Right:* Jit Gardner in Happy Valley.

The Yellow Brick Road, halfway to Laos.

A-6 "Intruder" bomber had shattered trees as thick as a few feet in diameter and left dirt, leaves and branches in tangled masses on the jungle floor, along with many twisted bomb fragments imbedded in the surrounding trees.

I wanted to make sure I had good communication so I had the team move into one of the large bomb craters just off the trail and had my radio operators take out their ten-foot whip antennas so we could establish positive communications for the team. Both radio operators soon signaled to me that they had solid communications with Ba Na radio relay site, the 7th Marines, and the artillery battery supporting the operation. This was welcome news, indeed.

I sent Gunny Webb and five Marines 100 yards to the west down the ridgeline's trail while I took Sgt. Pugh and three other Marines 100 yards to the east along the same trail. Both groups set up hasty ambushes just off the trail in the hope that any enemy contemplating attacking us would approach the team using this trail. We sat in our ambush locations for several hours but nothing materialized so I had both ambush teams return to the bomb crater for the rest of the day.

When I crawled into the bomb crater I was told by LCpl. Garner that there were "voices" on our frequency but he could not understand what they were saying. He handed the handset to me and I listened for an hour but heard nothing. Later that night, one of the men on radio watch woke me and handed me the handset again. This time I could hear Vietnamese and Japanese being spoken very clearly. In fact, their voices came in more clearly than the voices of the Marines operating only a few miles to our east. One of the Japanese voices on the radio referred to "A Shau" several times, which we interpreted to be the A Shau Valley several miles northwest of us in Thua Thien Province and a major enemy base area. Later on during this patrol we would again hear voices on our frequency talking in Vietnamese and Japanese. Sgt. Pugh was the only one in our patrol who could understand Vietnamese but he only listened to the voices once and he seemed to think the voices belonged to a friendly Vietnamese unit. I asked Ba Na to check to see if any friendly ARVN units were operating near us, and they reported back that no ARVN units were within 10 miles of us.

Charles Gillespie, a New Jersey native, near the Hai Van Pass.

After an uneventful night, the strange voices on our radio notwithstanding, Killer Kane moved out along the ridgeline trail to the east in search of a place where we could establish an OP overlooking the valley to the south. We left the bomb crater before sunrise and traveled for approximately two hours moving cautiously along the trail and making many stops to listen for enemy activity and to make sure we were not being followed. Then, at 0915, Sgt. Pugh turned to me and held up his hand in front of his face, the arm and hand signal for "enemy sighted." Ahead of him I could see LCpl. Slowick, the point man, in a crouching position looking to his left, his rifle in his shoulder. Pugh slowly moved toward me and raised his forefinger to his lips, and then he cupped his hand near my ear and whispered, "We hear VC voices below us." As he said this, I heard the voices also and they sounded like they were very, very close to us. I will now provide the reader with the actual words I used when I recorded the events of this patrol for the U.S. Marine Corps History Division as part of their Oral History Program:

> At first I thought these voices were so loud that they couldn't be VC; they must be Marines operating in the area, because they obviously felt very secure. However, after checking my map I decided no friendly units were anywhere near us. We moved up very carefully, very slowly until we came upon four VC sitting around a fire in a ravine below us. We heard other voices indicating there were more, but we had no idea how many there were at this time. I called up one of my machine gunners, Cpl. Hager, and along with our point man, John Slowick, our backup point, Sgt. Pugh, and me, we formed a tight line facing downhill into the ravine. The four of us opened fire almost simultaneously on the VC sitting around the campfire. Gunny Webb brought up the rest of the platoon, positioned them on line, and had them fire into the enemy position below. After ten minutes of intensive fire, we had complete fire superiority; the enemy only returned two bursts of automatic weapons fire during the entire exchange. We slacked up a bit and then we threw a dozen hand grenades and gas grenades down into the ravine. We did not have to don our gas masks since the wind carried the gas away from us and toward the enemy. About thirty minutes after the engagement was initiated, five men, myself included, moved down into the ravine in order to assess what damage we had done (Oral History Collection No. 1467, History Division, HQMC).

As we moved down into the ravine we saw that it stretched out on a flat surface that ran for nearly 100 yards to the north. On the eastern side there was a shallow stream about five feet wide that ran into the main stream in the valley 100 meters to the south. A high embankment ran the length of the stream on the eastern side. In front of us lay two enemy dead next to a small camp fire. I took some pictures of them and of the abundant weapons and equipment lying about the floor of the ravine. I wanted visual proof of what had transpired. I was not always confident that our patrol reports were taken seriously by our intelligence analysts back in Da Nang, but photos were impossible to ignore or refute.

It dawned on us that we had attacked a sizeable enemy force and they had abandoned all of their packs and supplies in their haste to retreat. I expected such a large enemy force to recover quickly and attempt a counterattack; I did not want this to occur while we were in the ravine with so much high ground surrounding us. We hastily picked up and carried the numerous packs and weapons lying around us, but we did not want to go too far down the ravine to recover all of it. I estimated we left at least half of the packs in the ravine. We carried those we recovered up to the ridgeline and conducted a quick inventory. It took five of us to go through everything we had collected.

We collected the following items: 16 packs containing 140 NVA uniforms, 15 sweatshirts, 19 towels, plastic sheeting, 15 ponchos, 15 pounds of medical supplies, six cooking pots, 16 sets of metal chopsticks, five ceramic cups, four field knives, eight gas masks, two Russian compasses, two Russian binoculars, twenty-two 30-round AK-47 magazines, 850 pounds of rice, and many personal items. In addition to the items in the packs, we recovered two new Chinese RPD light machine guns, two Chinese RPG-7 rocket grenade launchers, a Chinese AK-47 assault rifle, 19 Chinese potato masher-type hand grenades, 30 pounds of Czech plastic explosives, a wooden box containing blasting caps, and 30 feet of time fuse. Finally, one of the last items we brought up out of the ravine was a large, leather satchel that contained numerous documents, three communist flags, $256 in U.S. currency, $580 in U.S. military scrip currency, and 181,000 South Vietnamese piasters. We were stunned by this valuable haul of enemy equipment, cash, and documents. I sent a message to Camp Reasoner informing them of the captured items, and they immediately radioed back to us that we were to find the nearest LZ and stand by to have the items sent back to Camp Reasoner.

We needed to find an LZ that was close because the weight of such a large amount of gear would make it impossible to travel very far. I knew there was a strong likelihood that we would find an LZ in the valley to the south, so I dispatched Gunny Webb, Cpl. Hager, and PFC Glor to follow the stream in the ravine 100 meters south to where it intersected with the main stream on the valley floor. I felt confident we would find an LZ in that area.

Gunny Webb was gone only a few minutes when we heard rifle fire. A few minutes later, he reappeared with Hager and Glor and he was carrying a Chinese Type 56 carbine over his shoulder and smiling broadly. The three of them climbed up the trail to our position, and he told me that there was a good LZ just 100 yards south of our position and that he had encountered two NVA soldiers hiding by the stream bank. He had shot one, and Hager killed the other. He took the carbine off one of them but did not have time to search the other body.

Killer Kane with captured enemy weapons and flags. Back row, left to right: Lt. Mike St. Clair, me, Borecky, Bingham, Jit Gardner, John Slowick, Gy Sgt. Walter B. Webb, Major Charles Welzant; middle row, left to right: Captain Albert "King" Dixon, J. D. Glor, Combs, James Hauxhurst, Donald Conner, unknown; front row, left to right: Gy Sgt. Gabbert, Dave Pugh, James Hager, R. Garner, Donald Dobson.

I was relieved that Gunny Webb was unhurt and elated that he had found a good LZ so close to us. I radioed Camp Reasoner that we were moving to the LZ, and we expected to be there in 30 minutes. They radioed back that helicopters were on the way with a reaction force made up of volunteers from team Hateful led by Lt. Bob Drake. We had a devil of a time lugging all of the captured enemy packs down to the LZ even though we lightened the load by dumping the 850 pounds of rice all over the hill before we left. Still, it made for a difficult descent into the valley. Sweating profusely and laboring under the added weight, we finally made it to the LZ just as the helicopter's pilots radioed to tell us that they were inbound and only five minutes away.

When I had heard that a reaction force was being sent out to help us, I assumed that we would be extracted along with the captured gear. How wrong I was! As Lt. Drake's team ran out of the back of the CH-46, I could not help but notice that none of them were wearing any face paint or carrying any packs, a clear indication that they had no intention of staying on the ground. Any lingering doubt I had was dispelled when Bob Drake told me he had been sent out to help our team load the captured gear onto the chopper, and then he and his team would return to Camp Reasoner with it. Killer Kane was to remain in the field and continue on its mission. I was a bit incredulous, so I radioed Camp Reasoner and asked for confirmation that we were not going to be extracted even though we had just been in a firefight and the enemy certainly knew where we were. The terse message came back that we were to continue on our patrol.

Lt. Drake and his team helped us load the enemy gear on the Ch-46, and then he and his team boarded it and flew off to the east. Gunny Webb could not believe we were going to be left in the field after getting into such a big fight with a superior enemy force, and he made his displeasure known to me. I knew there was no alternative so I simply told him we needed to get out of the area fast! I did not want to make contact again with the enemy, so I decided to move closer to the 7th Marines and, hopefully, link up with them. To do this, we would have to move east along the valley floor following the major stream and "The Yellow Brick Road" in the valley. This was very dangerous, but I did not want to go west with the potential of leaving the artillery fan or to go north where the enemy had withdrawn after our firefight. Taking the patrol south was not an option either since that would take us into the NFZ of team Circumstance. My only real option was to move east quickly and then hide close to the trail so I could continue to screen the western approaches to the 7th Marines' AO.

As we moved out, I noticed that not every pack had been loaded on the helicopter. Gunny Webb was carrying an NVA pack in addition to his own. I also noted that one of the men was carrying the Chinese Type 56 carbine Gunny Webb had captured. I didn't say anything to either of these men since we were moving on a well-used trail and my mind was concentrated on this dangerous task. I told the point man to find a good OP site close to the trail as soon as possible but not to rush things since I did not want to alert any enemy who might be using the trail. I also told our rear point men to employ our tandem point system where they would leap frog with one man always covering the other as he moved. I did this because I thought it more likely the enemy would follow us and attack us the rear than from the direction of the 7th Marines to our front.

We crossed and recrossed the stream running in the valley, stopping each time to allow our rear point to obscure our foot prints in the mud. We moved along the trail for about 500 meters, and then we found a good spot to harbor for the night. It was close enough to the trail to observe movement, but far enough away to remain hidden. Around 1900, as darkness was beginning to fall, we observed a small group of VC moving southwest near the trail. We called in an artillery mission on them with excellent coverage, but we could not see any results. The foliage we were in was quite thick, and I did not want to risk moving in the dark to search the impact area.

After the fire mission, I went over to Gunny Webb and asked him about the pack he was carrying. At first, he told me he had simply forgotten to put it on the helicopter but I knew better and asked him why he had kept it. He told me that he did not trust the people in the rear to save the really good trading items for the team, and he predicted the "rear area poges" would steal most of what was valuable in the enemy packs. I sympathized with him and told him had I known we were going to be left in the field while the enemy gear would go back to Camp Reasoner without us, I would have probably combed the cache for all the valuable trading items myself. I knew many of my team members still did not possess all the equipment they needed, and the only way to obtain this valuable gear was to trade items we captured from the enemy with people who possessed the items we needed. For instance, we all needed camouflage uniforms, ARVN rucksacks, and survival kits, but only half of us possessed these things. I asked the Gunny what goodies he had stored in the pack, and he told me he had salvaged a Russian pistol, two NVA web belts with stars engraved on the buckles, a blue plastic wallet, a pair of Russian binoculars, a green notebook with poems written in it, some pictures, and a metal box the size of a standard shoe box. One of the pictures was a professionally done portrait of an attractive Vietnamese woman. When we returned from our patrol, an intelligence officer at division told us she was a famous prostitute and Da Nang brothel owner who passed out these pictures to her clients as a form of advertising. This woman later went into politics and owned a hotel in Da Nang. How an NVA soldier obtained such a photo was a mystery.

Just before dark, I noticed that Gunny Webb had left the harbor site to answer the call of nature. He had with him the entrenching tool we used to dig a cat hole for a hasty latrine. When he returned, the pack was not with him. I assumed he had transferred the items in the NVA pack to his own and ditched the empty enemy pack in the bush somewhere. I also noted that the man that I had seen carrying the Type 56 Chinese carbine was no longer carrying it. Following the usual procedure, he had disassembled it and hidden it in his rucksack. I knew it was wrong to not turn these captured weapons over to the Division G-2, but I also knew these weapons were prized trading items. Once they were surrendered to the G-2, we would never see them again.

The next day, the 23rd, our patrol continued in a southeasterly direction following the stream and trail in the valley. Where the valley began to open up, we found a VC farm that measured 200 meters by 100 meters with a well-constructed fence made of bamboo surrounding it. Millet and rice were growing in the farm's well-tended fields. Since Happy Valley was not inhabited, we knew the only people doing any farming in the valley were enemy soldiers. We expected to encounter the enemy at this farm but it was deserted, at least temporarily. We moved on a bit further and found several well-constructed bunkers had been placed every 100 meters along the "Yellow Brick Road" south of Hill 417. From their construction and orientation, it appeared these well-camouflaged bunkers were part of an elaborate ambush scheme. Fortunately for Killer Kane, the ambush site was not occupied.

At 1500 on the 24th, Killer Kane was extracted from an old, abandoned rice paddy field a few hundred meters north of the "Yellow Brick Road" (Team Killer Kane Patrol Report, 24 July 1967). When we arrived at LZ Finch, we were amazed by the number of people there to greet us. It looked like half the 1st Marine Division staff was there, along with a host of officers and men from the 1st Reconnaissance Battalion. There were also reporters and photographers from the *Sea Tiger* and the *Stars and Stripes* military newspapers. We were asked to pose for some photographs with the three communist flags and the weapons we had captured and then military reporters interviewed us before Lt. St. Claire had a chance to debrief us.

It was nice to be the center of all of that attention, but our enthusiasm was soon dampened when we asked where all the captured gear was. Mike St. Claire told me that when the helicopters landed at LZ Finch, several intelligence officers from division quickly took charge of the gear and removed it from Camp Reasoner so it could be analyzed. I asked him if we could get everything back after they were through with it, and he said he would ask. Capt. Dixon then told us that when the gear came in he was able to only retrieve the three communist flags and the weapons from the pile unloaded on LZ Finch. He told me he feared that the rest of it was in the hands of various staff officers at division.

I was very disappointed and angry over this news. I told Capt. Dixon that my team had captured that gear. Many of the items we had captured were of no intelligence value but of great value to the team for trade items. He agreed and said he would do his best to get everything back for us that was not deemed of intelligence value. I then told him that we had captured a lot of U.S. and Vietnamese money, and I wanted this returned to us so we could use it to have a platoon party and buy ARVN rucksacks for everyone who did not already have one. He looked at me strangely and then he produced an inventory made by the Division G-2 team of what they took with them when they left LZ Finch with our captured gear. The inventory did not contain any mention of money, and it was clearly a truncated list with most of the valuable items missing. My anger grew, and I nearly lost my temper. However, I knew Capt. Dixon and Lt. St. Claire were not responsible for this brazen thievery. This had to be the work of some person who was totally devoid of integrity.

To add insult to injury, Capt. Dixon informed me that Gen. Robertson, the division commander, had mentioned that he would like to have the weapons we had captured and the three communist flags so that these items could be put on display in the division headquarters and later given to the Marine Corps History Division. Now, I was really angry, and so was GySgt. Webb, who was standing nearby and overheard our conversation. I made some very profane and injudicious comments about senior officers and staff "pukes," all of which evoked looks of commiseration from Lt. St. Claire and Capt. Dixon, but did nothing to help the situation. Both officers told me to make a complete list from memory, and they would take it to the Division G-2 and ask them to return any items on our list, including the money that was missing.

After I had cooled down somewhat, Gunny Webb and I went back to my hootch where I took out the list of items I had inventoried, and we combined it with the list he had made. We then took the combined list to Capt. Dixon, who thanked us and immediately went up to the division headquarters, even though it was getting dark and most of the division staff had gone to chow. Gunny Webb and I went to eat chow at the recon mess hall, and while we shared a beer before eating he berated me as only a Marine SNCO can berate a lieutenant about trusting people living in the rear with captured goodies. I felt very bad about letting so much valuable gear out of our sight, and I apologized for my naïveté and misplaced trust in the Marine intelligence community.

As I was beginning to wax eloquent about how stupid I was, he confided in me, telling me that "all is not lost." He said he would talk to me in the morning about it, but for now we should just get some hot chow and a few more beers.

The next day, Capt. Dixon came over to my hootch, and I could tell he was angry. He told me that he had taken the list Gunny Webb and I had written to the Division G-2 and had been told they had only taken a few items and that someone else must have the rest. In effect, the Division G-2 told Capt. Dixon they were "lost." I could see that Capt. Dixon was as angry as I was, and he made several remarks about the perfidy of people who would take such items from a recon team. He then said he was going to discuss it personally with Gen. Robertson.

As it turned out, the missing items were never returned, but Gen. Robertson invited Capt. Dixon and me up to the command bunker so we could present him with the three flags we had captured, one of which was quite large and made of colorful silk. This flag had been presented to the 402nd Sapper Battalion by the Da Nang Central Committee of the Lao Dong (Workers) Party. At first, I told Capt. Dixon I did not want to go, but he convinced me that Gen. Robertson had nothing to do with the missing gear, and it would only make for some very bad feelings if I refused his request. Reluctantly, I agreed to go with him.

The next day, the two of us trudged up Hill 327 to the command bunker where Gen. Robertson had his office, and we dutifully reported to him. Capt. Dixon had the flags with him, and we both noticed that someone had already mounted the weapons we had captured on the command bunker wall for display. I managed to smile as a photographer took our picture as we presented the flags to Gen. Robertson. Then the general made a few complimentary remarks while a reporter from *Stars and Stripes* took notes. After the ceremony, we left General Robertson's office and walked back down the hill to Camp Reasoner.

When we returned to Capt. Dixon's office, he asked me to sit down while he pulled a flag out of one of the drawers of his field desk. It was the large, ornate 402nd Sapper Battalion flag we had just presented to Gen. Robertson. He put the flag back in the drawer smiling. At first, I thought maybe he had talked Gen. Robertson into giving back the flag but that was not the case at all. Some enterprising Marine, probably Gunny Webb, had suggested that the original flag be taken to a local seamstress in Da Nang and copied. This was done in a single night, and the copied flag was the one Capt. Dixon took with him and presented to Gen. Robertson. The original flag we captured was retained by the company. I never knew what happened to the original because, like everything else we captured, it later disappeared as well.

Several days after the ceremony in Gen. Robertson's office, I received a copy of the picture that had been taken showing Capt. Dixon and me presenting the flag to Gen. Robertson. An inscription written by Gen. Robertson on the photo read, "To Killer Kane, the most productive reconnaissance patrol from an intelligence point of view that has ever been conducted in Vietnam by the Marine Corps." This was high praise, indeed. When I showed the picture to my platoon and they read the inscription from Gen. Robertson, it had an immediate and dramatic effect on all of us. It lifted our morale and made us forget our disappointment over the lost trading items we had captured in Happy Valley.

I knew we had captured a treasure trove of enemy documents, and I was curious to find out exactly what these documents told us, so I went up to the Division G-2 shop to find out. There I found a SSgt. who had analyzed the captured documents, and he told me that our team had attacked the 1st Company of the 402nd Sapper Battalion, one of the most elite enemy units in I Corps. According to a roster we had captured, the company had an active strength of 43 troops with ninety percent of them coming from North Vietnam and only a handful from South Vietnam. The Marine SNCO went on to tell me this unit had been responsible for several attacks on the Da Nang Airbase in April and July, an attack on the ESSO fuel storage facility north of Da Nang, and the attack on the anti-

The presentation of false captured enemy flags to the commanding general of the 1st Marine Division in his office on Hill 327. From left, Andrew Finlayson, General Robertson, Captain King Dixon.

aircraft Hawk missile battery on Hill 327. He told me they were well equipped with new weapons from China and had received their sapper training with the 320th NVA Reconnaissance Regiment in North Vietnam before infiltrating south along the Ho Chi Minh Trail. The documents we captured included code books, unit rosters, unit code designations, maps with various NVA positions marked on them, correspondence with the Da Nang Central Committee and other communist military units and political committees in Quang Nam Province, and the names of several VC agents who were responsible for buying local goods for the unit and transporting them to Happy Valley. Several of these documents were highly classified and referred to an upcoming major offensive against targets in Da Nang and several district headquarters in Quang Nam Province. I asked the Marine SNCO when this "big offensive" was scheduled to take place, and he said the communists were always talking about major offensives and this probably had more to do with keeping up their morale than any real plans. He said he doubted they could mount any sustained attack on Da Nang, but they were capable of limited sapper attacks against any number of targets in the province. The last thing he told me was he had found a Marine utility uniform with the name "H. P. Ostdszewski" stenciled on it inside one of the enemy packs. I wondered if this enemy unit intended to use this uniform to try to infiltrate into the division AO to perform one of their sapper missions.

On 27 July, all the members of Killer Kane received the Vietnamese Cross of Gallantry for the patrol where we attacked 100 enemy soldiers near Hiep Duc. I was pleased by this but found it ironic that the South Vietnamese Government seemed more appreciative of our efforts than the U.S. Marine Corps.

After our platoon had finished a morning run to the Freedom Hill PX and back, Gunny Webb asked to speak with me about "a confidential matter." I asked him if he wanted to come to my hootch to talk, and he said he would prefer to have me come to his hootch since he wanted to show me something he had in his foot locker. I followed him to his hootch, where he invited me in and asked me to sit down at a small table he had fashioned out of spare lumber. He then went over to his foot locker and unlocked it. In a low whisper he said, "Lieutenant, when I was on the LZ waiting for Hateful, I knew they were going to take that gear away from us and we would never see it again, so I took one of the packs and stowed this money in it. We can use it for a really good party for the platoon." Now I understood why he told me the night before that "all was not lost." Two weeks later, we used the $256 of captured U.S. currency to purchase a case of 100 New York–cut steaks and several cases of Japanese beer from an Air Force friend of Gunny Webb's.

A few days after we had returned from our Happy Valley adventure, GySgt. Webb told me one of the Marines in my platoon, Cpl. Anthony Allen, wanted to request mast with me. *Request mast* is a naval term used by the Marine Corps to describe the formal procedure where a subordinate requests a personal audience with his immediate superior. I asked the Gunny what the problem was and the Gunny said Allen was having some "emotional problems" and "wanted out of the bush." I could tell that the Gunny was not very sympathetic toward Allen, so I asked him if he thought Allen really had a problem or he was just shirking. He said he thought Allen had "lost his nerve on the last patrol in Happy Valley" and he was "short," meaning he had only a few weeks to go before his tour of duty was complete. I told the Gunny to send him over to my hootch immediately, and I would talk to him.

Tony Allen normally went out with my other team, Brisbane, so I did not know him as well as some of the other men in the platoon. He always performed well and never caused me any trouble, so I was a bit surprised by his request to leave the field. We sat down together on my back porch while he told me he knew in his heart that he would die if he went out on another patrol. He said he had prayed to God for guidance, and he had "received the word of God" that he must leave the field or die.

I found his comments bizarre, but I also sensed that his fears were real and, given his long record of good performance, he was sincere in his beliefs. As he spoke to me, he began to cry and beg me to allow him to stay in the rear until his time of departure arrived. I was worried about setting a precedent for the other members of the platoon, so I argued that I could not allow every Marine who wanted to take a break from the bush to request mast and stay in the rear. He continued to cry and begged me to believe that God had decided he must die if he continued to go to the field. I sought a compromise because I could tell from his emotional state that he would be more of a liability on patrol than a help if I made him go on another patrol. I asked him if he would be willing to go to Hill 452 as part of a radio relay team, and he immediately accepted my proposal. We both assumed that spending a week on Hill 452 would be safe and would take him another week closer to his rotation tour date. I shook his hand, and we both went off to the company office to arrange for him to go with the next team scheduled for Hill 452.

Sadly, while Cpl. Allen was on Hill 452, lightning struck the RC-292 radio antenna on the main bunker, and this caused a case of fragmentation grenades to explode, killing Allen and another Marine, LCpl. Luther Stowe. I attempted to locate his mother in Philadelphia a year later, but no one answered the phone at her house. I wanted to tell her what a good Marine her son had been and what a good man she had raised.

After surviving another dangerous trip into Happy Valley, the members of Killer Kane thought we would get a respite with some easy patrol, but that was not the case. Originally, Maj. Welzant told me he intended to insert Killer Kane into the Que Son Valley area, and he had even given me the operation order and told me to begin planning for that patrol. However, just 24 hours prior to insertion, he canceled that mission and assigned us another one right back into Happy Valley.

III MAF G-2 had reason to believe the NVA were planning to launch missiles from Happy Valley

Tony Allen, who died on Hill 452.

using a new, long range missile. The enemy had used both 122 mm and 140 mm unguided rockets to attack targets in I Corps, but never anything with the range or payload this new missile possessed. If the enemy did, in fact, have such a missile and it had the range to reach the Da Nang Airbase from locations in Happy Valley, this would significantly degrade the security of this vital airbase. Adding to everyone's concern, we had to take a radiac meter with us to ascertain whether or not there was any source of nuclear radiation in the area. There was a fear that this new missile was now part of the inventory of the NVA's 368B Artillery Regiment, and it had both a conventional- and a nuclear-warhead capability. Killer Kane was given the mission of finding these missiles and to place particular emphasis on a hill on the north side of Happy Valley where an aerial observer had spotted what looked to him to be a construction site or a missile-launching pad. As if to stress the importance given our mission, Maj. Welzant told me that Gen. Robertson had specifically directed that Killer Kane be assigned the job of finding these missiles. Our patrol area was in a part of Happy Valley that had once contained rice fields but was now abandoned and overgrown with elephant grass and jungle. Because this mission had such high level interest in it, Maj. Welzant said he would go with us in the insertion helicopters to make sure we were inserted in the correct LZ and as close to the suspected launch site as possible.

On 29 July, Killer Kane, consisting of seven men, was inserted into a small LZ approximately 1,000 meters north of Hill 575, the location of the suspected missile site. Hill 575 was also known as Tam Dieo Mountain. On our approach into the LZ, we took ground fire from the northeast. As we settled into the LZ, Maj. Welzant asked me if I wanted to choose another LZ or abort the mission since we had taken fire on our approach. I told him we would continue, and I signaled everyone in Killer Kane to exit the helicopter. From the air, the ground in the LZ looked like it consisted of waist-high elephant grass. After landing, we found that there was nearly a foot of water in the LZ, and we sank into mud up to our boot tops as we waded toward the cover of some trees on the southeast side. As we approached the trees, we came across a very well-used trail running perpendicular to the direction we were moving. It was obvious that many people had been using this trail recently because the ground was beaten down firmly, and there were many Ho Chi Minh sandal tracks on it.

After the helicopters left us, we moved 100 feet into the trees and thick brush and listened to see if the enemy would react to our presence. PFC Glor and our new corpsman, HN3 Donald Conner, were our rear point and backup rear point respectively and were less than 30 feet from the trail. From where I was sitting, I could see Glor and Conner clearly; both were facing toward the trail we had just crossed and both were sitting, like me, with their backs resting on their packs. We had been sitting silently for nearly 30 minutes and I was just about to signal our team to get up and continue moving when Glor turned toward me and gave the hand signal that always sent a rush of adrenalin coursing through my body. He raised his hand in front of his face and then pointed to the trail. There moving across our line of vision was an old man dressed in white pajamas and behind him was a younger man dressed the same and carrying a large pack.

For a moment I wondered why peasants would be so far from the lowlands and walking through Happy Valley, a place many miles from the nearest village or hamlet and where only NVA and VC lived. My question was soon answered when I saw five young men in black pajamas and camouflage uniforms walking behind the men dressed in white. I could also see that they were carrying rifles at the ready and looking from side to side. They continued to walk east on the trail and out of sight. A minute later, two or three more men in white followed the first group, and one of them was carrying an RPG rocket grenade launcher. After they passed, I thought we might be in the clear, but then I saw one of the armed men come back and stop at the point where we had exited the LZ and crossed the trail. He looked in our direction but he did not appear to see us. Then he spoke to his companions and they gathered around him on either side. I was sure they were going to come into the bush looking for us. None of us moved since we were not yet sure they had seen us. Even Glor, who was no more than thirty feet from them, went unobserved. Glor was so close he could easily make out the details of the men's faces and uniforms as they peered in his direction.

Fortunately for our team, the enemy soldiers and their civilian companions did not come into the brush in our direction, but instead spread out and began to move away from us to search the marshy LZ. Evidently, they thought we were in the LZ hiding or they were hoping that we might attempt to follow them out into the open where they could fire at us. No matter what their intentions were, they moved away from us and out of sight. We did not move for several minutes, and soon we were left listening to only the normal sounds of insects and birds.

Our patrol's objective was Hill 575, the location of the suspected missile site, so I had the team form up and move slowly in that direction. We found a finger that led up to the summit of the hill, and we traveled along this for approximately 500 meters. Our movement was exceptionally slow because the undergrowth consisted of many vines and vegetation with thorns and briars. LCpl. Slowick often had to stop and quietly use his K-bar knife to cut a path for us through the tangles of this prickly vegetation. It was hot, hard going for him, so I relieved him with Sgt. Pugh an hour after we started. We would stop every 20 minutes to listen and watch in a 360-degree circle, but during these stops we heard nothing out of the ordinary. I worried about all the cutting we needed to do because I knew anyone following us could pick up our trail by just following the cut vegetation. Cut vegetation is a sure sign of humans, but I did not want to make any noise crashing through the bush so we went with what we hoped would be the lesser of two evils.

In the afternoon, we began to hear chopping and sawing sounds coming from the direction we were heading. At several spots along our route, we came across areas with trees that appeared to have been cut with a saw recently. The Vietnamese would often go into the mountains to cut firewood, so we did not automatically think this cutting and sawing was the work of the enemy. However, it was definitely the work of humans, and we did not want to encounter whoever it was. We continued to hear these woodcutting sounds for the rest of the day coming from the direction of the summit of Hill 575.

We were fairly close to the summit when we saw a small structure made out of logs and earth right in front of us. It looked like a bunker built between two large trees but it had a thatched roof over it about three feet above ground level. The earth used in its construction appeared to be fairly fresh, something that alarmed me and the other members of the team. We suspected that this structure might be part of a perimeter defense for whatever was on the top of the hill in front of us. We all agreed that this structure would be a great place to use as a machine gun nest since a machine gun would be able to fire at ground level directly down the finger we were using for 100 yards. Since it was getting late in the day, I decided to stop the patrol at the bunker and spend the night there. I did not want to make contact with the enemy late in the day since I knew the weather in Happy Valley often made it difficult or impossible for helicopters to fly, and we would need them to fly if we called for an emergency extraction. We formed a tight 360-degree "stand to" posture until an hour after sunset, and then we set up our radio watch. I knew it would be impossible for any enemy to approach us without making a terrific racket so I felt confident we were safe, at least until daylight. During the night, Sgt. Pugh woke me so I could stand my hour-long radio watch, and he told me that during his watch he had heard an elephant trumpeting north of us near our insert LZ.

Early in the morning of 30 July, just before daylight, we heard the distinctive sound of a mortar round fired over our heads. We estimated it had been fired from a location only 200 meters north of us, back in the direction of our insert LZ. It passed directly over our heads and landed approximately 1,000 meters to our south. We could not figure out why the enemy would fire one mortar round like this. It made no sense, but we did not think much of it aside from the fact that our enemy possessed this lethal indirect fire weapon and did not seem to mind firing it at nothing in particular.

There was a heavy mist covering the northern part of Happy Valley as Killer Kane set out on patrol. We could only see ten to 15 meters in front of us as we slowly began to ascend the finger leading to the summit of the hill. Just as we started to move, we heard some strange sounds that we could not identify off in the distance to our east and north. We stopped to listen but the sounds stopped, and no one had any idea what made them. The sounds we heard were similar to an animal screaming in pain.

I thought we could cover the remaining distance to the summit before noon. I hoped to get close enough to see what was on this hill without being spotted and then have enough daylight left to move down the hill and find a good place to hide for the night. I asked LCpl. Garner, my primary radioman, to let me know if we ever found ourselves in a radio "dead spot" because I did not want to make contact with the enemy when we did not have communications with the Ba Na radio relay site. Each time we stopped to rest and listen, he would give me a hand signal telling me whether or not we had solid communications.

We had been moving for about an hour when I decided to take another ten-minute "rest and listen" break. I looked at my field watch, and it said 0830. As we sat there in a slight depression, we began to hear the sound of brush breaking behind us. At first it sounded like it might just be bamboo creaking in the wind, but after a few seconds we all realized this noise was made by humans moving through the thick tangle of vines and brambles behind us. They were not far away. I was confronted with a dilemma. If the team stayed where we were, the enemy would certainly find us, and we would have to fight them off and then try to find an emergency LZ to be extracted. If we moved farther up the hill, we risked making a lot of noise and running into whoever was on the hill, maybe the same people who had built the bunker we had found not far behind us. In either case, it did not look like we were going to accomplish our mission of covertly observing the summit of the hill.

I knew from previous experience that the VC and NVA did not carry a lot of ammunition with them, usually only one or two AK-47 magazines and, perhaps, 100 rounds of linked ammunition for their machine guns. I also knew that they normally did not respond well to us when we initiated the contact and inflicted casualties on them. Instead, they often pulled back after taking casualties to assess their situation and receive instructions on what to do next. In order to escape, I knew we would have to initiate the contact at close range and try to kill as many of them as possible in the shortest time. I decided that we would stay where we were and wait until they were right on top of us and then we would hit them as hard as we could. Each man took up a firing position facing in the direction of the sound of the breaking brush, except for LCpl. Slowick and Cpl. Hager, who took up firing positions facing up hill toward the summit. I was facing toward the sound of breaking brush but only a foot away from Cpl. Hager who had the patrol's Stoner light machine gun. As my eyes strained to see through the dense jungle growth, I felt Cpl. Hager tap me lightly on the shoulder. As I turned toward him, I saw that he had his hand in front of his face, the signal that he had spotted the enemy. Almost instantaneously, I saw LCpl. Slowick point his M-16 rifle uphill. There, only a few meters in front of him, were two North Vietnamese soldiers, their AK-47 rifles at the ready, peering in our direction. Slowick fired and both NVA soldiers dropped. At the same time the rest of the patrol opened fire at NVA soldiers behind and below us. The NVA were shaken by this, but they did not withdraw. Soon, several NVA were firing back at us but their rounds passed harmlessly over our heads. I saw two of them to the right of the two shot by Slowick, and I fired at them from a range of no more than 20 meters, but I could not tell if I hit either of them. Around this time, we proved the value of the Stoner light machine gun, especially when in the hands of a brave and aggressive Marine. Cpl. Hager used it to great effect by firing short, five-round bursts at the enemy approaching us from the south. Cpl. Hager and his Stoner light machine gun gave the team the fire superiority we needed to survive this attack by a superior NVA force.

After five minutes, the enemy fire slacked, and we saw one NVA soldier dragging another off into the brush. LCpl. Garner told me he had the AO, Black Coat 1–0, on the radio and he was headed our way. Garner told him to tell Camp Reasoner that we were in heavy contact, and we needed an emergency extraction. I took the handset from Garner and asked the AO to help us find an LZ for us and to call in artillery and air on the enemy forces attacking us. I told him I would direct him over our position and give him a mark as soon as he passed overhead. I also told him I would pop a smoke to confirm our location. He acknowledged my request, said he would be over our insert LZ in 30 seconds, and asked me to direct him from there. I told him we were only 700 meters south of the insert LZ, and soon I could hear the engine of his plane passing north to south. When he was directly over our position and above the jungle canopy, I gave him a mark, and he said he knew where we were and did not need for us to use a smoke grenade. He began to mark the area south of us with white phosphorous rockets and a few minutes later we heard fixed-wing aircraft diving overhead and the thunderous explosions of 500-pound bombs ripping through the jungle near the summit of the hill. Black Coat 1–0 also called in an artillery mission to our north, which he walked up the finger from the insert LZ to only 100 yards from our position. I marveled at how good this AO was and how he was able to juggle both an air strike and an artillery mission so effectively and with such precision.

As I was coordinating with Black Coat 1–0 on the radio and beginning to feel fairly confident that we had sent the enemy on his way, Cpl. Hager stood up behind a tree and began firing his Stoner light machine gun at two enemy soldiers who were attempting to set up an RPD machine gun. He killed both of them. Other NVA fired at him but missed. Then they threw several grenades at us, wounding Cpl. Hager and our corpsman, "Doc" Conner.

Cpl. Hager's bravery surely saved us that day because no one had seen these two NVA soldiers until they were almost ready to fire on us. Had that machine gun been put into operation by the enemy, we would have certainly taken casualties. Cpl. Hager, wounded and bleeding, returned to the depression and told me that there was a large trail right in front of us and that this trail was how the enemy had gotten so close to us without being heard or seen. He said he saw three NVA dead lying on the trail, and he thought there were more enemy up ahead where the bombs from the air strike had landed. Neither Hager nor Conner were badly wounded, but at the time all I saw was blood on their faces and uniforms so I was not sure how serious their wounds were. I asked them about their condition, and both men laughed and said they were "fine." Despite having been wounded and just participating in one hell of a firefight at close range with a superior enemy force, these two men were still full of fight and looking for more targets to engage.

It was obvious now that the enemy had spotted our insertion on the first day and had begun to search actively for us shortly after we landed. They found our trail leading off to the south but decided not to follow us with just four armed men. Instead, they got reinforcements and set in motion a plan to herd us into the direction of an ambush on the large trail near the summit. They deliberately made a lot of noise behind us hoping we would move away from them and into the ambush they had set. Their plan did not work because we stopped before we reached the trail. This caused their colleagues to move along the trail looking for us: a deadly mistake on their part since we were able to see them and they could not see us. The old injunction that Clovis Coffman had told me several months previously proved right again: "Firefights are like fist fights, the one who throws the first punch usually wins."

Black Coat 1–0 gave me the grid coordinates of a good extraction LZ 200 meters west of our position and told us that helicopters were on their way to pick us up. I was afraid the enemy might be waiting for us to move out of the small depression we were in so I had each man throw a CS grenade along the path we would take and then we moved out between the clouds of gas. We moved downhill rapidly until we came to a rather large open space that had been used for agriculture long ago. Fixed-wing aircraft controlled by Black Coat 1–0 strafed ahead of us with 20 mm cannon. The LZ had waist-high elephant grass in it, and the ground was wet and in some places ankle deep with dark, muddy water. The helicopter landed over 100 meters away from us so we had to wade through the wet elephant grass to reach it, an arduous process that took nearly five minutes, all the time expecting the enemy to fire upon us as we moved toward the helicopter. No one fired on us until we lifted off in the helicopter, which took six hits in its fuselage. From the time we made contact with the enemy until the time we boarded the extraction helicopters just a little more than an hour had elapsed, but it seemed a lot longer than that. We stopped at Charlie Med on the way back to Camp Reasoner to drop off Conner and Hager so they could have their wounds treated (Team Killer Kane Patrol Report, 30 July 1967; see also *Newsweek*, 21 August 1967, pp. 40–41; and, Finlayson, Oral History Collection, No 1510, "Recon Team Killer Kane," History Division, HQMC").

At our patrol debriefing that afternoon, we told Lt. St. Claire that we had not reached the summit of Hill 575 or seen anything like a missile-launch site, but the fact that we heard a lot of woodcutting in the vicinity and that it was aggressively defended by at least 20 NVA or VC soldiers clearly indicated it was an important piece of real estate for some reason. We recommended that a Marine infantry force be inserted into the vicinity of Hill 575 to conduct a reconnaissance-in-force operation to ascertain whether the enemy was constructing a missile-launch site there. Our battalion commander, Lt. Col. Steinmetz, was present at the debriefing, and he made several very complimentary remarks about the team and conveyed the regards of Gen. Robertson, who had specifically requested Killer Kane for this mission. He also told us that I was to spend the better part of the next day talking to the 1st Marine Division and III MAF G-2 staffs about what I encountered on the patrol and my general impression of what was going on in Happy Valley.

On 1 August, I was asked to come up to the company office to meet a journalist from *Newsweek* magazine. When I arrived at the company office, I saw a rather portly, middle-aged man dressed in casual, civilian clothes accompanied by a Marine corporal from the division public affairs office. The man introduced himself as Mr. Perry, and he told me he wanted to do a story on our last patrol for his news magazine. He explained he had already interviewed an Army lieutenant who commanded a long-range reconnaissance platoon (LRRP) doing similar work, and he wanted to compare the two methods. He seemed friendly and genuinely interested in our work, putting me at ease. I had never spoken to the press before, and I knew nothing about the ground rules for dealing with the press, so I was initially reluctant to discuss anything of substance with him. He asked me if there was some place where we could talk without being disturbed, and I told him we could talk on the back porch of my hootch. The PR Marine said he would wait for us in the company office.

Mr. Perry and I sat down on two beach chairs overlooking the paddy fields of Phuoc Ly hamlet and talked while water buffaloes grazed just outside the perimeter wire. The journalist asked me to tell him about our last patrol to Happy Valley. In general terms, I told him the details of the patrol, and then he asked me some questions about the type of men serving in my platoon. I told him they came from all walks of life. He asked for specific details about the men, so I told him Mike Borecky had graduated from high school and spent a lot of time as a surfer on California beaches and doing underwater construction before joining the Marines. I also told him that another of my men had attended college for a year and dropped out to fight in Vietnam, while yet another had dropped out of high school before joining the Corps. He asked me if I had any draftees in my platoon. I told him there was only one, and he was one of my best men. I spent most of my time telling him about how brave and competent my men were and how much I valued their talents and abilities.

After a while he stopped taking notes, and he seemed to lose interest in my description of my men and began asking questions that put me on guard, even though he attempted to ask them in a rather friendly and low-key manner. He told me that he did not notice many black Marines at Camp Reasoner, and he asked me why that was. I told him I had not noticed this, but that two of the fifteen men in my platoon were black. He asked me how well they performed and whether there was any racial tension in my platoon. I told him that both of my black Marines performed very well, but all of my Marines performed their jobs well. He began asking me how many of my men were from the South. I told him I did not know, but I would check my platoon leader's notebook and provide him with this information. He demurred after I added that several of my Marines had led itinerant lives as kids growing up in different parts of the country.

Mr. Perry kept asking questions about race, so I told him I didn't think there was any more I could add to that topic. He agreed, but then he started to ask me about how my men felt about the anti-war movement in the States and whether what they were hearing from back home was affecting their perception about the morality of the conflict. I thought he was way off base asking such a question, and I told him so. I reminded him of his reason for our interview, which was to discuss the team's recent patrol in Happy Valley and to compare our patrolling methods with those of the U.S. Army. He only said that the anti-war movement was interesting to his readers in the U.S., and he had heard many military servicemen express disenchantment with the war. I was beginning to feel uncomfortable talking to him about this topic, so I said I needed to do some work and it was time to end the interview. I escorted him back to the company office, shook his hand, and turned him over to the PR corporal, who escorted him to our main gate.

Later that month, his story was published in the August 21 issue of *Newsweek*, and in his article he misquoted me, saying I had called my Marines "juvenile delinquents, beach bums, and high school dropouts." Naturally, the PR office at division was not pleased with the article, and they asked me to explain my comments, which I did. They warned me about being manipulated by journalists and told me I should, from now on, only talk to a member of the press in the presence of someone from their office. I told them that I had no desire to talk to any more journalists under any circumstances.

A month later, Mr. Perry returned to Camp Reasoner, and he denied that he had sent the alleged "quote" to his editor in New York City. He contended the editorial staff in New York had taken my words out of context when the article was edited. I learned a very valuable lesson from this first encounter with a member of the fourth estate and that was to always have a witness present when being interviewed. Unfortunately, this initial exposure to the press left me with a lasting sense of distrust. From that moment on, I was always on my guard when talking to the press, and I tried to avoid talking to them throughout my Marine Corps career. I never had the feeling they would represent my views fairly or accurately.

On 2 August, Capt. Dixon and I drove over to the III MAF headquarters on the west side of Da Nang. There I was interviewed for an hour by a team of senior officers from the Marine Corps Tactics Board who were in country to study the tactics used by our enemy. Gen. Robertson chose me to talk to the board because our team had had a lot of recent contact with the enemy and had been successful whenever we made contact. The interview was taped, and I was very impressed with how interested these colonels and majors from Washington, D.C., were in the tactics Killer Kane used whenever we got into a firefight with the enemy. Although the interview covered just about every aspect of ground reconnaissance tactics, they were especially interested in how we dealt with the enemy's counter-recon teams. They told me that the Army's Special Operations Group (SOG) and Marine reconnaissance units operating in western Quang Tri and Thua Thien provinces were suffering heavy casualties due to these enemy counter-recon teams, which they described as "special NVA units" trained and equipped specifically to deny U.S. recon teams access to certain key NVA base areas and infiltration routes.

On 3 August, Killer Kane was assigned a mission to establish an OP in the hills over-

looking the Hiep Duc Valley in support of the 1st Battalion, 5th Marines. To be honest, I was pleased our team was not going back into Happy Valley, even though I knew Hiep Duc was never an easy area to patrol. I was told I would be taking along Lt. Joe Taussig, a classmate of mine from the Naval Academy and a good friend. Joe had gone to Vietnamese language training after Basic School, so he came into country six months after I arrived. Joe came from a distinguished naval family that dated back to the Revolutionary War. He was the first in his family to serve as a Marine officer and not as a Navy officer. While at the Academy, he finished near the top of our class, far above me in the academic standings, and he also excelled at sports and public speaking. Everyone who knew Joe expected him to become a general officer one day. I was both happy and proud that my friend would be going out on his "snap in" patrol with me.

I spent most of the day doing all

Lt. Joseph K. Taussig, III.

the routine preparations for our insertion, including a thorough map study and an aerial recon of our proposed NFZ, along with issuing rations, ammunition and special equipment followed by my patrol order, the inspection of our equipment, and a rehearsal. Throughout this process, Joe took careful notes and asked great questions of me and the other members of the team. The evening before our patrol, Joe and I went up to the division officers' club to watch the nightly movie and relax for a few hours before turning in. It was great to see Joe again and talk about our time at the Academy. One of my best friends at the Naval Academy was Lt. Perry Graves, USMC, and Perry had married Joe's younger sister, Susie. Joe's father, who lost a leg at Pearl Harbor and won a Navy Cross for his heroism on that day, wrote the textbook we used at the Naval Academy to study military law. His father was a friend to every midshipman at the academy. He graciously allowed me to keep my TR-4 sports roadster parked in his driveway after I bought it since we were not allowed to keep our cars inside the grounds of the Academy until just before graduation.

On 4 August, our team was inserted into an LZ overlooking the Hiep Duc Valley and the main road running through it, but bombs dropped in the LZ started a brush fire that forced us to be extracted four hours later. Unlike the terrain in Happy Valley, the grass and brush on the slopes of the hills surrounding Hiep Duc Valley were tinder dry at this time of year. Also, many of the streams in the hills were dry, a situation that made thirst a primary concern for any patrol above the lowlands.

On 5 August, Killer Kane, consisting of two officers, six enlisted and one U.S. Navy corpsman, made a second attempt at insertion, and this time we had no brush fires in the LZ. Our LZ was a good one on flat, grassy terrain halfway up the southern slope of Nui Chom Mountain, an LZ approximately two miles from the LZ we used the previous day.

As usual, LCpl. John Slowick led the way as point, followed by Glor, Finlayson, Garner, Taussig, Hager, Conner, Williams, and Powell. We moved off the LZ, passed through a stand of tall trees, and then proceeded to climb a hill to reach our OP site overlooking the valley. On the way, we had to walk through a fairly open area that I feared made our presence easily detected by the enemy, but we had no other way to reach our OP. I had the patrol spread out, extending the interval between each man to nearly 30 yards and walking in a tactical staggered column, a precaution in the event we were observed by the enemy and fired upon. I did not want our patrol bunched up so a single enemy mortar round or grenade could cause multiple casualties. Although we walked in the open for nearly 300 meters, it appeared no one saw us, and soon we found a fairly good OP site on a narrow finger overlooking the valley.

The sun was brutally hot, so I chose an OP that had some five-foot-high brush, which afforded us a modicum of shade from the intense rays of the sun. Still, we were far above any source of water so all of us rationed our water as best we could. Lt. Taussig, Slowick, Garner, and I occupied the OP and started to scan the valley below us with our binoculars and spotting scope while the other five set up security higher up the finger behind us. We had to stay in the OP three days, something I did not like to do. The odds of the enemy finding us and organizing an attack were dramatically increased if we stayed in any one location for more than 24 hours. I took the risk because moving further down

Team Killer Kane waiting for their insertion helicopters at LZ Finch. Sitting in the back row, from the left, are Donald Conner and James Hager (the two men standing and the pilot in black squatting are unidentified); middle row: J. D. Glor and me; front row: Dave Powell, R. Garner, and Clarence Williams.

the finger toward the valley would expose us in open terrain, making it impossible to remain unobserved from the densely populated valley floor. If we moved higher into the canopy, we would have a very limited field of vision, and this would take us even farther from any potential source of water. It was one of the many Hobson's choices I had to make. I decided to stay put, accomplish our mission as best we could, and preserve our water.

From the 5th to the 7th of August, we made twelve separate sightings of VC and NVA troops moving north through the hamlets of Thuan Long (3) and An Long (1). We called in twelve artillery fire missions and directed two air strikes against the 121 enemy soldiers we observed. Even though we used a lot of artillery and air strikes on these targets, we only observed four confirmed killed due to the distance between our OP and the impact areas and the foliage where the artillery shells and bombs landed. We had very good response times from the artillery batteries supporting us and outstanding coverage of the targets, so we assessed an additional 27 probable kills. Several of our fire missions had to be delayed or abandoned because the enemy was moving through villages, and the South Vietnamese district headquarters would not grant clearance because they feared the artillery would kill or wound innocent civilians. I pointed out to Joe, who was getting a very good introduction to the use of supporting arms, that the enemy often traveled through densely populated areas deliberately because they knew we could not get clearance to fire on them if they were close to civilians. The enemy was also adept at moving along military unit and civilian administrative boundaries since this required more than one clearance. This enemy tactic often delayed many fire missions to the point where they could not be fired effectively, if at all.

By the 7th, despite our best efforts to conserve water, we found that we were taking our last sips from our canteens. The heat was becoming more and more intense. I knew we would need water soon, or I would have to ask for an extraction. I radioed Camp Reasoner, and they told me a water resupply would be sent that afternoon, and it would be dropped to us via poncho parachute from a low altitude so the likelihood of the enemy observing it from the valley would be minimal. I had my doubts, but I said we would be standing by for the drop.

In mid-afternoon a CH-46 flew over our position and dropped the water. The loadmaster in the helicopter dropped the bundle right on target but the speed of the helicopter caused the parachute to only partially open so all of the plastic bags of water were broken on impact. We watched with dismay and disappointment as the precious water sank into the parched ground. An hour later, we were told we would be extracted early the next morning. Throughout the rest of the day and into the night, I had dreams of ice-cold drinks.

In the morning of 8 August we were disappointed time and again as Camp Reasoner told us our extraction would be delayed for one reason or another. Finally, a little after noon, we were told the helicopters were on the way, and soon after that we were extracted from a rather poor LZ on a narrow finger east of the summit of Hill 623 (Team Killer Kane Patrol Report, 8 August 1967). When we landed at LZ Finch, our company Gunny, GySgt. Gabbert, had two gallons of ice water and a case of cold beer waiting for us. I paid the Gunny for the beer, and the entire team sat down and drank our fill of water and beer. I never tasted another cold beer as good as the one I had that day.

On 9 August, my old platoon sergeant, SSgt. Thompson, stopped by Camp Reasoner to say hello and to tell me about his new job with the CIA. He said his job was classified and it involved training former VC to conduct reconnaissance and espionage missions. I asked him to tell me where he was living now, but all he would say was he was living in an "embassy house" in I Corps, and his living conditions were a lot better than mine. He was interested in our most recent patrols, so I took out my maps and showed him where we had been and what we had done since his departure. When I reminded him of the patrol where he knocked himself out trying to retrieve a parachute drop that was supposed to be water but turned out to be rations and ammunition instead, his mood turned sour and he began to curse and rant about the time we nearly died of thirst while on that mission in the Que Son Mountains during Operation Union II. He was still angry about the fruitless three-hour climb he had to make in the blistering heat to retrieve rations instead of water.

Capt. Dixon asked me how well Lt. Taussig had done on the patrol, and I told him Joe was ready to take out a patrol immediately. Joe had called in several artillery missions during our patrol and had observed me calling in the air strikes, so I told Capt. Dixon Joe was certainly ready for any Stingray mission. I could tell Capt. Dixon was pleased with Joe and thought highly of him.

Almost in passing, Capt. Dixon told me that Killer Kane might be assigned to the

Special Landing Force (SLF) in September. He explained that the Marine Corps maintained a floating reserve of one battalion landing team (BLT) aboard U.S. Navy amphibious ships, a sort of 911 team in the event reinforcements were needed anywhere along the South Vietnamese coast. The SLF battalions had different units attached to them, such as an artillery battery, a tank platoon, an engineer platoon, an amtrac platoon, and a recon platoon, which gave these battalions as lot of extra firepower and capability. I told him I had hoped to be sent to scuba school in the Philippines, but I would go wherever I was needed. He said it might be possible to do both. Although it sounded to me that he had made up his mind to send Killer Kane for this assignment, he told me not to give it too much thought for now since the decision on what recon team would be going to the SLF had not been made.

When I asked Capt. Dixon what, if anything, I should do to prepare for the SLF, he recommended that I should begin training my platoon on the use of the company's rubber boats and participate in the upcoming parachute jumps scheduled for later in the month. This was the first I had heard of any contemplated parachute training, so I was intrigued as to why this training was beginning now. He told me that division was planning to insert our entire company by parachute in a future operation "out west," but he said he was not sure yet of the actual location. I would have to wait for a few weeks to find out where the destination for this parachute jump would be.

The evening of the 10th, Joe Taussig and I met with three of our Naval Academy classmates who were back in the 1st Marine Division's area to receive some training. We decided to take out a Weapons Carrier (WC) truck from the motor pool and drive to the Stone Elephant Officers' Club in Da Nang. This was my first visit to this officers' club since the unpleasant experience we had when we were asked to leave the club, and I wondered if the club manager would remember me or not. As it turned out, he did not remember me, and we all enjoyed a delicious steak dinner and some good music afterwards.

This night, there was a very attractive Vietnamese woman singing with the band. Her name was Khanh Ly, and she was one of the most popular singers in the country. She recorded many of the songs written by Vietnam's most successful song writer of the day, Trinh Cong Son. She sang both Vietnamese and American popular songs with great ability and emotion, even taking requests from the audience, demonstrating a rich knowledge of both country's musical tastes. I would encounter Khanh Ly again during my second tour of duty in South Vietnam.

On the 14th of August, Killer Kane was inserted on top of Hill 478, four miles south of Hiep Duc with the mission of observing the Hiep Duc area south of the Song Thu Bon River. Since we had encountered problems with brush fires started by fixed-wing bombing of our LZs on previous patrols, I had asked the pilots of our insertion helicopters not to request prep bombing on this insertion. However, my advice was either ignored or forgotten because 250 pound bombs were dropped on the insertion LZ, and this started a raging brush fire, making a landing on Hill 478 impossible. Instead, we had to pick another LZ more than a mile away. This LZ was a good one, but it was several hundred meters from the jungle canopy, requiring us to walk in the open where we could easily be observed by any enemy in the vicinity. When we reached the canopy, I stopped the patrol and we waited and listened for any signs of enemy activity. After I had used my compass and map to determine our exact location, I started to tell my radioman, LCpl. Dobson, to send a position report, but before I could finish a sentence, I heard a grenade explode toward the front of the patrol, no more than 30 meters away. There was a pregnant pause, and then I heard Cpl. James W. Hager begin to fire his Stoner light machine gun. He was soon joined by LCpl. John Slowick firing his M-16 rifle. Because the ridgeline we were on was steep and thick with secondary growth, only Slowick and Hager had seen the four NVA soldiers who had come down the ridgeline and thrown the grenade. I brought the patrol on line, and we began to fire and maneuver up the hill in the direction that Hager and Slowick had been firing. There were no return fire and no blood trails, but there were several sets of Ho Chi Minh sandal prints in the moist earth and an NVA pith helmet, which we quickly deemed outstanding trading material. Slowick placed it in his rucksack.

I asked Hager what had happened and he rather sheepishly admitted that he had laid his machine gun down when we stopped to take out his canteen to drink some water. As he was taking a drink he saw the enemy coming toward the patrol. When he moved to retrieve his machine gun, the enemy saw him and threw the grenade which, fortunately for him, hit a tree next to him and exploded harmlessly behind the tree. Aside from a ringing in his ears, he was unhurt. Slowick got a good look at the enemy troops as they ran away and told me they were wearing the ubiquitous gray-green field uniforms of the NVA. The lesson learned for Cpl. Hager and everyone else in the patrol was to always keep your weapon in your hands, even on a break. We lost a very good opportunity to kill or capture some NVA because of this mistake, but no one was more remorseful than Cpl. Hager, one of the best men in my platoon and a Marine who seldom made any mistakes while on patrol.

We moved southeast and came upon a well-used trail. Since we had made contact earlier, I decided it was too risky to travel on it. We noticed there were a lot of elephant spores on this trail, which surprised us since we were relatively high up in the hills. Normally, we only found elephant feces on low ground near sources of water. I moved the patrol off the trail and into an area of dense brush where we harbored the rest of the day and that night. During the night we heard elephants trumpeting repeatedly. It is often difficult to gauge distances by sound in the jungle, but we all agreed these elephants were fairly close to our position, perhaps as close as 100 meters. I wondered what action I would have the patrol take if the elephants decided to take a walk through our harbor site at night. I imagined the letter the Marine Corps would send home to my parents informing them that their son had been trampled to death by elephants.

The next day we moved to several different OP locations but we saw very little going on in the valley below us. At times, it seemed as if the valley was deserted, but periodically throughout the day, we would observe a few farmers doing the normal chores that Vietnamese farmers perform in the summer months, such as carrying shoulder poles with buckets of night soil for fertilizing their fields, or cutting wood, or maintaining their paddy dikes. During the three days we observed the valley, we only saw VC one time, and these seven enemy soldiers fled when we called in an artillery mission on them. Although we had good coverage of the target and we started some good brush fires near where we sighted them, we could not observe the results due to the distance and the terrain.

The only other thing we saw on this patrol of note was a tiger. One of my men was scanning the low ground to our north when he spotted a tiger prowling in an open area on the side of a hill approximately a half mile to our northwest. At first, I did not believe him since I knew tigers were nocturnal animals and usually avoided humans. But when I took his binoculars and looked at the open area he pointed out, I saw the tiger clearly as it moved back and forth on the side of the hill. Everyone wanted to see the tiger so we spent the next five or ten minutes sharing the binoculars until the tiger moved off into the jungle. That night, as I drifted off to sleep, I hoped that tiger did not pick up our scent and try to make a meal of us.

On the 17th at 1530 we were extracted from the same LZ we used for insertion and replaced by a recon team from Chu Lai (Team Killer Kane Patrol Report, 17 August 1967).

While we were back at Camp Reasoner our team participated in the first parachute training the company had done since coming into country. We made five jumps at the Red Beach drop zone (DZ) out of CH-46 helicopters: three without equipment and two with a full combat load. Lt. Charlie Campbell, a former SNCO who won a combat commission, was the jump master. The weather was perfect for our jumps, with clear skies and only a light wind, blowing off the South China Sea. The Red Beach DZ was large and

Parachute training at Red Beach.

Parachute training at Red Beach.

sandy, so we had no problems with injuries or damaged equipment. Many of the men were curious about the motive for this training, but no one, including our CO, seemed to know exactly what was being planned. Capt. Dixon told us that we would be told when we needed to know.

As the "Summer of Living Dangerously" came to an end, Killer Kane took its last patrol to Hill 452, spending an uneventful week on this rocky pinnacle overlooking the Song Thu Bon River and the Nong Son Coal Mine. Our twelve-man patrol occupied the bunkers on this radio relay site and spent each day looking south for enemy activity in the western entrance to Antenna Valley. In a letter home to my parents written the day after the patrol's return, and in our team patrol report of 29 Aug. 1967, I described this uneventful patrol this way:

> My patrol to Hill 452 was just seven days of looking at rice paddies, water buffaloes, farmers, villages and hills. We didn't see any VC the entire time so it wasn't a very interesting patrol. I did manage to read four books while I wasn't on watch and to eat plenty of C rations and to experiment with the new and very tasty Long Range Patrol Ration. In the afternoons and the early evenings it rained a great deal making it impossible to observe and very uncomfortable, as well. In the mornings the entire area below us was covered with fog and low clouds, making us feel as if we were angels in heaven looking down on the earth below. Never were "angels" so dirty, so unshaven, so mean-looking ... waiting to hurl 8-inch artillery thunder bolts at the slightest sign of the VC.

7

Happy Valley

I had expected to go out on patrol again on 2 September, but our mission was canceled because all of the CH-46 helicopters had been grounded due to a safety stand-down. The stand-down was the result of several fatal crashes caused by catastrophic tail rotor failures. While the problem was being investigated, we were told all future recon insertions would be made using Marine UH-34 helicopters, a sturdy and reliable helicopter, but one that was becoming obsolete. However, when one of these single rotor choppers went down in Happy Valley, all recon helicopter insertions were canceled for a few days.

There were national elections in South Vietnam on September 3rd, and the turnout was heavy in the Da Nang area, with long lines of voters at the polling stations. Vietnamese soldiers stood guard at most of the polling stations to prevent the VC from disrupting the elections, but U.S. Marines and other Americans were told to stay away from the polls so no one could say we were trying to influence the outcome. The voting went ahead with no apparent signs of fraud or voter ambivalence. In fact, every Vietnamese I talked to seemed to be genuinely interested in the election.

In Quang Nam Province there was a bitter rivalry between the two major contending parties, the Dai Viet and VNQDD, a rivalry both intense and violent. Despite this rivalry, it appeared that in the hamlets around our camp and the districts close to Da Nang the elections were carried out with no apparent problems. I learned later that things did not go smoothly in southern Quang Nam Province. There the VC attempted to disrupt the voting by intimidating some rural voters. The VC murdered 19 civilians in the province, 11 of whom were women and children, in a vain attempt to keep people in a few districts from going to the polls to vote.

Most Marines did not have any contact with the Vietnamese population, unless they were involved in some civic action or advisory job, so it was difficult for them to gauge the attitude of the average citizen in Quang Nam Province. I was fortunate to have made a few friends among the Vietnamese who worked near Camp Reasoner. I often talked to two Vietnamese women, Mai Ly and Dien, who worked as waitresses in the 1st Marine Division Officers' Club. They were in their late teens or early twenties, and both were the daughters of South Vietnamese military personnel. If I had a question about Vietnam or its people, I usually asked these two women.

Whenever I went to the division officers' club, they would greet me by name and ask me what drink I wanted. They were kept busy by the club manager most of the time, but once in a while I would spend a few minutes talking to them and flirting a bit. Although most of these conversations were short and did not cover weighty subjects, on occasion I would ask them questions about current events or how they felt about what the Americans were doing in their country. They both could be blunt and outspoken, traits that led me to believe their answers were honest and not crafted to simply appease me. For instance, Mai Ly once told me that while she valued the presence of the Marines in her province and understood the need for the security the Marines provided, she also was angry over the way Americans often treated the Vietnamese and the adverse effect the American presence had on the economy in Da Nang. Even though she personally benefited financially from the American presence and she was certainly not sympathetic to the communists, she admitted she was not happy with the impact the war had on the average South Vietnamese citizen. My friendship with Mai Ly and Dien grew to the point where they both invited me to their weddings and honored me by inviting me to their parents' homes, a really singular honor for an American. Both Mai Ly and Dien married members of the South Vietnamese Air Force, and for a time they lived with their husbands in the Da Nang VNAF housing compound before moving to civilian houses near the Da Nang Airbase.

Mai Ly, the waitress at the 1st Marine Division Headquarters Officers' Club, Hill 327.

These young women had effervescent personalities, brilliant smiles, and a not so subtle way of making fun of some odd physical or personal characteristic they found amusing in their American friends. Mai Ly, in particular, was hilarious when she would mimic a lieutenant colonel (Lt.Col.) she thought looked and walked like a duck. Dressed in their national dress, the Ao Dai, they always made for a welcome sight whenever I returned from patrol. Talking to them for a few minutes helped to dissipate the stress of a long-range patrol. While most of our conversations were restricted to light subjects, there were occasions when we discussed the impact the war was having on their lives and the lives of their family members. Both women were fervently nationalistic, strongly anti-communist, and completely devoted to the welfare of their families. During my year-long tour of duty, I would often ask these two women questions about Vietnamese culture and attitudes, and in each case they seemed eager to educate me about their country and its problems. For example, I asked Mai Ly why so many people seemed to support the VC in the rural areas, and she told me the rural peasants had no choice. When I asked her to explain what she meant, she replied, "In the villages, the VC force everyone to belong to an organization they control, and they use these organizations to force people to do what the VC want them to do. If you disagree, they will kill you, so they have no choice." When she spoke these words, it reminded me of the Chinese communist books

I had read while I was a midshipman at the Naval Academy. Specifically, I thought of Mao Tse-tung's emphasis on political mobilization using mass-based organizations, which he wrote about in his paper "On Protracted War." I thought of a quote from that paper: "The mobilization of the common people throughout the country will create a vast sea in which to drown the enemy, create the conditions that will make up for our inferiority in arms..., and create the prerequisites for overcoming every difficulty in the war" (*Selected Writings of Mao Tse-tung* [Peking: Foreign Languages Press, 1963], p. 228). These words of Mao's did not have any great significance to me when I first read them as a midshipman, nor did they seem particularly important to me when Mai Ly expressed a similar construct. This was because my war was not in the villages. It was in the mountains far from the rural population she spoke of and far from where Mao's guidance on the conduct of revolutionary war was being carried out. I would only come to realize the critical importance of political mobilization on my second tour of duty in South Vietnam when my war took me into the villages and I had to confront the reality of the enemy's mass-based organizations.

My friendship with Mai Ly and Dien was purely platonic, but it was strong and enduring. We remained good friends until I left South Vietnam in the summer of 1970 after my second tour. Once in a while, I would hear Marine officers bragging that they had dated one or both women, but I knew this was only wishful thinking on the part of these officers. To this day, I often wonder what happened to them after the communists conquered South Vietnam.

In the early fall of 1967, the Division G-2 received intelligence that the enemy was planning a big offensive in early 1968. In preparation for this offensive, the enemy was increasing their infiltration of soldiers and supplies down the Ho Chi Minh Trail to their base areas in eastern Laos and western South Vietnam. This enemy infiltration activity resulted in an increase in requests for recon patrols near the suspected NVA infiltration routes in the western regions of Quang Nam Province. More and more patrols were sent into Happy Valley, the Ong Thu Slope, and Base Area 112 in an attempt to locate the NVA units that seemed to be pouring into the province. Killer Kane was part of this effort to detect enemy troop movement and arms infiltration.

On 6 September, our team was inserted into the Quang Duc Duc area about ten miles west of the An Hoa Combat Base with the mission of observing the trail networks that traversed the Khe Gio tributary. This patrol area was in the foothills on the eastern slope of the Ong Thu Slope, the huge, flat plateau overlooking the Arizona Territory. The terrain in this area was very steep with unusually thick secondary growth which made movement slow and difficult. To compound this problem, there were also many open areas in the hills that made it easy for anyone living in the Arizona area's villages and hamlets to observe a patrol foolish enough to spend any time walking through them during the day.

Our two UH 34 helicopters landed in a fairly good, one-bird LZ, but I was concerned by the amount of time it took for both helicopters to make it in and out of the LZ. We had to use two helicopters to insert our nine-man team because of the weight limitations of the UH-34 helicopter. I did not have a choice in the matter, but it was something I did not like because it doubled the opportunity for the enemy to observe our landing.

However, since our normal means of insertion, the CH-46, was still in a maintenance stand-down, we had no other option available to us. We had to jump from the side door of the UH-34, a tricky evolution given we did not really know how deep the elephant grass in the LZ was by just looking at it. We literally took a leap of faith when we jumped. Fortunately for us, the grass was about waist high, but with 70 pounds of gear on our backs, the impact with the ground was jarring. We moved off the LZ and almost immediately found ourselves on a well-used trail leading north down into a small valley just south of Hill 199. I had the patrol follow the trail for 200 meters and then I decided to leave it and cut down hill to the west. Two hours later, we found ourselves at the bottom of a small valley with a fast-running stream running through it. There I had the patrol rest for 20 minutes and fill their canteens before making our ascent to the summit of Hill 199. On our climb up the hill, we encountered several nests of fire ants which were impossible to avoid, so we doused ourselves with insect repellent and soldiered on despite some very painful stings. The climb up Hill 199 was very strenuous, and the heat made it even more difficult. We took our time since we did not want to make any noise that would give our presence away. It was dark by the time we neared the summit, a problem for us since it meant we would have to find a safe harbor site in the dark. After a brief search of the summit, we found a suitable site to spend the night, a place that was thick with brambles and vines. We had not eaten since our insertion, so I gave the order to eat a cold meal of C rations before I established our night radio watch and radioed our position report to Camp Reasoner.

The next morning, the 7th of September, we found a good OP site on the summit of Hill 199 and began scanning the trail network that crossed the Khe Gio River to our east and southeast. We had taken more observation equipment than usual on this patrol because our map study indicated we would have excellent observation from Hill 199 and other high ground nearby. If we were to accomplish our mission, we needed to find an OP that gave us good observation of the trails that led from the Ong Thu Slope to the Arizona Territory. With this in mind, we took two 7 × 50 binoculars, one 8 × 30 binocular, and a Starlight (night vision) scope. While the OP site on Hill 199 was excellent for observation, it was not comfortable since there was little shade. I was also worried about the lack of any significant cover at the site, always a serious problem if we got into a firefight.

At 0925, we heard several loud voices speaking in Vietnamese in the stream bed below us. We called in an artillery fire mission, and the voices ceased. We were surprised that people could get this close to us without our observing them. Later that morning, around 1130 we observed six enemy soldiers moving northwest on a trail several hundred meters to our north. These enemy soldiers appeared to be searching for us, and they fired several signal shots from their rifles, probably as a warning to their colleagues that we were in the vicinity. I called in an artillery fire mission from an artillery battery at An Hoa Combat Base, and the coverage of the target was outstanding. However, since we could not observe any bodies due to dense foliage in the impact area, I gave the battery a rather conservative count of three probable kills. Assessing enemy casualties from artillery or air strikes was always an imprecise endeavor due the distance between a patrol and the target. When thick foliage concealed the impact area, the task was even more difficult. Still, we all felt very confident we had killed all six of the enemy soldiers. We just could not prove it.

Around 1830, Sgt. Dave Pugh and Cpl. Bill Ellison came to me and told me they had found two 250-pound bombs rigged as booby traps on the eastern side of the summit of Hill 199, not far from our OP. The enemy knew U.S. Marines and other American infantry units preferred to organize their defensive positions on prominent terrain features, such as hilltops, so they often implanted multiple booby traps on high ground. For this reason, I had everyone check the areas around them while I slowly followed Pugh and Ellison to where the bombs were located. After crawling up to them, but not touching them, I took down the fuse lot number of one of them so we could determine their origin.

Although no one reported finding any other booby traps or mines, I decided we should leave the area and find another OP site. Since we had encountered two lethal booby traps on the hill, I had the team move very slowly and cautiously to another OP site 150 meters away. At this new location, we had good observation over the trails in the southern portion of the Arizona Territory, especially those near the village of Khuong Dai (6). An agent report had indicated that this village had been used by the 3rd Battalion, 3rd NVA Regiment when it moved between the Ong Thu Slope and the An Hoa basin.

We spent the next two days in the vicinity of this OP observing to our east, but we did not see any enemy activity until the 9th when two enemy soldiers appeared only 20 meters from our OP. They seemed to be searching for us, and I was just about to take them under fire when they dropped over the side of the hill and disappeared. Soon after this, we heard more voices to our east and the squealing of pigs, but no one approached our position again. We suspected that the enemy knew where we were, but wanted to move their "pork on the hoof" and other supplies back up to the Ong Thu Slope without us calling in an artillery mission on them. Whatever their motives were, they did not attack us, and we were extracted from a good, flat, grassy LZ at 0900 on the 9th of September. The helicopters received small-arms fire as we lifted out of the LZ, and one round penetrated the deck of the helicopter, narrowly missing Sgt. Pugh, who was on his last patrol before rotating back to the U.S. As we left the area, fixed-wing aircraft came in and bombed the valley east of the extraction LZ (Team Killer Kane Patrol Report, 9 August 1967).

When we returned to Camp Reasoner, we were greeted with some very bad news. While we were on patrol two recon Marines were killed and another wounded on a patrol in Happy Valley. The seven-man patrol was hit by 15 NVA soldiers as the patrol waited in their LZ for extraction. Evidently, an NVA counter-recon team had followed the patrol and saw their chance to attack the Marines as they waited for their extraction helicopters to arrive. One of the men killed had only a few weeks left before returning home.

This bad news was compounded by the tragic events surrounding the first combat parachute jump by 1st Force Reconnaissance Company. Team Club Car, a nine-man team made up of parachute qualified men from my 5th platoon and a few other volunteers, led by my platoon sergeant, GySgt. Walter Webb, was parachuted into Happy Valley on the night of 5 September with disastrous results. High winds and poor navigation by the USAF C-130 transport plane carrying the Marine parachutists resulted in the team landing far from their intended drop zone and into high, 150-foot triple canopy. The team suffered many injuries and was unable to continue on their mission. Compounding the injuries was the loss of one of the team, HN2 Michael "Doc" Laporte, who went missing and was never found despite a long and thorough search. (Sgt. James W. Hager, Cpl. Robert J. Garcia, and LCpl. John Slowick from Team Killer Kane participated in the ill-fated jump [see also: Stubbe and Lanning, pp. 119–126]).

The parachute drop was necessitated by a combination of factors. First, intelligence had suspected the enemy had been staging Soviet-built Frog 3 missiles in Happy Valley, and they feared the enemy was preparing to fire these long-range missiles at the Da Nang Airbase. Second, maintenance problems with the CH-46 helicopter put a premium on the use of the few UH-34 helicopters available, so a parachute insert was deemed to be a good substitute. Finally, there were persistent rumors that the 1st Force Recon Company needed to prepare for a major operation planned for early 1968 in the northern end of the A Shau Valley very near the Laotian border, an operation that would require the entire company to parachute at night into this very dangerous area. I was told by a friend of mine in the division headquarters that the company would seize a hill in the northern part of the valley that overlooked the road that ran along the valley floor. Once we had seized this hill, two heliborne Marine infantry battalions would land in the southern part of the valley and sweep north toward us. We all knew such an operation would be a very high risk one, but I was told III MAF wanted to establish a blocking force on the hill as covertly as possible since they feared a daylight helicopter insertion would allow the enemy to escape into Laos where we were forbidden to follow. The best way to prevent the enemy from escaping was to establish a blocking force along the road leading into Laos and to do this under the cover of darkness, thus the use of a night parachute operation. While many of us questioned the wisdom of such parachute operations, there were many advocates who endorsed the parachute jump into Happy Valley. They believed it would serve as a means of proving the feasibility of similar clandestine airborne operation near the Laotian border, where the enemy had many logistics facilities and base areas. Although the Tet offensive of 1968 was the primary reason for abandoning the operation into the A Shau Valley, the disastrous results of the jump into Happy Valley was a major contributing factor in the decision to abandon the idea.

III MAF headquarters continued to receive numerous indicators that the enemy was planning "something big" for early 1968, but exactly what was not clear. Everyone knew that the enemy would need to reinforce their units in Quang Nam Province with more NVA troops if they intended to launch a really big attack against Da Nang, so it was only logical that they would soon be sending replacement drafts down the Ho Chi Minh Trail and along the infiltration routes leading to their staging areas in the province. As a result, the new S-2 of the 1st Reconnaissance Battalion, Lt. Paul Young, began to schedule additional patrols in the areas that were suspected enemy base areas or infiltration routes. The division wanted to know what the enemy was preparing for, and they hoped our patrols would produce more information about the enemy's plans. As part of this effort, Capt. Edwin H. Walker, the battalion's new operations officer, called me into the S-3 shop on 14 September and told me he wanted Killer Kane to try to determine if the 2nd NVA Division was moving from their traditional base areas in the west of the province into Antenna Valley, the large fertile valley south of An Hoa. With this objective in mind, he assigned us an NFZ around Hill 454 in the hope that we could find a good OP site on that hill from which we could monitor enemy activity.

After performing our routine preparations, including an overflight of the projected NFZ, Killer Kane was inserted at 0900 on 16 September into a large, two-helicopter LZ located in the hills overlooking the northern part of the valley. The insert helicopters took a lot of ground fire from a hamlet south of the insert LZ as we approached but no damage was done. Once we were on the ground, our eight-man patrol left the LZ for the safety of high jungle canopy and began to climb the steep slope of Hill 454. It took us only two hours to reach the summit, but the going was very rough, and the heat combined with the strenuous climb completely sapped our strength. Several of the men were near exhaustion by the time we reached the summit. After resting for a few minutes, I found a good OP site just west of the summit where we set up security and observed the valley to our south for the remainder of the day.

In the late afternoon, I began to search for a good harbor site for the night. As a security precaution, I sent out Cpl. Hager, my new assistant patrol leader who replaced Sgt. Pugh, with PFC Landis, PFC Ellis, and HN3 Conner to thoroughly search the entire summit area. After a few minutes, Cpl. Hager came back to me with a very worried look on his face, and he told me that "Doc" Conner was on the topographical summit of the hill, and he had stepped on a booby-trap mine. Since I was only 50 meters from the summit, I thought I would have heard an explosion if "Doc" Conner had triggered a booby trap, but Cpl. Hager explained that the booby trap was a "Bouncing Betty" pressure release mine and since Conner had not moved, the pressure-release mechanism had not been activated. If Conner moved, releasing the pressure his foot exerted on the mine, it would explode. As long as he continued to stand on the mine and not move, he was safe. I immediately moved up to where Conner was standing, but I moved very cautiously because I knew the enemy often "seeded" areas with mines, and I did not want to step on one in my haste to get to Conner. I had Hager take me back to Conner's position using the exact route he had used so as to minimize the chance of triggering another mine. When I got to Conner, I could see he was extremely agitated and distraught, as anyone standing on top of a pressure-release anti-personnel mine would be. This mine got its name of "Bouncing Betty" because once the pressure-release mechanism was activated, a spring-type device would propel the mine up into the air about three feet and then detonate, causing the shrapnel to enter the torso of its victim. It was just such a mine that killed Capt. Eric Barnes and Sgt. Blankenship months earlier.

I told "Doc" not to move and then I crouched low over his foot to observe the mine. What I saw gave me hope. I could see the prongs of the mine directly under Conner's toe, and I thought he may not have fully compressed them. The prongs had to be compressed to trigger the mine. We did not have helmets or flak jackets to lie around his foot to absorb or deflect the mine when it went off, but we did have our packs, so I gathered four or five packs around his leg. Then I had everyone move away, and I told Conner his best course of action was to fall directly backwards, holding a pack with a radio in it on his chest. In this way, any blast would go off above him, and the shrapnel would not penetrate the steel casing of the radio which would be protecting his vital organs. Conner was very scared, but he did what I told him to do. As he fell backwards, all we heard was the sound of him hitting the ground. The mine did not detonate, probably because Conner's foot had not fully compressed the activation prongs. I then had our entire team get on their hands and knees and feel for any other mines that might be planted nearby. Our search was meticulous and careful, taking us over an hour to feel every inch of the ground in an area 20 yards by 30 yards. We did not find any other mines, but I decided it would be best to avoid the summit from now on and remain near our OP site. Once again, we relearned the lesson of how the enemy employed their most lethal mines and booby traps. They planted them on terrain such as hill-tops where they thought Marines were most likely to establish defensive positions.

The next day, the 17th, I decided to get rid of the mine since it could kill some other Marine who happened to reach the summit of Hill 454. Cpl. Hager and I cleared the dirt away from the mine, and then I took an M-26 fragmentation grenade and unscrewed the top of it and inserted an electric blasting cap into the grenade housing. We took cover behind a rock and then detonated the grenade and the mine simultaneously. As we did this, we heard cheering and laughing coming from near the hamlet of Ap Ba (2), 2,000 meters south of us in the valley. My men wanted me to call in artillery on this hamlet, but I refused since I could not be sure we would not kill innocent civilians along with those laughing and cheering. It was not a popular decision, but I reminded everyone that we only called in fire missions on observed enemy and we had not observed any so far. As an afterthought, I told them that if the people laughing when the mine exploded were the same people who planted it, then they might come up here to check on their handiwork. If they did, this would give us a chance to kill them. This seemed to mollify the team somewhat.

We spent the remainder of the 17th and most of the 18th looking through our binoculars during the day and using the Starlight scope at night, but we did not see a single enemy soldier and we rarely saw any males at all. In fact, the valley appeared to be deserted except for some women working in the fields and some children tending water buffaloes. After we had moved into our harbor site on the night of the 18th, we heard movement only ten meters from our position. Careful not to make a sound, everyone was placed on alert and took up firing positions in anticipation of a possible attack. As a general rule, we never fired our weapons at night, unless it was absolutely necessary. Doing so gave our position away immediately, something the enemy wanted us to do. Instead, we normally responded with M-26 fragmentation grenades first since this did not give our position away, yet it could inflict casualties on anyone probing for our harbor site. In this case, I had Hager throw two grenades in the direction of the sound. After the two grenades went off, lighting up the jungle, we heard more movement and then silence. We waited silently for two hours, but we did not hear anything else that night.

In the morning, we searched the area where we had thrown the grenades and found Ho Chi Minh sandal prints near a Claymore mine we had set up just before dark. I suspected that the enemy, probably local VC from Ap Ba (2), had climbed up Hill 454 to see what damage their "Bouncing Betty" mine had done. Instead, they found our Claymore mine and were either trying to steal it or turn it around so it would fire back at us. It did not matter now because our grenades had clearly told them that U.S. Marines were on the summit of Hill 454. I expected them to return with reinforcements, so I moved our

OP and located our new harbor site in the densest jungle growth I could find. If they came back looking for us, they would not find us where they last encountered us, and they would have to make an awful racket moving through the tangle of vines and brush our new OP site provided.

From our new location we were able to see across most of the valley. It was still largely deserted, save for a few kids on their water buffaloes, but around 1500 in the afternoon an Air Force AO flew over the valley and four or five automatic weapons fired at his aircraft. The fire sounded as if it was coming from Ap Ba (2). We informed the AO and asked him if he intended to call in air strikes on the hamlet, and he told us he had no aircraft readily available. I then told him I would call in an artillery mission on the hamlet, which I proceeded to do. I fired thirty-six 105 mm artillery rounds into the hamlet teaching the inhabitants a grim lesson I hoped they would not forget. Two hours later, the AO returned, and this time when he flew over the hamlet no one fired at him.

On the 20th at 0900, we were extracted and returned to Camp Reasoner (Team Killer Kane Patrol Report, 20 Sept. 1967). When our team got off the extract helicopters at LZ Finch we were greeted by our new CO, Maj. Daniel J. Keating, a native of Larchmont, New York. I took to Dan Keating immediately. He had an easygoing manner that made him very approachable, but he was also thoroughly professional and serious when it came to leading our company. Dan and I were both Roman Catholic, but he was far more knowledgeable about the Church and its precepts. He often assisted the battalion chaplain with Mass. I learned he had a large family back in the States, and he loved to talk about his children and his wife, often taking a letter from them out of his uniform pocket and sharing portions of it with me. It was obvious that he loved his family deeply and missed them a great deal. Filling Capt. Dixon's shoes would require a truly superior officer, but we all agreed that Maj. Keating was the kind of officer who could meet such a standard. The thing I most admired about Maj. Keating was his ability to listen to advice from his officers and enlisted men and to stand up for us, when the need arose.

About this time, I first became involved with the Sacred Heart Roman Catholic Orphanage in Da Nang. At the suggestion of Father B. G. Ryan, the Catholic chaplain for the 1st Marine Division, I began sending monthly donations to the Sisters of St. Paul de Chartres, who ran the orphanage. Later on, I often asked Commander (Cdr.) Ray Stubbe, a Lutheran priest and Navy chaplain, to take my donations to the orphanage if I was unable to make the trip myself. Cdr. Stubbe was a much beloved chaplain, who served as the chaplain for the 26th Marines during the siege at Khe Sanh, and after the war he wrote a book about this important battle; along with John Prados, titled *Valley of Decision: The Siege of Khe Sanh.*

The war had produced a lot of orphans, and many of them were now living with the Vietnamese and Filipino nuns at the Sacred Heart Orphanage in Da Nang. In between patrols, I would often stop by the orphanage to give my $10 contribution to the nuns and chat with them about their work. I was greatly impressed with them. Their love for the children entrusted to their care and the backbreaking work they performed in their badly understaffed and underfunded orphanage reminded me of the Scottish missionary priest in A. J. Cronin's inspiring book *The Keys to the Kingdom.* Surely, I thought, there must be a special place in heaven for these dedicated and compassionate nuns. My association with this orphanage would last until a few months after the fall of Saigon in 1975, when all communication with the orphanage was severed by the victorious communists.

On 21 September, I was called up to the S-3 shop for a meeting with Capt. Walker and Lt. Paul Young. They told me that there was to be a B-52 strike against a large enemy target far to the west, only ten miles from the Laotian border and farther west than any Marine recon patrol had ever been before. They told me the enemy was stepping up infiltration of both men and supplies in anticipation of a major offensive, and the people at III MAF and MACV wanted everything done to locate and destroy these infiltration groups before they reached their staging areas near the lowlands. Lt. Young said a special reconnaissance plane had flown over an area of Western Quang Nam Province near the junction of the A Vuong and the Tam Talou Rivers, 15 miles west of Happy Valley, and had located a large number of enemy troops. This plane carried a new technology that could detect the presence of humans and animals by the chemical makeup of their sweat. I had my doubts about such a capability, but I continued to listen as they described this "people sniffer" technology and how it produced an estimate of nearly 1,000 people within a mile of the abandoned montagnard hamlet of Trao deep in the Annamite Mountains.

With great enthusiasm, they went on to tell me that the Division G-2 wanted Killer Kane to land in this area immediately after the B-52 strike to conduct a bomb damage assessment (BDA). At first I was incredulous, but then I saw they were completely serious. I asked them, "You want my team to land in an area where 1,000 NVA soldiers are located, and to do so right after they have been pissed off by a B-52 bombing raid? That sounds like a very dangerous mission with a high probability of my team getting wiped out."

Capt. Walker acknowledged the danger involved, but stressed that there was only one way to determine whether or not the enemy was in the area and that meant the insertion of a recon team. He then went on to tell me that the Division G-2 had specifically asked for Killer Kane to take on this mission. I suppose he thought I should be flattered by this request, but that was the furthest thing from my mind. Lt. Young, who had a lot of patrol experience before his assignment as the battalion S-2, was far more sympathetic than Capt. Walker, who had never been on a recon patrol in combat. However, I could tell from Paul's demeanor that the decision to use Killer Kane for this BDA had been made, and there was no turning back. I resigned myself to the fact that the mission would be carried out and Killer Kane would be the team to do it. Capt. Walker added to my apprehension when he told me there would be no overflight of the NFZ, because "we don't want to alert the enemy before the Arc Light strike." Now, I knew I would be going into an area thought to contain 1,000 NVA soldiers, and I would also be going in blind. I had a sick feeling in my stomach that remained with me until well after we were inserted two days later.

Lt. Young took me into his office later on, and the two of us went over everything he had on the area where we would be conducting our BDA. There wasn't much. I respected Paul for many reasons. He was a proven patrol leader with many successful patrols to his credit, he possessed a keen intellect, and he was a highly competent intelligence officer. Most of all, I respected him for his genuine compassion and concern for the recon teams he sent out. He was eager to provide all the information available to each team's leader. In my case, about all he could tell me was our patrol area was virgin territory as far as the Marine Corps was concerned. No Marine unit had ever been within miles of it. He thought the U.S. Special Forces had conducted a few "Road Runner" and CIDG patrols in the general area, but he did not know what they had encountered on these classified operations. One piece of useful information he provided was the Special Forces operations had often encountered NVA units using the trail networks leading south from the A Shau Valley and from eastern Laos, and the area I would be patrolling contained one such trail system. Paul mentioned that some of the U.S. Special Forces patrols near my NFZ had suffered heavy casualties. He briefly touched on the highly classified work of the Special Operations Group (SOG) that had its Command and Control North (CCN) headquarters near the U.S. Marine base at Phu Bai in Thua Thien Province, but nothing specific to my patrol area was produced. I had heard about SOG and CCN, but their work was so highly classified I knew very little about their mission. All Paul could tell me was SOG had "special long-range reconnaissance units" that operated in "the border area," a term used to describe eastern Laos. At this time, very few people knew about SOG or their patrols into Laos, but I could tell from Paul's cryptic comments that something like this was going on. Our patrol would not take us into Laos, but listening to Paul's remarks, I could tell he thought the area we were going into was BAD.

Fortunately for me, the composition of Killer Kane for this BDA was exceptionally strong and experienced. I would be taking only seasoned men with me, another "All-Star Team" of recon men. My assistant patrol leader was Cpl. James W. Hager, who had many patrols under his belt and was exceptionally brave, intelligent, and knowledgeable. I came to rely on his judgment and knowledge frequently and had complete confidence in his ability to take over Killer Kane, if I was killed or wounded. He was uniformly respected and admired by everyone in the platoon. Cpl. John Slowick, a native of Philadelphia, Pennsylvania, was the point man, while LCpl. David Powell, of Washington, D.C., handled the rear point duties. My corpsman for the patrol was HN3 Conner, who was not only an expert at first aid but also a skilled reconnaissance man. My two radio operators were LCpl. Garner from Minneapolis, Minnesota, and Cpl. Clarence Williams from Brooklyn, New York. Reliable, steady, and courageous, LCpl. Glor from Batavia, New York, carried the team's M-79 grenade launcher. I knew this mission would be very dangerous, but I also knew I had a first-rate team of Marines going with me. This made me both proud and confident that we could accomplish this mission safely, if we were careful and had a little luck.

At 0600 on the morning of the 23rd of September, Killer Kane gathered together in the S-3 office to hear Capt. Walker's briefing to the helicopter pilots who would be taking us on our BDA mission far to the west. We were told the B-52 "Arc Light" bombing raid had been carried out successfully a few hours before and that over a hundred 500-pound bombs had been dropped inside a rectangle 1,000 meters wide and 2,000 meters long, covering the area where the "people sniffer" had detected the presence of the enemy. Capt. Walker reminded us that our NFZ was many miles outside of the range of the nearest artillery battery, so we would have to rely solely on air support if we got into trouble. With this in mind, he had arranged for an AO to be on station over us the entire time we were on the ground, and he ordered two F-4 Phantom jets to be on "strip alert" at the Da Nang Airbase, ready to fly to our assistance if the AO called for them. While I was grateful for the extra support he had arranged, I knew the distance between the Da Nang Air base and our BDA NFZ meant we would have to wait at least 20 minutes for those jets to reach us. Twenty minutes in a firefight could be an eternity.

The atmosphere in the S-3 shop was tense, and the pilot leading the insertion package made a few caustic comments near the end of the briefing about the sanity of landing in a base area right after an "Arc Light" strike. I remained silent until the briefing was complete, but as I walked out the door into the light of a gathering dawn, the lead pilot turned to me and whispered, "I pray to God we don't find any VC out there. This mission is crazy." I could not think of anything better to say, so I simply said, "I guess we will soon find out."

It took us a long time to reach our insertion LZ. As we sat in the helicopter shivering from the cold air and the long ride west, I thought about what I would do if we encountered 1,000 NVA soldiers on the ground. None of the options I explored in my mind ended well for us. Finally, we arrived over the insertion LZ. I could see out the Plexiglas window behind me that the jungle was still smoldering from the B-52 strike that had occurred a few hours earlier. Helicopter gunships could also be seen diving over the LZ firing their machine guns. The crew chief gave me the handset of the intercom so I could talk to the pilot, who informed me that the gunships had received some ground fire. He then suggested we abort the mission.

For some illogical reason, probably rooted in hubris and the knowledge that if we did not go in now we would surely go in later, I told him we should go in now. He and his copilot looked at each other after I told them this, and it was pretty evident they did not have a lot of faith in my powers of reasoning. After a jolting and rapid descent with everyone aboard expecting disaster at any moment, Killer Kane was on the ground in a large open area surrounded by high, steep, mist-shrouded mountains. The helicopter pilot stayed in the LZ for nearly 30 seconds because he thought we might decide to abort the mission, and he did not want to land again if he did not have to. As I moved off the LZ, I gave the pilot a hand signal that we were all secure, and he saluted from his cockpit. A second later the helicopter lifted off the ground. As the helicopter struggled to gain altitude and head back to Da Nang, we heard eight or ten rifle shots coming from the valley to our east. The enemy knew we were on the ground, and it was a sure bet they were not happy about it.

The evidence of the tremendous devastation a B-52 Arc Light bombing raid could inflict was everywhere: splintered and uprooted trees, large bomb craters, small brush fires, and the air thick with the smell of wet earth and pungent explosive fumes. After pausing for 20 minutes to rest and listen in a bomb crater, the patrol moved due east along the valley floor. As we did so, we heard several signal shots coming from the vicinity of the A Vuong River to our west, a sure sign that the enemy was nearby and aware of our presence. Although the terrain was covered with thick bamboo and high elephant grass in most areas and the environmental damage caused by the bombs compounded the difficulty of traversing the terrain, we quickly moved out of the LZ. On the valley floor, we found several well-used trails, most of which were effectively camouflaged from the air by trees. We located five different trails running into the valley, all of which had evidence of recent and extensive use. We also found a large cultivated area just east of our insertion LZ and several other cultivated areas to the east along our patrol route. We could not identify all of the crops in these areas, but some we easily recognized as tobacco and corn. The crops appeared to be well-tended, both in terms of irrigation and weeding. Most of these cultivated areas were either camouflaged among other jungle growth or hidden entirely under trees. Hiding a farm on low ground was not the way Montagnard tribesmen farmed. They used slash and burn agriculture along the slopes of mountains. So we knew these cultivated areas were the work of the NVA.

As we progressed east along the valley floor, we found several large, recently occupied harbor sites, over 20 well-made log bunkers, two tunnels, 50 meters of covered trench, two pits that were obviously field latrines, and 30 fighting holes that were flush with the ground and well concealed. On one trail, we noticed that a single, narrow rut ran through the center of the trail as if some type of wagon with one wheel had been used to transport heavy loads on it or, more likely, many bicycles had traveled along this trail and over time their wheels had dug the deep rut in the trail. The NVA were known to use bicycles to transport weapons, food, and equipment along the Ho Chi Minh Trail, and this rut certainly appeared to us as something the continued use of bicycles could produce. We also found numerous Ho Chi Minh sandal prints, all pointing to the east.

In one place where a trail crossed the small stream that ran in the valley, we saw that the bank on the eastern side of the stream was completely collapsed and there were hundreds of Ho Chi Minh sandal prints in and around the collapsed earth. It was evident that a large number of enemy troops had rapidly crossed the stream at this place and headed east. At this same embankment, we saw two very large pools of blood, too big to be from humans and more likely from a large animal like an elephant or a water buffalo. Further on we found another pool of blood, but this one was more likely human since it was right beside a fighting hole that had collapsed from one of the bombs. Despite the blood and the numerous indicators that the area was a large enemy complex used for transiting troops, we did not find a single enemy body or even a single piece of enemy equipment or personal gear on our five-hour patrol. At every turn, we expected to encounter a large enemy force, but it was eerily quiet as we moved slowly along the valley floor uncovering one enemy bivouac site after another for a distance of 1,000 yards.

As we came to the end of our BDA, we found another large cultivated area with the remains of several fresh campfires that probably were no more than 48 hours old. Nearby we saw thousands of corn cobs strewn around in a haphazard fashion, as if something had interrupted the meal of several hundred enemy soldiers and caused them to drop everything and leave abruptly. Finally, not far from the corn cobs, we found several large wicker baskets filled with approximately two tons of corn. We did not have time to destroy the cache of corn, so we marked it with an air panel so an air strike could be used to destroy it after we had been extracted.

When we boarded our extraction helicopters around noon, we felt that we had definitely "dodged the bullet" on this patrol. Our five hours on the ground had determined that a large enemy force had indeed occupied the target of the B-52 "Arc Light," but the enemy had either gotten advance warning of the bombing or they were in the process of leaving this transit base on their way east at a very propitious time. In either case, they escaped destruction by only a few hours. For our part, we found a large transit or rest area capable of sheltering and feeding at least a battalion of enemy troops on their way east toward the lowlands of Quang Nam Province, an area that would receive future attention by American air power thanks to our discovery of it (Team Killer Kane Patrol Report, 23 Sept. 1967).

Killer Kane had little time to rest from the BDA patrol because just two days after we had returned from that mission we went out on patrol again, this time in the Hiep Duc and Que Son Valley area in support of Operation Wheeler. We were inserted into an abandoned rice paddy on the southern slope of Hill 224 in the early morning of 29 September. We quickly found a spot where we could observe the prominent trail running through the mountains between the hamlet of An Long (2) to the north and An Son (1) to the south.

At first, all we saw were a few civilian woodcutters using the trail, but at 1120, we saw 17 VC moving southwest along the trail toward us. They were dressed in khaki uniforms and black pajamas with camouflage helmets. Five of them were carrying rifles and packs. We called in an artillery fire mission, but we could not observe the results.

Three hours later at the same spot, we observed five more enemy soldiers moving southwest along the trail. They were dressed the same as the previous group, and all of them were carrying AK-47 assault rifles. They noticed the results of our previous fire mission, either the dead bodies or shell holes, so they began to trot quickly along the trail and disappear before we could get an artillery fire mission cleared. That night, we harbored near our OP, and the next morning we began moving east through some very difficult terrain. At times, we had to haul ourselves up the steep and slippery slopes of rain-drenched ravines, even crawling on our hands and knees at times in order to get from one place to another. It rained most of the day since this was the beginning of the monsoon season, and the rain made our journey through the jungle more difficult and unpleasant than it normally would have been.

For the next five days we searched our NFZ but failed to turn up any more VC, although we did hear Vietnamese voices and AK-47 fire coming from a deep ravine south of Hill 381 on the 27th. Although we did not find any more VC on this patrol, we did find a very well-used trail that led up to Hill 381. Near the summit, we found a portion of the trail that had been fortified recently by the enemy. There were numerous fighting holes just off the trail facing downhill to the southeast. We had encountered these well-constructed and well-camouflaged fighting positions before, and this knowledge gave us a healthy respect for the skills of the enemy when it came to preparing their field fortifications. Any American unit trying to fight their way up Hill 381 would encounter stiff opposition from any enemy force occupying these positions. We also found an abandoned battalion-size harbor site about a mile southwest of Hill 381 surrounded by fighting holes and bamboo punji stakes. We concluded that the enemy had used Hill 381 for some purpose in the recent past, but had abandoned it at least a month earlier.

On our last day of the patrol, the 29th of September, we found a good extract LZ and waited for our helicopters to arrive. While we were sitting in some trees on the side of the LZ, we found an empty 12.7 heavy machine gun fighting position with a well-constructed ammunition bunker beside it. Since it had been raining heavily during the past few days, the condition of this machine gun position told us it had been built very recently, probably within a day or two. This put us on an increased alert because we knew that normally only NVA units possessed such heavy weapons, and such a weapon could easily bring down our extract helicopter. I radioed this information to Camp Reasoner, and they passed this information on to the extract helicopters. In mid-morning, after 105 rain-soaked hours on the ground, we were extracted without incident. Back at Camp Reasoner, we recommended that the well-used trail through the mountains between An Long (2) and An Son (1) be ambushed or used for a prisoner snatch because it had many good ambush sites along it. The enemy we saw using it seemed to be less alert than most enemy personnel we had seen in the past, even walking very close to each other, carrying their weapons at sling arms, and talking loudly (Team Killer Kane Patrol Report, 29 Sept. 1967).

On 30 September, I attended an awards ceremony at the 1st Marine Division Headquarters where my friend from the Naval Academy, Kenny Moore, received two awards for his bravery as a platoon commander with the 5th Marines during Operation Union II. He and his company commander, Capt. Stoney Burke, came over to our company area after the ceremony, and we ate lunch together in the mess hall. Kenny was impressed with how well I lived in comparison to his Spartan existence with his infantry company. I felt a little embarrassed talking to him in my hootch with all the comforts it contained. Still, he and his company commander said they thought the kind of war I was fighting was just as dangerous as their war, and they confided that they preferred engaging the enemy with a rifle company in the lowlands than with a small recon patrol deep in the mountains. As Kenny was leaving he told me he intended to take R & R leave in Bangkok in early November, and he asked me if I had taken R & R yet. I told him I had

not, but maybe we could go on R & R together, if my battalion had a quota open. This was the first time I had really given much thought to R & R, but I decided I would take the subject up with Maj. Keating.

October began with another "interesting" patrol in Happy Valley and, similar to every other patrol in this infamous valley, it resulted in contact with the enemy and an early emergency extraction. It seemed as if every patrol in Happy Valley was destined to involve heavy contact with the enemy forces living there. Our mission on this patrol

Patrolling in Happy Valley.

was somewhat different from previous missions. We were told to locate "possible rocket-launching sites, storage areas, fortifications and routes of access," all objectives we had been given previously on other patrols, but in addition to these objectives we were also given a secondary mission of "capturing a prisoner." The reason this mission had been added to our objectives was due to some recent intelligence III MAF had received, probably from radio intercepts, that elements of the 368th Artillery (Rocket) Regiment, an NVA unit that was reported to possess Frog-3 long-range rockets, were believed to have recently infiltrated from North Vietnam to the vicinity of Happy Valley. Our intelligence people suspected that this unit would be used to provide support for the upcoming enemy offensive due in early 1968. While no one I had spoken to at this time suspected there would be anything like the nationwide Tet Offensive, I was aware that our intelligence services fully expected a major enemy attack somewhere in I Corps in early 1968 around the Tet holiday. We were told that many NVA units were moving from North Vietnam to South Vietnam in anticipation of this major battle. Capturing a prisoner from one of these infiltrating NVA units would help solve the puzzle concerning the size and objective of this upcoming attack.

Conducting a "prisoner snatch," as we referred to this activity, was the most dangerous activity a recon team could engage in since it meant a small team of American Marines operating in enemy-controlled territory had to physically compel an enemy soldier to surrender. Many things could go wrong with such an endeavor, and they usually did. Prisoner snatches were rare, and most of them went badly, so I was not very enthusiastic about conducting such a mission, especially in a place as dangerous as Happy Valley. Still, orders were orders, so I decided to take my entire platoon on the mission. I would need the manpower to fill the three elements required to successfully pull off a prisoner snatch: two security elements and an assault or capture element. I had Killer Kane rehearse both an ambush and prisoner snatch several times using different configurations since I was not sure what opportunities we would have on the ground. The basic configuration called for my 14-man patrol to be divided into two four-man security teams which would be positioned along a trail approximately 100 yards on either flank of the six-man capture team. The security teams would have radios so they could inform the capture team what was coming down a trail toward them. If the enemy moving along the trail consisted of one or two men, the capture team would prepare to capture them. If the approaching enemy was more than two, the capture team would either initiate an ambush or let the enemy pass, depending on the size of the enemy force. Such a configuration would require us to take three radios with us on patrol instead of the normal two since it was essential that each of the three elements be able to communicate with each other. There was no standard organization for a prisoner grab. I developed our system relying on ambush doctrine I had learned at the Basic School and information I had gleaned from reading about such operations conducted by the British in India, Kenya and Malaya. After two hours of practice on LZ Finch, including methods for securing prisoners using lengths of parachute cord and blindfolds, Killer Kane was ready for its patrol.

Since the entire 5th Platoon would take part in this patrol, I had to adjust the job assignments for each Marine to take advantage of their individual talents and experience.

Sgt. Hauxhurst, the team leader of the platoon's other team, Brisbane, would be my assistant patrol leader on this patrol, with Cpl. Hager as his backup. Both men were exceptionally good recon Marines, possessing an abundance of field experience, common sense, and courage, so I felt very confident having them help me with the patrol's preparations. With one or two exceptions, every man on the patrol was a seasoned veteran with multiple patrols under their belt.

At 0730 on the morning of 4 October, Killer Kane landed in a small LZ 1,500 meters northeast of Hill 749 and 300 meters south of a stream called Tam Kho. When we landed in the LZ, we were greeted by team Circumstance, which had been patrolling in the area east of the LZ for four days and had observed many enemy troops using the trails on the valley floor. I spoke with the team leader of Circumstance for a minute before he boarded the helicopter to leave, but the noise from the rotor blades of the UH-34 insertion helicopter drowned out most of what he said. What I did understand was he thought his team had been followed during most of their patrol. Since Killer Kane would be assuming the mission of Team Circumstance and using their NFZ, we hoped the enemy would just think Circumstance was leaving and not suspect Killer Kane had replaced them.

After team Circumstance departed, I started to move Killer Kane uphill to the south and into some trees. I wanted to get to the top of Hill 749 and then move along a ridgeline west. I was not sure, but I thought any ridgeline in Happy Valley would have a trail on it, and I needed a trail to set up an ambush or prisoner snatch. We moved very cautiously uphill through thick brush and jungle canopy for two hours until the point man, LCpl. John Slowick, stopped the patrol and motioned for me to come forward. Slowick pointed to an open area in front of him that looked like a small, montagnard hill farm. A path skirted the western edge of the cultivated area and along this path there was a low fence made of bamboo striplings. We watched the area for nearly a half hour and were able to make out a bamboo and thatch lean-to just inside the tree line on the far side of the field, the only indication of human activity we could observe. This was definitely a danger area since anyone moving in the open cultivated area would be vulnerable to fire coming from the tree line above. I brought up Hauxhurst and Hager, and the three of us discussed the situation. We decided that it would be best to skirt the cultivated area to the west and use a natural depression in the terrain to give us cover as we moved uphill.

As we were preparing to move, the tree line 100 meters above us erupted with rifle and automatic weapons fire. Killer Kane returned the fire, employing both our M-60 machine gun and our M-79 grenade launcher to good effect. The enemy fired a single B-40 rocket grenade at us, but it passed harmlessly over our heads and exploded in the trees 100 meters behind us. Fortunately for us, we had good cover in the natural fold in the ground. The enemy fire was heavy but inaccurate, passing over our heads by several feet. After just a few minutes, the enemy ceased firing. Cpl. Hager said he hit one enemy soldier and saw him fall, but the rest of us only saw muzzle flashes coming from the tree line, so we did not know if we hit anyone or not. LCpl. Garner, my lead radio man, had contacted an AO flying nearby and soon the AO was directing an air strike on the tree line above us. Napalm canisters and 500-pound bombs, a lethal combination we called "Snake and Nape," rained down on the enemy and sent large clumps of dirt and burning debris flying into the air. The air strike silenced the enemy and reduced the tree line to a smoking, torn up pile of charred and splintered wood. Since the enemy appeared to be withdrawing to the east, I decided to take the team west and uphill toward the summit of Hill 749.

About an hour after our firefight at the hill farm, our team reached the main ridgeline of Hill 749 where, as expected, we found a well-used trail nearly three feet wide. We moved west along the trail over the summit of Hill 749, searching for a good place to try our luck at a prisoner snatch. We descended gradually for 1,000 meters, moving with deliberate care and stopping frequently to see if we were being followed. On one stop, our rear point, PFC Glor, saw two enemy soldiers wearing camouflage uniforms and carrying Chinese Type 53 carbines approaching the patrol, and he took them under fire at close range. He thought he had killed one of them, but we decided it was too dangerous to walk back up the trail to search for his body since we did not know how many friends he had with him. We continued to move west to lower ground until the setting sun made movement too difficult and dangerous for us. I found a good harbor site 50 meters off the trail, and we spent the night there with mosquitoes and leeches feasting on our blood.

The next day, we came to the western base of Hill 749 on the floor of Happy Valley at a point where the trail leading off the hill intersected a larger trail running north-south along the eastern side of the Song Yang River. Our map showed this trail to be on the western side of the river, but either trails ran along both banks of the river or the map was wrong. This north-south trail ran from Happy Valley south ten miles through dense jungle along the Song Yang River until it reached the small village of Thuong Duc on the Song Vu Gia River. It was a very obvious infiltration route for any enemy unit wishing to gain access to the lowlands of Western Quang Nam Province. For this reason there was a U.S. Special Forces camp near Thuong Duc, which was often aggressively attacked by elements of the 2nd NVA Division. The intersection of the trail leading down from Hill 749 and the major north-south trail leading to Thuong Duc seemed to me to be a perfect spot to lay an ambush for any transiting enemy soldiers. As we set up our ambush, we noticed that there were two newly constructed bunkers on the north side of the hill facing south. These bunkers were well concealed and camouflaged, offering their occupants excellent fields of fire against any person walking down the trail from the south. Fortunately for Killer Kane, the bunkers were empty.

We had been in our ambush site only a few minutes when three enemy soldiers dressed in khaki and black pajamas walked into our killing zone from the south. The ambush element used a Claymore mine to trigger the ambush, and then we opened fire. Two enemy soldiers were killed immediately, but the third staggered back down the trail and off the side of the hill into deep brush. We quickly searched the bodies and retrieved a Chinese-made SKS rifle and a pack with assorted personal items inside it, including three sets of black pajamas, a journal, some pens, several packs of U.S. Marlboro cigarettes, three USMC socks filled with rice, several cans of Japanese mackerel in tomato sauce, and two photos of the dead soldier with some other soldiers in the jungle. Following my policy not to turn over any captured weapons that were not fully automatic or crew-served, I had the SKS rifle broken down and hidden in one of our rucksacks. I was still angry over the way our booty had been rifled and stolen from a previous patrol into

Happy Valley, and I vowed never to let that happen again. We moved the bodies off the trail and covered them with brush and reset our ambush.

Two hours later, we triggered our second ambush. This time, we ambushed three enemy soldiers walking north on the main north-south trail toward Happy Valley. Unlike the first group of enemy soldiers, who were happily walking along without a care in the world with their weapons slung over their shoulders, this group had obviously heard our ambush. They were alert and carried their AK-47 rifles at the ready while they maintained a five-meter interval between them. Instead of walking at a normal speed, they approached our ambush site slowly, looking from side to side as they progressed. Again, our silence, our camouflage clothing, and our face paint prevented them from seeing us until it was too late. This time we triggered our ambush with rifle fire and again two of the three died in our killing zone while the third, obviously hit, tumbled off to the side of the trail and down into a steep ravine toward the river. We heard moans coming from the ravine for nearly 20 minutes, but I would not allow my men to search the ravine since I did not know if this enemy soldier was actually wounded, or he was just trying to lure us into the ravine where he could attack us. Finally, I had Sgt. Hauxhurst and PFC Charles Gillespie throw several hand grenades into the ravine, and the moaning ceased. We searched the two bodies of the enemy soldiers we had killed and retrieved a new Chinese AK-47 assault rifle from one of them and an SKS rifle from the other. Again, we broke down the SKS and hid it in one of our rucksacks. We also hid the ammunition belts we took off the bodies. I noticed that all of the enemy we had killed that day were young, wore clean uniforms, carried new weapons and equipment, and had short, military-style haircuts, all of which indicated they were NVA and not local VC. They also had numerous, fresh scars on their legs from leech bites, a sign they had been living in the mountains for some time.

There was now a lot of blood on the trail, even though we had moved the bodies into the brush and hidden them from sight. I was afraid the blood would give our ambush site away, so three of us found some fresh dirt and covered the pools of blood that had accumulated on the trail. When we had finished, I decided we had done enough damage to the enemy that day, and it was time to find a harbor site for the night. We moved 200 meters to the east, found a fast-running stream, refilled our canteens, located a good harbor site, ate a quick meal of C rations, sent in a position report to Camp Reasoner, set our radio watch, and waited in the shadows as the deep purple darkness of night descended upon us. As the last light faded away, we heard two distant rifle shots to our north. We suspected these were warning shots made by NVA "trail watchers" or a counter-recon team informing any enemy in the area that Marines were present in Happy Valley. Aside from the nuisance of leeches trying to make a meal of our blood, the night passed peacefully with no other sounds to disturb our sleep but the screeching of some monkeys who seemed to dislike our presence on their turf.

The next morning, I decided we should still continue to ambush the trail running north and south between Thuong Duc and Happy Valley since it appeared the enemy was using it regularly. I still wanted to try for a prisoner grab, so Sgt. Hauxhurst and I moved north on the trail until we found a large rock a few feet off the trail where we both could hide until an enemy walking on the trail was within arm's length. I had designated Cpl.

Williams, our biggest man, to be the prisoner grabber while Sgt. Hauxhurst and I would deal with a second potential prisoner or help Williams if there was only one. Our fourth man was LCpl. Dave Powell, and his job was to cover the rest of us as we moved onto the trail to either secure the prisoner or search bodies. We positioned this four-man "snatch team" and positioned the other two elements of the team on the trail leading off Hill 749 and at the intersection of that trail and the main north-south trail. In essence, we had three security elements and three ambush elements with this arrangement. Once we were all set in, we only had to wait for some hapless NVA soldier to walk down one of the trails.

Our wait was not long. At 0830, three NVA soldiers wearing light green uniforms and carrying Chinese Type 53 carbines and a captured U.S. M-79 grenade launcher walked into the ambush covering the trail from Hill 749. Unfortunately, the ambush was triggered prematurely, and only one of the enemy soldiers was hit. The wounded NVA soldier was able to run back up the trail away from the ambush. Cpl. Hager, who was in charge of this element, had told his men that he would initiate the ambush, but one of his men panicked at the sight of the enemy so close to him and fired a single shot from his M-16, which gave the three NVA soldiers a second to duck off the trail and run back uphill. The man who fired his weapon without authorization felt confident he had killed the man he shot, but I did not find a blood trail or anything else indicating the enemy was even wounded. Cpl. Hager, one of the best men I have ever served with, was extremely angry with the Marine who disobeyed his orders and promised to "take care of him" when we returned from patrol. Knowing Hager as well as I did, I did not relish the punishment Hager would mete out to the man who disobeyed his orders.

Later in the day, at 1430, we had another contact with the enemy and again it did not turn out as well as we would have liked. The "snatch team" heard Vietnamese voices to our north and downhill from where we were set in. The north-south trail had a steep incline of nearly fifty feet up to the ambush site, so steep that handrails had been built along it and there were several steps cut into the trail and reinforced with logs. The voices seemed like they were not on the trail but off to the west and fairly close. I decided to take a look downhill to our north to see if we could see who was talking. LCpl. Powell accompanied me for the short, 20 meter crawl to where we could look directly down to the bottom of the trail for a distance of 100 feet. As soon as we peered down the trail, we saw two NVA soldiers walking up the trail toward us. Because the trail was steep, both men had their heads down looking at the ground and one of them was holding onto one of the bamboo railings to help himself up the steep incline. LCpl. Powell and I immediately opened fire on the two enemy soldiers hitting them multiple times. Instinctively, LCpl. Powell fired at the lead NVA soldier while I fired on the second. Both enemy soldiers fell on the trail below us but one of them moved slightly so we both fired another magazine into the two of them to make sure they were dead. I noticed that one of the enemy soldiers we had killed had a red armband and a red neckerchief, items we had never seen before on NVA soldiers. We were about to go down and search the bodies and retrieve their weapons when we began to take fire from the trail behind them. It was obvious that this was an attempt at "recon by fire" by the enemy since the rounds did not come close to us but impacted harmlessly many meters below us. We estimated another three or four enemy soldiers were behind the ones we had just killed.

Since we had now encountered the enemy coming toward us from the east, north and south, I knew it would not be long before they knew exactly where we were, and they would come after us with a large force. With this in mind, I decided to collect the entire platoon and move back to a good defensive position near the intersection of the two trails. I did not want to move any farther along a trail since the enemy would surely have the trails watched by now and would establish ambushes along any route we might take.

We had other options but I did not think any of them were better than the one we adopted. For instance, I could have moved west off the hill, but then I would have to cross the Song Yang River, which would be a very dangerous thing to do. It would not only force us out into the open to cross the river, it also might carry us away in its swift current. The depth and current of the rivers in the Annamite Mountains were deceptive. Even a narrow stream that appeared shallow could have an extremely fast current or a deep, hidden channel. Marines had drowned in these mountain streams and rivers because of these deceptive characteristics. I decided the best thing for us to do was to stay where we were and request an AO so he could direct us to the nearest LZ.

It was not very long after we established our new position that the enemy struck. At 1515, two groups of enemy soldiers began firing at us. One group was coming from the south and the other was coming from the north in what appeared to be a coordinated attack. They did not know our exact position because they were firing erratically. Unfortunately for them, the group coming up from the south exposed themselves, and we were able to take them under fire from less than 50 meters distance, resulting in two enemy soldiers killed. Slowick and Hager, along with several others, drove back the southern

Davis Powell (left) and W. P. Kelly (right).

group, while Sgt. Hauxhurst, LCpl. Gardner, PFC Adams, PFC Ellis, and Cpl. Kelly beat back the attack from the north. Along with the rest of the patrol, I covered the eastern approach to the patrol since I was convinced the enemy would attempt to distract us by their two-pronged attack along the main north-south trail while they maneuvered to get behind us, thinking we might attempt to withdraw in that direction. I realized the enemy now knew exactly where we were, and it would not be long before they concentrated their forces and attempted to destroy us. I radioed Camp Reasoner and told them we needed an emergency extraction immediately, but they asked me if I was capable of carrying on my mission. Evidently, they did not understand how precarious our position was so I sent them another message that said, "Killer Kane loves to kill Cong, but the time for extraction is now." This message was not intended to be humorous, but the officers in the Division G-2 thought it was. In any event, an AO soon appeared over our position, and I asked him to give me the grid coordinates of the nearest LZ. A minute later, he told me there was a good LZ just 100 meters west of our position, but it was on low ground surrounded on three sides by hills. He warned us that it was also adjacent to the Song Yang River, and there were some trails leading into the LZ from the north. He added that while he thought it was a good LZ, it also was a dangerous one. I told him we would move to the LZ as soon as we heard that our extraction helicopters were on the way to pick us up. He replied that he was going to bring in some fixed-wing aircraft to prep the LZ before we were extracted since he suspected the enemy was waiting for us there.

Around 1600, we were told to begin moving to the extract LZ and to relay through the AO when we had arrived. We could not begin to descend to the valley floor immediately since the AO was calling in air strikes on the area surrounding our LZ. For about an hour the AO directed bombing runs on the LZ and the hills overlooking it with very good coverage. If anyone was in the LZ or on those hills, they would have been beaten up badly since the fixed-wing aircraft really worked over the area with their bombs and napalm. At 1700, we began to move downhill and to the west toward the LZ after telling the AO we were doing so and asking him to shift the air strikes to the west so the enemy would not know exactly what LZ was our intended destination. The tension was intense because we had recently had so much contact with the enemy, and we expected them to hit us at any moment. We did not have a long distance to move, but we had to move slowly since the terrain was both steep and thick. It took us nearly a half hour to move the 100 meters. When we arrived we were told the helicopters were only 15 minutes away and to be prepared to pop smoke as soon as the lead helicopter pilot asked for it.

As soon as I threw the yellow smoke grenade into the LZ, I saw the extract helicopter coming in from the west, guiding on the Song Yang River. As he drew nearer, he confirmed he saw my smoke in the LZ and he asked me to confirm the color. Then when the helicopter was only 200 yards away, the highly competent and always reliable Marine Air Wing put on a splendid display of choreographed support. Two Marine F-4s streaked over the LZ in a dummy run to keep any enemy at bay, while two Marine helicopter gunships strafed the hills on either side of the lead extract helicopter's approach. It was beautiful to see such superb airmanship and reinsuring to Killer Kane that their awesome firepower was at our disposal. When the helicopter touched down in the LZ, eight Marines ran forward and scrambled aboard. Because of weight limitations, we could not board the entire team on one helicopter, so the remaining six of us waited in the LZ for the second helicopter to land. A few seconds after the lead helicopter lifted off and the second one began to hover over the LZ, we saw three NVA soldiers dressed in khaki uniforms moving into position on the far side of the LZ near the banks of the Song Yang River. We fired at them, killing one and sending the other two running for cover. The helicopter opened fire on them with their door-mounted .50-caliber machine gun. As we ran to the helicopter, we continued to fire on the enemy on the far side of the LZ. At the same time, one of the gunship pilots radioed to us that he saw another group of NVA running away to the west parallel to the river. In order to escape ground fire, the helicopter lifted off and banked sharply to the right following the Song Yang River south before gaining altitude, thus avoiding flying over where we had last seen the enemy. Once again, Killer Kane had been unable to avoid making contact with the enemy in Happy Valley, and once again the enemy had aggressively attacked us there. It was becoming obvious that the enemy did not want American reconnaissance patrols in Happy Valley or the trails leading west from it. They were hiding something there, but we did not know what (Team Killer Kane Patrol Report, 7 Oct. 1967).

Back at Camp Reasoner, Maj. Keating listened to our debrief and said he wanted me to write up several members of the patrol for personal decorations since we had so much contact with the enemy and had killed nine of the enemy with small-arms fire and not suffered a single casualty. The next day, I immediately went to work on the award recommendations, gathering written statements for the four men who were to be recommended for the awards and typing up my own statements for them. When I delivered them to Maj. Keating and SSgt. Cole in the company office, I asked both of them to do whatever they could to convince the awards board at division headquarters to approve them. I pointed out that if we told a Marine he was being recommended for a certain award and later he found that the award was downgraded or not even approved, this had a deleterious effect on that Marine's morale. I told them it would be better not to make the recommendation if the awards board did not approve them. Both men agreed with me and promised to work behind the scenes to make sure the awards were approved as written. I had a lot of confidence in these two men, but I was beginning to have very little confidence in the 1st Marine Division's awards board, especially when it came to giving awards to enlisted Marines.

About this time, my mother sent me a letter from home, including a local newspaper clipping, which quoted one of my state's senators, Clifford Case, clearly stating his anti-war position and calling for a negotiated settlement. Since Senator Case was an elected official, I could not write or say anything controversial about him or confront him, so I asked my father to write a letter to him expressing how wrong I thought he was and how his statements would not help the morale of the troops fighting the war. This was the first time that the anti-war issue at home had any real impact on my morale and my reaction to it was very emotional and negative. Here is a portion of the letter I sent home:

> Tell him (Sen. Case) that the men over here will never forgive any politician who allows us to accept any other solution but total victory. Any solution other than victory is a slap in my face and the face of my men and I strongly resent it. Many of the troops over here are getting a little ticked off at some of the politicians advocating peace ... we are going to win this war despite

these people. I would be ashamed to call myself an American if the people of the U.S. allowed themselves to be duped by these political opportunists and allow these idiots to appease the communists. Please send me an absentee ballot so I can vote for the biggest hawks there are and any man running against Senator Case.

During my tour of duty in South Vietnam I never gave much thought to the anti-war movement in the U.S., but during those rare occasions when I did think about it, I never allowed it to diminish my support for the war or my commitment to the defeat of the communists. However, it did puzzle me. My parents and others who wrote to me told me the anti-war movement in the U.S. was very small and had little support from average Americans, but when I read U.S. newspapers, which were seldom available to us, and magazines from the PX, such as *Time* and *Newsweek*, the articles seemed to tell a different story. I began to wonder whose side the press was on and where they were getting their information about the war. Since I only had direct contact with a member of the U.S. press twice during my 32 months serving in South Vietnam, it was difficult for me to determine where the press obtained their information or why their reporting seemed so at odds with what I experienced. What I did know was I did not agree with much of what I read, and I often found their portrayal of events on the ground out of line with reality. My frustration and anger with the Western press in South Vietnam would grow as the war progressed.

Maj. Keating felt Killer Kane had had its fair share of contact with the enemy and was due for a rest, so he had us scheduled for another week on Hill 452, our radio relay site that provided continuous communications for the recon patrols working at the extremes of the 1st Marine Division's southern TAOR. Since this mission required us to man four bunkers, I took both of the teams in my platoon. Jim Hager had been just promoted to Sgt., so I decided to take him along as an assistant patrol leader, sharing this duty with Sgt. Hauxhurst. Both men were very capable and brave men, and I wanted both of them to become team leaders in their own right. This "milk run" to Hill 452 allowed me to spend many dedicated hours with Hager and Hauxhurst going over the details of leading a team. In addition, I hoped that I would be able to conduct some much needed training so every man in the platoon would have at least a working knowledge of what to do if any of the team leaders were killed or wounded. With this in mind, I took along some lesson plans from my Basic School classes and the SOP for the battalion. I also asked Doc Conner to prepare a few classes on basic field first aid. I did not want this valuable opportunity to pass without getting in some training in our weak areas.

At the last moment, I packed four books I had recently received in the mail from home: Mikhail Sholokhov's novel about Russia, *And Quiet Flows the Don*, Paul M. Angle's *A New Continent, A New Nation*, Isaac Deutscher's biography of Stalin, and Burke Davis's biography of the legendary Marine, Chesty Puller. I read all four during my seven days on the mountain, which says a lot about how routine and uneventful such duty could be. When I wasn't on watch searching for the enemy in the terrain south of us toward Antenna Valley, I would read. Sitting in the shade of a poncho atop one of the bunkers, I would lie back and read for several hours at a time, immersing myself in whatever book I was reading. This would be a habit of mine throughout my career. Reading was my favorite pastime for the 25 years I spent in the Corps, although I have to admit my reading was often focused on just a few areas of interest. I read very little fiction, but concentrated instead on history, political science, economics, anthropology, foreign languages, and military strategy. If I did read works of fiction, most of them would be the works of John Updike, Thomas Hardy, Joseph Conrad, and Ernest Hemingway, but I also read many of the great Asian classics, such as *The Tale of the Genji, KimVan Kieu, The Water Margin,* and *The Romance of the Three Kingdoms.*

Each evening around 1700, I convened a class for the team. We would gather around one of the bunkers, and I would give an hour-long class on subjects such as map reading, calling and adjusting artillery, small unit tactics, the use of intelligence reports, and "Know Your Enemy." Killer Kane had several new men in the platoon, so I had one class where I pointed to a location south of Hill 452 and told the group to locate where I was pointing to on a map I had laid out in front of them, use a compass to obtain an azimuth toward the target, then write down a call for fire for the target: all in less than a minute. We made a game of it and awarded several C ration cans of the much valued sliced peaches to the winners. When I was not giving the evening course, Doc Conner would instruct us in how to treat gunshot wounds, stem bleeding, clear airways, and build a poncho litter. After each class, we would watch the sun go down and eat a hot meal of C rations cooked over our field stoves before setting the night watch and going to sleep.

During this trip to Hill 452, we did not observe a single enemy soldier. Everything seemed peaceful and quiet in the villages far below us. We did, however, have one significant contact with the "enemy," a colony of very large and aggressive rats! Since so many Marines had occupied the summit of Hill 452 for over a year, trash had accumulated, making it ideal for all sorts of wildlife. Rats were the biggest problem. One night shortly after I had settled into my bunker to sleep, a rat fell right on top of me and scurried away out the bunker door. An hour later, another fell on my foot, waking me up and squealing as I tried to kick it off. The next day, Sgt. Hager, Sgt. Hauxhurst, Cpl. Powell and I formed a "Committee for the Eradication of the Rodent Problem" and set in motion a plan to rid our bunkers of these nasty critters. We found the holes in the rocks on the summit where they lived, and then we put smoke grenades in a few of the holes and covered the others with our M-16s. Each of us picked a hole to watch and positioned ourselves so we could fire on the rats without hitting each other or anyone else on the hill. Within seconds of the introduction of the smoke grenades into the holes, rats began to pour out of the other holes. We killed eleven of them, and from that time on we did not have any midnight encounters with rats in our bunkers. Despite our victory over the rats and the easy life on Hill 452, we were all happy to leave when our week-long patrol ended (Team Killer Kane Patrol Report, 19 Oct. 1967).

When Killer Kane returned, we learned that two recon patrols from the 1st Reconnaissance Battalion had suffered heavy casualties in our absence. The two patrols were hit hard by the NVA, suffering a total of seven Marines killed and 21 wounded. It was the bloodiest week for the battalion since their arrival in South Vietnam. This news underscored how lethal our job was, especially when a recon team encountered a strong enemy force far from friendly lines. We mourned the loss of our friends and studied the events leading up to the two deadly encounters with the enemy in an attempt to ascertain the causes for these two tragic events. From the comments of the survivors, it appeared NVA counter-reconnaissance teams had located the patrols soon after the teams were inserted and the teams spent too much time in one location, allowing the enemy to concentrate their forces for an attack. These facts reinforced in our minds the standing policy to never spend more than 24 hours in one location while on patrol.

8

Swift Scout Makes Its Debut

On 20 October, I received my first American decoration, nine months after arriving in country. Gen. Robertson presented the Bronze Star to me and several of my men at a ceremony on the dirt field we euphemistically called "the parade deck" at Camp Reasoner. While I was pleased that the actions of Killer Kane were finally getting some official recognition, I was painfully aware that these awards had been downgraded from Silver Stars by the division awards committee. My team and I felt that the men serving on the awards committee did not understand how difficult and dangerous our work was, or they did not believe the statements made by me and my men about what actually transpired on our patrols. In any event, Killer Kane began to wonder why our team was always called upon by the Division G-2 to conduct the most dangerous missions and to brief every visiting dignitary to the 1st Marine Division, yet we never seemed to get the official recognition that other units in the division received. Later on, I would have an opportunity to speak to the recorder of the committee's meetings, and he would tell me that the philosophy of "They are just doing their job" permeated many of the comments of these staff officers, along with comments relating to the paucity of "independent confirmation," meaning statements from witnesses outside of the membership of the patrol. The fact that only seven or eight men went on these patrols did not seem to figure in their evaluation of the value of the statements submitted with the award recommendations. My frustration with the division awards committee eroded my confidence in the Marine Corps' award system, and I began to question the utility of even submitting award recommendations to them. In fairness to the officers serving on the awards committee, they had certain criteria to meet when approving an award. The higher the award, the more substantiated evidence was required. There were few witnesses on a recon patrol who could substantiate the facts since the recon teams were small, covert and far from friendly lines. All the awards committee had were the statements of a team leader and a few members of the patrol, many of whom lacked the writing skills needed to produce graphic and compelling statements.

Adding to our disenchantment with the awards policy of the 1st Marine Division, Killer Kane learned on 20 October that our code name had been changed. We would now be called Swift Scout instead of Killer Kane, and this did not go down well with us at all. Everyone recognized the need to change call signs for security reasons. Still, we had become very attached to our call sign. It prompted respect for the team whenever it was mentioned in reports and briefings. Although disappointed about the change, we did not complain, and vowed that we would make our new call sign as famous as the previous one.

In addition to receiving the news that our call sign had changed to Swift Scout, I was also informed of a new mission for our team. We were to provide reconnaissance and screening for two U.S. Marine infantry battalions, which were conducting Operation Knox south of Hue. Our mission was to observe any enemy activity in the Loc Tu Sector of Phu Loc District, Thua Thien Province, paying special emphasis on the main coastal road, Route 1, and the strategic Phu Gia Pass north of Da Nang. We were to keep 2/3 and 2/7 informed of any threat coming at them from the south and to call and adjust artillery on any enemy forces we observed.

As I received this mission from the S-3, I was informed that I would be taking a journalist along with me on the patrol. I had only one exposure to the press before, and that one had not turned out well, so I was reluctant to take a civilian journalist with me on a recon patrol where every man had a critical role to play. I saw no value in taking a civilian with us and a lot of problems. It was soon apparent that I had no real say in the matter since division had approved it. I reluctantly accepted the inevitable, but I voiced my views to Capt. Walker and to Capt. Kicklighter, the new S-2. They were sympathetic, but said there was no recourse since III MAF had granted the journalist's request to go on a recon patrol. As far as I knew, few if any journalists had ever accompanied a recon patrol before, and I wondered why this journalist and my team had been singled out for this highly unusual endeavor. Since I had no say in the matter, I resigned myself to make the best of a bad situation.

Later that day, I met the journalist who would be going on patrol with Swift Scout. His name was Eric von Dorp, and my initial impression of the 28-year-old was positive. He told me he had traveled the world ever since he graduated from college and had recently taken a canoe down the Mekong River alone from Laos to the Mekong Delta. He had come to Southeast Asia only 11 months ago, but had been able to sell several of his articles to major publications. He said he was a freelance journalist, a point he stressed made him "totally objective." I was to find out, however, that he harbored some sympathetic views of the VC. He gave away these views when he said he thought the aspirations of the Vietnamese communists were not a threat to the U.S., and their policies were more like those of "nationalist revolutionaries and agrarian reformers" than communists. The more I spoke with him, the more I began to question the wisdom of taking this man on patrol with me, but I decided to do nothing to prevent him from getting his story. Perhaps, I might even make him more sympathetic to our cause by showing him what we did and why.

When I told my team we would be taking a civilian journalist with us who I suspected of having some strong anti-war views, they were not pleased and let me know it. For a few minutes, I thought I might have an actual mutiny on my hands, but after I explained we had an opportunity to show this man that we were performing a necessary service, and to possibly change his views, they settled down. Of course, this was wishful thinking, but it helped to assuage the anger that this man's presence had on the team. I told them to focus on the patrol, and that I would call an emergency extraction if the actions of Mr. von Dorp placed the patrol in jeopardy.

I allowed Mr. von Dorp to listen to my patrol order, leaving out the intelligence portion, which I gave the team afterwards when he was not present. I also allowed him to observe our other preparations for the patrol, including our rehearsals and weapons test-firing. The day before we departed on patrol, I made sure he had the necessary field equipment and rations needed for the patrol, and I reminded him that once we were in the field, he was to obey every order I gave. I warned him that if he failed to do as I told him, I would have him removed from the patrol immediately and ask III MAF to pull his press pass. He agreed and assured me he would not be a burden.

On 22 October our team, consisting of 11 Marines and one U.S. journalist, was inserted by two UH-34 helicopters on the western slope of Dong Nhut Mountain, only a few hundred meters east of Dam Cao Hai Bay, a large body of water that emptied into the South China Sea. During the 110 hours of the patrol we did not observe any enemy forces because the OP sites we thought would give us good observation of Highway 1 were too far away and too high. Our first OP was on Hill 592, and the thick, gray mist that shrouded the summit made it impossible to see the terrain below. We moved to another OP on a finger at a lower elevation, but observation here was also very poor due to the mist and fog that rolled in from the sea. All of the trails we found in the NFZ seemed quite old, with the only sign of human activity a significant amount of wood-cutting all along the patrol route. We also found an old U.S. Marine defensive position on top of Hill 592, but no sign of any enemy activity in the area. After a rather uneventful and rain-soaked patrol, we returned to Camp Reasoner (Team Swift Scout Patrol Report, 26 Oct. 1967).

Having spent four days with Mr. von Dorp, I was interested in his views about our patrol and my men. In a letter home, I recounted what he said to me and my impressions of him:

> He was quite impressed with two things, so he said. First, he thought my Marines were better than the average Marine, and, second, he thought I was a military fanatic but a rational one. He could not believe how we moved so slowly and quietly, never talking for hours on end and then only in whispers. When he left (Camp Reasoner) he said he would put me in two chapters of a book he was writing and classify me as "a stereotypical Annapolis man." I laughed and told him that I would put him in a few sentences of a letter home and classify him as a stereotypical bum. He gave me his address and said that if I ever got back to the States, he would treat me to some of the wine from his father's vineyards.

Two months later, I received a letter from Eric. He had returned to his parents' home, a winery in California, and was looking for employment. He thanked me for allowing him to accompany Killer Kane on patrol, an event he considered the high point of his journalistic endeavors in South Vietnam. I often wondered if the impression we made on him changed his mind about the war and those who fought in it. Since he did not send me a copy of his article, I suspected we had not changed his views.

On 27 October, I made another parachute jump from an Air Force Caribou transport plane. About 50 Marines from our company made the jump at Red Beach, the large logistics facility near Da Nang. There were a lot of Vietnamese kids on the drop zone (DZ), and they seemed delighted with the show as we drifted down into the sand among the numerous graves that dotted the area. Miraculously, no one was hurt during our jump, although several of us narrowly escaped landing on top of the grave stones. As we always did after a parachute-training jump, the Marines speculated as to why we were being prepared for such an operation since it was so out of the ordinary for us and none of our commanders seemed to know what the objective of this training was. The members of my platoon were curious about how we might be employed as parachutists against the enemy, but I could never provide an answer for them that made much sense. There were continuous rumors about a jump into the A Shau Valley or, perhaps into some other place in Laos, but nothing definitive was ever revealed to us.

The evening after the parachute jump, I had a visit from Lt. Dave Gillespie, a Marine supply officer who had just returned from R and R in Bangkok. Dave graduated a year ahead of me at Merchantville High School, where he had been an All-State football star on our dismally unsuccessful football team. He had preceded me to the Naval Academy, and we had been good friends there. In addition to being a standout athlete, Dave was also very smart and had the kind of charismatic personality that endeared him to everyone who came in contact with him. We ate dinner together in our mess hall and later went to the division officers' club for a few drinks and the nightly movie. He told me that I should take advantage of the many opportunities in Bangkok to buy Christmas presents for my family, and he gave me business cards for stores in Bangkok that sold Thai silk, jewelry, porcelain, cameras, and other products, as well as instructions on where to go to have the presents I purchased shipped to the U.S. I went back to my hootch that evening and matched what Dave told me with a list I had prepared of Christmas gifts for my family and "Jane." It felt good to know that I would be able to use my R and R to get each person a nice gift for Christmas and have it shipped home in time for the holidays.

On 29 October, I was called into the S-3 shop and given another "prisoner snatch" mission. This time, team Swift Scout would try its luck capturing an enemy soldier in the Mortar Valley area. Mortar Valley lay directly north of Charlie Ridge, and the trail that ran through this deserted valley ran west until it connected with the main east-west trail in Happy Valley, the infamous "Yellow Brick Road." It was also only eight kilometers from one of the three main roads between Da Nang and the An Hoa Basin, so it was a logical place for enemy units to hide while on their way to launch rocket attacks against the Da Nang Airbase. Recent intelligence had confirmed the presence of a new NVA artillery unit in or near Mortar Valley, and III MAF wanted to interrogate a prisoner from this unit to find out what their mission was. III MAF intelligence had confirmed the arrival of several large NVA units that had spent the last few months moving south from North Vietnam and southern Laos along the Ho Chi Minh Trail. Most of these enemy units seemed to be concentrating near the U.S. Marine base at Khe Sanh in western Quang Tri Province, but some were thought to be heading toward Quang Nam Province. I could tell from the tone of the conversation that there was real concern about these developments, and division wanted an NVA prisoner badly so they could find out which units were moving into the division TAOR. I suspected that signals intelligence had picked up the enemy movement, but the locations and missions of these enemy units were still unknown.

Maj. Keating asked if he could observe my preparations for the patrol and go on the overflight with me. I was flattered by his interest and impressed with his desire to see how my team went about preparing for a mission such as a "prisoner snatch." None of my previous COs had asked to observe our preparations. From the initial map study and analysis of previous patrol reports, to the overflight and issuing of the patrol order to my team, Maj. Keating accompanied me and quietly observed. He even watched the test-firing of our weapons, the inspection of each man's rucksack and equipment, and the two hours of rehearsal in the scorching sun beside LZ Finch. The more I saw of Maj. Keating, the more I liked him. I asked him what he thought of the team's preparations and he only said one thing. Hearing it filled me with pride. He said, "Andy, now I know why your team is so good. Nothing is left to chance." I told my team what he had said, and they all beamed with pleasure and pride. His comment did wonders for our morale.

Early in the morning of 31 October team Swift Scout, consisting of one Marine officer, ten Marine enlisted men, one Navy corpsman, and one scout dog landed in a grassy LZ on a narrow ridgeline at the western edge of Mortar Valley about one mile south of Hill 502. The LZ was one of the few open areas in the vicinity where a helicopter could land, which concerned me since I knew it increased the likelihood that it was under observation by the enemy. However, I knew our objective was to reach the summit of Hill 502 and the trail running east-west through the summit, so this LZ would have to do if we hoped to get to the summit before dark.

As we moved off the LZ, we noticed there were several fighting holes overlooking it, and one of these fighting holes had blood in it. The fighting hole was old, but the blood was fresh. Evidently, the strafing runs by the escort helicopter gunships had produced at least one enemy casualty. We cautiously searched the area, but could not find who had left the blood. After waiting and listening for 20 minutes, I had Cpl. Slowick lead the patrol up the slope of Hill 502. The terrain was steep with tall canopy and very thick undergrowth. Some of the trees were 150 feet tall with trunks over six feet in diameter. We followed a small stream for a few hundred yards, stopping frequently to listen for the enemy and to allow our scout dog to drink from the cool water. As we progressed, we found there were swift-running streams in all of the ravines we passed. The streams not only provided us with a fresh and abundant supply of water, they also muffled any sounds we made as we moved uphill toward the summit of Hill 502.

It soon became apparent, however, that our scout dog, Major, was having a difficult time of it. I had been talked into using the scout dog because Marine units had had good success with these dogs in the lowlands of the province. It was believed they would alert on the presence of the enemy well before any humans could, but my previous experience with scout dogs on recon patrols had proven just the opposite. They were excellent for guarding static positions or searching lowland villages, but they tired easily in the mountain jungles and needed more water than a human did. Major was no exception, and his handler, Cpl. McWilliams, had to ask us to stop constantly so his dog could recover from the heat and the exertion of the climb. In some instances, McWilliams had to physically carry Major when the undergrowth was too thick. I hoped to reach the summit of Hill 502 before dark, but that goal soon became moot as we spent most of our time resting the dog and filling canteens for him so he would not suffer heat exhaustion. We harbored for the night in a less than adequate site, one that had a slope of nearly 30 degrees, forcing some of us to sleep with our legs between tree trunks so we did not slip down the hills as we slept during the night. A heavy and persistent rain throughout the night only added to our discomfort.

The next day, the 1st of November, we finally reached the summit of Hill 502 at around 0900. Hill 502 had been the scene of a bloody battle fought in February 1966, and the terrain around the summit bore witness to the ferocity of this battle. Trees were still splintered and felled from the artillery and air strikes on the hill nearly two years before. There were also old U.S. Marine–style fighting holes, now filled with water and mud along with some old sandbags and empty shell casings.

More ominous to us were the signs of recent travel on the trail that ran east and west from the summit and two recently constructed NVA bunkers on the eastern side of the hill. Cpl. John Slowick and PFC J. D. Glor took up security on the trail of the eastern slope of the hill while Cpl. W. F. Kelly and PFC Jon Ellis took up a security position on the trail facing downhill on the western slope. As I was giving LCpl. Robert Garner, my radioman, a SITREP to send to Camp Reasoner informing them that we had reached the summit of Hill 502, I heard shots coming from the direction of Kelly and Ellis. Sgt. Hauxhurst and I ran to where these two men were and found that they had been surprised by an enemy soldier who had probably followed the patrol as soon as it reached the summit.

Team Killer Kane with scout dog "Major," preparing for patrol. Back row: Pfc Boyd, me, Dave Pugh, John Slowick; front row: Mike Borecky, McWilliams, J. D. Glor, Doc Willis, Clarence Williams.

Sgt. W. P. Kelly examining an NVA bunker on Hill 502.

Kelly said he had just taken up his security position behind a tree where he could look down the trail when he saw a single enemy soldier dressed in a camouflage uniform standing in the middle of the trail looking up at him. Kelly froze for a moment, afraid any movement on his part would alert the enemy solider. For a few seconds the two men stared at each other, and then PFC Ellis fired several shots at the enemy soldier. Ellis felt he had hit the enemy soldier, but no body or blood trail was evident on the trail where he was last seen.

I was not pleased with this encounter. I felt a stationary Marine in a camouflage uniform with his face covered in green and black face paint should have been able to get the jump on any enemy soldier walking up a trail. I cautioned both men that they needed to be more alert, and then I had them move back to a new position near the summit. I knew if the enemy escaped and returned, he would have his friends fire on the site where he had last encountered my security team. To bolster the two-man security team covering the western approach to the summit, I had LCpl. Donald Dobson and LCpl. Charles Gillespie join Kelly and Ellis. I also called in an artillery fire mission on the western approaches to the summit, hoping we might get lucky and hit any NVA planning to attack us from that direction.

A few hours after Sgt. Hauxhurst and I had returned to the summit, we again heard gunshots, and this time the rounds were going both ways. The security team on the eastern slope of the hill saw ten NVA soldiers wearing green uniforms, carrying Chinese AK-47 assault rifles, and moving up the trail from the east. This time, the experience of Slowick and Glor paid off as they initiated contact with the enemy soldiers, killing one and wounding another in their initial burst of fire. Sgt. Hauxhurst, Cpl. Williams and I joined Slowick and Glor and began to pour a torrent of rifle fire down the trail until we gained fire superiority, and the enemy withdrew back down the trail to the east. Using gas grenades, Hauxhurst, Williams, and I went forward to search the dead NVA soldier lying 30 feet in front of us and retrieve the wounded NVA soldier who was attempting to crawl behind a large rock just off the trail. Sgt. Hauxhurst fired his M-79 at a tree above the rock. We did not know how badly wounded the enemy soldier was or whether he had a rifle or grenade he could use against us. We heard him moan after the M-79 showered him with shrapnel. Although it was highly risky, I decided we needed to take a chance retrieving this wounded enemy soldier if we hoped to obtain a prisoner. I crawled down the trail, keeping as low to the ground as possible with my rifle pointed toward the rock where the wounded enemy lay. For a moment, I considered throwing a hand grenade behind the rock, but rejected this since I knew that would probably kill the enemy soldier.

An NVA soldier killed in a Killer Kane ambush.

I looked around the rock and found the enemy soldier lying unconscious, bleeding from a bullet wound in his stomach and shrapnel in his back. He was still breathing, but I could tell he was in shock. We needed to get him on a medevac helicopter soon, or he would die. While Sgt. Hauxhurst searched the other body and retrieved a pack and an AK-47 rifle from the dead NVA soldier, I had Williams help me carry the wounded NVA soldier back up to the summit where I hoped we could use a helicopter hoist to lift him through the high jungle canopy. As we lifted the wounded enemy soldier, we noticed he had a Russian pistol lying under him. I quickly picked up the pistol and put it in my shirt.

When we got the wounded man to the summit, Doc Conner began to work on him trying to save his life. He put a bandage on the stomach wound, inserted an IV into his arm, and began to fan his face with a wet field handkerchief he always carried. I radioed Camp Reasoner and told them I had a wounded prisoner and that we needed an emergency medevac immediately if we wanted to save the prisoner. I told them what had just transpired and gave them information about enemy activity to pass on to the medevac pilots. I was told a medevac helicopter would be over our position in 20 minutes.

The wounded NVA soldier slipped in and out of consciousness as Doc Conner worked over him. When he was conscious, he would stare at us with undisguised hatred in his eyes. He was quite young, perhaps only 17 or 18 years old, in excellent condition, with close-cropped hair and a wiry, well-muscled physique. Thirty minutes passed, but no medevac arrived. I radioed Camp Reasoner and asked about the status of the medevac helicopter, but all they would say was the choppers were on the way and should be over our position soon. As I gave the radio handset back to Bob Garner,

Donald "Doc" Conner administering first aid to a wounded NVA lieutenant.

Doc Conner looked over to me and whispered, "He's gone." I could see the wounded NVA soldier had stopped breathing and was turning blue around his lips. Doc Conner attempted CPR, but after a few minutes we could see it was futile. I radioed Camp Reasoner and told them the prisoner had died. They radioed back that they would cancel the medevac. I requested an extraction since we had obviously lost any chance of capturing a prisoner and would be lucky to get off the hill without making contact again. I was told to continue on my mission. Reluctantly, I did as I was told.

After wrapping the dead prisoner in one of our ponchos and attaching a short note

James Hauxhurst preparing a demolitions charge to clear a tree from an LZ.

to his shirt informing those who retrieved his body that we did everything we could to save him, I had the team prepare to move off the hill back down in the direction we came. It was always risky to use the same patrol route twice, but I knew the likelihood of the enemy coming after us was good. I hoped to find our insertion LZ and wait there until we could be extracted. I did not want the patrol searching for an alternate LZ if we made contact again. I was worried that the enemy knew exactly where we were now, and they would be laying a trap for us along the trail where contact had been made. I thought the best course of action was to move away from the trail and down the southeastern slope until we came to our insertion LZ. I told Sgt. Hauxhurst to take the team 100 meters down the hill and wait for me to follow in five minutes. I wanted to see if we were being followed.

As I saw my team drop out of sight over the southeastern slope of the hill, I positioned myself behind a tree where I could observe the trail. After only a few minutes, I heard a Vietnamese voice directly in front of me, but I could not see the source of the voice. Another minute passed and then standing no more than 30 feet away was a single NVA soldier carrying an AK-47 assault rifle. He had come up to the summit of Hill 502 from the north, avoiding the east-west trail. He looked down the trail in both directions and began to move west in the direction of the topographical summit of the hill where we had laid the body of the NVA soldier wrapped in one of our ponchos. As he turned toward me, I fired at him and saw him drop back down off the hill. I had fired a single shot from my M-16 rifle, a well-aimed shot that I was sure hit him. After a pregnant pause, all hell broke loose as several enemy soldiers began firing in my direction from the trail. I could not see them, but I could hear the distinctive sound of the crack of an AK-47 rifle over my head, and I noticed that my bush hat was no longer on my head. I returned fire and then proceeded to run down the hill in the direction of my team where I found them waiting for me. We expected the enemy would follow us down the hill and attack us so I had the team move another 100 yards south and then take a ninety-degree turn to the east and move for another 50 feet. I did this because I knew if the enemy followed our trail, we would have a distinct advantage over them if they were 50 feet to one side of our path as they moved through thick brush and vines.

Once in position, I had the team set up a 360-degree defense weighted toward our old trail and waited for the enemy's pursuit. We did not move. We did not talk. We did not whisper. We hardly breathed. All we did was watch and wait for what we expected to be a very bad firefight. Hours passed, but we heard nothing and saw nothing. The stress of such a situation made all of us tired and anxious. We did not even dare to whisper into our radio to send a message to base. LCpl. Garner would only key his handset to indicate we were "all secure" but Camp Reasoner knew we were in trouble and told Garner that they were sending an AO, our old friend Black Coat 1–0, to assist us. The AO came on station around 1500 and began directing artillery missions on the east-west trail on both sides of Hill 502. After an hour, the AO departed but told us to contact him again if we needed help. I told him we needed an extraction, but first we had to find an LZ. He flew over our position and passed on the locations of two LZs 1,000 meters southeast of our position. I thanked him for the information and hoped he would relay our request for an emergency extraction back to Camp Reasoner.

The rest of that day, the 1st of November, we spent sitting in silence waiting for an attack that never came. Taking time only to sip some water from our canteens, we kept watching and listening for any indication that the enemy was searching for us. We could not help but notice that we were sharing our small space in the jungle with dozens of thick, black millipedes. These harmless creatures, unlike their orange-colored cousins the centipedes, did not bite and were not poisonous, but they were not welcome in the small space we shared with them. Some of the men squirted insect repellent on them and watched them twitch in agony, but most of us just brushed them aside.

Our scout dog, Major, required a lot of water to fend off heat exhaustion, and soon his desire for water became a source of irritation for all of us. Water was precious in the hot jungle, and each of us only had five canteens, most of which were empty. We dared not move to search for a stream in fear of alerting the enemy to our location. We did not know when we would be extracted, so we rationed our water carefully. This worked for us, but Major only knew he was thirsty and hot. He let his handler know this by whining. The sound of a dog whining in the jungle was bizarre, and we all knew that if the enemy heard it, they would know exactly where we were. I gave one of my canteens to Cpl. McWilliams, the dog handler, because he had indicated that Major had finished all of the water he had been carrying for him. The dog seemed insatiable and drank the contents of my canteen in less than an hour. Cpl. McWilliams knew that his dog was a burden and a danger to our team so he whispered to me that, if necessary, he would kill Major. I told him to forget it. We would all get out, but only if he was able to keep the dog as cool and quiet as possible.

As night approached, I set the radio watch and decided to take the first watch myself. As I held the handset of the PRC-25 radio to my ear and listened to the reassuring hum it made in my ear, I looked at the group of men surrounding me. In the gathering darkness, the jungle foliage changed colors from dark emerald and light green to shades of grey and purple, before finally disappearing into black shadows. The Marines turned into sepia lumps, hardly distinguishable from the trees and rocks around them. As I took the handset away from my ear, I heard the night sounds of the jungle, sounds that always seemed to soothe my spirits. The hum of insects, the gentle calls of birds, and the buzz of mosquitoes, these were the normal sounds of the jungle I had become accustomed to hearing on patrol. I could also see the fluorescent streaks of light that clung to the dead and decaying foliage on the ground or hung in the moss that covered many of the branches and vines surrounding our harbor site. I could smell the jungle with its pungent odor of decaying vegetation. For many people, the jungle is unpleasant to the senses, but I always found these sights and odors reassuring because they were not the sounds and smells I feared. The sounds and smells I feared indicated the presence of the enemy. As the night dropped its blanket of darkness around us, I felt comforted.

The next day, our team went on alert at first light and remained on alert until around noon when I decided it was time to move to one of the LZs our friend, the AO, had told us about. We slowly made our way down Hill 502 until we found the LZ exactly where the AO said it was. On our way to the LZ, we came across a 60-man NVA harbor site that appeared to be recently used since we found fresh human feces in a small pit on its edge. The bamboo used to reinforce the side of the shelters looked like it had been cut only a few days previously. We found a good harbor site nearby and radioed Camp Reasoner that we were prepared to be extracted. We were told it was too late in the day for an extraction, but we would be extracted the next day, the 3rd, as soon as an extract package could be launched. The next day, at 0900, we were extracted and returned to Camp Reasoner's LZ Finch (Team Swift Scout Patrol Report, 3 Nov. 1967).

Although we were unsuccessful in our mission to obtain an enemy prisoner, we did manage to obtain some very useful information from the documents we found on the dead NVA soldiers. These documents identified the soldiers we had killed as belonging to the 368B Artillery (Rocket) Regiment of the NVA, a unit that possessed 140 mm rockets. One set of papers indicated we had killed a NVA lieutenant who had recently returned from a reconnaissance mission near Da Nang. The captured AK-47 assault rifle had been made in China less than a year earlier and had a new fiberglass stock instead of the normal wooden one. It appeared the NVA were now being equipped with the latest models of this highly effective rifle. As I listened to the enthusiastic comments our S-2 debriefer made about the new Chinese rifle, I was tempted to tell him I had also captured a new Russian pistol. However, I could not forget what had happened previously to the captured weapons we had turned over to the intelligence officers at division, so I remained silent. A week later, I traded the pistol to a U.S. Air Force NCO for a case of 100 New York–cut steaks.

I made several recommendations to the S-2 debriefer. Foremost among them, I said that we should never take another scout dog along on a recon patrol. I said the dogs and their handlers were great, but the dogs tired easily, and when they were tired, they did not alert us to the enemy's presence. Not once during our patrol did our dog, Major, signal the enemy's presence, but Slowick, Hauxhurst and Glor all sensed the enemy's presence as soon as we reached the summit of Hill 502. I had far more faith in my human colleagues than I did in the dogs we took into the jungle.

Many of us wondered about this ability to sense the presence of other humans near us when we were on patrol. Some of the men had developed an unusually keen ability to do this, and I also experienced it at times. When we talked about it, we were never sure why some men possessed it and others did not. Those of us who had this ability to sense humans were glad we were able to do so. Perhaps it was actually a long dormant trait that our ancestors, who were hunters and gatherers, possessed. Our senses became more acute when we were under the stress produced by patrolling in areas where death lurked around every corner. None of us could tell whether this unique ability to sense the presence of the enemy without seeing or hearing him was due to any logical explanation. It was just something we knew in our minds. I do know this: I lost this sense when I stopped seeking out the enemy in the mountainous jungles of South Vietnam, and I never experienced it again.

From 8 to 11 November, Swift Scout patrolled in an area south of Highway 1, the coastal highway that ran from the DMZ all the way to Saigon. This part of Highway 1, which was in the southern portion of Thua Thien Province, was called the "Street without Joy" by the French during the First Indo-China War, and it was the scene of several large and savage battles between French forces and the Viet Minh. It continued to be the scene of battles during the Second Indo-China War and remained an area where the VC political cadres held sway over many of the villages nearby.

The monsoon season had begun in central South Vietnam, and with it came days of rain and colder temperatures. Due to the bad weather and the increased likelihood of poor flying conditions, our patrols planned for more than the normal four days in the bush. We took more food with us to tide us over if our patrol was extended, and we often increased the size of our patrols in case we had to walk out and move through the villages in the lowlands. Taking all of this into account, I decided to take most of my platoon on this patrol, a force of 13 Marines. Our mission was to establish an OP near Phu Loc and observe any enemy infiltration in that area. Marine intelligence sources continued to inform us that the enemy was planning to attack Da Nang and several other military and civilian sites sometime after the first of the year. They wanted the recon teams to find out where these enemy units were staging for the attacks. For some reason unknown to us, they suspected the hills south of Hue near Phu Loc as one of these enemy staging areas.

We did not spot any enemy during our patrol, primarily because the monsoon rains kept everyone with any common sense indoors and dry. Of course, we had no sense. We spent a soggy four days in our ponchos trying to keep the lenses of our binoculars dry while we scanned the empty terrain below us through a veil of continuous rain. There was some traffic on Highway 1, mostly U.S. and ARVN military vehicles and civilian trucks, but that was about all we saw. The incessant rain not only made us wet and uncomfortable, it tended to sap our morale as well. By the time the patrol ended on the 11th of November, we looked like prunes, and some of my men were suffering from the onset of trench foot (Team Swift Scout Patrol Order, 11 Nov. 1967).

One thing we did during this patrol did lift our spirits. We celebrated the Marine Corps Birthday on November 10th. No matter where Marines are in the world, we always find some way to celebrate the Corps' birthday. I knew we would be in the field on November 10th, so in anticipation of this important event, I filled a canteen with rum prior to leaving Camp Reasoner. On the evening of the 10th, I gathered the patrol around me in the rain and read the Commandant's Birthday message to them. Then I gave each man a sip of rum as we toasted the Corps. At the end of this little ceremony, I heard one of my men whisper, "Good night Chesty, wherever you are." Of course, he was referring to the legendary Marine Chesty Puller, the Corps' most famous hero of World War II and the Korean War. Everyone repeated the phrase, and then I set the night watch as the rain continued to pour down on us in sheets.

Since the fog and rain were so intense, we were unable to be extracted by helicopter on the 11th of November, as planned. Instead, we had to walk out to Highway 1 where we met trucks from Company G, 2/7 and traveled to their CP. When we got there, we were impressed with their formidable base perched on high ground overlooking the South China Sea. On the top of their position stood an old French concrete machine gun bunker, a crumbling vestige to siege warfare and static defense. The French built many of these concrete bunkers throughout Vietnam during the First Indo-China War, usually along strategic roads, but they were not effective in preventing the Viet Minh from infiltrating along these roads or conducting ambushes of French military convoys. Now, a small three-man recon radio relay team lived inside the old bunker. They had the mission of providing secure communications for recon teams operating north of the Phu Gia Pass. We talked with these men for an hour or two about the situation north of Company G's position, and then around 1700 as the weather cleared, we were picked up by two UH-34 helicopters and returned to Camp Reasoner. After four days and nights spent shivering in the cold and rain, we were happy to get into some dry clothes and eat a hot meal at the mess hall.

The day after our return, the 12th of November, one of my men came to me after our morning run and told me he needed to talk to me. He was an NCO who had spent a couple of years in college before volunteering for the Marines. Like most of my men, he was intelligent and brave. He had been on at least a dozen recon patrols with our platoon and had always performed well. I thought of him as very competent, quiet, thoughtful, and disciplined, not the kind of Marine who would have a problem that needed my attention. We sat on the back porch of my hootch, and for the next hour he gave me an insight into how he and others perceived me. He began by saying that he thought he was a conscientious objector, based upon his religious beliefs and his aversion to killing. I asked him why, after nearly two years in the Marine Corps and at least a dozen recon patrols, he had suddenly had this religious conversion. He said he had always been deeply religious, but only recently had decided that there was a basic contradiction between his long-held religious beliefs, which were Baptist, and his attitude toward the taking of life. My intuition told me that his change of heart had something to do with his experiences on a recent patrol to Happy Valley. The way he answered a few more questions confirmed my suspicions.

I was not a chaplain or a theologian, so I knew I would not be able to convince this excellent Marine that he was not a conscientious objector using theological arguments. Instead, I appealed to his sense of loyalty to our team and the adverse impact on the team his absence might cause. During this exchange, he began to talk about me in a way that both surprised and saddened me. He said that I was different from the other men in the team and just about everyone else he had ever met. He said he and the other men in the team felt I was obsessed with killing the Vietnamese communists, and they were all concerned about the requests I made to take patrols on dangerous missions to Happy Valley and other locations where contact with the enemy was likely. He was polite and respectful, but I could tell he feared me and resented what he perceived to be an unreasonable willingness to risk the lives of the men in the team "chasing down and killing every VC in South Vietnam."

What he said disturbed me since I did not think of myself as he did. When I began to argue with him that this was not true, he asked me some pointed questions. Why had I requested the missions in Happy Valley? Why had our team, and no other team, been given the mission of capturing prisoners? Why was I always looking for an opportunity to ambush the enemy when our mission was just to observe and report on the enemy's movement? I began to realize that this Marine and perhaps others in our platoon had a very negative opinion of me and actually feared my aggressive approach to patrolling. What had begun as a conversation about his newly found religious convictions turned into a critique of me as a leader. The more I talked to this young and articulate NCO, the more I realized his observations about me might be widely shared. This hurt me deeply. I told him he really needed to talk to the battalion chaplain, and I would arrange such a meeting as soon as the chaplain was available. He thanked me and then said something to me that haunts me to this day. He said, "Sir, I have only been in the Marine

Corps for two years, but you are the best Marine officer I have ever known. You are brave and really know your job, but you are like Capt. Ahab in *Moby Dick*. Do you understand what I am saying?" I did understand him. Painfully, I realized his words had the ring of truth. This was not the first time someone had cautioned me about my aggressive approach. Maj. Lowrey had brought up the same subject with me and now one of my own team members had spoken to me about it. I took both of their comments to heart, but I decided I would not change how I conducted patrols. Instead, I would try to explain in more detail to the team why it was important for us to use every opportunity to attack the enemy, if the circumstances allowed us to do it without incurring excessive risk. In retrospect, I think my decision was correct. After all, we inflicted heavy casualties on the enemy, and we did so without the loss of a single Marine. As far as I was concerned, the results dictated we continue to patrol aggressively.

Strangely, the day after he spoke to the battalion chaplain, he came to me and said he had changed his mind about being a conscientious objector. He wanted to stay in the platoon and continue to go on patrol. I did not want to pry into what had transpired between him and the chaplain, but I told him I was grateful for his honest comments about me and that I was giving them a lot of consideration. I should have let the matter rest, but I made a lame attempt at humor by saying, "I know you think I am a cold, psychopathic killer, don't you?" He looked me straight in the eye, unsmiling, and said, "Yes sir, I do, but we need you."

Upon my return to Camp Reasoner I was given my orders for R and R in Bangkok and told I would be spending five days there from 18 to 23 November. The uniform for my trip was to be wash khaki, a uniform I had not worn since coming to South Vietnam. Fortunately, I had two wash khaki uniforms in my foot locker that had escaped the ravages of mildew. I had lost a lot of weight since arriving in country, so I tried the uniforms on to see if they still fit me. They did, but rather loosely. I had both uniforms cleaned and starched by Mr. Smart in Da Nang since I did not want to risk having them washed in the fetid rice paddy water normally used at our regular Vietnamese laundry. Mr. Smart assured me that he would have them cleaned and starched by a woman he knew in Da Nang who could be trusted to launder uniforms properly. The next day he returned with the two uniforms folded and wrapped in brown wrapping paper and secured with a red ribbon. The clothes smelled fresh and clean. I was delighted and gladly paid the extra cash for this first-rate service. I also packed a few civilian shirts and trousers to wear while in Bangkok.

The flight from Da Nang Airbase to Bangkok was uneventful, aside from seeing some really attractive American flight attendants serving us our meal and joking with us. I had almost forgotten what an American woman looked like after ten months in South Vietnam — almost!

At the Bangkok airport we boarded busses and traveled to several hotels. A dozen or so men exited the bus at each one. My hotel was modern and clean, but not large, with less than 100 rooms. I immediately changed into civilian clothes as soon as I reached my room and ran into the toilet to flush the commode several times, enjoying the marvel of it since I had not used a flush toilet since departing from Okinawa. I had not seen a television for ten months so I turned on the television, staring with incomprehension at a few local Thai programs until my thoughts turned to food. I ordered a banana split from room service. When the waiter brought the banana split to my room, I thought I had never seen such a delicious sight before in my life. I had dreamed of such a treat many times during the previous ten months, but now in all its glory it was sitting right in front of me just begging to be consumed. I sat by the window looking out onto the hotel's swimming pool and dug into this object of my culinary desire. I ate the entire dessert in a minute or two and immediately called room service to order a second one. I ate the second banana split just as quickly as the first one. Before the day was out, I would order three more banana splits from room service and consume each one ravenously.

The five days of my R and R were enjoyable for the most part, but I felt rather lonely during my stay. I did not know any of the other American men staying at my hotel, and I was not interested in getting drunk with them and making an ass of myself. They had all acquired Thai "girlfriends" shortly after arriving, probably via the hotel switchboard. I received a call shortly after I checked into my room from what I thought was the hotel's front desk. As it turned out, the hotel had contacted a local brothel and informed them that a group of U.S. servicemen had just checked in and given them the room numbers. A woman who spoke excellent English introduced herself as the "hotel entertainment coordinator," and she asked me if I needed some female company during my stay at the hotel. I told her I would think about it and call her back, if I needed such a service. I asked her for her telephone number and she refused to give it to me. When I asked her why she would not give me her telephone number, she just hung up on me. An hour later, she again called my room and asked me if I needed female companionship. This time, I hung up on her.

I was not engaged to "Jane," but I was in love with her, and I did not want to do anything to jeopardize my relationship with her. I was also aware that there was a huge problem with venereal disease in Thailand, a fact that was graphically pointed out to us by the R and R liaison officer at the airport. I had no desire to contract one of the many forms of VD then prevalent there. For these reasons, I decided to avoid contact with any women while I was on R and R and concentrate on my main objectives to buy presents for my family and "Jane" for Christmas and to relax as best I could after ten months of patrolling in South Vietnam.

My first priority was shopping, so I spent my first full day in Bangkok going to the stores Dave Gillespie told me about. I arranged for a private car from the hotel to take me around the city. I gazed at the gorgeous and exotic city of Bangkok, so clean and modern, and so different from the war-ravaged city of Da Nang. It bustled with commercial activity including a wide variety of shops devoted to products from Western Europe and Japan. There were also many shops that sold locally produced items, such as Thai silk and jewelry. Dave's list of good stores was very helpful, and before the day was done, I had made a huge dent in my Christmas gift list. I bought Thai silk, sapphire rings, top-grade leather and alligator wallets, jade pendants, and a complete dinner set nicely contained in a wooden carrying case. At each store, the proprietor offered me a cold beer to drink while he brought out his wares to display. I thought to myself that there could not possibly be any better way to shop.

On my second day, I decided to take a tour of the city. The hotel concierge arranged for me to join a small group of other U.S. military men for an all-day tour of the major sights in the city. A white van pulled up in front of the hotel early in the morning, and the driver and our guide, an attractive young woman, greeted me. Two young enlisted Army soldiers and their Thai girlfriends were also in the van. The men were from Montana and Nebraska, friendly and talkative, informing me proudly that they both came from farming families and telling me all about their brothers and sisters back home. For the most part, their Thai girlfriends just smiled sweetly and hung on their arms throughout the day. Our guide, whose name was Nid Theenthang, took us to see the solid gold Buddha, the floating gardens, Thai boxing, several temples, a Thai craft store, and finally an opulent Thai restaurant where we had a traditional Thai dinner. At the end of the evening, she dropped me off at my hotel and asked me if I wanted to go on another tour the next day to see the Bridge on the River Kwai. I told her I had things to do the next day, but she should contact me the following evening to see if I had time to take another tour. She said she would stop by the hotel the next evening to check on my plans.

I spent my third day visiting the U.S. Embassy and the American JUSMAG compound because both places had stores that sold imported products at reduced rates. I still had a few items I needed to buy for my family and for friends back at Camp Reasoner. In the afternoon, I met an American businessman, Mr. Ames, a family friend. My family had called him and told him I would be in Bangkok on R and R. We had lunch together at a local restaurant, where he impressed me with his ability to speak Thai and to read the Thai menu. Over lunch, he told me about what it was like to live and work in Thailand as an expatriate. It was obvious that he enjoyed a lifestyle in Bangkok that would have been impossible to duplicate on his salary in the United States. For instance, his home was a spacious and modern villa, and he had several servants who lived in the house with him, taking care of his every need.

After we finished our lunch, he took me to a Buddhist temple for a bath and massage. Most Thai bath houses are merely fronts for prostitution, but he told me this bath house at the temple was run by blind Buddhist monks, and I would actually get a good massage there. When we arrived at the temple, we paid for our bath and massage in advance and then removed our clothes and placed them in lockers. We were taken into a large room with a pool of very hot water and directed to wash for at least 20 minutes before our massage. Then we were taken into a room with several massage tables and introduced to two rather large, blind monks who proceeded to beat the hell out of us using their exceptionally strong fingers, forearms and elbows. This was definitely not the kind of massage one would normally expect in a Thai massage parlor in the red light district of Bangkok. While I was being "massaged," I began to doubt the wisdom of meeting up with Mr. Ames. In fact, for a few minutes, I even harbored the thought that he was playing some kind of trick on me. However, when the massage was over, I was surprised by how well I felt. When we stepped out of the temple into the bright sunlight, I felt as if ten months of stress and strain had been lifted from my shoulders, and my body and soul had been thoroughly reinvigorated. An hour later, I fell asleep in my hotel room and slept soundly for several hours.

That evening, Nid returned to the hotel, as she had promised, to see if I wanted to take another tour. We sat in the lobby and chatted for a few minutes before she suggested

I take the tour to a Thai nightclub. I said I might be interested, but I was hungry and wanted to eat some good Western food first. She told me that there was a restaurant called Nick's Hungarian Restaurant that was very popular with Westerners, but she had never been there so she could not vouch for how good the food might be. I asked her if she would like to go to Nick's for dinner, and she said she would, but she would have to make a phone call first to let her husband know she would not be home for dinner that evening. This was the first time she had mentioned she was married, and I wondered about the propriety of taking a married Thai woman out to dinner. However, she assured me that her husband was used to her having dinner with clients because her job as a tour guide required her to take clients out all the time. The two of us caught a cab to Nick's Hungarian Restaurant where we enjoyed an excellent meal and pleasant conversation. During the meal she told me that her family was actually Chinese, and her ancestors had immigrated to Thailand from southern China many years ago. She went out of her way to explain that she and her husband were Thai citizens but they did not consider themselves Thai.

After dinner, we went to her tour office and got into the office tour van, so we could pick up several clients who had signed up for the nightclub tour. We drove through the crowded streets to a nightclub that featured cabaret style entertainment, such as traditional Thai dancers and singers, as well as a troupe of female impersonators who mimicked Marilyn Monroe and Marlene Dietrich, among other famous female celebrities. Nid informed me that one of the female impersonators on stage was actually a woman and asked me if I could guess who she was. I had to admit I could not tell which one was "real," so she told me. "Look at the hips." she said, "The female impersonators don't have prominent hips, but the real woman does." Taking her advice, I quickly spotted the real woman. It was a fun evening, and I thanked Nid for her company when we reached the hotel. She gave me her husband's business card and told me to stop by his barber shop before my R and R ended.

My remaining time in Bangkok was devoted to eating well, hanging out at the hotel's swimming pool, and going to see two movies, one of which was the latest James Bond release. I also got a good Marine Corps regulation "high and tight" haircut at the barber shop Nid's husband owned. Despite all of this, I was becoming depressed with each day I spent in Bangkok. I felt very lonely, and I thought a lot about "Jane." I had wanted to take R and R in Hawaii and meet "Jane" there, but the policy of our battalion made that impossible. All of our R and R quotas for Hawaii were reserved for married Marines, and I was single. It may seem strange, but at the end of my five days in Bangkok, I was eagerly looking forward to returning to Camp Reasoner and my recon platoon. I found that I missed the company of my men, and I felt I should be with them in the jungle rather than enjoying myself in a nice hotel in Bangkok. When I got off the plane at Da Nang Airbase on 23 November, I was actually happy to be "home" again.

Shortly after my return, I was informed that there were orders from Headquarters Marine Corps waiting for me. These orders were to report to the Marine Barracks, Washington, D.C., as soon as my 13-month tour of duty in South Vietnam was completed. I had mixed feelings about these orders. I was flattered that I had been chosen for such a prestigious assignment, but I had several concerns about my suitability for such a job. I wondered why I had been chosen for this assignment and came to the conclusion that it was probably the result of a comment in my Basic School fitness report that said I should be considered for a "ceremonial assignment." I suspected this cursory recommendation had caught the attention of one of the detailing officers working in the Personnel Department of Headquarters Marine Corps, and they decided I was a good fit for this type of assignment.

I talked to Maj. Keating about the orders, and he said he was surprised I had been given them considering I was not "six foot two with eyes of blue," meaning I was too short for such a billet. He told me that every officer had to be at least six feet two inches tall at the Marine Barracks in Washington, D.C., because they had to be perfectly sized for the evening parades held at the barracks every Friday night during the summer. I asked him how I might escape such duty and he told me the only way to do it was to extend for six months more in South Vietnam. He strongly advised against such a rash action.

While we were talking about my orders, Maj. Keating told me that Lt. Col. Broman C. Stinemetz had recently told him I was being considered for assignment to a new company that was forming in the 1st Reconnaissance Battalion. He told me the Marine Corps was adding an additional company to each of its recon battalions in South Vietnam due to the increasing need for recon patrolling. Company E would soon be formed and join the other four companies of the battalion. Lt. Col. Stinemetz had indicated he wanted me to be part of this new company since all of the enlisted Marines would be new to South Vietnam, and he wanted experienced officers to train and lead them. I did not want to leave my platoon or 1st Force Reconnaissance Company, but I also knew my preferences would not figure prominently in any consideration about where I should be assigned.

On 29 November, I went on my last recon patrol with my platoon, although I did not know this when our helicopter lifted off the helipad at LZ Finch. Swift Scout's mission was "to detect possible VC troop movement or arms infiltration in the vicinity of the Nong Son Coal Mine area with particular emphasis on the trail networks that traverse the Khe Dienne River between Hills 406 and 89." We were also assigned a secondary mission of capturing a prisoner and were given a piece of new, experimental equipment that could detect movement near it. Since it was considered a classified piece of equipment, the technicians who gave it to us did not tell us much about it, aside from how to use it. One of the technicians called it a "seismic intrusion device" and informed us that it could detect movement by any enemy who passed near it. We were told to place the device on a well-used trail and then monitor it from a distance using a small handheld radio transmitter. The technicians assured us that we would have plenty of advance warning of the enemy's approach using this device, enough time to prepare an ambush or prisoner grab.

Because our mission called for a prisoner grab, we took more men than we would normally. Our patrol consisted of nine enlisted Marines, one Navy corpsman, me, and Capt. Fred Vogel, who had just joined the company and was going along as an observer. Fred had been in my company at the Naval Academy and graduated a year ahead of me. He was the son of a Navy admiral, and he was one of the first upperclassmen at the Naval Academy to offer his friendship to me during my plebe year. He was extremely intelligent with a unique gift for languages and the kind of engaging and friendly personality that appealed to both men and women. I felt honored that I would be taking him out on his first recon patrol.

At 0830, our team landed in a rather poor LZ on the north bank of the Khe Dienne River. Our CH-46 was exposed to the high ground surrounding the LZ, and the heavy monsoon rains had flooded the LZ to a depth of nearly a foot. LCpl. Dave Powell was on point, taking us toward the high ground southwest of the LZ. It began to rain heavily as we slowly made our way through thick undergrowth. The monsoon rain was a blessing since it masked any noise we might make moving through the thick brush. We walked along the north side of the Khe Dienne River until we came upon a trail that crossed the river just as it was shown on our map. The trail was well-used, but we decided to follow it for a few hundred meters to see if there was a good spot on it for an ambush. We found several trails intersecting with the main trail that followed the river, all of which showed signs of recent use, but we did not find a location that looked promising for an ambush or prisoner grab. We found many Ho Chi Minh sandal tracks and some odd cut marks on trees, which we guessed were trail markers telling the enemy which trail to take.

It was overcast and raining all day, and our movement was impeded by the mud and water in the low ground near the river. After several hours of fruitless search, we finally found a good location near two old enemy harbor sites. We took our seismic intrusion device 200 yards farther west along the trail and set it up. We tested it several times to make sure it was working properly, and then we returned to our ambush site, a sharp bend in the trail that had some large trees we could hide behind and allowed us to spot anyone walking down the trail from the west. We set out our security elements on the flanks of our ambush, making sure they were positioned in such a way as to protect the two approaches into the ambush site and to kill any enemy troops we did not capture. I chose PFC Castellano and Cpl. Williams for the actual prisoner grab team, since both were very strong and could easily handle any Vietnamese they might have to subdue physically. I covered them both from a few feet away and placed several lengths of pre-cut parachute cord in my web belt so I could tie up any prisoners we captured. Fred Vogel, who was the most familiar man with the intrusion device, was given the job of monitoring it and informing me if an enemy soldier activated it. According to Fred, any person moving within a few

Captain Fred Vogel on patrol.

feet of the device's sensors would trigger a silent alarm, giving us plenty of time to alert the grab team of the enemy's approach.

At approximately 1300, Capt. Vogel gave me the hand signal that the intrusion device had indicated several VC were walking toward us from the west. We waited for several minutes but no one came down the trail. An hour later, the intrusion device again indicated the enemy was approaching us, and this time the size of the force appeared to be quite large. I was worried about taking on a large enemy force with only a five-man assault force, but I thought it unwise to try to move our team away from the ambush site with the enemy so close. We waited for nearly an hour, but no one appeared on the trail. I decided either the enemy had turned back or the intrusion device had malfunctioned. I had the team assemble and move east toward the river and Hill 89, where I hoped to find a safe place to harbor for the night. From our new position, we hoped to continue to monitor the intrusion device sensors we left near the trail.

As darkness approached, we climbed to the top of Hill 89 and set up security on the top. Hill 89 was a perfect defensive position for an infantry squad and also a perfect OP for a recon team. Its summit was an oblong ridgeline approximately 50 yards long running north to south with several large rocks at each end of the oblong, which afforded excellent observation of all the surrounding terrain, especially the main east-west trail. The slope of Hill 89 was quite steep, making it easily defensible for whoever occupied its summit. I split the patrol into two sections and set up two OPs on each end of the summit among some large rocks. We barely had time to prepare our positions when darkness enveloped us, and it began to rain heavily. I was worried that the enemy who triggered the intrusion device might be nearby and had observed our ascent of Hill 89. Consequently, I had the entire team on alert for several hours after dark, but all was quiet throughout the night. Sheets of cold rain swept across Hill 89 all night long making sleep difficult and adding to our apprehension that the enemy might use the sound of thunder and rain to mask their movement toward us.

On the following days, we would leave Hill 89 before dawn and patrol along the river to the west, charting the trails in the area and resetting our ambush. We would occupy the ambush site for a few hours monitoring the intrusion device, but unlike the first day the device did not indicate the presence of the enemy. All we did was sit and shiver in the rain with our eyes straining for the slightest movement on the trail, our muscles sore and stiff from the lack of movement. Each afternoon, we would take a different route back to Hill 89 and set up our defense on the summit of this steep little hill.

On the last night of our patrol, the 1st of December, the weather cleared, and we could look up at the night sky and observe the terrain around us in the moonlight for several hundred meters. The stars shone brightly, like diamonds on black velvet, and for the first time the starlight and the light of the moon made it possible for us to see anything that moved along the narrow valley floor. There was a strong, cold wind, and most of us wrapped ourselves in our poncho liners to ward off the cool night air. Around midnight, I was awakened by our new Navy corpsman, HM1 J. B. Christy, who whispered in my ear that PFC C. L. Adams and LCpl. J. D. Glor thought they saw enemy soldiers moving around the south slope of the hill. I crawled over to where Adams and Glor were and they both pointed down the hill toward the river where it doglegged under the hill. I could see clearly all the way to the river which was only 100 meters away but I could not see any movement. The other Marines on the south side of the hill were all awake now and crouching behind the large rocks that formed a natural defensive position on this side of the summit. We looked for an hour but all we could see were the small trees at the bottom of the hill swaying in the wind and the shadows of tree branches that danced on the river's surface.

Since I had not seen any indication of the enemy, I told the men not to use their weapons to open fire on the enemy but to throw grenades if they saw anything out of the ordinary. I did not want to give our position away needlessly. I wanted the enemy to open fire first and give their position away before we hit them. We had not taken a machine gun with us on this patrol, and now I wished we had. Although we had a very good defensible position with large rocks to protect us from small-arms fire, we were not dug in, a big problem for us if the enemy used grenades or mortars to attack us. Glor and Adams swore they saw several enemy soldiers moving around the base of the hill near the river but whatever they saw was not there now. I had half the team remain on alert for the rest of the night but all remained quiet.

Due to heavy rain, we were not extracted until late in the day of the 2nd of December. We radioed Camp Reasoner around 1500 and told them the LZ had several hundred feet of visibility which should make it possible for a CH-46 helicopter to land, but we had our doubts that we would be picked up given the erratic weather. However, at 1600, like the sound of angels' wings from heaven, we heard the welcome sound of helicopter rotor blades in the gray, misty skies approaching our LZ from the east. I popped a smoke grenade in the LZ, and within seconds we saw the glorious sight of a CH-46 descending into the small LZ we found a few hundred meters west of Hill 89. We clambered aboard and flew back to LZ Finch, passing by the Nong Son Coal Mine complex on our left as we followed the Song Thu Bon River north to Da Nang and Hill 327 (Team Swift Scout Patrol Report, 2 Dec. 1967).

After our debrief at Camp Reasoner, Maj. Keating told me that I would be transferred to the 1st Reconnaissance Battalion where I would be assigned to the newly formed Company E. Company E was in cadre status, meaning it was only manned at a fraction of its full strength. He told me the Marines needed to bring the company to full strength would be arriving from the U.S in a week or two. This news, along with my orders to Marine Barracks, Washington, D.C., filled me with a deep sense of melancholy. The officers in my hootch could not understand my disappointment and unhappiness with my new situation. They said I should be happy that I was finally out of the field after nearly eleven months of recon patrolling. They also pointed out that I would soon be assigned to the most prestigious Marine Corps Barracks in our Corps where I would be able to enjoy all the perks that went along with such an assignment in our nation's capital. I would be going back to "the world," as we called the U.S., and I should be elated and grateful, instead of morose and dejected. I could not make them understand that I hated to leave my platoon and the excitement of making long-range reconnaissance patrols. It was difficult for me to explain my feelings to my fellow officers, feelings that only seemed to grow with the realization that I would no longer do the one thing I felt I was truly good at and which garnered the respect and admiration from my colleagues that I craved. Odd as it may sound, finding and killing the enemy was a task that seemed to define my purpose in life. My new assignment left me with a feeling that my future no longer involved meaningful or exciting work.

I tried to hide my disappointment with my situation, but I did not just accept my fate. I wrote to the officer at Headquarters Marine Corps responsible for assigning lieutenants, a person whose title was the "Lieutenants Monitor," and requested that my orders to Washington, D.C., be changed to the Basic School at Quantico, Virginia, or the 2nd Marine Division, so I

This picture of me reflects the strain of long-range patrolling. Compare this photograph with the photograph of me as a midshipman, taken only two years previously.

could escape the ceremonial duties associated with duty at "8th and I." I also drove a jeep to the CP of the 1st Battalion, 5th Marines, and asked them if I could extend my tour of duty in South Vietnam so I could spend my last six months with them in an infantry company. Lt. Col. Duncan, their C.O., told me he would gladly have me in his battalion if I extended my tour, and he even promised me that he would give me a rifle company to command, unless a more senior officer reported before I was assigned.

In another attempt to remain with my platoon, I went to see the G-1 of the 1st Marine Division and told him I wanted to extend my current tour for three months so I could avoid my transfer. His response to my inquiry was both vehement and angry. He told me one did not turn down orders to "8th and I" since that was "the Commandant's Home" and "Marine officers for that assignment were handpicked." He then berated me for writing to my monitor at Marine Corps Headquarters without first consulting him about trying to get my orders changed. He said, "Where do you get off, lieutenant, thinking you know more than the Lieutenant's Monitor about where you should be assigned? Why are you so special? Why don't you do something really unique, like obeying orders and not thinking of yourself?" I stood in front of his desk taking one hell of an ass-chewing from a real expert in that business, but he failed to understand that I had received far worse rebukes at the Naval Academy and I was inured to such outbursts by now. I simply listened to his tirade until he was finished, and then I asked him what I had to do to extend. I thought he was about to come across his desk and hit me, but instead he simply told me to go back to my company office and fill out an AA (Administrative Action) form requesting the extension.

When I walked back down Hill 327 to Camp Reasoner, I stopped off at my company office and asked SSgt. John Cole for an AA form. I told him why I wanted it, and he seemed genuinely concerned about my motivation for such a drastic action. He gave me the form, but he told me I should hand deliver it directly to Maj. Keating after I had filled it out.

John Cole was unique. He spent many years in South Vietnam, never rotating back to the U.S. until there were no other options open to him for staying in country. He was an expert in administration and had spent several years prior to Vietnam with force reconnaissance units in the U.S. Later on, he was commissioned and retired as a colonel. I suspected that John spoke to Maj. Keating about my request for the AA form because the next day when I gave it to Maj. Keating, he did not even look at it. Instead, he had me sit down in his office for a "heart-to-heart" talk. He started off by complimenting me on all that my team had accomplished while I commanded the 5th platoon and even went so far as to tell me I was the best reconnaissance team leader in his company, and possibly the best in the battalion. He gave me a copy of my final fitness report and asked me to read the narrative section, where he had written a few sentences outlining my performance of duty while assigned to his command. Those sentences contained many glowing terms and superlatives. I told him I did not deserve such a good fitness report, especially in light of the trouble I had caused him concerning my unhappiness with the awards system and the rather caustic way I described my unhappiness in front of senior officers. He simply nodded, and then he spoke to me like a father:

> Andy, I am truly concerned about you. I find it difficult to really understand you, and I am not the only one. I have no complaints about how you do your job. In fact, I think the results speak for themselves. What worries me about you is how you seem to take this war personally, as if it is some sort of personal crusade. Capt. Dixon told me you were overly aggressive and seemed to seek out every chance to make contact with the enemy, and he warned me to keep an eye on you because of this. I have come to see what he was talking about. During your patrol debriefings, you seemed to take a perverse delight when you described the way you and your team killed the enemy. You embarrassed the Commanding General a while back when you were doing a "dog and pony show" for those congressional staffers because you said the only way to win wars is to kill the enemy, and your team actively goes looking for trouble. I am not sure whether or not you really believe what you said, but comments like that don't go down well with civilians. I have to be honest with you. Some of your men are also concerned about you. Two of them came to me last month and told me you are taking too many risks and that all you think about is killing the enemy at every opportunity. Don't get me wrong. These men admire you and care about you more than you know, but they are fearful that your aggressive attitude is placing the team in danger. Are you aware of their concerns?

I suspected that Maj. Keating had had a conversation with the chaplain, although he did not indicate that this was the case. However, I could not ignore the message he was conveying since it was a message that I had heard before. I fought to find the right words to explain to him why I did what I did. I told him some of my men seemed afraid while on patrol, but no one, aside from two men who had talked to me about getting out of the bush, had told me about their concerns. I then felt tears well up in my eyes, because I felt I had always tried to protect my men as best I could while still trying to accomplish our mission. I loved the men in my platoon and considered them like brothers to me. It hurt to know that some of them no longer had confidence in me and considered me a risk to the team. I began to choke on my words, overcome with emotion. I blurted out, "So that is why I am being sent to Company E. I am being relieved of my duties, aren't I?"

Maj. Keating said, "No, you crazy bastard, that is not why you are going to Company E. You are going to Company E because those new men from the States need you and your experience to help them survive when they go on patrol. Most patrol leaders only spend six months in the field, but you are working on eleven, an unheard-of amount of time in the bush for a lieutenant. It is time for you to turn over your platoon to someone else. Not because of anything bad you have done, but because everyone wants you to survive this war. You cannot win this war by yourself. If you keep going like this, you will certainly be killed. I don't want the law of averages to catch up with you. Now take this AA form and put it away for now. Go to Company E and train those new men so they are as good as the men in Killer Kane. In a few months, if you still want to extend to go to the infantry, you can still take the AA form to your new C.O. at Company E, and I am sure he will forward it."

Maj. Keating was probably no more than ten years older than I, but I considered him vastly more experienced and far more knowledgeable about how the Marine Corps worked and how to judge the character of men. I respected him as a leader and teacher. His talk to me that day had both hurt me and helped me. It hurt to hear him say that my men worried about my perceived fixation with killing the enemy at the risk of their lives. It helped, however, to know they thought highly of me as their patrol leader and that Maj. Keating thought I could use my experience to improve the chances of survival of the men of Company E. I took the AA form and tucked it into my jungle utility pocket and walked back to my hootch, chastened in the knowledge that I would soon be helping Marines to survive in combat.

My last day with my platoon was 4 December. In the morning, I went on a run with them in the rain along our usual route, the road that led from Camp Reasoner to the Freedom Hill PX. As we ran, we chanted the same cadence calls we always had on countless other runs along this road. Jeeps and trucks passed by us with their occupants staring at us and wondering who these crazy men were out running in a downpour. After taking the obligatory cold shower and putting on my jungle utility uniform, I packed my belongings into my two footlockers and went to the company office to get my orders to Company E. While I waited, Maj. Keating reminded me that there was a going-away party for me at the Camp Reasoner Officers and SNCO mess hall that evening, and it was "a command performance." As I walked back to my hootch, Sgt. Hauxhurst came over to me and told me the platoon wanted to see me before I shoved off, and would I come over to their hootch before evening meal? I told him I would.

Around 1600, Sgt. Hauxhurst came to my hootch to remind me of the platoon gathering. I walked over to the SEA hut that was the home of my platoon, and there all of my men were assembled. As I stepped into the hut, Sgt. Hauxhurst yelled, "Attention on deck!" and then each man came up to me, shook my hand, and told me they would miss me. Sgt. Hauxhurst presented me with a framed picture of the entire platoon and a small, compact 35 mm Canon camera they had bought for me at the PX. I thanked them for the gifts, but when I started to tell them how much I appreciated them, I found it very difficult to speak without getting emotional. I had not expected my men to do anything special for me, so when I heard their kind words and expressions of affection for me, I nearly broke into tears. Sgt. Hauxhurst rescued me from further embarrassment by breaking out a prized bottle of whiskey he had been saving for an important occasion and offering me a drink. Everyone sat down on the cots and footlockers near me and each of us had a drink. It was rather awkward at first, but soon we began to talk about some of the patrols we had gone on and some of the men who had left the platoon and returned to the States. As evening meal approached, we broke up and each man again shook my hand and wished me luck. I wished them luck also and then, fighting back tears, I walked up to the Officers and SNCO mess hall for dinner. As I walked the 100 yards to the mess hall, I suddenly found myself saying a prayer. I thanked God for the privilege of serving with such remarkable men, and I asked Him to take care of them and protect them in my absence.

Later, after dinner, Maj. Keating gathered the officers and SNCOs of our company in the mess hall where he presented me with a unit plaque and wished me well in my new job. What struck me during this little ceremony was the way he addressed me. I was not Lt. Finlayson or Andy—I was Killer Kane. He, like many others in the unit, associated me with my team. I was part of Killer Kane and it was part of me forever. (Sadly, Maj. Keating was killed in action on 22 May 1968, in the A Shau Valley, Thua Thien Province. He was conducting recon in support of the U.S. Army's 1st Cavalry Division at the time.)

When the ceremony was over, the lieutenants from my company and several other officers from the battalion asked me to go up to the division officers' club to watch a movie and enjoy a few drinks. The entire time I was at the club that evening, my favorite Vietnamese friends, Mai Ly and Dien, would not let me pay for a single drink. Probably more than anything else that happened to me that last day, this simple gesture of friendship by two young Vietnamese women touched me. These young women did not have much money; they essentially lived off the meager tips they received from the officers at the club, yet they wanted to express their friendship to me by buying me drinks. The club manager told me he had never seen these two women buy a drink for another Marine. When I left the club that evening, Mai Ly and Dien gave me portrait photos of themselves and told me not to forget them. I promised I would remember them and I did. I did not know it at the time, but I would be seeing both of them again in less than a year.

9

Okinawa and Home

With my transfer from 1st Force Reconnaissance Company to Company E, 1st Reconnaissance Battalion, the remainder of my time in country was devoted to training the men of Company E. I no longer took out recon patrols. There was not enough room for

Company E at Camp Reasoner, so the new company was given excess billeting in SEA huts within the 1st Tank Battalion cantonment on Hill 35, southwest of Da Nang Airbase. For the next six weeks, we joined new Marines arriving from the States, issued them equipment, and began a rigorous physical training program. We also took them to a local ARVN rifle range where each man test-fired his new M-16 rifle, zeroed his sights on a 1,000-inch range, and fired several hundred rounds at targets placed 300 meters down range to make sure their battle sights were correct. This was done to ensure each rifle was "battle zeroed," meaning the point of impact at 300 meters was the point of aim. I taught classes on map reading, patrolling techniques, ambushes, immediate action drills, calling and adjusting artillery, the proper employment of the Claymore mine, and basic demolitions, and gave a three-hour lecture on how the NVA operated against recon patrols and how to counter them.

Each day began at 0500 when everyone in Company E fell out in the company street for physical training (PT) with 1st Sgt. Maurice Jacques, the company 1st Sgt. and a legend in the Marine Corps for his bravery and leadership. (He's even the subject of a biography, *Sergeant Major, U.S. Marines*, by Maj. Bruce H. Norton, Ivy Books, 1995. His time with Co. E is on pages 309–330.) After a half-hour of rigorous calisthenics, 1st Sgt. Jacques would turn the company over to our CO, Capt. James P. Cahill, who would lead us on a company run in formation. These runs increased from a single mile at a slow pace on our first day to three miles at a fast pace two weeks later. Marines arriving from the States were usually in good shape, but the heat and humidity put a strain on anybody who was unused to tropical weather. We tried to increase gradually both the tempo and duration of their physical training until the new Marines were thoroughly acclimated to their environment. After PT, 1st Sgt. Jacques led us in some additional calisthenics, and then we took a cold shower, dressed, and fell back in formation for a personnel inspection. At 0700, we ate breakfast in the 1st Tank Battalion's mess hall, where the food was not as good as the food at Camp Reasoner but still far better than the cold C rations we ate in the field. During the remainder of the morning, the officers and SNCOs taught classes. After lunch, there were more classes, followed by another hour of PT before dinner. The time after dinner was free time, during which the enlisted Marines wrote letters, played cards, drank a few beers, or watched a movie in the enlisted club on the cantonment. The officers and SNCOs in our company usually followed Capt. Cahill each evening to the 1st Tank Battalion's Officers and SNCO club, a very small building no larger than the standard SEA hut. Here we enjoyed each other's company and the limited selection of libations available. Despite the austerity of the club, it provided a welcome respite after a hard day of physical training and classes. I spent little time in this club, because I had to prepare lesson plans for my classes, and this took up several hours each night. Since Capt. Cahill had no experience as a patrol leader, he delegated most of the planning for our training to Pete Badger and me. Pete had been a patrol leader also, and he brought with him a wealth of valuable patrolling information. He was also a gifted organizer and coordinator, obtaining choice training facilities for us and arranging for the 1st Motor Transport Battalion to take us to the various training venues in and around Da Nang. Between the two of us, we produced most of the training documents for the new company.

Because we were in a forming company and in a training status, we did not have to participate in the normal guard duties for the cantonment, but we did have our own interior guard and fire watch system. Pete Badger drafted our guard orders, and our SNCOs managed the interior guard system. Capt. Cahill was a terrific administrator and a good leader, as well as the kind of officer who instantly elicited loyalty and respect from his men, making him an ideal choice to lead our new company. We were also blessed with an exceptionally strong set of officers and SNCOs, making the difficult task of forming a reconnaissance company from scratch and preparing it for combat a relatively easy one.

The highlight of our training before our departure for Okinawa was a two-day course on rubber boat drills and scout swimming at Nam O Bridge north of Da Nang. These two skills often atrophied for most recon Marines in South Vietnam because the need to focus limited training opportunities on scouting and patrolling often crowded out any opportunity for amphibious reconnaissance training. 1st Sgt. Jacques and the SNCOs were in charge of this training, and everyone enjoyed it with the possible exception of those Marines who had never experienced salt water and surf. For me this time at Nam O Bridge was joyful. Whenever I had the opportunity to swim in salt water, it always reminded me of my childhood swimming in the surf of the Atlantic Ocean at Cape May, New Jersey. I actually felt a twinge of homesickness at various times during this training. Standing on the beach after an hour of swimming in the surf, my body warmed by the sun, and the taste of sea salt on my lips, I felt at peace with the world. As I looked at the steel gray mountains that descended gracefully into the South China Sea to the north, it struck me that this place combined both mountains and the sea, the two elements of nature that most appealed to me. Although there was a war being waged nearby, I could not help but think this place would make a perfect spot for a tropical resort one day.

On Christmas Day, 1967, our company enjoyed a special dinner in the mess hall. Turkey with dressing, sliced ham, mashed potatoes, candied yams, green bean casserole, mixed nuts, and apple and pumpkin pie were on the menu for that day, a rare feast as only the Marine Corps can put on far from home in a war zone. I attended Catholic Mass, and afterward, the chaplain for the 1st Motor Transport Battalion asked me to be the Catholic lay leader for the remainder of my time at the cantonment. Since I had been a Catholic lay leader at Camp Reasoner, I gladly agreed. Although I enjoyed the Christmas dinner and the break from training, the day filled me with an intense feeling of homesickness. I could not help but think of the wonderful Christmas dinners my mother prepared for my family and the delicious cookies and pies she baked at that time of year. Like many children, I often took the love and sacrifice of my parents for granted. This Christmas far from home, I had time to reflect on the many things my parents did for me, especially the way my mother made the Christmas holidays so special for her children.

Despite the wonderful Christmas dinner, I don't think anyone felt jubilant or happy that day. The incessant monsoon rain, the overcast skies, the mist-shrouded hills, and the ever present mud put a damper on the holiday spirit. I tried to think of the religious significance of Christmas and how fortunate I was to be alive and out of combat, but a lingering feeling of impending danger blocked out all the positive aspects of the celebration of Christ's birth.

Shortly after Christmas, Capt. Cahill told Pete Badger and me that he had received word that the enemy was planning to attack Da Nang Airbase and the I Corps compound in Da Nang sometime around New Year's Day. He informed us that a "very reliable source," which we assumed meant a signals intercept or a spy, had warned of a large scale attack on these targets. According to Capt. Cahill, the enemy would use a rocket attack against the airbase as the signal for the attack to begin. In this way, the enemy did not have to rely on less secure methods, such as written orders or radio transmissions, to signal the attack.

Capt. Cahill told us the enemy would launch their ground attacks using VC and NVA sapper units, small highly skilled units trained in covert infiltration and demolition techniques. Once these sapper units had successfully breached the defenses of these two targets, elements of the 2nd NVA Division would follow them and exploit their success. He then went on to explain how an elaborate American ruse, code-named Operation Claxon, would be used to fool the enemy into making a premature attack. First, Marine recon teams would be positioned along likely avenues of approach for the NVA units while Marine infantry and ARVN units would move to locations where they could ambush the local VC units before they reached their targets. Artillery observation teams in the hills near Da Nang and "Spooky" gunships would be ready to attack any enemy units caught moving toward their attack positions. In order to fool the enemy, Marine engineers had placed demolition charges inside the Da Nang Airbase and would set them off shortly after midnight on New Year's Eve in the hope that the local VC units would think the airbase was under rocket attack and then launch their attacks prematurely. If they took the bait, it would confuse the enemy's leadership and cause many of the units from the 2nd NVA Division to move in an uncoordinated fashion.

Pete and I listened with fascination as Capt. Cahill told us about this bold attempt to precipitate an enemy attack. I had listened to several intelligence briefings at Camp Reasoner and at the 1st Marine Division G-2 office that talked about a "large scale enemy attack in early 1968," but I had thought it unlikely the enemy would be able to mount such a large attack. My thinking, which evolved out of conversations with other like-minded officers at the time, was that the enemy had suffered too many casualties during the summer to be able to mount much of an offensive in I Corps. I expected only a few attacks by fire on isolated friendly positions and a few sapper attacks on targets such as district headquarters. I did not think they had the capability to mount a ground attack against the Da Nang Airbase or Da Nang City. I was wrong.

On New Year's Eve, the three of us watched as the Marine engineers began to set off their explosive charges at the airbase. From a distance of a few miles, it looked exactly as it was intended to look, like a rocket attack. We saw the yellow bursts of light on the horizon and then heard the sound of the explosions as dozens of charges went off over the space of five minutes. Our cantonment was on full alert, and our company was standing by in full battle gear to reinforce the perimeter if the enemy had us on their target list. We waited in the darkness for several hours, but there was only silence. The ruse had not worked, and Pete and I jokingly talked about how foolish it was to believe the enemy would be able to get through our defenses to attack the airbase or Da Nang. We wondered who it was who informed us of this impending attack and whether he could be believed again. Years later, I was to find out that the source of this information came from a CIA informant who lived in Da Nang. He was a member of the communist infrastructure in the city and had been recruited by the CIA only a few months prior to Christmas. He provided accurate information to the CIA about the targets for the Tet offensive, but he was not able to provide the exact date and time for these attacks until 24 hours before the enemy struck. Still, the information he provided allowed the U.S. and South Vietnamese to counter effectively these attacks and inflict very heavy casualties on the attackers when they struck on 31 January during the Tet holiday.

In early January, it became increasingly obvious that something big was afoot. Recon patrols spotted several very large groups of NVA soldiers moving into positions in the lowlands west and south of Da Nang. One recon team reported seeing an enemy force of 300 well-armed NVA soldiers, and another team spotted 167 NVA troops carrying rockets and mortars. Such large sightings were highly unusual, clearly indicating the likelihood of a major enemy operation. We also heard reports that the rate of infiltration by NVA units from North Vietnam through Laos had increased dramatically during late 1967, another indication that some serious fighting would take place in early 1968.

While most of the press was reporting on the developing battle at the Khe Sanh Combat Base in Quang Tri Province to the north, the NVA launched an attack on the Da Nang Airbase in early January, an attack that was clearly meant to test the defenses of the airbase in preparation for their main attack to follow during TET. A barrage of rockets was launched 3,000 meters southwest of our cantonment and in the middle of 1/7's TAOR. The enemy paid a heavy price for this rocket attack because artillery and tank fire responded immediately, inflicting heavy casualties on the NVA unit firing the rockets before they could launch all of them. A reaction force found three bodies, numerous unfired rockets, and a huge amount of abandoned web gear and equipment where the artillery and tank fire impacted. They also found numerous blood trails leading west toward Happy Valley. The next day, Capt. Cahill and I went to an OP near the scene and used our binoculars to observe the mess the tanks and artillery had made. We both agreed that there were probably more attacks coming as Tet approached, but we also felt confident the American and ARVN forces would be able to defeat easily any such attacks. We believed the enemy simply did not possess the forces needed for a serious, sustained attack on any target in the 1st Marine Division TAOR.

My frustration with the actions of our political leaders in Washington, D.C., was growing as I saw the enemy consistently disregard the various truces inflicted upon us. The enemy exploited these truces to speed up their infiltration of men and supplies from North Vietnam, and I could not understand why our leaders were agreeing to these truces when they had no effect on the enemy. In a letter I wrote to my parents on 9 January 1967, I summed up my feelings on this subject: "The NVA moved in a new regiment during the 'truce.' The result: several Marines killed and many wounded. If the politicians have one more 'truce,' I doubt if the Marines will observe it. Recon has seen too many violations already, and the patrol leaders feel that, even if they can't get permission to use artillery because of the 'truce,' they will open fire on the enemy with small arms. *I can't wait to vote in the 68 election!*"

On 14 January, I flew to Okinawa along with a small number of enlisted men from our company. We were the advance party for Company E, and our mission was to prepare the way for the rest of our company, due to depart for Okinawa in a few days. We arrived at Kadena Airbase and took a truck up to Camp Schwab where we immediately set to work on a list of things we needed to accomplish before our company showed up. Our advance party made sure Company E had everything they needed when they arrived: billeting, armory, mess facilities at Camp Schwab, bus transportation from the airbase to Camp Schwab, and clean linen for their first night on the island. I also coordinated with the Operations Officer for the 9th Marine Amphibious Brigade at Camp Schwab and worked on the details of a tentative training schedule for the company. He was very helpful and said he would do everything in his power to make sure we had the highest priority for training areas and resources.

On 18 January, Company E boarded C-130 transport aircraft at the Da Nang Airbase and flew to the island of Okinawa where it was scheduled to complete its reconnaissance training before returning to Da Nang in early March. Soon after the planes touched down on Okinawa, I met Capt. Cahill and the company with busses for the troops and trucks for their personal gear and equipment. Within a few minutes, our convoy was headed north along Okinawa's winding roads toward Camp Schwab. I had not slept much during my first few days on Okinawa. A combination of worry over the short time our small advance party had to accomplish the many tasks needed before the arrival of the company and the long hours needed to meet our schedule left all of us overly fatigued. The small team of junior enlisted Marines and I had to work some very long hours and to beg for transportation to get ourselves around to the various offices we needed to coordinate with. Due to the lack of sleep and the change in weather between South Vietnam and the much colder Okinawa, we all came down with bad colds. I had arranged with the mess hall at Camp Schwab to serve a late meal for Company E, and the cooks did a great job of preparing a full meal service for the newly arrived visitors from South Vietnam, despite the inconvenience and the late hours. It was after midnight before we finally had all of our Marines billeted in their barracks. Capt. Cahill held a short meeting so the officers and SNCOs could go over the next day's events, and then I went to my room at the BOQ and collapsed.

I only had a few hours of sleep when reveille sounded at 0500. I had to shake off the effects of my cold and turn out for PT with 1st Sgt. Jacques and the rest of the company. My cold made life miserable for me during that first week of training, but I had no other choice but to endure it. Only Pete Badger, 1st Sgt. Jacques and I had the recent combat experience needed to organize and conduct a training plan for our company, so there was no possibility of my reporting to sick bay or taking a day off. We were the only people in the company who had been on reconnaissance patrols in country. Most of our SNCOs and NCOs had been assigned to us from 1st Marine Division infantry battalions, which meant all of their previous training had been infantry related and not focused on reconnaissance. As a result, 1st Sgt. Jacques, Pete and I found that we not only had to plan and organize the training program for the company but we also had to teach the majority of the classes. We constantly had to refine the training program for the company because the staff officers at 9th MAB headquarters had prepared a reconnaissance training program based upon their understanding of what was needed, but their syllabus was often inadequate or contained training events we did not need for the mission of a reconnaissance company. Of course, every change we made caused consternation among the 9th MAB's staff because it meant new lesson plans, new schedules, and new demands for training areas, ammunition, rations, and transportation. I soon found that my face was not a welcome sight in the operations office of the 9th MAB.

Despite these problems, our training program progressed on schedule. The five platoons of Company E were all at full strength as we began our training on Okinawa, and all of our men were volunteers, which meant their morale was high and their motivation to learn was keen. The fact that all of our Marines in the ranks of LCpl. and below had come to the company from the reconnaissance school at Camp Pendleton, California, and already had the basic reconnaissance MOS of 8651 meant each of them had a very good foundation for the more advanced skills we were teaching them. They were a pleasure to train. I also was impressed with the quality of SNCOs in the company. Despite their paucity of recon experience, they were all good leaders, and many of them had previous combat tours in Vietnam with Marine infantry units, giving them a good understanding of the enemy and the terrain. All in all, I thought the men in Company E were highly motivated and well disciplined.

Since I was the senior lieutenant in the company, I was given the job of executive officer in addition to my initial job of training officer. The executive officer of a company is the second in command, and he is also responsible for ensuring the administration of the company is carried out properly. As such, I had to spend a lot of time on administrative duties which took me away from the field training. Capt. Cahill, who was scheduled to rotate back to the U.S. a few weeks before I was, saw that giving me both the executive officer and training officer jobs was too much for one man, so he had me turn over my training duties to Pete Badger. This was a wise decision, although I would have preferred to concentrate on training and not paperwork. In retrospect, I benefited from Capt. Cahill's decision since it gave me an opportunity to gain some staff proficiency and practical experience with Marine Corps administration procedures. It also allowed me to recover my health since my cold continued to hang on, and it weakened me to the point where I was having difficulty with our daily PT routine.

I soon found out that the job of executive officer was a full-time job. I spent long hours in the company office, usually working from 0730 each morning until late at night. I was fortunate to have an expert in company administration assisting me as my administration chief: Sgt. Schlapp, a Marine reservist who volunteered to come on active duty out of a strong sense of patriotism and gave up a well-paying job in the U.S. to serve his country. I learned a great deal about Marine Corps administration from this man. Although I was no longer the training officer for the company, I found that most of my time as the executive officer was devoted to making sure the training schedule that Pete Badger and 1st Sgt. Jacques developed was properly supported. I had to make sure that little things were done according to plan, such as the delivery of M-16 ammunition to the proper range at the proper time, or the preparation of late rations when the troops came in from the field late at night.

A normal day for me went something like this: after PT and breakfast in the morning, I went to the company office at 0730, where I made a quick check of my in-box to see if any important documents were there. Then at 0745, I held a short meeting with key staff and the platoon commanders to pass on any word pertaining to the training day. After company formation at 0800 I relieved the old Duty NCO and posted the new one. From 0815 to 0930, I read all the directives and messages that were routed to me since close of business the previous day, and then I passed them along to Capt. Cahill for him to read. From 0930 to 1130, I coordinated with the 9th MAB's staff sections so they would know how to support the next day's training schedule. After noon meal, I would return to the company office and spend the remainder of the afternoon reading the Marine Corps Personnel Manual and Marine Corps publications, drafting and signing letters, and doing other routine administrative work. At the end of the day, I would attend a meeting with Capt. Cahill and Lt. Badger on the next day's training, followed by an hour of PT with the company. After dinner, I would return to the company office until 2100, going over the unit diary with Sgt. Schlapp and preparing for the next day's work. Although the hours were long, I did not find this work stressful, and Capt. Cahill did not over manage me. The work was enjoyable, although not as interesting or rewarding as field work.

The majority of our training took place in the Northern Training Area (NTA) on Okinawa, a large tract of land on the northern tip of the island that had terrain and vegetation very similar to the mountainous jungle of I Corps in South Vietnam. As a result, it was an ideal place to provide practical instruction to the Marines of Company E. We knew the best training for our men was training that was as realistic as possible, so we developed a system of patrols that allowed each platoon to work against each other, a sort of recon team versus recon team training system. First Sgt. Jacques and some of our SNCOs acted as lane graders, going out with the patrols and evaluating them on the spot and providing instantaneous feedback to them as they progressed on their patrols. Pete Badger and I established a radio relay site for the teams and acted as the battalion headquarters, feeding the patrols instructions and recording their SALUTE reports for later evaluation once the patrols returned. Most of the patrols were of short duration, only a day or two, because we wanted the patrol leaders to have as much experience as possible preparing their patrols and conducting them. The culmination of this realistic training in the NTA was a three-day patrol where we had several small aggressor teams dressed as VC soldiers operating against the teams, forcing the teams to evade, use supporting arms, or ambush, depending on the situation. When we returned to Camp Schwab from the NTA, we gathered the evaluators and lane graders and went over each team's performance, highlighting their strengths and weaknesses and recommending remedial training where it was appropriate. Most of the teams scored well, but a few needed additional work, primarily in the use of supporting arms and the proper way to respond when a team made contact with the enemy. Pete Badger developed an innovative way to conduct this remedial training by setting up several training stations at Camp Schwab where the team members could rotate between each station, accomplishing a set of tasks at each one. In this way, the teams obtained the necessary repetition to achieve proficiency. I marveled at how well both Pete and 1st Sgt. Jacques found ways to expedite and improve training, and I took notes of how they did this so I could benefit from it in the future.

My impression of Okinawa at this time was not a good one. I did not like the seedy bars, massage parlors, and cheap restaurants I saw outside the camp. There was a lot of tension between the Marines and the people of Okinawa, so I did not go out in town more than once during my entire stay there. Japanese communist agitators were prevalent on the island, and they often placed provocative signs outside the main gate or conducted staged rallies near the base against the U.S. presence on the island. Several U.S. lawyers who belonged to the communist front group, The National Lawyers Guild, aided and abetted the communists in Kin Village by assisting in the preparation of propaganda leaflets and the printing of a crude newspaper promoting communist causes in Asia. I felt far more ill at ease on Okinawa than I ever felt in South Vietnam. While I was there, communists infiltrated a fenced ammunition bunker at Camp Hansen and stole several thousand rounds of rifle ammunition. In a letter home to my parents, I told them that the Marine guards at Camp Hansen saw the ammunition being stolen but "were afraid to shoot" because they were "afraid of causing an incident." The entire time I spent on Okinawa, I felt as if I was in a hostile country.

The event that had the greatest impact on me while I was on Okinawa was the North Korean attack on the USS *Pueblo* and the capture of its entire crew. When this occurred, it took the U.S. military leadership completely by surprise, and they were woefully unprepared to react to it. Our reconnaissance company was the only ground combat unit on the island, and we were too far away to do anything. On the day of the *Pueblo*'s capture, we were told to end our training, report to our barracks, and be prepared to move out to the Kadena Airbase in one hour. We were hastily issued chemical, biological and nuclear protective clothing, called MOP gear, and some sophisticated equipment used to monitor radioactivity, but we were not issued ammunition.

We remained in our barracks for a day awaiting orders from higher headquarters, and then we were told to stand down. It is highly unlikely that any serious consideration was given to moving us to Korea, but we went through the drill anyway. As it turned out, the U.S. military forces in Northeast Asia were impotent when it came to responding to this blatant attack on one of our ships. We looked bad in the eyes of the world, deservedly so. An officer in the 9th MAB operations office told me the U.S. had sent a U.S. Navy ship into harm's way without any adequate means of protecting it. I shared his frustration and anger as he went on to explain that we had compounded our shame by doing nothing to punish the North Koreans for this attack, which constituted an act of war under international law. I felt ashamed as these events unfolded, but worse things were to happen shortly. Again, we would be too far from the action to do anything about it.

On 31 January 1968, the communists in South Vietnam launched a country-wide offensive against dozens of political and military targets in the hope of precipitating a general uprising among the people of South Vietnam. I listened to the radio and television reports that were coming from South Vietnam with incredulity. I simply could not believe what I was seeing and hearing. Despite months of warnings that the enemy was preparing for a major assault in South Vietnam in early 1968, the U.S. and South Vietnamese military were taken completely by surprise. During the first chaotic 48 hours of the communist Tet offensive, the news we received was fragmentary and contradictory. The press corps in South Vietnam seemed to have panicked, and their reporting took on a decidedly negative and defeatist tone. As things began to settle down in South Vietnam and it became apparent that the enemy's objective of fomenting a general uprising against the South

Vietnamese Government had failed, we began to receive daily classified briefings from Marine intelligence officers. These briefings painted a different picture of events from those we read about in the U.S. press or saw on the television news programs from the U.S.

Each day, I attended the 9th MAB intelligence briefing and took notes so I could brief Capt. Cahill and the other officers about the events unfolding in South Vietnam. These notes clearly showed a progression in the analysis of events that initially reflected shock and dismay by intelligence officers inside South Vietnam at the intensity and scope of the communist attacks, but changed over the subsequent days and weeks to a much more sober and realistic assessment of the attack. One daily briefing chart in particular interested me: a list of the primary targets attacked by the enemy and whether or not the targets were still held by the enemy or were contested. This chart showed a dramatic change in the situation in South Vietnam. While the enemy had attacked most of the South Vietnamese provincial capitals and many of the district headquarters during the first few days of their offensive, only Saigon and Hue remained as pockets of resistance a week after the initial communist assaults. The chart also told a dramatic story of the success of the South Vietnamese military forces, who quickly repulsed the communist attackers and reestablished control of their political centers after only a few days of fighting. There was no general uprising as the communists had hoped, and many NVA units which were intended to be used to exploit VC successes either failed to reinforce their communist brethren or deliberately left them to their fate. The Marine intelligence officers were perplexed as to why the NVA forces did not follow up the attacks by the local VC. It began to look like many of the NVA units deliberately chose to stay in their base areas or staging positions despite the frantic cries for help from the VC units leading the attacks. Hue was the only significant exception to this NVA failure.

What began to emerge after two weeks was a picture of massive failure on the part of the enemy to achieve any significant objective while suffering huge losses in the process. I was particularly heartened to hear of how the ARVN had crushed the VC attacks in Quang Nam Province, especially at the I Corps Headquarters in Da Nang. U.S. recon teams had spotted several large NVA units moving toward Da Nang and Hue and devastated them with artillery and air attacks. I felt relieved when I heard these intelligence briefings on the status of the war and hoped we could quickly exploit this enemy defeat with counterattacks into their base areas to clear out the NVA units that were still not engaged. What I was completely unaware of at the time was the impact televised reports of the fighting in Saigon and elsewhere was having on the American public. All the news the American people were receiving from correspondents in Saigon was negative. As they looked at selective and spectacular scenes of the fighting on their television screens and they listened to the breathless commentary of American newsmen in Saigon, the American people received a far different and a far more inflammatory story of the Tet Offensive than the U.S. military and South Vietnamese people heard and saw. The American public saw television reporters claiming a huge victory for the communists, while I saw a huge defeat for the VC and NVA emerging from the reporting from MACV. I found it impossible to understand how the American press and television crews could portray the Tet Offensive as a communist victory when there was so much evidence to the contrary. Unfortunately, this failure of the press to report the results of the Tet Offensive accurately would have a profound impact on American politics in the coming months. It would also have a profound effect on me when I returned home. (For more detailed information, see Peter Braestrup, *Big Story: How the American Press and Television Reported and Interpreted the Crisis of Tet 1968 in Vietnam and Washington*, 2 vols [Boulder, CO: Westview Press, 1977] and James Robbins, *This Time We Win: Revisiting the Tet Offensive* [New York: Encounter Books, 2010]).

On 23 February 1968, I boarded a commercial plane at Kadena Airbase and flew to Travis Airbase in California. After debarking and going through customs, I took a cab to San Francisco International Airport and boarded a plane for Philadelphia and home. When I arrived at the Philadelphia airport, my parents, my cousin Joe Kelley and his wife, Franny, and my girlfriend, "Jane," met me. I was overjoyed to be home and happy to see my parents and "Jane" again after a separation of nearly 15 months.

When we reached my hometown of Merchantville, the realization that I was finally home struck me. It was a bright, sunny, winter day when we drove up the driveway of 310 Volan Street, a day that seemed so normal that it almost felt as if I had not been gone for over a year. I was back in this quintessential little American town, a town that embodied all that I loved about my country. My father had the American flag flying on our front porch; aside from that, there were no visible signs that their warrior son had returned. Inside the house, I was reunited with my older brother, John, my younger brother, Bruce, and younger sisters, Nancy and Jean. I sat in the living room of our home talking to everyone while my mother went about cooking my favorite meal of roast pork, sauerkraut, applesauce, and roasted potatoes. I was so overcome with the happiness of being home that I felt almost giddy. That night, I slept in the same bed I had slept in for most of my life. As I drifted off to sleep, I could hear the soothing and familiar sound of the wind blowing through the trees in the front yard. I was at peace with the world and with myself. For the first time in over a year, I felt completely at ease with my surroundings.

For a few days, I basked in the realization that the war I had fought for the past year was far away, and I was now safe. "Jane" and I got reacquainted and spent several days doing the things we both enjoyed doing together before I left for Vietnam. We would take long walks at Cooper River Park and go out to dinner at local restaurants or see a movie at one of the theaters in the area. "Jane" had to return to college in Washington, D.C., and her departure seemed to take the air out of any good feelings I had. I soon found myself alone for most of each day.

Despite the best efforts of my parents and siblings to make me feel at home, I soon became bored with the unstructured routine at home. In addition, nobody in the community came to see me or called me, and this eroded my pleasure in being home. My feeling of alienation increased each night as I watched the evening news on television. All three of the broadcast stations in Philadelphia carried negative news about the progress of the war, filling our home and the homes of every American with stories of defeat and chaos. My parents listened to these news reports every night during my absence. Now that I was home, they did not seem interested in news about the war. I could not blame them. All I saw on television was a dreary litany of defeat and no mention of any victories against the VC and NVA. Commentators such as Walter Cronkite, Daniel Schorr and

Dan Rather told the American people that the war in Vietnam was lost. Their comments appeared to suggest that the communists had won the hearts and minds of the South Vietnamese people, and this was the reason for the enemy's success on the battlefield. Of course, I knew this to be untrue, but my comments about the war surprised my parents because all they had heard from our nation's news media was contrary to what I was telling them. When they asked me why I thought the reporting was biased and untrue, I told them that the American journalists in South Vietnam seldom ventured out to where the fighting was actually taking place. They had made up their minds before coming to Vietnam that the VC were the good guys and the South Vietnamese Government and military were evil, corrupt, and inept. I told my parents that I only saw two American reporters during my entire thirteen months in South Vietnam, and both of them made comments to me that reflected contempt for the South Vietnamese and admiration for the North Vietnamese communists.

I also told them that it was common knowledge among the American military that these American reporters spent most of their time in Saigon with their mistresses drinking at the Caravel and Continental Hotels and talking to South Vietnamese café politicians who represented a constituency who could easily hold a convention in a phone booth. What most American soldiers and Marines saw in the dangerous areas of South Vietnam were South Vietnamese and Taiwanese photographers and sound men, who gathered film footage of combat and did the really dangerous work for the Americans back in Saigon. When the American journalists did venture to the field, it was usually for a very short visit via helicopter so they could get a good visual in front of some burning hut or wounded GI and then fly back to Saigon to file their story and enjoy the comfort of their air-conditioned offices and hotel rooms. They got most of their stories from staff officers in Saigon who had never heard a shot fired or from malcontents, such as John Paul Vann, who harbored a grudge against the South Vietnamese or the U.S. Government. I tried to tell my parents that most of us had only contempt for the misfits covering the war for the major media organizations. I tried to explain to them that the Western press in Saigon had panicked during Tet because it was the first time their sheltered little world had been rocked by the real war, and they were frightened and disheartened by it. They were also angry about what they perceived to be the mendacity of the American military telling them the war was going well and then finding street battles going on in Saigon. When Tet disrupted their comfortable and secure lives, they went out of their way to convey to the American public that the U.S. military was incapable of telling the truth. Each evening, it became a tiresome ritual of watching the news on television and telling my parents that what they were seeing and hearing was either false or one-sided.

Along with my anger over what I considered biased and untruthful reporting from South Vietnam, I increasingly wondered why no one came to our home to welcome me back from the war. As a young boy, I saw how several local men were greeted when they returned from the Korean War, and their welcome home stood in sharp contrast to mine. For them, there had been block parties with neighbors gathered in their front yards or on porches festooned with red, white and blue bunting, but I saw none of that on my street. I remembered my mother baking a cake for one of these young men, Marine Cpl. Danny Stewart, and going with her to give it to him at his home. In my case, not a single person came to see me or even call me on the phone to welcome me back during the three weeks that I was at my parent's home. Everyone seemed demoralized by the reports about the Tet offensive and how bad things were going in South Vietnam. Anyone who told the truth about the terrible beating the enemy took during Tet was looked upon as crazy or untruthful.

After two weeks of relaxing at home, reading and working out, I became so bored and disheartened that I began to think it was a waste of time to continue taking any more leave. In some strange way, I missed the tempo of life and the camaraderie of my life in South Vietnam. I found myself longing for my life as a recon Marine. The things that used to excite me and fill me with anticipation and enthusiasm no longer did so. Life had lost its edge, and I had the feeling that I would never recapture any of the feelings I used to have for the life I knew before I went off to war. I kept thinking of a passage from a novel by Hemingway I had read in Vietnam, one that spoke of how men who had hunted men were never satisfied with life after they had done this.

I suppose all of this came to a head when my youngest sister, Jean, a junior at our local high school, told me one day that her history teacher was very much against the war in Vietnam, and he did not share my views on why we were there and how the war was progressing. I told Jean that I would be delighted to visit the high school in order to debate this teacher, and she carried this message to him the next day. I received a call from the principal of the school, Mr. William Flynn, and he told me that instead of a debate, he thought it would be better for me to come to the school and give a talk to Jean's history class and then answer any questions the students might have. I agreed, and the next day I found myself in a classroom of 16- and 17-year-olds quietly waiting for me to tell them about the war. My talk focused on a series of questions I thought needed to be asked about the war and then I provided answers to these questions, based upon what I had observed during my year in South Vietnam. Standing in the back of the room was the teacher with his arms folded across his chest. It was evident he was not about to let me simply present my case unopposed.

I began my talk by telling the students that the information they were receiving from newspaper and television accounts of the war was either false or misleading, especially those reports that pertained to the recent Tet offensive and to alleged atrocities carried out by South Vietnamese and American military personnel. I explained to them that during my entire time in South Vietnam, I never once saw a television news crew, and I only met two journalists during my year in South Vietnam. Neither of them had spent much time covering the war from the field. I also told them that I never saw an American or South Vietnamese atrocity or even heard of one that I could verify. As I made these statements, I could see the teacher in the back of the room bristle and roll his eyes.

I went on to say I had defeated the enemy every time I came in contact with them, and not a single man in my platoon had been killed in combat with the enemy. I told them that I lost only one man due to an accident, a lightning strike on Hill 452. I wanted to blunt the idea that every operation conducted resulted in huge casualties for American forces.

Finally, I spent several minutes going over my impressions of the South Vietnamese people, including their military and political leadership. I admitted that not every South Vietnamese supported the central government and that in many places the VC actually governed the people instead of the South Vietnamese Government. I also told them that there was a lot of corruption and economic dislocation fueled by the war. I pointed out to the students that the South Vietnamese Government was not similar to the style of government U.S. citizens recognized, but the village and district chiefs I saw in Quang Nam Province were doing a pretty good job of taking care of their people and providing them with basic governmental services. I also told them I had witnessed several large-scale civic action projects carried out by the South Vietnamese government, such as the construction of hospitals and schools. I went on to tell the students about the success of the village elections I had witnessed.

A student raised his hand and asked me if the South Vietnamese military was good or bad. I told him that my impression of the South Vietnamese military was mixed. I felt the airborne, marine, and ranger units were quite good, but some units were poor. On the whole, however, the South Vietnamese soldiers I encountered were brave and competent, but not as well armed or equipped as either the Americans or the North Vietnamese, which made their task of fighting NVA units more difficult for them than for the Americans. I said most of the equipment used by the South Vietnamese military was obsolete World War II American equipment, ill-suited for them or the war they were fighting. As an example, I told the class the South Vietnamese Army was equipped with the American M-1 Garand rifle, a heavy weapon that only fired eight rounds, while the North Vietnamese and most of the VC were equipped with the Chinese or Russian AK-47 rifle, which was much lighter, more reliable, and had a magazine capacity of thirty rounds.

Another student asked me, "We hear that the VC are more popular than the Saigon Government because they are closer to the people and do more for them." My response to this student made the teacher wince. I said the VC only had the support of approximately 20 percent of the population, and this support stemmed from three factors: terror imposed by VC assassination teams, the promise of land distribution if the VC won the war, and the success of VC propaganda that portrayed the Americans as colonialists similar to the French. I stressed that each of these things had a powerful hold on the minds of many rural South Vietnamese and made the task of winning the war very difficult. At this time, I did not fully understand how pervasive and effective the social organization programs of the communists were, so I did not discuss this important aspect during my talk. It would take me another tour in Vietnam before I fully understood the highly effective means of controlling the rural population employed by the enemy.

A young girl sitting right in front of me asked me if I had seen any atrocities committed by the VC. I told her I had witnessed the results of several atrocities committed by the VC, but none by the NVA, who were more disciplined than the VC. I added that I knew of several instances of VC corruption where VC political officials were involved in extortion, tax-skimming and land-grabbing for personal gain. I admitted that corruption was also a major problem for the South Vietnamese Government, but it was not the major reason for people taking the side of the VC. I could tell that this last idea was new to the students and several of them took notes about it. The teacher had a visibly negative reaction to my comment about VC corruption, one that told me this subject would surely be discussed after my talk concluded.

At the end of my talk, which lasted approximately 40 minutes, I asked the students if they had any more questions. A few tentative hands went up in the air. One girl asked me about what I did to amuse myself when I wasn't fighting. Another girl asked me how I felt to be home. A boy asked me if I had ever seen any Marines burning the homes of Vietnamese civilians. I answered that I had not seen a home burned. I told him many Vietnamese homes had bunkers in them, and the enemy often used these bunkers to hide in or to fight from, making them targets for destruction whenever the enemy chose to fight inside a village.

Then the teacher asked me a question. He said, "You spoke about only 20 percent of the people supporting the National Liberation Front (NLF). If that is true, why aren't the U.S. and South Vietnamese more successful? It seems we are losing the war against these 20 percent."

My reply was rather simplistic, and I regretted making it as soon as the words left my mouth. I said, "As far as I can see, we are not losing the war. The enemy loses every battle. More and more land and people are coming under the control of the central government. We are pushing the VC and the NVA back into the mountains and out of the villages."

The teacher, a young man close to my age, took on the demeanor of the all-knowing teacher and began to lecture me on why what I had just said "was obviously incorrect." The gist of his argument went like this:

> All we are hearing from South Vietnam is the enemy has attacked all the provincial capitals and struck at the heart of Saigon. It seems to me that it is the Americans who are being pushed out of the towns and into the mountains, not the National Liberation Front (NLF). If they are losing and they only have support from 20 percent of the people, it is highly unlikely that they would be able to do this. I think they have the support of most of the people and that is why the NLF is winning and able to attack everywhere in South Vietnam. What you are describing sounds very hard to believe when we see a totally different picture every day on television. Pictures don't lie; we are losing this war because we are on the wrong side. The NLF fighters are the true nationalists. As I see it, the NLF people are like our own anti-colonial fighters during the American Revolutionary War when we fought against England. That is why we cannot win, and I don't think we deserve to win.

I could tell from the expressions on the faces of the students that his words were telling and made sense to them. All I could say to counter his argument was that I had been to Vietnam, spent many months there, had observed the people and their daily lives, and had come to the conclusion that we were winning the war. I felt that our side would provide a better future for the South Vietnamese than the communists. As if to put an exclamation point to my statement, I said it was really a fight between a future based upon democratic institutions and free markets and one based upon one-party, authoritarian rule and a collective economic system. I thought the differences were stark, and the South Vietnamese people would finally decide which future was best for them. On that note, I left the classroom and returned home.

When I reflect on this incident at my old high school I am far less angry and disappointed now with the words and reactions of the teacher and the students than I was at the time. I realize that their views on the war were logical given the way the war was being portrayed in the newspapers and on television at that time. Had I not recently returned from the war and only had the news media reporting to form my views, I most likely would have had the same opinion on the war they had. In early 1968, this encounter filled me with dread because I felt for the first time that the war was being lost in the hearts and minds of the American people, and I knew this was the center of gravity for the enemy's strategy. Once a people lose faith in the justification for a war, their will is eroded and it is only a matter of time before they are defeated. As I walked home that day, I realized that the people living in my hometown were beginning to lose heart and were even susceptible to the enemy's propaganda. For the first time, I began to feel the war could be lost.

The next day I called the Marine Barracks, Washington, D.C., and told them I would be reporting for duty a week early. That evening, I told my parents I wanted to get back to work so I would be leaving in two days for my new assignment. They said they understood, and they thought it would probably be good for me to be close to "Jane" again. I packed my uniforms and other personal items in my car and told my parents I would call them when I arrived in Washington, D.C.

Nineteen sixty-eight was one of the most traumatic years in our nation's history. It was the year of the Tet offensive in South Vietnam, the announcement that President Lyndon Baines Johnson would not run for another term, the assassinations of Martin Luther King, Jr., and Bobby Kennedy, and the riots at the Democratic convention in Chicago. At times, it seemed as if the nation was coming apart, and civil war might erupt. There were demonstrations on college campuses against the war and radical groups endorsed violent action against the state. When I returned to the U.S. in February of 1968, I soon found myself engulfed in this national fury, and I was stationed at the epicenter of the political turmoil — Washington, D.C.

I reported on 2 March to the Marine barracks, Washington, D.C., arguably the most famous post in the Corps and the home of the commandant of the Marine Corps. For most Marines, this barracks is more often referred to as "8th and Eye" because it is located at the intersection of 8th and I streets in southeast Washington, D.C. Located just a few blocks north of the Washington Navy Yard, the barracks occupied an entire city block and housed several Marine units, whose primary duty was to support government and military ceremonies. In addition to the impressive living quarters for the commandant of the Marine Corps, the barracks also served as the home for the Marine Corps Band, the Marine Corps Drum and Bugle Corps, the Guard Company, and the Marine Corps Institute (MCI). Its primary function was, and still is, to serve as the public face of the Marine Corps and to provide ceremonial support for various White House, Pentagon, and Arlington National Cemetery functions.

These duties call for perfection in every endeavor, no matter how trivial or mundane. From the Friday night Sunset Parades held each summer on the barracks parade ground to the White House and Pentagon arrival ceremonies or the burial details at Arlington National Cemetery or the posting of the guard each evening on the parade ground, every little detail associated with these ceremonies had to be executed to perfection. Errors or miscues were often punished severely in both official and unofficial ways. The reputation of the Marine Corps was at stake, so any mistakes occurring at these public functions was an embarrassment to the Corps. It was bad enough to make a mistake in front of the general public, but it was a disaster when these mistakes were viewed by the senior political leadership of the U.S. and foreign dignitaries. Any Marine, regardless of rank, was informed of the necessity for perfection from the moment he or she reported on board, and they were held to this exacting standard throughout their assignment to the barracks. The Marine Corps is noted for its ceremonial acumen and its devotion to "spit and polish," but at the Marine Barracks at 8th and I Streets, these traits were elevated to almost religious significance and observance.

On March 2nd, I departed home very early in the morning so I would be able to

Me at Marine Barracks, Washington, DC, April 1968.

report to the barracks at 0800 sharp. My little TR-4 roadster, packed with all of my worldly possessions, made the journey in less than four hours, even taking into account the confusion I found with the street signs in our nation's capital with their northeast, northwest, southeast and southwest designations. I pulled up to the barracks' main gate, Gate Number 1, took the salute from the sentry, and then parked my car in the visitor's parking space at the south end of the parade field. The sentry at the gate told me where to report, and within a minute of exiting my car, I was standing before the duty officer, presenting him with my orders.

I then made an office call to the commanding officer of the barracks, Col. Joe Fegan. Col. Fegan was a veteran of World War II, Korea, and Vietnam, with an impressive chest full of medals to attest to his heroism in battle. He was tall, with dark features, and had a face that looked like aged leather. He greeted me warmly, as if he had known me all of his life, and he spoke to me more like a friend than the senior officer at a key Marine Corps installation. He had seen my Officers Qualification Record (OQR) previously because he immediately began to talk about my hometown, my parents, and my experiences in Vietnam. His friendly comments made me feel at home and appreciated. But he had a very serious side to him, and he began to impress upon me the high standards expected of me and the importance of demonstrating to the public the professionalism of our Corps. He told me that many people who viewed our Sunset Parades at the barracks or the evening parades at the Marine Corps Memorial at Arlington National Cemetery would only see the Marine Corps on display at these events once in their lives, and they would carry away from these ceremonies their only impression of the Corps. As such, it was essential that the Corps impress these people, regardless of their position or station in life. Because of this, everything we did at the barracks, down to the minutest detail, must be done with professionalism and the highest standards of excellence. He warned me that I would be spending a lot of time drilling, including many hours of standing in front of a mirror rendering sword salutes, and polishing leather every day. It was often dreary and repetitious work, but it was absolutely necessary if I was to project perfection on the parade ground or at some other ceremony where the public would see me.

Near the end of our conversation, Col. Fegan asked me if I was interested in doing some extra work for the Marine Corps that had nothing to do with my duties at the barracks. I asked him what this "extra" work entailed, and he said he had a friend at Headquarters Marine Corps who was doing a study on ground reconnaissance. Since I had recently returned from South Vietnam and had a great deal of practical experience with the subject, he thought I might prove helpful to this colleague of his. As it turned out, I helped with two projects. One was a ground reconnaissance study being done by Maj. Alex Lee and my old friend from Vietnam, MSgt. Clovis Coffman, at the Marine Corps Development and Education Center at Quantico, Virginia. The other was a classified study that was part of "Project Agile," an effort by the Department of Defense and the Battelle Memorial Institute to develop a system of electronic sensors to monitor enemy movements of men and equipment. In both cases, I spent a day or two working on these studies at Quantico and the Pentagon, respectively. My input involved providing information on how Marine ground reconnaissance operations were conducted in South Vietnam and identifying areas where I thought technological and tactical improvements could be made.

Before I left Col. Fegan's office, he invited me to attend a Mess Night that evening. A Marine Corps Mess Night is a formal dinner without spouses. I told him that I did not have my Dress Blue uniform pressed for such a formal dinner, but he said he would send someone over to the Center House BOQ, where I would be billeted, to collect my uniform and have it pressed and returned to me in time for the Mess Night in the Band Hall. I thanked him for his kindness, but secretly I wished I did not have to attend a formal affair on my first night. I always felt ill at ease at such formal affairs, and I did not relish spending my first night at the barracks attending a Mess Night.

After my introduction to Col. Fegan, the adjutant showed me to my room at Center House, situated on the west side of the parade ground and the first house north of the main gate in a row of several other identical brick houses. The other houses were homes for the assistant commandant, Gen. Lewis W. Walt, and other senior Marine officers and their families. On the north side of the parade ground was the stately and beautiful home of the commandant, Gen. Leonard F. Chapman, Jr. The commandant's home was the oldest continuously occupied government building in Washington, D.C., and the scene of many official functions hosted by the commandant for congressional, military, and corporate leaders.

Center House was a unique BOQ. Unlike the usual BOQ on most military bases, Center House was a stately house with a very homelike feel to it. There were only five officers living in it when I reported aboard. I was given a room on the second floor. My room was not like the standard government issue BOQ room with nondescript metal furniture of ancient origin. My room was a large bedroom that one would expect to find in an upscale home. There were a queen-size bed, two end tables, a large mahogany wood desk, a sofa, coffee table, and several large, comfortable leather chairs. There were framed paintings on the walls and large photos of Marine Corps scenes from around the world. The window of my bedroom looked out on to the manicured parade ground and red brick barracks opposite. It was plush, indeed, and I felt very privileged to be living in such splendor and comfort.

Two Marine orderlies took care of Center House and cooked our meals. They prepared breakfast, lunch and dinner for the six of us each day, and they served every meal to us in grand style. If we wanted, the small bar on the first floor would be open at 1630 each day, and one of the enlisted orderlies was there to provide us with our favorite libation. At 1800 sharp, dinner would be announced, and we would adjourn to the dining room where we would sit around a table set with white linen and sterling silver place settings, complete with sterling silver napkin holders with our names engraved on them. We were required to wear either our service uniform or a civilian coat and tie at dinner. Elegant porcelain dishes and crystal stemware were set at each place. An orderly would serve each course from a large silver tray and pour wine for us from a crystal decanter. I felt as if I had stepped into some aristocratic Victorian home whenever I sat down to dinner at Center House, and I was sure no other officer in the Marine Corps enjoyed such luxury and comfort.

The other officers living in Center House with me were Major Herbert Seay, Captains James Cooney, Thomas Campbell, Nick Grosz, and Lieutenant Frank "Ike" Izenour. All of these officers were single, had the infantry MOS, and had recently served in Vietnam. They were also highly decorated. At the Mess Night my first evening at the barracks, I enjoyed the traditional meal of roast beef and the friendly and collegial atmosphere that was a reflection of Col. Fegan's inspiring leadership style.

During the table conversation, I found out why I had been sent to "8th and Eye" and not to some other post or station in the Corps. It turned out that a year ago an influential congressman had attended a Friday Evening Parade and noted that none of the officers or enlisted Marines on the parade deck were wearing the Vietnamese campaign ribbon or any other decoration indicating they had served in South Vietnam. The commandant took note of this and immediately changed the long standing policy of sending carefully screened Marines directly from basic training to the barracks. Instead, he ordered Headquarters Marine Corps to start sending officers and enlisted Marines from Vietnam to fill the ranks. This policy change resulted in some significant changes in the types of Marines sent to the barracks. For instance, it had previously been the normal procedure to assign only Marine officers who stood six foot two inches tall to the barracks since the commandant wanted to have all of his officers tall and imposing and of uniform height. Since I was only 5'11" tall, under the previous assignment process I would not have been selected for assignment to the barracks. Several other returning Marine officers also did not meet the height requirements, but that did not matter to Gen. Chapman; he wanted Marine officers wearing decorations and campaign ribbons that clearly showed they had been to Vietnam. While this new policy meant the ranks were being filled with combat veterans, it also meant the Marines in the ranks made for a less uniform and imposing appearance.

The next few days were devoted to honing my ceremonial skills. I spent endless hours of sword drill under the careful eye of the 1st Sgt. of Guard Company and several officers. I seemed to learn quickly the distinctive drill maneuvers particular to the barracks, such as the parade flank movement, the rigid hand salute, and the parade gait that made an officer look like he was walking on eggs. After two weeks, I was pronounced ready for basic ceremonial duties.

I was temporarily assigned to the Marine Corps Institute (MCI) at the Navy Yard to help complete one of their correspondence courses called *Reconnaissance Marine*. This work took only a few weeks to complete, since it was largely finished before my arrival. I amended a few items in the course to reflect some of the lessons learned in Vietnam before it was published and sent to the field. Once my work at MCI was finished, I received my permanent assignment to Guard Company, also located in the Navy Yard. I reported to my new CO, Capt. Barry Beck, and he told me to take over the 1st Platoon.

I shared my new office on the second floor at Guard Company with my platoon Sgt., SSgt. Johnson. He was on his second tour at Guard Company, having served there as a junior enlisted man several years ago. He was thoroughly professional, and knew everything about the duties of Guard Company. We got along well from the beginning, and I came to rely on this seasoned SNCO for his expertise and counsel throughout my time at the barracks. We spent countless hours together in our small office rehearsing the intricacies and nuances of our ceremonial duties and shining leather gear, polishing brass, and ironing our uniforms as we prepared for the ceremonies that Guard Company participated in. Ever the thoughtful SNCO, he would always go over each ceremony with me so I was thoroughly familiar with how it was performed and what dangers lurked for an unsuspecting platoon commander. These duties included the Sunset Parade at the barracks each Friday during the summer and the Evening Parade at the Marine Corps Memorial each Tuesday, as well as White House and Pentagon dignitary arrivals, and Tomb of the Unknown and funeral processions at Arlington National Cemetery.

We also had other duties that did not involve ceremonies, but still required a very high level of professionalism and attention to detail, such as presidential security at Camp David and security for visiting dignitaries staying at Blair House, located across the street from the White House. Before leaving for a ceremony, we would inspect ourselves in front of a large full-length mirror in our office and then turn to face each other for one final visual inspection before we left the office. Each of us spent the last few minutes before departing for a ceremony using Scotch brand tape to remove every speck of lint from our uniforms. This ritual of personal inspection became routine for us and ensured we were both properly turned out. We left nothing to doubt.

During my first month at the barracks, I received a call from Col. Fegan telling me I was to report the next day to a room in the Pentagon to perform some of the "extra" work he had mentioned on my first day of duty. He did not tell me anything about the work, only that it involved my recent experience in South Vietnam and that I did not need to do anything to prepare myself for it. He told me parking was difficult at the Pentagon, so he graciously volunteered the use of his staff car and driver to take me there.

The next day I was driven to the Pentagon, where I soon found out I was to help with "Project Agile," a Department of Defense study on the use of new technologies to detect and deter enemy infiltration into South Vietnam. At this meeting, I began to learn about the strategic thinking of the military and civilian leaders working on the war. As part of the meeting, I received some background on why my input was needed. The analysts working on the study wanted to have the opinion of officers familiar with the enemy's infiltration methods so they could use technology to impede the movement of North Vietnamese troops and supplies down the Ho Chi Minh Trail. It was very obvious that the civilians at the meeting were keen to get me to endorse their ideas because they went out of their way to be solicitous to me, a mere lieutenant, and to ask leading questions. Their briefing covered how they intended to use "The McNamara Line" to form a barrier running from the South China Sea near Dong Ha in South Vietnam to the Mekong River near Savannakhet in Laos. They explained that the 1962 Geneva Accords on Laos prohibited the U.S. from employing U.S. troops in Laos, and they hoped to get around this problem by using a host of technological innovations to compensate for the absence of U.S. ground troops in Laos. They spent most of their time asking me whether or not I thought these various devices could be covertly placed by indigenous reconnaissance teams working inside Laos and how best this could be accomplished.

After they had briefed me on several of these detection devices and their means of delivery, one of the Army staff officers opined that the entire idea of a barrier to infiltration was fraught with problems, and he did not think a system could be developed that would stem the movement of NVA troops and supplies down the Ho Chi Minh Trail. I could tell the technical people from Battelle and the civilian Pentagon bureaucrats at the meeting did not welcome this officer's comments. One of the people from Battelle responded by saying, "Then I guess the war is lost, because unless you do something about the Ho Chi Minh Trail, you will never defeat these people." The Army officer, who represented the Joint Chiefs of Staff at this meeting, countered by saying, "We could build a barrier from the South China Sea to India, but those little bastards would find a way to get around it. Unless you put American forces on the ground in Laos to over watch your electronic systems and have plenty of firepower to back them up, it is futile to believe this will work. We all know the only way to stop them from coming south is to occupy Laos, but we also know State won't stand for that."

An Air Force officer began to argue with the Army officer about the feasibility of the electronic barrier, but after a few minutes of hot discussion, all talk ceased when the senior person at the meeting, a political appointee, told everyone to calm down and to stick to the agenda for the meeting, which he said was to get recent field input from Marine and Army reconnaissance operators to ascertain whether or not they thought the equipment described by Battelle would work.

He asked my opinion on two pieces of experimental equipment, and my response was I thought these two seismic detection devices would only be useful if they worked continuously in all types of weather, were constantly monitored, and there was some way to attack the targets they identified quickly. Another recent returnee from the Vietnam War, a U.S. Army Special Forces captain, said essentially the same thing. He added that to be effective, one would first have to know which trails the NVA troops were using, which was not an easy task since these trails often changed or were constantly expanding into new areas. I came away from this meeting thinking some very smart people were devoting a lot of time and money to the Ho Chi Minh Trail, but not everyone was in favor of the solutions put forth and not everyone was confident that there was a solution to the NVA use of the Ho Chi Minh Trail, given the proscription on the use of U.S. ground forces in Laos.

My first month at "8th and Eye" passed quickly and, largely, uneventfully. In addition to working on my drill and other duties, I spent my weekends with "Jane" and attended several social functions she had at her sorority house at George Washington University. We both felt very strongly about each other, and we enjoyed getting to know each other again after the year of separation. Many of "Jane"'s friends in her sorority had wedding plans for June, a fact that became very apparent to me as I listened to them eagerly discuss their impending marriages at the conclusion of their university studies.

"Jane" and I began to discuss our relationship and where it might lead, but our long separation had prevented us from really developing that relationship in a normal way. We had known each other for less than five months before I went to Vietnam and just about everything we knew about each other was drawn from the weekly letters we wrote to each other. We had a lot in common and were very much attracted to each other, but we both needed time to find each other again and have our love mature and grow before we made a permanent commitment to each other. Unfortunately, several events in April damaged our relationship beyond repair and altered my life in ways that would affect me for years to come.

The first of these events took place on April 4th when news reached the barracks that Martin Luther King, Jr., had been shot and killed at the Lorraine Motel in Memphis, Tennessee. We were all shocked by this news, but our shock soon changed to revulsion as we began to see a general breakdown of law and order in the capital when many citizens in the African American community began to riot. As the rioting spread, the police force was either unable or unwilling to contain the lawless behavior of the rioters. President Johnson saw that the police were not able to contain the rioting, so he called out federal troops to restore order and protect the government workers and facilities. The Marine Corps Guard Company's riot company, a 250-man-strong unit, was called out to clear Pennsylvania Avenue of rioters and protect the Capitol Building. The Army's 3rd Infantry Regiment, a ceremonial unit like the Marine Corps' Guard Company, was also called out to restore order and to protect the White House. These two federal forces were the first of over 13,000 federal troops called out to quell the riots.

Since I was new to Guard Company and had not drilled with my platoon when they practiced the various riot control formations, I was not called out the first night of the riots. Another officer from the barracks took my place. However, I was told to go along with the company to observe how they operated, so I would be able to take over from this officer when my platoon took up a static defense of the Capitol Building. What I observed that first night of rioting literally sickened me. It seemed the only people doing their duty that night were the Marines and soldiers; the police simply stood around and did nothing to stop the looting and burning going on in front of them. When our officers asked them to help by arresting the numerous people running down Pennsylvania Avenue with looted television sets, clothing, and other items stolen from the stores on that street, the police on Pennsylvania Avenue said they had orders from their police chief and Mayor Walter Washington not to arrest the rioters unless someone's life was threatened. I could not believe my ears. The police also warned us that we were not to make any arrests because martial law had not been declared, and they still had jurisdiction over Washington, D.C. They invoked the Posse Comitatus Law, a vestige of the Civil War that forbids the use of federal troops to enforce laws.

Several store owners, most of whom were African American, came up to the Marines during the night and begged them to clear the street and protect their businesses which were being systematically looted by hundreds of gleeful, rampaging rioters. Despite the warnings by the police not to intervene, the officers of the Riot Company requested permission from their military chain of command to respond, and soon the entire company of Marines was on line and moving down Pennsylvania Avenue with their bayonets fixed and held at high port. Several rioters made the unwise decision to disregard the Marine officers' orders to drop the items they had stolen, and these looters were quickly brought to the ground by four-man flying squads and turned over to the police for processing. Those who resisted were introduced to the business end of the heavy, wooden stocks of the M-1 rifles carried by the Riot Company. The gleeful, boisterous attitude of the mob quickly changed to fear as they ran away from the Marines as fast as they could, dropping their ill-gotten goods in the street and adjacent alleys as they fled. Over one hundred looters were captured and turned over to the police that night. Later, owners of several local stores came up to the Marines and thanked them for protecting their property and requested that the Marines post a guard on their stores because they did not trust the police to prevent further looting.

Early in the morning of 5 April, I returned to the barracks to catch a few hours of sleep and some breakfast before I relieved the lieutenant who had commanded my platoon the first night of its deployment against the rioters. When I talked to the officers at the barracks that morning, I found that all of them were shocked and saddened by the deplorable breakdown of law and order and the absence of any civilian control of the situation. They were particularly scornful of the police and the mayor for their lack of courage and indecisive behavior. I also learned that the dry cleaning shop across the street from the barracks, where all of our uniforms were taken for alterations and cleaning, had been looted and burned the first night of the riots, as were most of the other stores in the neighborhood. The sentry on the main gate had seen the rioters break into the dry cleaning shop, but he did not receive permission from the police to respond, so all he could do was watch as the store was looted and burned. Several thousand dollars of Marine dress uniforms were destroyed.

Because the Marines had inflicted some serious injuries to resisting rioters, the mayor's political friends began complaining to the press that the Marines had overstepped their authority. He demanded that the Marines restrict their presence to the Capitol Building. As a result, the Riot Company was pulled off Pennsylvania Avenue and moved to the Capitol Building where we set up an interior guard consisting of an inner and outer ring of security posts manned 24 hours a day. We also began to conduct squad-sized foot patrols in the streets leading up to the Capitol Building as a sort of "show of force."

My platoon was given responsibility for several posts on the western and northern sides of the Capitol Building. When my Marines were not on duty at one of the posts, they rested in one of the corridors in the lower floors of the building in the vicinity of several offices belonging to Senate staffers. This led to a rather unpleasant confrontation between me and a staffer from Senator Edward Kennedy's office. As I was standing on the veranda of the Capitol Building looking out in the direction of East Capital Street, I was approached by a rather officious young man who demanded to know who was in charge of the "soldiers" sleeping in the corridor near his office. He said the Marines sleeping there were "dirty and smelly" and they were "in the way" of his colleagues who had "important work to do." I told him the men were not soldiers, but U.S. Marines, and the reason they were in the corridor was because the capital police had told us to put them there. I also told him that they had spent the past 48 hours defending him and his colleagues from people who wanted to tear the Capitol Building apart and that this little detail might explain why they had not had the time to shower.

He did not like my answer and began to tell me that the presence of the Marines made his female colleagues "feel uncomfortable," and he wanted the Marines "removed immediately." I was trying to suppress a strong desire to rip the man's face off when the commander of the Marine security force, a colonel from the Marine base at Quantico, came over and told the staffer that busses from the barracks would soon be taking the Marines back to their quarters for a shower and a clean change of uniform. He pleaded with the staffer to have patience until then. He also promised the officious young man that he would locate another place for the Marines guarding the building to sleep. This did not seem to impress the staffer who continued to complain about having Marines in combat gear carrying weapons near his office. Before he left, he hurled what I am sure he thought was the ultimate warning to the colonel when he said, "Senator Kennedy will hear about this, and I don't think he will like it." My opinion of the colonel was elevated considerably when I saw him bristle at this last comment and he retorted, "Son, you do that. You tell Senator Kennedy that you are unhappy with the troops protecting him and his staff. I will be glad to talk to the good Senator whenever he would like to see me about this matter."

The colonel spoke with me after the staffer had left, and he told me not to judge everyone working in the building by the words of this one Senate staffer. I did not. I noticed, however, that during the entire time my platoon guarded the Capitol Building, not a single congressman or staffer thanked us for protecting them. In fact, they seemed to go out of their way to ignore us. The only interest shown to us was that of several journalists who sought out our African American Marines to ask them questions about how they felt about the assassination of Martin Luther King, Jr.

On April 9th, my platoon was relieved of its duties at the Capitol Building, and we returned to the barracks. The streets outside the barracks looked like a war zone with burned out shops and stores lining the street and debris everywhere. Police patrolled the streets with shotguns pointing out of the windows of their squad cars. I heard several stories from Marines at the barracks about the vandalism and general lawlessness that had transpired nearby, including one incident where an African American Marine from Quantico who had been assigned to guard a looted store across the street from the barracks was taunted by some teenagers to the point where he hit one of them with the butt of his M-14 rifle, seriously injuring the teenager. I was told this Marine had been taunted continuously for nearly an hour by the teenagers, who were showing off in front of some girls nearby. The Marine took the taunting, including some particularly vicious racial taunts, until one teenager made the mistake of touching the Marine on the chest, daring him to respond. This constituted assault, and thus the Marine was justified in responding as he did. He knocked the teenager unconscious with one blow, and the boy went to the hospital where he was treated for significant facial injuries.

In another incident, a woman was raped in an alley across the street from the barracks. Only half-dressed and bleeding, she came to the main gate asking the Marine sentry for assistance. The sentry called the police, and she went to a local hospital for treatment of her injuries. These tales, and the extensive damage I witnessed to the community surrounding the barracks, sickened me. I could not believe that such things could happen in my country, let alone my nation's capital.

I blamed the mayor, Walter Washington, and his cowardly police chief, Jerry Wilson, for the 12 people killed, the 900 stores looted, and the widespread devastation visited upon the city, much of which took decades to heal. Their lack of decisive action when the first rioting broke out along the 14th Street corridor on April 4th led to the rapid spread of lawlessness and violence. Their bad decisions forced the president to call out 13,600 federal troops and to place these troops in a situation that forced them to make arrests and protect the lives and property of law-abiding citizens, something they were not trained to do or expected to do when they joined the U.S. Marines.

True to form, the press, who were noticeably absent on the streets of Washington, D.C., while I was there, quickly took up the cause of the mayor and portrayed him as a hero who tried not to overreact and make matters worse. They shamelessly protected both the mayor and his police department. In the days following the riots, my fellow Marine officers and I were unanimous in our condemnation of the actions of the mayor and astounded by the way the press described the riots. My faith in the federal government and in the press was seriously eroded by what I saw and experienced during these riots.

Shortly after the riots, I decided to visit the grave of Lt. Tom Dowd, my good friend who was killed in South Vietnam. My platoon provided a burial detail at least once a week at Arlington National Cemetery, so after one of these burial details, I took the opportunity to visit Tom's grave and pay my respects. While I looked down on his grave and read his tombstone, I felt a deep sense of guilt. I felt guilty that I had survived the war and Tom had not.

I had spoken to Tom many times before we shipped out for Vietnam, and I knew he never intended to make the Marine Corps a career. He had decided that he would put his personal plans on hold and serve his country. That was his sole motivation for joining the Marine Corps. He had heard the words of President John F. Kennedy, "Ask not what your country can do for you, but what you can do for your country," and he had responded. In the purest sense, he was a patriot. His life's ambition was to teach at the university level and, perhaps, coach soccer. He also wanted to raise a large family. Now, he was dead and those dreams died with him. I felt that a fairer outcome would have been for me to die, not Tom. Had Tom lived, I am sure he would have achieved great things in his life. He had all the attributes needed to reach the pinnacle of success in any field of endeavor he chose. Unlike Tom, I did not aspire to any civilian calling, and I was largely ambivalent about marriage and family. For me, the Marine Corps was the sole focus of my existence, and any satisfaction I derived from my life would come from serving my country as a Marine. I wished for nothing else.

I felt that very little would be lost if I died. When Tom Dowd died the world lost a man who had great promise, a man who was destined for great things. All I could do was stand in front of Tom's grave and promise him that I would not abandon the cause he died for. He believed the Vietnam War as a crusade, an opportunity to give the people of South Vietnam a government based upon democratic principles and an economy based upon the free market. He believed it was immoral to abandon them to the totalitarianism of a communist state and the misery of a collective, command economy. As I walked away from his grave, I thought of Tom's favorite song, "The Impossible Dream," and how apt that song was, given Tom's short life and how he had "charged into hell for a heavenly cause." I would visit Tom's grave several more times in the coming years, and I would always think of him whenever I heard his favorite song, "The Impossible Dream."

Sometime in April, I received a letter from Maj. Dan Keating, my former CO of the 1st Force Reconnaissance Company. It had taken two weeks to reach me. In the letter, he informed me that my platoon had been nearly wiped out during the Battle for Hue and was now listed as "combat ineffective" due to casualties. He did not tell me how many had been killed and wounded, but he told me the platoon had been part of a hastily formed reaction force that was used more like a standard infantry platoon. They had been hit either on the bridge leading to the Hue Citadel or immediately on the north side of the Perfume River. The lieutenant who had taken over my platoon was one of the wounded.

My heart stopped when I read his short letter with its chilling story of my platoon's demise. I felt both sorrow and rage. Here I was, sitting in my comfortable room at Center House, waiting to eat a steak dinner with wine prepared and served by orderlies, safe and secure, living in luxury while my men were being killed and wounded in Hue. I felt remorse at their loss and guilt that I had left them. I felt that had I been there, this terrible thing would not have happened; I would have found a way to save them. Nothing terrible like this had ever happened while I commanded my platoon, but now they had suffered because I had gone home and left them. It is impossible to know if I could have avoided the disaster that my platoon suffered, but I had taken my platoon into some very dangerous situations before and always found a way to overcome the obstacles we faced. My platoon was not trained or experienced in urban combat, so they were at a distinct disadvantage when they were employed in an infantry role in Hue against heavily armed NVA troops. At the very least, I know I would have questioned the rationale behind using a lightly armed recon platoon of only fifteen men in an urban combat scenario.

As I was reading Maj. Keating's letter, Lt. "Ike" Izenour came into my room to tell me it was time for dinner. He saw that I was upset, so he asked me what was wrong. I looked up at him, and suddenly I began to weep. I blurted out, "My platoon is dead, wiped out, because I left them." Ike, always a jovial and upbeat man, looked really concerned and just stood there in the doorway with an odd expression of concern on his face. I showed him Maj. Keating's letter and then he simply said he was sorry about the bad news, but I should not feel guilty over it. He tried to console me, but his efforts were to no avail. He went down to dinner, but I remained in my room. I did not want my fellow officers to see me in such an emotional state. I reflected on the news of my platoon's destruction and, no matter how hard I tried to rationalize the information contained in Maj. Keating's letter, I still came to the conclusion that this terrible event would never have happened if I had remained in South Vietnam with them. That night I decided that I would ask to be reassigned to South Vietnam immediately.

The next morning, I told my CO at Guard Company, Capt. Beck, that I wanted to go back to the war, and he needed to find a replacement for me. Not surprisingly, he was shocked by my decision, and he asked me why I wanted to go back when I had just recently returned to the U.S. He asked me if I was unhappy with my job as a ceremonial guard officer, or if I had some personal problem that motivated me to take such a drastic step. I told him several things had made me reach my decision. First, I told him I was sickened by what I saw during the riots in Washington, D.C., and this was undermining my faith in the U.S. government and the society I was sworn to protect. I then told him about the recent destruction of my recon platoon in South Vietnam and how I felt guilty that I had not been there to prevent their tragic fate. These two things taken together, along with the irony of my living a life of luxury and relative ease while my comrades in South Vietnam were suffering, made it impossible for me to continue to live in the U.S. while there was a war going on. Capt. Beck, who was married to one of President Johnson's personal secretaries, had already decided to leave the Marine Corps to pursue a law degree in Texas. He found it very difficult to understand my decision. He tried to talk me out of it, but I remained adamant. He then said I should wait a day or two before calling my assignment monitor in the Personnel Department of Headquarters Marine Corps so I could weigh all of my options. I told him I would wait a day, but I didn't think it would make any difference. I thanked him for his advice and left his office.

An hour later, Col. Fegan's secretary called me and asked me to come up to his office at the barracks that afternoon. Shortly after noon, I was standing in front of Col. Fegan's desk. He asked me to sit down, and then he stood up from his desk and walked to his window that overlooked the parade field. He was silent for a moment, and then he said, "What's this I hear about you wanting to waive your overseas control date and go back to Vietnam?"

I told him the same thing I had just told Capt. Beck, and he listened intently, never taking his eyes off me. After I had finished speaking, he was silent for a moment, pausing several times to look out his window, as if weighing what he would say to me. I think he sensed that I was very serious and he needed to choose his words with care. As far as I was concerned, no words of any kind would deter me from returning to Vietnam.

He began by telling me he shared my disgust with the riots and that he understood how bad it felt to know one's comrades had been killed and wounded. He told me about his own experiences as a young lieutenant during the Battle for Iwo Jima and how he was so upset with the chaos and incompetence he saw there that he thought seriously about submitting his resignation from the Marine Corps. I could tell he was trying to find some way to dissuade me, some line of argument that would cause me to change my mind.

He then surprised me by asking me if I intended to make the Marine Corps a career or not. I told him I had never wanted to do anything else but serve in the Marine Corps. I had no aspirations to do anything else with my life. When I told him this, he changed his demeanor, relaxing a bit and leaning back in his chair. He then told me that the normal tour of duty at the barracks was three years and, if he wanted to, he could prevent my transfer until then. However, he said he had no intention of doing that. Instead, he asked me to stay at the barracks until the parade season was over in October. If I would agree to stay until then, he would approve my request to leave the barracks and return to Vietnam. I agreed to Col. Fegan's terms because I really had no other alternative. I also knew that it would be difficult to replace me on short notice during the parade season. I had faith in Col. Fegan, and I knew he was a man of his word, so I decided to take his advice and remain at the barracks until the parade season ended before going back to Vietnam.

When I informed "Jane" of my decision to return to Vietnam, it ended our relationship. She was the daughter of a naval officer and understood my commitment to the Marine Corps, but she said she was not prepared to go through another year of separation so soon. She doubted my sincerity, telling me that it was unfair to her to make her wait another year or more before making a decision on marriage, and she had no intention of doing so. She thought my decision meant I lacked any true feeling for her, and I was using the decision to return to Vietnam as a means of putting off a decision on marriage. I tried to explain to her how strongly I felt about the need to return to the fight, but I knew she did not believe me. I realized I was being unfair to her, but I knew I would never forgive myself if I did not return to Vietnam while the war raged on. I told her it was impossible for me to get on with my life while the war was unresolved. The war had become my mission in life, and I did not want to abandon it until I was sure the U.S. had achieved victory. We both agreed that, given my convictions, it was best to end our relationship and allow "Jane" to find someone else who could give her the life she deserved. She married someone else six months later.

When I called my monitor in the Personnel Department to tell him that I wanted to waive my overseas control date and schedule my departure for South Vietnam as soon as the parade season ended, he was at first incredulous. I had only been back in the U.S. for less than three months, and I was not scheduled to go overseas again for three years. I convinced him of my sincerity, and he said he would send the paperwork over to me to sign in a day or two. I later found out that he called Col. Fegan to confirm the feasibility of allowing an officer to leave "8th and Eye" after less than a year on station. Col. Fegan told the monitor that he thought I would change my mind, but he would not stand in my way to leave if that was what I wanted to do.

Since I had seen how happy my parents were now that I was safely back in the U.S., I did not immediately tell them of my intention to return to South Vietnam. I told them that "Jane" and I had decided to break up, but I did not tell them the real reason for this development. They had driven down to see me and attend an award ceremony at the barracks where I received a Navy Commendation Medal. They seemed to be happy for me during the ceremony on the parade ground and the reception following it in Center House. I could tell they basked in the glow of the entire event. I did not share in their enthusiasm and felt very awkward having the entire Guard Company fall out on the parade ground, along with the drum and bugle corps, for an award ceremony in my honor.

I declined another award ceremony later on when my "end of tour" Bronze Star medal arrived at the barracks. This did not go down well with Col. Fegan, who felt it was necessary for the Marines at the barracks, many of whom would be going to South Vietnam after their tour of duty at the barracks ended, to listen to an award citation given for heroism in combat. I told Col. Fegan why I did not want even to accept the award, and the forcefulness of my explanation had its effect on him. He reluctantly allowed me to receive the award in a private ceremony in his office with only Capt. Beck and one other officer in attendance. I think he was surprised by my contempt for "end of tour" awards and the entire Marine Corps awards system. I suppose my vehemence had an effect on him because he told me he intended to take the matter up with the 1st Marine Division CG, Gen. Robertson, a personal friend of his. That award was the last personal award I allowed the Marine Corps to present to me. I even turned down a retirement award when I left the Corps 23 years later.

When I first arrived at the barracks, I discovered that I was replacing Capt. Charles "Chuck" Robb, who had recently married President Johnson's daughter, Linda. Capt. Robb was also a ceremonial guard officer, and one of his additional duties at the barracks had been that of a White House social aide, a job that meant he often assisted with social and ceremonial events at the White House. Through this position he met Linda Johnson, dated her, and eventually married her. I found out that there were only four Marine officers assigned the additional duty of White House Social Aide, all of whom came from the Marine Barracks at "8th and Eye."

One night, shortly after the riots, Capt. Cooney, a fellow bachelor officer who lived in Center House with me, came into my room and asked me if I was interested in taking on the additional duty of White House social aide. He explained that both he and Capt. Robb were vacating their positions, and he offered to recommend me for one of the opening slots. After a brief description of the duties entailed and his assurance that he thought I could handle the job, he informed me that I would only get the job after I had successfully passed a screening interview with the White House social secretary, Mrs. Bess Abell. Naturally, I was flattered that I would be considered for such a prestigious job, so I readily accepted his offer to take on this extra duty.

Capt. Cooney and I later went over what I needed to do during the interview to ensure that Bess Abell would be favorably impressed. He said she would light up a cigarette during the interview, and if I pulled out a lighter and lit her cigarette, I was a shoo-in for the job. If I did not, or made some other social faux pas, then I would not be accepted. It all depended on impressing Mrs. Abell with my social skills and manners. He followed up his advice with a strong injunction never to speak about what I saw or heard while working in the White House since discretion was essential in this job. If I talked to the press or anyone else about what was going on in the White House, it would result in a lot of embarrassment to the Marine Corps and my immediate dismissal from the White House Social Aide detail.

A week later, I traveled to the Social Office of the White House. I was dressed in my best Summer Service A uniform. I tucked a brand new cigarette lighter in my sock so nothing would crease my uniform or appear as a bulge in my pocket. When I entered Mrs. Abell's office, I was struck by her elegance and beauty. However, this initial impression lasted only a minute or two. Mrs. Abell was a force to be reckoned with. She did not get her job because of her beauty and charm, and this was clearly evident after speaking to her for only a minute or two. Her explanation of how important social contacts were to the president and the role protocol played in his ability to grease the machinery of politics in Washington demonstrated to me that she was an extremely intelligent and capable woman. Everything about her exuded intelligence, education, style and breeding.

She asked me to take a chair in front of her desk, and I waited for her to seat herself before sitting down myself. She then began to ask me questions about my background, education, and family. It was obvious that she was gauging my experience with social situations similar to those I might encounter in the White House. She asked me what I thought was the most important thing I had done in my life. I answered immediately and without reservation: leading Marines in combat in South Vietnam. She asked me if I supported the war, and I told her I did. I added that I thought the policies of President Johnson were correct, and that I was disappointed the president had decided not to run for reelection. She seemed satisfied with that answer, and then she reached across her desk to a wooden box and retrieved a cigarette from it. I immediately rose from my seat and moved quickly to light her cigarette for her. She asked me if I smoked, and I said I did not. She then asked me why I was carrying a cigarette lighter and I told her, "Because I may encounter a lady who might have need of one." After taking a long draw on her cigarette, she rose and told me that she thought I would make a good social aide, and she would soon arrange for the president's military aide to send orders to the barracks asking that I be assigned to her office.

Throughout the summer months of the parade season, I carried out my duties as a Guard Company officer, but I was often called upon to work at the White House, usually during the evening hours, but on occasion during the day. During parade season, I participated each Friday in the Sunset Parade at the barracks and each Tuesday evening at the Marine Corps Memorial outside the Arlington National Cemetery. I also participated in the other ceremonies and events commonly performed by Guard Company, such as funerals and wreath-laying ceremonies at Arlington National Cemetery and arrival ceremonies at the White House and the Pentagon. In between, I often went to the White

House in my capacity as a White House social aide to help with ceremonies there, usually State dinners for visiting heads of state or legislation-signing ceremonies where the president would sign important legislation into law before national television cameras in the company of the congressmen who were responsible for the legislation.

My time as a White House social aide was short, less than seven months, but I had several interesting experiences during this time. On 11 September 1968, I was assigned by the White House Protocol Office to assist at a State Dinner in the White House in honor of the prime minister of the Barbados and his wife, who were visiting the country. It was an elegant and very formal affair that required careful timing and perfect execution. The social aides were responsible for ensuring the entire event went flawlessly, from greeting the guests and organizing the receiving line to shepherding the guests into the dining room and being available to dance with the female guests if the president decided that dancing following the dinner was appropriate. As the guests for the dinner began to arrive, the social aides escorted them into the White House and began to mingle with them, making small talk and ensuring they were given drinks. These guests represented a literal "Who's Who" of Washington's political and social elite, as well as influential people from around the country. It was pretty heady stuff for a 24-year-old lieutenant, and I must admit I felt very privileged to talk to congressmen, journalists, entertainers, and leaders of American industry. At this particular State dinner, I had the opportunity to escort Senator and Mrs. John J. Sparkman of Alabama, Senator and Mrs. Mike Mansfield of Montana, and the famous Broadway singer, Mr. Gordon MacRae and his wife. I also spoke briefly with the actress Merle Oberon and was struck by how beautiful she was and how young she looked even in her sixties. However, as I went about my duties I began to feel that I was looked upon by the guests as someone filling the role of footman on some aristocratic estate. Some of them would even ask me to obtain items like ashtrays or pens for them, treating me more like some ornately dressed servant than a military officer.

As I was going about my job of making these guests feel welcome and at ease, Mrs. Abell came up to me and Lt. Ike Isenour with a rather worried look on her face. She said, "Thank God you are here. I have a mission that only the Marines can handle." She then went on to explain that a married couple had arrived at the White House drunk, and they had loudly insulted Senator Symington and others. She told us we had to make sure this man and woman, two major contributors to the Democratic Party from New York City, were not seated at dinner, but were diverted somehow when the other guests moved into the East Room. She pointed out the couple and told us to figure out some way to prevent these people from doing any more harm. Ike and I had not anticipated such a problem, and for a moment we simply looked at each other as if to ask, "Well, what do we do now?" After a moment of reflection, we decided we would tell this couple they would be eating dinner with the social aides in the White House's Navy Mess, instead of the East Room. In order to carry out this plan, we enlisted the aid of the senior Mess attendant and two members of the Secret Service detail. I asked the wife, who was less inebriated than her husband, if she knew where they had parked their car, and she told me she did not. I asked for a description of their car and the license number, and requested she give me the keys to the car, which she obtained from her husband, who appeared completely oblivious to why she was rummaging through his trouser pockets. I informed the Secret Service detail they needed to bring the couple's car around to the West Wing entrance as soon as they located it. I gave them the car keys and hoped they would find it quickly. I made small talk with the couple while Ike saw to it that name cards for the couple were placed at the table in the White House Navy Mess and two extra meals were laid out for them. Since the social aides always ate their meals in the Navy Mess during a State dinner, I knew the meal we ate would be identical to the one served to the guests in the East Room, minus the wine. We were confident the inebriated couple would not be disappointed with the fare provided. I escorted them downstairs to the Navy Mess and sat them at one of the tables and had the Filipino mess men serve them their meal. While they were eating, the husband kept asking where the president was, while his wife tried to keep him from noticing that they were definitely not in the East Room. She saw what we were doing and wanted to avoid any more embarrassment, so she went along with our game and actually kept her husband from running upstairs to look for the president. After ten minutes of awkwardness, the Secret Service returned and informed me that they had the car waiting by the West Wing, and one of their agents would drive the couple to their hotel. A few minutes later, we had the couple in their car and on their way. Later that evening, Mrs. Abell came up to me and Ike and thanked us, adding, "I knew I could count on the Marines." Mrs. Abell was always gracious and kind, but she was sparse with her praise. Ike and I felt we had done a good job that night and prevented a situation that had the potential for real embarrassment to the president.

On two occasions at the White House, I got into trouble. The first occurred during the State dinner described above. As the guests assembled for cocktails prior to the dinner, I saw a journalist from the *Cleveland Plain Dealer* newspaper dropping cigar ashes on the new and very expensive rug in the Green Room. I found an ash tray and came over and presented it to him saying, "Sir, I think you may have need for this." He was embarrassed, and I found out later he complained to Mrs. Abell about my "rude comment in front of the other guests." In this instance, Mrs. Abell saw fit to forgive me, probably because she indicated the man in question was not to her liking and should not have been dropping ashes on the rug. Still, she scolded me and told me to never embarrass a guest again. The fact that Ike and I had helped with the drunken guests from New York City that night may also have had a softening effect on Mrs. Abell's chastisement.

My second, more serious, blunder occurred during a bill-signing ceremony in the East Room of the White House. President Johnson was signing an environmental bill, and my job during the signing ceremony was to make sure no one to the president's right was in the wrong position. Another aide was positioned on his left. In front of the president's desk was a bank of microphones, several still photographers, and three television cameras. Mrs. Abell had instructed us prior to the ceremony that under no circumstances should we allow anyone to come between the president and the cameras during the signing. Since the president used nearly fifty pens to sign the bill, the actual signing of it took nearly five minutes to complete. He would sign only a small portion of his signature and then turn to present one of the pens to each congressman who had had some role to play in the bill's passage.

I thought this would be an easy task, and for a moment I forgot what my role was at such a function. I became distracted by the cameras and the act of the president signing the bill, and I neglected to observe Senator Stuart Udall moving in front of the president's desk to receive his pen. In so doing, Senator Udall came between the president and the television cameras, exactly what Mrs. Abell had warned us about no more than 30 minutes before. It happened very quickly, making it impossible for me to do anything about it once the Senator moved. As he took the pen, I immediately came to his side and guided him back to his position and made sure that no one else followed his lead when retrieving their pen.

When the ceremony concluded, a civilian staffer came up to me and told me to report to Mrs. Abell's office immediately. My heart sank because I knew I had made a serious mistake, and one that she had explicitly told me not to make in her briefing to the social aides prior to the signing ceremony. As expected, once I was in her office standing at attention in front of her desk, she commenced to berate me for my lack of attention to duty during the signing ceremony. Ever the elegant and correct lady, she did not resort to expletives or raise her voice, but she let me know in no uncertain terms that she was very disappointed in me and she expected much better from a Marine officer. She then said that under normal circumstances my assignment at the White House would be terminated, but she wanted to speak to Capt. Tom Campbell, the senior Marine social aide, before making a decision on whether or not to fire me.

I was dejected and embarrassed when I left the White House and drove back to the barracks. When I got there, Tom Campbell was waiting for me, and I fully expected he would tell me that I was no longer a White House social aide. He started out by giving me the normal kind of "ass-chewing" a Marine officer could expect from his senior on such an occasion. After a minute or two of strong language and expressions of intense disappointment in me, he told me that he had talked Mrs. Abell out of firing me and that I would continue as an aide at the White House. He cautioned me that normally there were no second chances for mistakes. I must never allow my attention to wander again, or I would surely be fired and probably receive a letter of reprimand in the bargain.

I owed my salvation to Tom Campbell, and I was grateful. I also knew I was obligated to him for going out on a limb on my behalf. He had spared me from the humiliation and the consequences of reporting to Col. Fegan and telling him I had been fired from my social aide job. That evening at dinner, Tom acted as if nothing had happened. He did not tell anyone else at the barracks about my less-than-stellar performance at the White House that day. Tom Campbell was a class act in every respect and throughout my career I admired this man for his professionalism, courage, and intelligence. To this day, I do not know why he came to my rescue. I certainly did not deserve it. Nonetheless, I am grateful and will always be grateful to Tom for his act of kindness to me.

While my time at the barracks entailed less than nine months and my service at the White House less than seven, both jobs afforded me some unique insights into the last year of the Johnson presidency. One example of this occurred at Camp David, the presidential retreat.

The Marine Corps, along with the Secret Service, was responsible for presidential security at Camp David. Camp David is a highly secure Navy facility that has been used as a presidential retreat since 1939. It is located 60 miles NNW of Washington, D.C., in the Catoctin Mountains near the town of Thurmont, Maryland. In 1968 one platoon from Guard Company provided the exterior guard force for Camp David, which meant that for two weeks out of every six, my platoon would travel to Camp David for this duty. We would be responsible for guarding the main gate and the perimeter fence, conducting security checks along the perimeter road every two hours, and maintaining a quick reaction force to reinforce the Secret Service.

While at Camp David, I routinely conducted a "no notice" drill each day for the reaction force. This normally involved having the reaction force move by foot from their quarters to several locations near the president's lodge, code-named "Aspen." We took this job very seriously, as did the Secret Service detail assigned to the camp. Each quick reaction response was treated exactly as if there was an actual threat to the president's security. For each drill, the Secret Service personnel on duty in a small guard shack outside of "Aspen" would call me and use a password to tell me that the president's cabin had been breached and they needed the reaction force immediately. I would call the Sergeant of the Guard and order him to respond, again using a code word, to deploy the reaction force. From the time we received the call from the Secret Service, we were required to have a dozen heavily armed Marines at their positions outside of Aspen in less than one minute.

President Johnson seldom spent time at Camp David. He preferred his ranch in Texas if he wanted to relax, but his family members and members of Congress often spent time at Camp David. I recall only one time President Johnson visited Camp David while I was on duty there, and his stay was a short one. On this one occasion, I nearly had a serious problem involving presidential shotgun ammunition. The day before President Johnson was due to take his helicopter, Marine One, from the White House south lawn to Camp David, SSgt. Johnson came into my room at Camp David and told me he had a "small problem" that needed my immediate attention. I could tell that he was worried and the problem was not "small," but serious. After I told him to stand at ease, he informed me that all of the shotgun ammunition used by the president for skeet shooting was gone. The presidential skeet-shooting range was located next to the Camp David helipad, and on the rare occasions when President Johnson visited Camp David, he would often take an hour or so to enjoy shooting skeet. I did not see this as much of a problem because I knew that the Navy, which was in charge of Camp David, had a generous budget for such items. I told SSgt. Johnson to go to the Navy Chief in charge of purchasing supplies and get a purchase order to replace the ammunition. SSgt. Johnson then went on to explain that the reason the shotgun ammunition was gone, all 500 rounds of it, was the Marines from the barracks had used it for their personal entertainment several weeks earlier and had told no one about it since it was not authorized for them to use the president's ammunition stocks.

Now the magnitude of the problem was dawning on me. The president of the U.S. was less than 24 hours away from a visit to Camp David and all of his shotgun ammunition had been used up by Marines from the barracks. I saw great embarrassment to the Marine Corps and a major dent in my next fitness report if the president decided to shoot skeet and was told he could not do so because the Marines had used all of his personal ammunition.

Like all good Marine SNCOs, SSgt. Johnson had an answer to my dilemma, but his solution was about to lighten my paycheck substantially for that month. He told me there was a general store in the town of Thurmont at the bottom of the hill leading to Camp David, and that store sold shotgun ammunition. If I hurried, I could purchase the replacement shotgun ammunition before the store closed. I looked at my watch and saw I had a little over an hour to cash a check, drive down to the general store, and buy the ammunition. I rushed out of my room, checkbook in hand, and went to the Navy paymaster, who allowed me to cash a personal check. I then got into my car and raced down the hill to the store where I found the owner in the process of closing for the day. I told him I needed his best skeet-shooting ammunition, and he produced the last of his stock, six boxes containing 25 shotgun shells each. I hurriedly paid for all six boxes and said a little prayer that the president would not want to shoot more than 150 clay pigeons.

That evening I gave the ammunition to SSgt. Johnson and he took the shells and placed them in the empty boxes with the presidential seal on them. Fortunately for me, the ammunition that I had just purchased was identical to the Winchester Arms Company ammunition used by the president. As it turned out, the president did not choose to shoot skeet during his visit, much to SSgt. Johnson's and my relief. The day after the president's departure for the White House, we placed an order with the Navy for new presidential ammunition for the skeet range; however, I never recovered the money I spent.

Because Marine officers at "Eighth and Eye," especially those assigned as White House aides, were often working with or around senior staffers at the White House, we often overheard sensitive conversations and rumors. Discretion was key. A White House social aide had to keep his mouth shut. We never signed a nondisclosure agreement, but we learned that anything we heard or saw there was not to be repeated outside the walls of 16 Pennsylvania Avenue. I took this injunction seriously and never talked to anyone about what I observed or heard while I worked in the president's residence or at Camp David. We heard many rumors about the president, but I have no personal knowledge of their veracity. What I did see of the president leads me to dismiss these rumors as nothing more than idle gossip. I will relate two things I overheard as a result of my work at the White House but only because I think they may be of some interest to a historian.

The first were the comments by several military and civilian workers at Camp David concerning President and Mrs. Kennedy. I often heard these people, many of whom had worked at Camp David on multiple assignments, talk about how friendly President John F. Kennedy was to the military personnel when he stayed at Camp David, often speaking with them in the mess hall or on his walks around the perimeter. He was, in their words, "military friendly." While they spoke highly of President Kennedy, they were very negative toward Mrs. Kennedy, whom they described as "very aloof and openly hostile toward anyone in uniform." They told me that she would refuse to eat in the mess hall if she saw anyone in uniform there, even the Marine helicopter pilots who flew Marine One for them. These Camp David workers had very warm words for President Johnson and his family, especially Lady Bird Johnson, the president's wife. From what I observed while I was in the White House, I would echo their sentiments about Mrs. Johnson.

Although I was often present in the same room in the White House with President

Johnson, I never had an opportunity to talk to him. As a White House social aide, I was instructed never to speak to the president unless he spoke to me. We were also told not to salute him or greet him since this might burden the president by forcing a response. We were told we were in the White House to help the president conduct certain protocol events, and that was all. Although I never had a conversation with President Johnson, I was often present when he was conducting official duties, and I did observe his interaction with his immediate staff. I also overheard several conversations he had with both his staff and visitors. What I noticed most about the president was the duality of his demeanor. When he was with his staff in private, he was rather stern and, at times, profane. But when he was in front of a group of people or the television cameras, he adopted a very charming, folksy demeanor, probably honed from many years of political campaigning. It was difficult for me to see which of these personalities was real and which was contrived. Perhaps both were real.

One incident that gave me a strong, positive impression about President Johnson occurred while I was helping with a State Department dinner. I was mingling with the guests in the Green Room when I noticed a young couple standing in a corner looking rather uncomfortable and shy. Since part of my duties involved making the president's guests feel welcome in the White House, I went up to them and introduced myself. They told me their names and said they were from Texas. I said, "Are you friends of the president?" and they replied that they were not friends but employees on his ranch. They were both 19 years old and were on their honeymoon in Washington, D.C. I asked them why they had chosen Washington, D.C., for their honeymoon venue, and they excitedly told me that they had not planned on a honeymoon at all. The president had said they should spend their honeymoon in the White House, and he would pay for everything they did for a week.

I was surprised by this information and impressed that the president would do such a nice thing for one of his employees. I told them not to feel nervous, but to enjoy themselves. Everyone felt a bit ill at ease at the White House, so they were not alone. They smiled, and I could tell they were worried about what to do and say at such a formal dinner. Until the dinner was served, they clung to me and only spoke to other guests when I introduced them.

The young man told me he was a cowboy, and his deep tan and rugged features clearly identified him as someone who worked hard outdoors. I could not help but notice when he shook my hand that his hands were huge, nearly twice the size of mine. His wife was a lovely young woman with a smile that set the room alight. She told me that Mrs. Johnson insisted they attend the State dinner even though neither she nor her new husband had any formal attire. President Johnson arranged for the rental of a tuxedo for the cowboy and a beautiful gown for his new bride. This thoughtful and kind gesture on the part of the president left me with a very warm impression of the human side of him and told me that, despite the many cares and concerns he had running the country, he still had time to provide a honeymoon in the White House for a cowboy who worked on his ranch.

Some of the most controversial things I heard while I was working as a White House social aide came from one of the domestic political advisors on the White House staff.

This political appointee had been working with the president for a few years, and he was intensely loyal to him. He was, as one would expect, an ardent Democrat. I first met him in early June during a coordination meeting in the White House for a State dinner in honor of the Shah of Iran. He asked me about my service in Vietnam and mentioned that he was personally unhappy that President Johnson had decided not to run for reelection. He attributed LBJ's decision not to run to the need to concentrate on the president's domestic agenda and negotiations to end the Vietnam War, although he admitted the president's poor showing against Eugene McCarthy in the New Hampshire primary was a factor.

I told him I was also disappointed that the president would not be running for reelection. We did not have a lot of time to talk on that occasion, so we agreed to meet later when we could continue our conversation. Since both of us had very busy schedules during the week, we decided the best time to talk would be on a weekend evening. He initially suggested we meet for dinner at a restaurant he liked near the White House, but I said such a venue might impede our conversation. I suggested it might be more relaxing and more conducive to privacy if we met at Center House. He agreed, and that weekend he joined me and the other bachelor officers at Center House for dinner.

After a pleasant dinner, the two of us adjourned to the small bar for an after dinner brandy and the opportunity to resume the conversation we had started in the White House. He told me again of his disappointment with the president's decision not to run for reelection. He personally thought the president's decision was a mistake. He contended that he did not think the primary reason for the president's decision was based upon the showing of Senator McCarthy in the New Hampshire primary or the president's fear of a presidential bid by Robert Kennedy, two reasons commonly alluded to by the Washington press corps at that time. Instead, he believed the president was motivated entirely by his desire to end the war in Vietnam and the president's belief that he could not negotiate effectively with the North Vietnamese and run for president at the same time. He described the president's decision as "courageous but unnecessary." He was convinced that the president could defeat any opponent in either party and still manage the war.

He lamented the advice the president was receiving on the war, especially the reports he was getting from the U.S. State Department and the CIA, which he described as "bad news on top of bad news with absolutely no ideas about how to reverse the negative trends." He also was very critical of Gen. Westmoreland and the Joint Chiefs of Staff for "constantly asking for more troops and more money, but offering little in the way of new advice on how to win the war." He referred to Robert McNamara, who had resigned the year before as "a real back-stabbing son of a bitch and an incompetent defeatist." He even went so far as to accuse McNamara of being a source of leaks to the press that made the president look weak and ineffectual.

Since he seemed to know a lot about the big picture and was privy to classified material that was not available to me, I decided to ask him about his ideas on whether or not the U.S. had a coherent strategy for winning the Vietnam War. He said military strategy was not an area he felt comfortable discussing, but he told me he had read enough classified information about the war to form the judgment that the U.S. military was not fighting the war correctly and the North Vietnamese were. I told him that my experience in South Vietnam told me the North Vietnamese were losing every battle, but I had to admit their losses on the battlefield did not seem to be having the effect we thought they would. I then told him I did not think the strategy of "graduated response" was a good one since it did not seem to have any effect on the will of the North Vietnamese to continue the war. He asked me if I thought the bombing halts initiated by President Johnson would have any effect, and I told him I honestly did not know. After all, I was just a lieutenant, and I had no idea how our bombing raids on North Vietnam were affecting the communist leadership in North Vietnam. I did say I had seen some very dramatic evidence that the enemy had taken advantage of the various bombing halts to increase their infiltration of men and supplies from North Vietnam, a fact that did not make my job any easier on the ground in South Vietnam.

He went on to say the president was getting conflicting advice on the bombing campaign as to its military and political effectiveness. He said the State Department and the CIA thought the bombing was ineffective, while the military thought it was effective, at least in terms of hurting the enemy logistically. However, the military seemed to be also saying the bombing was not effective politically because it was "not applied aggressively or broadly enough." He complained that it was impossible to obtain any definitive information on the effectiveness of the bombing, aside from the knowledge that the bombing did not seem to have much effect on the level of violence inside South Vietnam. As an aside, he mentioned that Harry C. McPherson, a good friend of the president and his special counsel, and Bill Moyers, the president's press secretary, were strongly opposed to the bombing campaign against North Vietnam and were constantly advising the president to halt the bombing.

I then asked him whose advice the president most valued on the conduct of the war, and he replied, "Averell Harriman has the most influence on the President. LBJ doesn't trust the judgment of the Kennedy team, and I cannot understand why he still keeps any of them on. They treat us like Red Headed Step Children. You would not believe how arrogant those bastards are. He doesn't think much of the professional soldiers either and for good reason. They lie to him all the time."

I wanted to draw him out on the specifics of the lies the military were telling the president, but I did not get the chance because he changed the subject and began talking about his frustration with the Kennedy administration holdovers working in the government. He used the word "traitors" several times when describing them. He also attacked the Washington press corps and accused them of working with the "Kennedy wing" of the Democratic Party to undermine President Johnson. He even went so far as to describe the press as "the running dogs of the Kennedy wing of the Democratic Party."

In retrospect, I wish I had discussed in greater detail with him why the President valued the advice of Averell Harriman on the Vietnam War. I knew very little about Averill Harriman at that time. I knew he was our chief negotiator at the Paris peace talks, but aside from that, his name simply registered as another Washington insider to my unsophisticated mind. Since my friend was so irate about the Kennedy administration holdovers, I asked him if Mr. Harriman was part of the Kennedy cabal still working as a key advisor to the president. My friend confirmed that Harriman was, indeed, part of the Kennedy team, but he was not working in the Johnson administration. I later found out that Harriman left the State Department in 1963, five years earlier, so my confusion as to why Harriman was so influential only deepened. I never did find out from my friend what it was that made Harriman so influential with President Johnson, especially if he was part of the hated Kennedy administration.

Since the riots in Washington, D.C., were fresh in my mind and a source of great anguish to me, I changed the subject and asked him his opinion on the matter. I wanted to see if he would reveal how the president felt about them. I was shocked by this White House staffer's response. With a voice tinged with passion and anger, he told me that Martin Luther King, Jr., "lied to the president and reneged on a promise to support the president in exchange for legislation that would eliminate the Jim Crow laws." He made a forceful defense of LBJ's commitment to the cause of civil rights, telling me that no one in America was a stronger or more effective advocate for the civil rights of African Americans. My friend told me that Dr. King and his supporters "turned on the president" after all the president had done for them. He went on to say that LBJ understood how slavery and racial prejudice had scarred our nation, and the president was determined to do whatever he could to correct these injustices. He reminded me that LBJ had ignored the advice of his own party's leadership and worked hard to get the Voters Rights Act of 1964 passed, an accomplishment that my friend said could not have been achieved by any other president.

Like most Americans at that time, I was shocked and saddened by the murder of Dr. King, so I felt very uncomfortable hearing this White House staffer speak so disparagingly of such a beloved civil rights leader. I tried to get him back to talking about the Vietnam War, but he was so angry my efforts led nowhere. He told me that political freedom was not enough for Dr. King; he wanted economic equality also. My friend said President Johnson also wanted to correct the economic injustices that made the poor suffer, and he had fought hard to have legislation passed that would improve the economic situation of all Americans, even if these actions posed great political risks to himself and his party. According to my friend, this wasn't good enough for Dr. King. Dr. King was impatient for change, and he wanted expensive welfare programs immediately, he did not want to hear about the cost of the Vietnam War, inflation, or anything else he considered an excuse, not a reason, for taking action. Dr. King wanted the money that was being spent on the war spent on the poor. Because LBJ was not forthcoming, Dr. King turned on the president and did everything he could to undermine the president on the war. He went to the president's political enemies and told them that he would throw his support behind them if they would cut off spending on the war and divert that money to "The War on Poverty." The president knew that Reverend King had broad support among African Americans and the rest of the country, so this turn of events was a serious threat to LBJ's hopes for reelection. According to my friend, the foundation of African American political power in the U.S. was in their churches, and the ministers in these churches could turn out their flocks in solid voting blocks. The president knew he could not win a national election without strong support from African American voters, so when Martin Luther King, Jr., turned against him, he knew his reelection chances were greatly diminished. In order to win the support of Reverend King, President Johnson would need to find some way to end the war in Vietnam as quickly as possible, so the money saved could be devoted to helping the poor with increased welfare spending and other programs.

These remarks shattered any illusions I had that President Johnson would take the actions needed to win the Vietnam War or that any Democratic candidate for the presidency in 1968 would support the war. It was apparent to me, for the first time, that the Democratic Party was intent upon finding the quickest way to end the American involvement in the war, and to do so even if it meant negotiating from a position of weakness, not strength. My friend was a fervent, partisan Democrat and a political appointee who was extremely loyal to President Johnson. Since I worked in the White House as he did, he assumed I was also a member of the Democratic Party. I do not think he would have shared his candid thoughts with me had he known I was not a member of his party. I had told him I liked President Johnson, supported his policies, and would have voted for the president had he chosen to run for reelection, all of which were true; but I never told him I was a Democrat. I think he used our conversation as a means of venting his frustrations, and I had no doubt his comments were sincere. However, I wondered then, and I continue to wonder to this day, why he chose me to talk to about such sensitive subjects. I do not know if they were accurate or whether they truly reflected President Johnson's views. All I can say is they reflected the views of a political appointee working on the personal staff of the president during the summer of 1968. (According to this White House staffer, secret negotiations with Dr. King and several of his advisors were held periodically in Texas and Georgia to discuss the coordination of White House policy with them and to gauge their support before these policies were announced. He led me to believe that he attended these negotiations and was a leading participant. President Johnson never attended these meetings, but received briefings about them from this domestic policy staffer. It was very clear to me that this individual was highly sensitive to racial issues in the country and was a strong advocate of all of President Johnson's legislation that advanced the civil rights of African Americans and other minorities. I have not revealed his name because he made me promise never to reveal his identity.)

After my dinner guest had left, I immediately went to my room and attempted to write down the essence of our conversation. I wanted to share his comments, anonymously, with my friend, Robert Asprey, whom I had been corresponding with ever since he had helped me with my senior year research paper at the Naval Academy. Mr. Asprey, who was writing his two-volume history of guerrilla warfare, *War in the Shadows,* in Oxford, England, at this time, often would solicit my input on the Vietnam War and, on occasion, send me rough drafts of his chapter on the war for me to read and comment upon. Whenever I thought I had some information he might find useful or interesting, I would write to him. Up until this time, my correspondence with him had been totally focused on guerrilla war tactics and strategy, but I thought this political information was so important I sent him an airmail letter the next day giving him the essential details of my conversation. A week later he called me from England. He told me that he thought the president had decided to not run for reelection because he wanted to devote his energies completely to finding a way out of Vietnam and that Martin Luther King, Jr., had nothing to do with the president's decision not to seek another term. He also disputed the idea that Averell Harriman was the most influential advisor to President Johnson on the war; he felt Robert McNamara, McGeorge Bundy, and Dean Rusk had been far more influential. He blamed the president and his advisors for fighting the wrong war in Vietnam: that is, using conventional forces and conventional tactics to defeat a revolutionary, guerrilla enemy. I respected Mr. Asprey and considered him one of the foremost experts on guerrilla warfare in the world, so I took his analysis of the president's motivation not to run for reelection as correct. Still, the comments of the White House staffer haunted me and convinced me that even at the highest level of our government, there was no clear understanding of how to win the war in Vietnam.

I met this White House domestic policy staffer several more times before I left for my second tour in South Vietnam, but on those occasions we seldom had time to talk about anything of substance. The last time I saw him was at a White House lawn barbecue dinner that the president put on for his staff. According to my friend, "The President had always wanted to have a real Texas-style barbecue at the White House," but had been dissuaded by his staff because of concerns about how such an event "might be viewed by the Northeast establishment and the press." His advisors feared that a Texas-style barbecue with informal dress and Southern country entertainment would be ridiculed by the press and viewed by some as a step down from the more formal affairs held at the White House, thus offending some invitees who expected formality, pomp and ceremony at such functions. I was told that Bess Abell had finally convinced the president to hold this event. Despite the success of this White House barbecue, it was a singular event, never repeated. I considered it the only event at the White House I truly enjoyed.

During this alfresco barbeque, I had a very pleasant conversation with Linda Johnson Robb as she mingled with the Marine aides, even joking about her pregnancy saying, "See what you Marines have done to me," and pointing at her burgeoning stomach. Linda always presented herself as self-assured, yet very approachable and friendly. Although I only spoke with her on a few occasions and never about anything serious, it was obvious she was extremely intelligent and confident, as well as poised and charming. She was clearly a favorite of the social aides who worked at the White House.

The comment of another White House staffer, a young woman who worked in the social secretary's office, added to my loss of faith in President Johnson's willingness to win the war in South Vietnam. One day in the fall of 1968, this young woman was put in charge of a small event at the White House honoring the Future Teachers of America. It was held in the Lincoln Library for approximately 30 high school students who had been invited to hear a short speech by Mrs. Johnson and to receive some White House mementos of the occasion. Since it was a small event, there were only two White House social aides handling the protocol for it, along with the young woman from Mrs. Abell's office. About a dozen reporters were also invited to cover the event, among them a young Connie Chung and the seasoned White House reporter Helen Thomas. The First Lady's press secretary, Liz Carpenter, was also in attendance to make sure the gaggle of press were kept on a short leash.

Once the students and Mrs. Johnson were seated in the library, I noticed there were no chairs for the press. Helen Thomas came up to me and asked me if there were any chairs for the press to sit on, so I asked the young woman in charge of the event if I should go across the hall and bring some chairs in for the women reporters to sit on. The young woman gave me an icy stare and told me to forget about getting any chairs for the press. Her words surprised me and told me a lot about the administration's relations with the

Washington press corps. She said, "Andy, those people are not our friends; they can stand until their legs give out." This young woman, who was the epitome of grace, charm and exquisite manners, surprised me with the venom in her voice. When no chairs were forthcoming for the press, Helen Thomas spoke up in a voice that everyone in the room could hear. She said, "That's all right, lieutenant, we are used to this sort of treatment around here."

After the brief ceremony concluded, I lingered for a while in the Lincoln Library and struck up a conversation with the young woman, trying to find out why she was so angry with the press covering this event. When I broached the subject, she immediately became very agitated and cut me off short. It was obvious she did not want to discuss the matter with me. Instead, she took a deep breath and said, "I just heard you are going back to Vietnam. Didn't you just return from there?"

I suppose it was the directness of her question and the lack of time I had to reply that forced me to tell her honestly why I had decided to go back to Vietnam. I blurted out that I did not feel comfortable with what I was doing in the U.S. and needed to be back where Marines belong during wartime. My answer to her question produced a quizzical look on her face, one that told me she did not understand the logic behind my answer. She asked me why I felt uncomfortable, so I told her it was a combination of things, including my work at the White House. The quizzical expression remained on her face: it was obvious she was having difficulty comprehending why I would give up the chance to work at the White House to go back to the war. I read her unspoken words immediately and started to explain to her why I felt compelled to do what I was doing. I told her that in peacetime I would enjoy all that I was doing, but in wartime it was impossible for me to enjoy things I considered so trivial in comparison. Putting on parades for the public, conducting ceremonies around Washington, D.C., escorting people at the White House and talking to political leaders and celebrities, all of this would be thrilling if there wasn't a war being fought. I told her I felt guilty about the lifestyle I was leading while other Marines were fighting and dying. This young lady, who had recently been married, listened intently to what I had told her, and then said, "I think you are making a mistake. I just can't understand why anyone would leave their family and go off to fight in a hopeless war if they did not have to. You realize, of course, that you could very easily get killed and your death would be just a terrible waste? Surely, there must be something you can do better with your life."

Her words jolted and angered me. I assumed that since she was a member of the president's staff, she supported the president's war, but her words gave away her true feelings. It was an awkward moment for me since this young woman's words hurt me deeply, and I really did not know how to reply to her. I simply said what came into my mind at that moment: "It really isn't something I choose to do; it is something I must do."

After the parade season ended, Col. Fegan made good his promise to let me return to Vietnam. I packed all of my belongings into my car, bid farewell to my fellow officers and the men in my guard platoon, and stopped off at Colonel Fegan's office to thank him for allowing me to leave his command early. As usual, he was both friendly and cordial to me when I entered his office. He gave me some advice on the importance of supervision and the need to ensure every precaution was taken to prevent needless casualties, and then he shook my hand and wished me luck. A moment later I was driving out the main gate and heading north to my hometown and my parents.

As I sat in my parents' bedroom in the gathering darkness of an autumn afternoon, I looked at my mother, desperately searching for the right words. A month earlier, I had written to my parents to inform them that I was volunteering to return to the Vietnam War. I was now home for a month's leave before departing, and I knew I owed them an explanation about why I felt compelled to return to the war. They were disappointed with my decision, a fact my father explained the previous evening. During this stressful conversation, he told me that my choice to return to the war was having a traumatic effect on my mother. While he did not argue with my decision and seemed satisfied with the rationale I provided, he reminded me that I was not the only one affected by what I was doing, a subtle way of telling me I was both selfish and unsympathetic for not considering how my family might feel about my return to the war. He even quoted from the poem, "No man is an island," to make his point. He insisted that I talk to my mother and help her understand what motivated me.

My mother sat on the edge of my parents' bed only a few feet in front of me. Seeing her sitting in the shadows and outlined against the window behind her, I thought back to the time when I went to her on a similar autumn afternoon as a crying child. I told her then that I was unable to remember how to say the Apostles' Creed, a prayer the nun in my catechism class would test me on the next day. My mother had sat on her bed, and we recited the prayer together several times until I memorized it. When she saw that I had mastered the prayer, she told me to pray to God that night so I would remember it when the nun called on me to recite it. That night, I repeated the Apostles' Creed until I drifted off to sleep, content in the knowledge that I would be able to repeat it again in my religious education class the next day. Many times after that autumn afternoon, I would turn to my mother for her assistance and guidance and remember her advice always to pray to God for His help. As I thought back to that day when I was six years old, I felt a lump in my throat. Struggling to maintain a check on my emotions, I began to explain to my mother why her son was risking his life when no one was forcing him to do it. In a slow, deliberate voice I began:

> Mom, I am not sure the words I choose to explain my decision will satisfy you or Pop. I realize I did not consult either of you when I made this decision, and that was wrong of me. I think I did that because I was afraid you might talk me out of it. I realize it doesn't make much sense to either of you that I would voluntarily give up a plum assignment in Washington, D.C., to go back to a war that everyone here seems to think is lost. All I can say is I think that is where I belong. I have wanted to be a Marine ever since I heard that Marine recruiter speak to me at school, but my decision goes far beyond my calling as a Marine. I took my reconnaissance platoon through nearly a year of danger without losing a single man and having only a few wounded. I think I am good at the job of fighting, and there are Marines who need me. I think I can keep them safe and not make the kind of mistakes that get good men killed. This is not arrogance on my part. My recon platoon was nearly wiped out soon after I left Vietnam, and I cannot help but think that had I been with them they would not have suffered the casualties they did. I know that experience in combat saves lives, and it is selfish for me to stay in a cushy job like the one I have now while Marines need experienced combat leaders. I don't think I could live with myself if I did not return to the fight. I would be ashamed.

My mother's face seemed to disappear as the room darkened, but I could feel that she was tense and was choosing her words carefully. After a moment of silence, she clasped her hands tightly together and said, "You are an adult, and you know better than anyone else what you want to do with your life. I am curious, however, as to why you cannot wait until your tour of duty in Washington, D.C., is complete before going back to the war. After all, you told your father and me that you wanted to go to graduate school if you had the time, and you certainly won't be able to do that if you go back to Vietnam. I just don't understand why you are rushing back after such a short time."

"Mom, do you remember when I was in high school and I told you and Pop that I wanted to go to the Naval Academy in order to become a Marine officer so I could serve my country? Well, it was more than that. I felt that I was not an exceptional person, but I needed to do something for the people in my hometown, to protect them, I guess. More than anything, my desire to have the people of Merchantville respect and love me motivated me to choose the path I am on. If we lose this war, I don't think I could ever face the people of this town again. America has never lost a war. If we don't do something soon, we will lose this war. I must go back and try to win the war. It sounds crazy to you, I know, but I must do this. I must do everything I can to win this war, and I can't do that living the easy life back here in the U.S."

My mother sat in silence for a moment and then she got up, came over to me, leaned over and gave me a kiss on the cheek. As she walked out of the bedroom, she said, "It is almost time for dinner, and I need to get started on it." As she left, I touched my cheek, and I felt the tear she had left there. My parents never mentioned my decision to go back to the war again.

A few weeks later, my parents took me to the Philadelphia International Airport just as they had done when I first departed for the war. No one else was with us to see me off. At the airport, I shook my father's hand and kissed my mother. They both asked me to write often and to be careful. For my sake, they tried to be cheerful, but I could see quite clearly that they were very worried about me. I walked to the boarding gate and glanced back to wave one last time before boarding the plane. I saw my father had his arm around my mother, and she was crying. I waved goodbye and boarded the plane. I did not realize it at the time, but my second tour in South Vietnam would last nineteen months and give me an entirely new understanding of the war. Although I knew the risks I would be facing and regretted the anxiety I caused my parents, I felt truly at ease with myself for the first time since I had returned from the war. I was now going back where I belonged.

Glossary

AK-47 The standard weapon carried by communist forces. This assault rifle was ideal for combat in Vietnam since it was simple to operate, was easy to maintain in the harsh tropical environment, and was capable of providing both semi-automatic and automatic fire. Most NVA troops were equipped with this reliable and effective infantry assault rifle.

AO Aerial observer. The AO was trained to control artillery and air strikes while flying as the observer in the back seat of a single engine prop-driven aircraft.

ARVN Army of the Republic of Vietnam.

CAP Combined Action Platoon. A village defense platoon made up of three squads of Popular Forces and one squad of U.S. Marines.

CAS Close Air Support.

CHICOM Chinese Communist.

CIA Central Intelligence Agency.

CIDG Civilian Irregular Defense Group. South Vietnamese military units made up of ethnic minorities, such as Montagnards and Cambodians, and initially organized by the CIA and commanded by U.S. Special Forces but later turned over to the South Vietnamese Special Forces.

CO Commanding Officer.

COC Combat Operations Center.

CORDS Civil Operations and Revolutionary Development Support. A program established in 1967 to manage all U.S pacification activities in South Vietnam.

COSVN Central Office for South Vietnam. This organization served as the headquarters of the Lao Dong Party in South Vietnam. It directed the military and political activities of communist insurgency. Until 1967 it was located inside South Vietnam but was driven into eastern Cambodia by U.S. military forces.

Deep Reconnaissance The insertion of Marine Corps reconnaissance teams outside the range of friendly artillery and deep into enemy-controlled territory. These missions were the most dangerous missions assigned to Marine Corps reconnaissance units during the Vietnam War.

DRV Democratic Republic of Vietnam, the name of the communist state of North Vietnam.

DZ   Drop Zone (for parachutists).

GVN   Government of Vietnam. The name of the South Vietnamese Government.

H&I   Harassment and Interdiction. This term applies to artillery fire that is unobserved and used to harass or disrupt the enemy.

Hamlet   The smallest administrative entity in South Vietnam, usually a small grouping of houses within the larger entity of a village. Hamlets varied in size from 100 to 1,000 people.

KIA   Killed in Action.

Lao Dong Party   The name of the communist party of Vietnam. It literally means "Workers Party." All communist forces and political organizations in South Vietnam were commanded and controlled by the Lao Dong Party, but the communists often tried to hide this reality by creating front organizations, such as the National Liberation Front, or bogus political organizations, such as the Provisional Revolutionary Government, to make it appear there were non-communists in leadership positions within the insurgency.

LP   Listening Post.

LZ   Landing Zone (for helicopters).

M-16   The assault rifle used by U.S. and South Vietnamese forces after 1967. Initially, there were many problems with this rifle due to deficiencies in design, lack of training, and faulty ammunition.

M-26   The standard U.S. anti-personnel fragmentation grenade.

M-60   The standard U.S. machine gun.

M-79   A 40-mm grenade launcher that had a maximum effective range of approximately 250 meters.

MACV   Military Assistance Command Vietnam.

MR   Military Region. There were four South Vietnamese military regions. Military Region 1 consisted of the five northern provinces in South Vietnam. Military Region 2 consisted of the next twelve provinces. Military Region 3 consisted of the ten provinces surrounding Saigon. The remaining southernmost sixteen provinces were in Military Region 4.

NFZ   No Fire Zone.

NLF   National Liberation Front.

NVA   North Vietnamese Army. Sometimes referred to as the People's Army of Vietnam, or PAVN.

OP   Observation Post. An OP can be either overt or covert.

PF   Popular Forces. Lightly armed South Vietnamese village militia organized in platoon strength.

Phoenix   The American name for the South Vietnamese pacification program called Phung Hoang. This was a program, which began in 1967, aimed at defeating the communist political infrastructure in the villages of South Vietnam by forcing all of the American and South Vietnamese organizations involved with defeating the VCI to cooperate and coordinate their efforts at every administrative level of the South Vietnamese Government. The Phoenix Committees at the national and regional level addressed policy, while the Phoenix committees at the province and district level dealt with operational matters.

Phung Hoang   The South Vietnamese organization that paralleled Phoenix with committees at each administrative level of the South Vietnamese Government down to district level.

POSREP   Position Report. A report used by American forces to give their location using grid coordinates.

PRG   Peoples' Revolutionary Government.

Province   A grouping of districts.

PRU   Provincial Reconnaissance Unit. This was the primary action arm of the CIA's war against the Viet Cong political infrastructure

PSDF   People's Self Defense Force. A local anti-communist militia made up of rural villagers.

R and R   Rest and Recuperation. A five-day holiday that allowed U.S. servicemen to travel at U.S. Government expense to various locations in Asia and Hawaii.

Radio Relay Site   A location, usually on a prominent terrain feature, that allowed for the retransmission of radio traffic. Such sites were frequently employed by U.S. Marine reconnaissance units since many of their patrols were conducted in areas of steep mountainous terrain where line of sight radio transmissions were masked.

RF   Regional Forces. These were South Vietnamese company-sized light infantry militia units at district level. They were used by district chiefs to reinforce PF units who were under attack by communist forces.

RPD   Light machine gun used by communist forces.

RPG   Rocket Propelled Grenade launcher used by communist forces that was often called the B-40 for the earliest version and the RPG-7 for the later, improved version.

RVN   Republic of Vietnam. The name for South Vietnam.

RVNAF   Republic of Vietnam Armed Forces.

S-1   The administrative staff section for a unit below brigade level.

S-2   The intelligence staff section for a unit below brigade level.

S-3   The operations staff section for a unit below brigade level.

S-4   The logistics staff section for a unit below brigade level.

SALUTE Report   A report used by American forces to identify and describe enemy activity.

SEA Hut   Southeast Asia Hut. A wood framed structure with a corrugated steel roof and screened siding which was commonly constructed by U.S. engineer units for rear area cantonments and bases.

782 Gear   Individual field equipment issued to Marines, such as cartridge belt, ammunition pouches, canteens, packs, etc. Also called deuce gear or web gear.

SITREP   Situation Report.

SKS   A semi-automatic rifle used by communist forces.

Snake and Nape   A combination of fin-stabilized bombs and napalm canisters used by fixed-wing aircraft in support of ground troops.

Stingray   A Marine Corps reconnaissance tactic that used small reconnaissance teams to call in supporting arms on the enemy, often far from friendly lines.

TAOR   Tactical Area of Responsibility. This term applies to the geographical area assigned to a combat unit and for which that unit is responsible for security and operational control.

VC   Viet Cong. The name used to identify southern communists. In actuality, all communist forces in both North and South Vietnam were either military or civilian organizations controlled by the Lao Dong Party headquartered in Hanoi.

VCI   Viet Cong Infrastructure. The term used to describe the Lao Dong Party's political organization in South Vietnam.

Village   A grouping of hamlets that constituted the basic rural administrative entity in South Vietnam. They ranged in size from 1,000 to 10,000 people and often were spread over significant terrain due to dispersed land holdings and rice fields separating hamlets within the village structure.

VNQDD   Viet Nam Quoc Dan Dang, a South Vietnamese anti-communist political party.

VR   Visual reconnaissance. A term used to describe a helicopter overflight of a projected reconnaissance patrol area.

XO   Executive Officer. The second in command of a unit, who normally was given the responsibility of managing the staff of a unit.

Recommended Reading

Ahern, Thomas L., Jr. *CIA and Rural Pacification in South Vietnam.* Langley, VA: Center for the Study of Intelligence, Central Intelligence Agency, 2001.

Andrade, Dale. *Ashes to Ashes. The Phoenix Program and the Vietnam War.* Lexington, MA: Lexington Books, 1990.

_____, and James H. Willbanks. "CORDS/Phoenix: Counterinsurgency Lessons from Vietnam for the Future." *Military Review,* March–April 2006, pp. 9–23.

Asprey, Robert B. *War in the Shadows: The Guerrilla in History.* 2 vols. Garden City, N.Y.: Doubleday, 1975.

Braestrup, Peter. *Big Story: How the American Press and Television Reported and Interpreted the Crises of Tet 1968 in Vietnam and Washington.* Garden City, N.Y.: Anchor, 1978.

Clausewitz, Carl von. *On War.* Princeton: Princeton University Press, 1976.

Colby, William, and Peter Forbath. *Honorable Men: My Life in the CIA.* New York: Simon & Schuster, 1978.

Colby, William, with James McCargar. *Lost Victory: A Firsthand Account of America's Sixteen-Year Involvement in Vietnam.* Chicago: Contemporary, 1989.

Corson, William R. *The Betrayal.* New York: W. W. Norton, 1968.

Davidson, Phillip B. *Vietnam at War: The History 1946–1975.* Novato, CA: Presidio Press, 1988.

Fall, Bernard B. *The Siege of Dien Bien Phu: Hell in a Very Small Place.* New York: Da Capo Press, 1985.

_____. *Street Without Joy: From the Indochina War to the War in Vietnam.* Harrisburg, PA: Stackpole, 1964.

_____. *The Two Vietnams,* New York: Frederick Praeger, 1967.

Finlayson, Andrew R. Marine Advisors with the Vietnamese Provincial Reconnaissance Units, 1966–1970. History Division, United States Marine Corps, Quantico, Virginia, 2009.

_____. "The Tay Ninh Provincial Reconnaissance Unit and Its Role in the Phoenix Program 1969–70." *Studies in Intelligence* 51–2 (2007): 59–69.

_____. "Vietnam Strategies." *Marine Corps Gazette,* August 1988, 90–94.

Giap, Nguyen Vo Gen. *People's War People's Army: The Viet Cong Insurrection Manual for Underdeveloped Countries.* New York: Frederick Praeger, 1962.

Grant, Zalin. *Facing the Phoenix: The CIA and the Political Defeat of the United States in Vietnam.* New York: W. W. Norton, 1991.

Gravel, Mike, ed. *The Pentagon Papers.* 5 vols. Boston: Beacon Press, 1971.

Griffith, Brig. Gen. Samuel B. *Mao Tse-Tung on Guerrilla Warfare.* New York: Frederick Praeger, 1967.

Hannah, Norman B. *The Key to Failure: Laos and the Vietnam War.* New York: Madison Books, 1987.

Herring, George C. *America's Longest War: The United States and Vietnam 1950–1975.* New York: John Wiley and Sons, 1979.

Herrington, Stuart A. *Silence Was a Weapon: The Vietnam War in the Villages.* Novato, CA: Presidio Press, 1982.

Hickey, Gerald C. *Village in Vietnam.* New Haven: Yale University Press, 1964.

Karnow, Stanley. *Vietnam: A History.* New York: Viking, 1983.

Kissinger, Henry. National Security Council Memorandum 3173-X (Declassified), Subject: Lessons of Vietnam, dated 12 May 1975.

_____. *White House Years.* Boston: Little, Brown, 1979.

Komer, Robert W. *Bureaucracy Does Its Thing: Institutional Constraints on U.S.— GVN Performance in Vietnam.* Santa Monica: The Rand Corporation, 1972.

Lansdale, MGen. Edward G. *In the Midst of Wars: An American's Mission in Southeast Asia.* New York: Harper & Row, 1972.

Lehrack, Otto J. *Road of 10,000 Pains: The Destruction of the 2nd NVA Division by the U.S. Marines, 1967.* Minneapolis: Zenith Press, 2010.

Mao Tse-Tung. *Selected Military Writings of Mao Tse-Tung.* Beijing: Foreign Languages Press, 1963.

McNamara, Robert S. *Argument Without End: In Search of Answers to the Vietnam Tragedy.* New York: Public Affairs, 1999.

Moyar, Mark. *Phoenix and the Birds of Prey: The CIA's Secret Campaign to Destroy the Viet Cong,* Annapolis: Naval Institute Press, 1997.

Norton, Bruce H. *Sergeant Major, U.S. Marines: The Biography of Sergeant Major Maurice J. Jacques, USMC.* New York: Ivy Books, 1995.

_____. *Stingray.* New York: Ballantine, 2000.

Oberdorfer, Don. *Tet!* New York: Doubleday, 1971.

Palmer, Gen. Bruce, Jr. *The 25-Year War: America's Military Role in Vietnam.* New York: Da Capo Press, 1984.

Pike, Douglas B. *PAVN: People's Army of Vietnam.* Novato, CA: Presidio Press, 1986.

_____. *Viet Cong: The Organization and Techniques of the National Liberation Front of South Vietnam.* Cambridge: MIT Press, 1966.

Polk, Charles P. *The Annals of Merchantville.* Merchantville, NJ: Merchantville Historical Society, 1997.

Prados, John. *The Blood Road: The Ho Chi Minh Trail and the Vietnam War.* New York: John Wiley and Sons, 1999.

_____, and Ray W. Stubbe. *Valley of Decision: The Siege of Khe Sanh.* Boston: Houghton Mifflin, 1991.

Pribbenow, Merle L., trans. *Victory in Vietnam: The Official History of the People's Army of Vietnam, 1954–1975.* Lawrence: University Press of Kansas, 2002.

Race, Jeffrey. *War Comes to Long An: Revolutionary Conflict in a Vietnamese Province.* Berkeley: University of California Press, 1972.

Robbins, James S. *This Time We Win: Revisiting the Tet Offensive.* New York: Encounter, 2010.

Rodriguez, Felix I., and John Weisman. *Shadow Warrior: The CIA Hero of a Hundred Unknown Battles.* New York: Simon & Schuster, 1989.

Sorley, Lewis. *A Better War: The Unexamined Victories and Final Tragedy of America's Last Years in Vietnam.* New York: Harcourt Brace, 1999.

_____, *Westmoreland: The Gen. Who Lost Vietnam.* New York: Houghton Mifflin Harcourt, 2011

Stanton, Shelby L. *The Rise and Fall of an American Army: U.S. Ground Forces in Vietnam, 1965–1973.* Novato, CA: Presidio Press, 1985.

Stubbe, Ray W., and Michael L. Lanning. *Inside Force Recon: Recon Marines in Vietnam.* New York: Ivy Books, 1989.

Summers, Col. Harry G. *On Strategy: A Critical Analysis of the Vietnam War.* Novato, CA: Presidio Press, 1982.

Tang, Truong Nhu. *A Vietcong Memoir: An Inside Account of the Vietnam War and Its Aftermath.* New York: Harcourt Brace Jovanovich, 1985.

Thucydides, text and translation by C. F. Smith, I–IV (Loeb), London and Cambridge Mass., 1919–1923.

Westmoreland, Gen. William C. *A Soldier Reports.* Garden City, N.Y.: Doubleday, 1976.

Young, Paul R. *First Recon — Second to None: A Marine Reconnaissance Battalion in Vietnam, 1967–68.* New York: Ivy Books, 1992.

Young, Stephen. "How North Vietnam Won the War." *The Wall Street Journal* (August 3, 1995), A8.

Index